Rent Seeking and Development

Rent seeking continues to be a topic of much discussion and debate within the political economy. This new study challenges previous assumptions and sets out a new analysis of the dynamics of rent and rent seeking in development, using Vietnam as a case study.

This book provides an alternative approach to the study of economic development and illuminates new perspectives in a contemporary context. It argues that not only has there been an incomplete understanding of Vietnam's industrial development over the last three decades, but that neoclassical economics do not adequately address many of the issues endangering Vietnam's development.

A significant observation of the Vietnamese experience is the analytical view that rents can be developmental and growth enhancing if the configuration of rent management incentivizes industrial upgrade and conditions firm performance. Underlining the need to reexamine how economic actors and the state collaborate through formal and informal institutions, this study fills a gap in the scholarship of the political economy of rent and rent seeking and how rents might be used for developmental purposes.

Christine Ngoc Ngo is an Assistant Professor of Economics at Bucknell University. She received a PhD in Economics from the School of Oriental and African Studies (SOAS), University of London, and a Juris Doctor from the University of California, Hastings College of the Law.

Routledge Studies in Development Economics

The Service Sector and Economic Development in Africa
Edited by Evelyn F. Wamboye and Peter J. Nyaronga

Macroeconomic Policy for Emerging Markets
Lessons from Thailand
Bhanupong Nidhiprabha

Law and Development
Theory and Practice
Yong-Shik Lee

Institutions, Technology and Development in Africa
Jeffrey James

Urban Policy in Latin America
Towards the Sustainable Development Goals?
Edited by Michael Cohen, Maria Carrizosa and Margarita Gutman

Unlocking SME Finance in Asia
Roles of Credit Rating and Credit Guarantee Schemes
Edited by Naoyuki Yoshino and Farhad Taghizadeh-Hesary

Full and Productive Employment in Developing Economies
Towards the Sustainable Development Goals
Rizwanul Islam

Information and Communication Technologies for Development Evaluation
Edited by Oscar A. García and Prashanth Kotturi

Rent Seeking and Development
The Political Economy of Industrialization in Vietnam
Christine Ngoc Ngo

For more information about this series, please visit: www.routledge.com/series/SE0266

Rent Seeking and Development

The Political Economy of Industrialization in Vietnam

Christine Ngoc Ngo

LONDON AND NEW YORK

First published 2020
by Routledge
2 Park Square, Milton Park, Abingdon, Oxon OX14 4RN

and by Routledge
605 Third Avenue, New York, NY 10017

First issued in paperback 2021

Routledge is an imprint of the Taylor & Francis Group, an informa business

Publisher's Note
The publisher has gone to great lengths to ensure the quality of this reprint but points out that some imperfections in the original copies may be apparent.

British Library Cataloguing-in-Publication Data
A catalogue record for this book is available from the British Library

Library of Congress Cataloging-in-Publication Data
Names: Ngo, Christine Ngoc, 1981– author.
Title: Rent seeking and development : the political economy of industrialization in Vietnam / Christine Ngoc Ngo.
Description: Abingdon, Oxon ; New York, NY : Routledge, 2020. | Series: Routledge studies in development economics ; 150 | Includes bibliographical references and index.
Identifiers: LCCN 2019056073 (print) | LCCN 2019056074 (ebook) | ISBN 9781138100763 (hardback) | ISBN 9781315657493 (ebook)
Subjects: LCSH: Industrialization—Vietnam. | Economic development—Vietnam. | Rent (Economic theory)
Classification: LCC HC444 .N398 2020 (print) | LCC HC444 (ebook) | DDC 338.9597—dc23
LC record available at https://lccn.loc.gov/2019056073
LC ebook record available at https://lccn.loc.gov/2019056074

Typeset in Bembo
by Apex CoVantage, LLC

ISBN 13: 978-1-03-223729-9 (pbk)
ISBN 13: 978-1-138-10076-3 (hbk)

DOI: 10.4324/9781315657493

For Dad

Contents

Figures

Tables

About the author

CHRISTINE NGOC NGO is an Assistant Professor of Economics at Bucknell University in Pennsylvania. She received a PhD in economics from the School of Oriental and African Studies (SOAS), University of London, in the United Kingdom, and a Juris Doctor from the University of California, Hastings College of the Law in San Francisco. She has published papers in the *Journal of Evolutionary Economics, Review of Political Economy, Journal of Economic Issues, Canadian Journal of Development Studies, Journal of Contemporary Asia*, and the *European Journal of East Asian Studies.* She has worked as Associate Economic Affairs Officer for the United Nations Conference for Trade and Development (UNCTAD) in Geneva, Switzerland, and as a consultant for the United Nations Development Programme (UNDP), the World Bank, German Society for International Cooperation (GIZ), and a number of government agencies in Vietnam. Her current research explores the impacts of artificial intelligence, robotics, and the Internet of Things on the future of work in the United States and in developing countries.

Foreword

This excellent book makes an important contribution to our understanding of the role of institutions and policies in driving economic and social development. It builds on and develops an alternative approach to development – the political settlements approach – which says that institutions and policies work in ways that depend on the behavior of the organizations affected by them. Organizations in developing countries can be formal organizations but also powerful informal networks of politicians, businesses, and bureaucrats. The effectiveness of institutions and policies cannot be understood without identifying the powerful organizations in each context. Organizations have interests, and their relative power gives them the capability to resist or support the implementation of particular rules. Organizations act to support or resist rules because rules have implications for resource allocations. If the organizations subject to particular rules want to change or distort them in their own interest, and they have the power to do so, the operation of these rules will clearly be affected. As a result, when economists talk about the efficacy of particular institutions and policies, they are really describing how rules have interacted with powerful organizations to produce outcomes that can be judged to be economic success or failure.

There can actually be no general theory of institutions on their own, but we can have a general analytical frame for looking at the effects of particular institutions in particular contexts of organizational power. The distribution of economic and political organizational power in a society is its *political settlement.* The book is part of a research agenda that studies how political settlements, institutions, and policies interact to produce different types of economic and social development. The ongoing interaction between institutions and political settlements leads, over time, to outcomes that we can judge to be economic success or failure. The book develops a range of pluralist perspectives on rents and rent seeking, and in particular, it develops the analysis of how institutions and political settlements interact. It should be of great interest to economists, development policy analysts, and policymakers.

The analysis of policy design in different contexts has not been helped by ideological debates between liberal free marketeers on the one hand and supporters of developmental states on the other. Proponents of these positions have often used theory and evidence selectively to support their particular positions.

These debates have not helped developing countries identify feasible policies that are implementable in their context and that can accelerate and sustain their development paths. In some social, political, and economic configurations, institutional and policy combinations that approximate free market ones have indeed triggered and sustained development, though always with substantial state interventions that are often underplayed by proponents of free markets. It is also true that in other power configurations, institutional and policy combinations that appear to be driven by an autonomous developmental state have achieved transformative results, though always with a strong commitment to markets and competition in critical areas. The limitation of these analyses has been that their proponents rarely recognize the very specific configurations of social and political factors that enabled particular institutions and policies to be as effective as they were. Most importantly, they do not investigate how the bargaining power of different types of organizations in each country affected the outcomes of their institutions and policies.

The book draws on the analysis of political settlements, social transformations, rents, and rent management and puts them together in a framework the author describes as developmental rent-management analysis. This is a useful synthesis of the most essential components of these approaches for understanding and developing policy. Policies, institutions, organizations, and political settlements are all linked through policy rents and rent seeking. Policy rents are income flows that are created by policies in the context of existing institutions with the objective of achieving specific objectives. The achievement of the desired policy outcome depends on how changes in incentives and resource flows, both of which can be described in the language of rents, induce changes in behavior in society.

For instance, policy may create revenue flows to schools or hospitals to improve education and health outcomes and combine these with institutional rules about how these resources should be used and who is to monitor and govern them. These revenue flows create potential incomes for many different actors and organizations that may be essential for achieving the policy outcome but may also seek to benefit from the income flows as individuals and organizations. Any policy that creates policy rents therefore inevitably induces a variety of rent-seeking activities. All activities that try to affect the allocation, use, or alteration of policy rents are rent-seeking activities. The actual social outcome achieved by the policy will therefore depend on the relative power and interests of the different individuals and organizations engaged in rent-seeking, monitoring, and governance activities, all of whom may also be critical players for delivering the desired social outcomes.

The distribution of organizational power in developing and emerging societies is very different from that in advanced countries, but they have also differed greatly among themselves. This is why institutions and policies that work in one developing country have often not worked in another and also why those that worked at one time have often stopped being effective when either the political settlement substantially changed or new technological, social, or other challenges emerged. The best practice for delivering health outcomes in developing countries is therefore a meaningless concept. There is a pressing need to move beyond ideological models that occasionally fit a few cases but fail to provide a way of thinking about policy in the general case where power configurations may be quite specific. The political settlements approach offers a way of developing higher-level theories and analyses of how institutions, organizations, and rents interact, which can allow us to develop context-specific policy in a rigorous way.

Consider a policy that seeks to direct resources for health-service delivery in a developing country. The policy rents can flow in a number of ways and rent-seeking activities by doctors, private providers, public sector interests, NGOs, politicians, and patients will inevitably try to influence policy design. The policy and institutional design that emerges will determine whether the money goes primarily through the public or the private sector or a mix of both, through corporates or NGOs, and so on. Rent seeking will not only influence the emergence of this institutional and policy structure, it will also influence the implementation of the policy from then on. It will help to determine how resources are used within the delivery system once it is set up. As the rent-seeking activities can have positive or negative outcomes, which in any case can never be ruled out, the reasonable strategy is to understand rent-seeking activities, limit it and influence how it works, not try to rule it out, as some early neoliberal analysts of rent seeking attempted to suggest.

If the political choice is made to direct the flow of resources through public hospitals, the ultimate delivery of services will depend on the governance and monitoring of resources going to salaries, purchases of medicines, the mix and quality of services provided, and so on. Will qualified doctors and nurses be hired or those who have political connections? Will medicines be overpriced and the margins shared between buyers and sellers? Many similar questions have to be answered to understand the overall outcomes that are likely to be achieved through this institutional and policy structure, and this is what this book describes as a rent-management system. The latter describes the constellation of interests and agencies whose interaction determines how policy resources are used in specific contexts. The configuration of relative power and capabilities of the organizations and agencies involved is therefore critical for understanding what is going on.

A very different set of rent-seeking questions will arise if private providers are selected as the delivery mechanism. Will they be able to overprice their services by colluding with or hiding information from politicians and bureaucrats giving the contracts? Which agencies are empowered to check this, are they likely to collude with private providers, and do they have the power and technical capacity to regulate them? Will the private providers receiving public money deliver the right mix of services to maximize social welfare or focus on services that are cheaper or where private co-payments are made? How effective will governance agencies be, given their power, relative to these private sector players? These questions and others like them will describe the rent-management system in this case. Whether public or private delivery or some combination offers the best way forward depends on our assessment of these comparative rent-management problems. Policy always begins with a historical inheritance of institutions and policies that may be delivering results that are better or worse than expected, and the task of policy analysis is to analyze the existing rent-management structure with feasible alternatives and then to nudge the system toward better systemic outcomes using feasible and incremental institutional and policy changes.

Drawing on this pluralist literature on political settlements, rents, and rent seeking, as well as the closely related literature on the analysis of industrial policy and structural change in developing countries, Christine Ngo provides a user-friendly and very useful synthesis of many of these ideas in her developmental rent-management framework. When institutions and policies create incentives and compulsions to use resources in effective ways, rapid and sustainable growth can follow. For this to happen, the combination of policies, institutions, and organizations has to be such that the rules (both formal and informal) create the right incentives and compulsions for achieving the socially desired results. The right incentives are created if the rules create incentives for individuals and organizations to behave in developmental ways. But the rules also have to create compulsions for developmental behavior because incentives are usually insufficient. Powerful individuals and organizations may want to behave in privately beneficial but socially damaging ways. To achieve socially acceptable outcomes, their capacity to do this must be limited. The interaction of specific rules with different agencies and organizations must create credible pressures and sanctions on critical individuals and organizations to make it difficult for them to capture or use resources in unproductive ways and indeed to create pressures on them to behave in socially desirable ways. Feasible ways of doing this will clearly depend on the initial distribution of organizational power and capabilities and the political settlement at national or sectoral levels. If these policy conditions hold for important formal and informal institutions and policies at a national or even a sectoral level, rapid growth and transformation can happen. Indeed, rapid transformation can happen at a sectoral level as a result even if the state does not look anything like a classic developmental state and the market does not look like a rules-based market economy. This is why the application of this framework to the Vietnamese case is so useful.

Vietnam's success in developing several critical manufacturing sectors has been at the heart of its social transformation over the last 20 years. However, its policy and institutional structures have been far removed from a classic market economy with stable private property rights, a rule of law, and effective institutions supporting competition. Vietnam's policy and institutional structure have also been far removed from the classic developmental state of the East Asian type. The Vietnamese state has displayed limited capacities of the classic developmental state to allocate policy rents from above, monitor the relative success of the firms or sectors getting the policy rents, and then continue with the allocation or withdraw these rents according to performance. Like most developing countries, Vietnam has powerful networks of lower-level politicians and bureaucrats, even though it is a single-party system, and these networks have the power to influence the allocation of rents in important ways. As a result, policy rents often get captured by powerful subgroups of politicians or businesses or state-owned enterprises, and the management of these policy rents has sometimes not been very successful.

However, in many important sectors, the configuration of interests and capabilities and the relative power of the players allowed rent management that was indeed highly developmental. The argument in this book shows how we can make sense of and explain how Vietnam achieved its very creditable success by looking at policies, rents, and rent seeking in a new way in the sectors that drove its growth. Even more importantly, this understanding may help policymakers in Vietnam and elsewhere build on their successes by replicating what works and trying to nudge other sectors and regions into similar outcomes. By providing an analysis of Vietnam using this framework, Christine is adding to a growing body of literature on how we can understand these nonconventional cases, which actually turn out to be the norm. The more we understand success and failure in cases that do not fit the archetypal liberal market or developmental state models, the better will we be able to advise developing and emerging countries on feasible policy changes that can have an impact in their context.

Finally, while the political settlements and rent-management analysis were developed to make sense of the anomalous operations of institutions and policies in developing and emerging countries, these tools are becoming increasingly relevant for advanced countries too, as their institutions come under stress. In developing countries, the interaction of institutions and organizations has always been important to understand because formal rules were often violated or contested by powerful interests that frequently accessed rents informally. Many advanced countries that once appeared to do very well with the institutional structures of competitive market economies did so because these institutions had legitimacy and were supported by a range of powerful organizations ranging from political parties, corporations, trade unions, and the media, and this was because the institutions delivered enough to all powerful interests, given the interests and capabilities of the latter.

However, as market economies evolved with increasing globalization, they excluded large numbers of people from effective power to influence policy, and policy then evolved to exclude them further. These changes in the political settlements of advanced countries have concentrated income and power in new organizations while older ones like trade unions have become weaker. Business organizations that deal in digital data or finance have become incomparably more powerful than older manufacturing firms or their unions. These changes in relative power allowed further institutional and policy changes in advanced countries that further exacerbated the distribution of incomes and power. The contemporary emergence of populist and nationalist mobilizations in many advanced countries is symptomatic of these underlying tensions and the declining legitimacy of existing institutions. They demonstrate that unless progressive organizations are able to mobilize the excluded and use new organizational forces to support policies that can be gradually implemented to address the new challenges, extremist movements are likely to gain greater ascendance. Effective new policies and institutions not only have to be appropriate for addressing the new social, technological, and environmental challenges, they also have to be designed in such a way that powerful organizations will not or cannot obstruct or distort these changes. The rent-management framework provides a way of thinking through these challenges and checking whether policy proposals, whether in developing, emerging, or advanced countries, pass the test of feasibility and impact.

Mushtaq H. Khan
Professor of Economics
School of Oriental and African Studies (SOAS),
University of London

Preface

I was born in Ho Chi Minh City (formerly Saigon), and I remember it well: the wide boulevards of the first district lined with large, mature trees; the elegant opera house, with its stone statues and adornments; the delicious street food, available on every corner of the city at any hour of the day; and the courtyard of my childhood home, where friends visited to study, debate politics, play games, sing pop music, and dream about the future of Vietnam.

My generation witnessed one of the most radical transformations of Ho Chi Minh City and the country as a whole. Within a couple of decades, Vietnam transformed from a war-torn country – impoverished but proud – to a middle-income country. I remember a time when bicycles were the favored mode of transportation in Ho Chi Minh City, a stark contrast to present-day streets clogged with motorcycles. Vietnam transitioned from wet, open-air markets to air-conditioned shopping malls, with fashions and price tags matching the Western world. Bookshops filled with communist books have become modern bookstores, stocking only English titles. The changes are remarkable. When I visit Vietnam, nostalgia draws me to the narrow alleys for fresh-made breakfasts or to the old woman pushing a beverage cart through traffic. I marvel at the changes, when riding a motorbike around the Saigon River, the Notre-Dame Cathedral, and Le Duan Street in the evening. The city is sprinkled with a layer of light rain, freshening the air and blurring the sharpness of a crowded, over-charged Southeast Asian metropolis.

My love for Vietnam is rooted in a specific point of view. I left the country at the beginning of the new millennium, when I was 18 years old. My strongest memories are of the 1990s, during the first wave of economic transformation. In the evening light of my family's courtyard, friends and I would discuss the opening of the country, the lifting of the U.S. trade embargo, and its impact on us. We wondered with excitement and hope, what will the future hold for our country? It is this love, those experiences and memories, that inspired me to return, to witness and understand how this beautiful country grew and transformed into something that seems entirely foreign to my childhood home. What happened? Was the transformation inevitable? And now, can Vietnam find a richer, more socially inclusive, and environmentally sustainable version of itself?

My personal story of Vietnam and its development is set within the troubled backdrop of hyper-globalization. During my course of study in economics, the world economy and its orthodox view on trade was turned on its head. In college, I was taught that globalization lifts people out of poverty and hunger and into jobs that provide personal and social development. However, I now live in a world where globalization has caused tremendous inequality at multiple levels, as economic, social, and political disparity have unraveled the postwar order. The rise of populism, the distress in the developing world, and the growing resentment among the Western working class promise to bring global peace, security, and prosperity to their knees, if we fail to act bravely and confront inequality head on. The meaning of development has changed, and the masses demand not just economic growth, but social, environmental, and political inclusion in the development process.

Much has changed in Vietnam since I began my research in 2004. I document some of these changes in this book and explain how they impacted the country's rocky road to development. In some ways, this book is about Vietnam. In others, it is about the intricate process of development more broadly, offering a means to scrutinize the complexity of development through changes that are organic, planned, and driven by special interests. Development is not just a process. It is a powerful force of economic, social, and political evolution that influences millions of lives and ways of living. I hope to capture this powerful force in explaining Vietnam's path to development but also to project where it may lead in the future. In many ways, Vietnam is not unique; other developing countries face similar constraints and limitations. If development theory and policy are to be grounded in the experience of the countries themselves, then Vietnam offers useful lessons to the rest of the developing world.

Christine Ngoc Ngo
Lewisburg, PA
November 2019

Acknowledgments

Many have played instrumental roles in enabling me to complete this research project. Professor Mushtaq H. Khan offered stimulating intellectual engagement, prolific guidance, and generous support during my course of study at the University of London, School of Oriental and African Studies (SOAS), and beyond. I am greatly indebted to all the people and institutions that helped me, in one way or another, undertake my fieldwork in Vietnam. Many individuals and firms offered their precious time, information, and insights that together comprise the data set used in this book. I thank them for their incredible generosity and kindness. The University of Denver and Bucknell University offered vibrant academic environments, where I tested and refined the research ideas and arguments presented in this book.

Finally, I would like to thank my family, friends, and colleagues in the United States, Vietnam, and Europe for their unequivocal support over the years. In particular, I thank my husband, Michael, for being a tower of strength throughout the writing process. My mother, Huong, has stood behind me unconditionally every step of the way, and I am tremendously grateful for her backing. And above all, my father, Thuan, has been an enduring source of inspiration and admiration. He was instrumental in encouraging me to pursue my ambitions and dreams. This book is dedicated to him.

★

I am grateful to the Taylor and Francis Group for granting me permission to reproduce the following articles: "The political economy of industrial development in Vietnam's telecommunications industry: A rent management analysis," *Review of Political Economy*, vol. 29, no. 3, 2017, pp. 454–77; "Local value chain development in Vietnam: Motorcycles, technical learning and rents management," *Journal of Contemporary Asia*, vol. 47, no. 1, 2017, pp. 1–26; "Developmental rent management analysis: Learning, upgrading, and innovation," *Journal of Economic Issues*, vol. 50, no. 4, 2016, pp. 1045–68; "Economic development in a rent-seeking society: Socialism, state capitalism and crony capitalism in Vietnam" (coauthored with Dr. Vlad Tarko), *Canadian Journal of Development Studies*, vol. 39, no. 4, 2018, pp. 481–99. I am also thankful to Springer-Verlag GmbH

Germany, part of Springer Nature, for granting me permission to reproduce "Rethinking rent seeking for development and technological change" (coauthored with Dr. Charles Robert McCann Jr.), *Journal of Evolutionary Economics*, vol. 29, no. 2, 2019, pp. 721–40. In addition, I am grateful to BRILL for granting permission to reproduce "Industrial development, liberalisation and impacts of Vietnam-China border trade: The case of the Vietnamese textile and garment sector," *European Journal of East Asian Studies*, vol. 16, no. 1, 2017, pp. 154–84. Professor Mushtaq H. Khan, and Springer Nature; Professor Ricardo Hausmann, Professor Dani Rodrik, Professor Andres Velasco, and Oxford Publishing Limited; Professor Hal Hill; Dr. Fujita Mai, and the Institute of Developing Economies; and Dr. Nguyen Duc Tiep permitted me to use some of their research materials, for which I am extremely appreciative. Finally, my colleague and past coauthor, Dr. Charles Robert McCann Jr., has been more than supportive of this book project. I am indebted to him for sharing his time, expertise, and encouragement.

1 Rent management as development

1.1 Economic development in transitional economies

Economic development is a *process* of change that enables a poor country to achieve progress for its people and society at large. It also allows individuals and communities to strive for better livelihoods by improving economic and social infrastructures, income, opportunities, and aspirations. However, development is not a linear process of a few economic factors moving from one development level to the next. Rather, it is a series of dynamic, evolutionary factors and forces that move in unsynchronized and unpredictable directions. Much of the transformation involves individuals and firms learning not only to create innovative and sought-after products but to make risky investment decisions within a short time horizon. There is also the crucial role of the state in coordinating investments, infrastructure planning, education, training, technology adoption, and backward and forward linkages among firms, industries, markets, and research institutions. If history is any guide, it is an extremely challenging process. Few countries in the last century successfully became newly advanced and industrialized economies. These include Japan, the East Asian Tigers, and to some extent, China.

The objective of this book is to highlight the dynamic transformation in economic development and to understand it from a developing country's perspective – in this case, Vietnam. Understanding dynamic transformation reveals the strengths and weaknesses embedded in a developing economy and how they influence the actions of the state, firms, entrepreneurs, and the labor force. This objective is achieved through careful study of country history and context, and the actions of economic agents, while incorporating economic theories and practices. History reveals not only the origin of institutions but also the existing economic, social, and political arrangements. Meanwhile, context provides implicit knowledge about social norms, customs, and motivations. These contextual features help explain the behavior of individuals and groups, given the constraints in resources and weak institutions. Finally, economic theories provide cursory guidance and intuition to spot-check issues, analyze processes of change, and identify policy solutions.

Development is an ever-changing process, as is the context in which poor countries often find themselves in the course of history and global relations. In recent decades, developing countries have encountered new sets of opportunities and challenges against the backdrop of hyper-globalization; the rise of China; changes in geopolitics; and unprecedented rates of technological change, climate change, and rising inequality within and across nation states. Opportunities emerge from rising global wealth and market demand, innovative production techniques that boost productivity and outputs, and hungry capitals looking to make profits across the world. Nevertheless, the new set of challenges is encompassing and unprecedented, so much so that development models and examples offered by Western countries and East Asian economies are no longer sufficient. For example, the world has never seen an economy rise at the speed and size of China. Presumed trade-offs among growth, environment, and inequality are no longer tolerable for the earth and for poor workers around the world. Hyper-globalization and its innovative institutions have not only reduced the policy space for developing countries but also created a backlash from around the world. These events have led to a great deal of turbulence in international cooperation that, in the past, was crucial to reducing poverty, elevating development, and promoting progress in poor countries.

Economic development in the twenty-first century is a quest with narrowing global support, time, trust, and policy space (United Nations Conference on Trade and Development, 2018). The first two decades of the twenty-first century squarely placed countries and people in a new age of hostile politics and conflicts across the social classes; growing, powerful multinationals; and diminishing liberal democracy. Developing countries, therefore, must manage their own processes of development and navigate the winds of change in global markets and affairs. It is within this perspective that this book aims to contribute. The objective is to provide an alternative approach to the study of development and policymaking and to illuminate new understandings in a contemporary context. The "alternative" theoretical and analytical approaches adopted in this book are uncommon within mainstream economic literature, with special attention to recent contributions in the field of the political economy of development.[1] This strand of literature offers much-needed theories, perspectives, and research methods to analyze and understand economic transformation without the unrealistic assumptions of competitive markets, perfect information, costless technological change, savings-determined investment, and constant income distribution found in mainstream economics. I will begin by locating the political economy approach in the vast body of economic development literature, motivations for this research, and the research questions and methodology used.

1.2 The political economy of development

The political economy literature focusing on economic development has been instrumental in explaining why some countries are more successful than others in achieving development and growth (Amsden, 1989; Chang, 2000; Cimoli,

Dosi, & Stiglitz, 2009; Lall, 1992; North, 1990; Rodrik, 2004; Stiglitz, 2013). Scholars and field practitioners have identified several important factors that enhance or impede development. In addition, analyses uncovering economic progress in Japan, China, the newly industrialized East Asian countries, India, and Africa deliver significant insight into the mechanisms that contribute to successful or failed development efforts (Amsden, 1989; Amsden, 2009; Bardhan, 1999; Booth & Golooba-Mutebi, 2012; Fine, 1997; Fung, 1989; Khan & Blankenburg, 2009; Lall, 2004; Wade, 1990; Whitfield, Therkildsen, Buur, & Kjaer, 2015).

The analytical approaches used to analyze development processes in these studies come from a variety of schools of thought in development economics, development studies, and area studies. For example, neoclassical economists attribute development success to improvements in rules of law that allow for market freedom, trade liberalization, foreign investment, and entrepreneurship in poor countries (Krueger, 2012; Sachs & Pistor, 1997; World Bank, 1991, 2008). Development scholars highlight the role of the government in those countries and how "getting relative prices wrong" could provide incentives and resources for firm performance that lead to industrialization and development (Amsden, 1989, 2001; Chang, 1999; Chang, Cheema, & Mises, 2002; Wade, 1990). Corruption literature provides additional insights into how cronyism and corruption can be productive in the context of development because they provide stability to the political economy, motivation for state agencies to enforce certain growth-enhancing policies, and the possibility for firms to focus resources on productivity growth (Acemoglu & Verdier, 2000; Gray, 2015; Hanousek & Kochanova, 2016; Méndez & Sepúlveda, 2006). Finally, the literature on rent, rent seeking, and rent management analyzes economic development from the perspective of resource allocation; structures of incentive and conditionality; and political settlement within specific political, institutional, and industry dynamics (Abegaz, 2013; Booth & Golooba-Mutebi, 2012; Khan & Jomo, 2000b; Ngo, 2016; Whitfield et al., 2015). These different strands of literature are complementary, in that they highlight interplays between the crucial roles of the state, functioning of the market, technological change, and firm incentives that can explain economic growth in developing countries since the second half of the twentieth century.

This book employs important theoretical contributions in the political economy of development using the theory of rent and rent seeking to analyze the dynamic process of economic transformation. Rent is defined as income over and above the amount that would be received under a competitive market system. Rent seeking is the expenditure of resources by individuals, firms, or policymakers to create rent or to maintain and transfer existing rent (Khan, 2000).[2] Although the concept of rent was first discussed by classical economists such as David Ricardo and Alfred Marshall, analyses of rent and rent seeking were only carefully developed in the public choice and neoliberal literature of the late 1960s to reinforce the support of free-market driven economies and claims against state intervention (Buchanan, Tollison, & Tullock, 1980; Krueger, 1974; Tullock, 1967). The public choice and neoliberal approaches have since been questioned and broadened by institutional and political economists. These economists point out inconsistencies in assuming that rent and rent seeking could be removed without political and economic costs. In addition, the institutions used to remove rent and rent seeking effectively create alternative rents and rights. Therefore, rents cannot be eliminated entirely (Khan & Jomo, 2000b; Medema, 1991; Samuels & Mercuro, 1984). From this point of view, political and institutional economists suggest to first analyze the origins and types of rent being created, the individuals and groups that benefit from rent, and the economic outcomes produced by the use of such rent. Then, policy solutions with considerations of rent outcomes can be devised to promote development (Gray & Whitfield, 2014; Khan & Jomo, 2000b; Ngo, 2016; Whitfield et al., 2015).

From this perspective, political and institutional economists broaden the conceptual framework of rent and rent seeking used by the public choice and neoliberal literature, allowing it to become a constructive and insightful analytical tool in the field of the political economy of development. This broadened conceptual framework addresses the limitations of the mainstream's approach to economic development. For instance, the presumptions of perfect market competition and rational economic men are ill suited for understanding development in poor countries where power, norms, and market failures are omnipresent. More importantly, by enriching the conceptual framework of rent and rent seeking, this strand of literature helps explain the dynamics, complexity, and nuances of economic transformation.

1.3 Research motivation and question

Early literature on rent creation and rent seeking tends to narrowly depict these phenomena as inherently inefficient and growth-reducing, and rarely attends to how they may have contributed to positive developmental outcomes (Buchanan et al., 1980; Krueger, 1998; Posner, 1975; Tullock, 1967). More problematic is the claim, widely spread by donor agencies, that development failures in poor countries are mostly due to the pervasive damage of rents and rent seeking (Coolidge & Rose-Ackerman, 1999; Mauro, 1997). Given this perspective, donor conditionalities in many poor countries are often meant to curb rent creation and rent seeking on the grounds that they necessarily undermine economic development. Vietnam is one country where this argument has been advanced. Experts on Vietnam frequently attribute the country's development challenges to rent seeking. The warning from the World Bank 2003 Development Report is representative:

> [Vietnam] may fail to remove the obstacles in its reform path, let the vested interests capture government transfers to offset their inefficiencies, and see an unhealthy relationship develop between enterprises and government officials. A weak macroeconomic situation, slower growth, increased inequality and generalized corruption could be the outcomes.
>
> (World Bank, 2003, p. 4)

As mentioned, an emerging body of political economy literature challenges this narrow perspective on rent and rent seeking. Research by institutional economists such as Khan and Jomo (2000b); North, Wallis, Webb, and Weingast (2007); Whitfield et al. (2015); and Gray (2018) provide evidence that certain types of rent can be value enhancing and that rent seeking can lead to development. In the words of Khan and Jomo (2000a): "In a world where learning and innovation have to be rewarded, distributive conflicts dealt with, where incentives have to be created to deal with asymmetric information and where scarce natural resources have to be conserved, many types of rents are socially desirable" (p. 8). An illustrative example of this political economy scholarship is the Africa Power and Politics Programme, which introduced the concept of "developmental patrimonialism" (Booth & Golooba-Mutebi, 2011, p. 1). In the case study of Rwanda, research from this program points out:

> The interest and ability of the ruling elite to impose a centralised management of the rents which are an unavoidable feature of early capitalism . . . have provided Rwanda with the "early-stage venture capitalism" it needed to achieve economic recovery post-1994 and to maintain respectable rates of investment and socio-economic progress under otherwise unfavourable conditions during the last decade.
>
> (Booth & Golooba-Mutebi, 2011, p. 1)

Political economy scholars suggest that a beneficial analytical approach to development is to consider rent seeking a process and rent as the outcome of political and economic contests (Gray & Whitfield, 2014; Khan & Jomo, 2000b; Ngo, 2016; Whitfield et al., 2015). This can be done through incorporating political and institutional variables to explain (1) the types of rights and rents created as a result of rent seeking and (2) the mechanism of how these new rents create the incentives and pressures to strengthen firm efforts and capability. In the present context, a rent-management mechanism[3] is defined as the configuration of politics, institutions, and industry organization[4] that underlines the incentives and pressures of economic and political agents in their behaviors and activities. In this book, I argue that rent is better understood as a policy instrument that could either be damaging or developmental, depending on the rent management operating within a specific industry and the country's political economy.

1.3.1 Research question

The present research project considers three primary theoretical issues: (1) the political and institutional factors that incentivize economic transformation, (2) the underlining forces that enable technological change and technology adoption that allow for successful industrialization and growth,[5] and (3) the role of rent and rent seeking in the development process. Because development research is context specific, I analyze Vietnam's economic transformation as a case study to inform the aforementioned theoretical issues.

The Vietnamese experience is valuable for understanding economic change from the dimensions of rent and rent seeking for two reasons. First, as a transitional economy, Vietnam has faced a number of constraints and market failures during its growth process. Understanding how Vietnam handled these constraints to transform itself from a low-income to a middle-income country provides important lessons for other poor countries on a similar developmental path. Second, debates on industrial development to date have focused largely on improving a country's transparency; adopting good governance practices; and enhancing its trade openness, privatization, and market liberalization. However, there has been insufficient attention to decipher the ways in which rent and rent seeking enhance or impede development, especially from the perspectives of industrial upgrading. Vietnam's measured success in industrialization and development provide important information on how rent seeking took place and how politics and institutions shaped the path of development in the industrial sectors. In sum, the Vietnamese experience contributes to key theoretical and empirical knowledge of developmental processes.

Given this context, this research project asks: *what are the key political and institutional processes that shaped the structures of incentives and pressures for technology adoption and capacity building in the Vietnamese industrial sectors since the country's economic reform in 1986?* I explain the methodological approach in the next section.

1.4 Methodological approach

This book employs three methodological approaches to answer the research question: one approach is to incorporate a new theoretical foundation of rent and rent seeking; another is to use a developmental rent-management analysis framework; and the third approach is the study of eight cases to analyze different aspects of the Vietnamese industrial experience.

1.4.1 Theoretical foundation: rent, rent seeking, and technological change

The first methodological approach involves surveying the literature on technological change, rent, and rent seeking, as applied to economic development (see Chapter 2). I first review the literature on the characteristics of technology adoption, capacity building, and growth from the neoclassical and heterodox perspectives. Next, I analyze how key market failures are associated with technical learning and industrial production. The classical view asserts that the transformation of institutions to address market failures and promote technological adoption inherently alters social relations, creates rents, and incentivizes rent seeking in transitional economies. From this perspective, a nation's promotion of its firms, industries, and development must necessarily confront issues of rent creation and rent seeking as part of its evolving growth process. I therefore survey the theoretical foundations of rent and rent seeking from the perspective of classical, neoclassical, and heterodox economists. Finally, I present a theoretical assessment regarding the role of the state in enabling institutions to resolve critical market failures, manage rents, and regulate rent seeking. The literature survey supports the assertion that the process of development and industrialization requires understanding the mechanisms of rent management – a configuration of incentives and pressures that fully corresponds to existing political, institutional, and industrial structures of a developing economy. This particular theoretical approach emphasizes the diversity of empirical and historical contexts across and within countries.

1.4.2 Analytical framework: developmental rent-management analysis

The second methodological approach involves using an analytical framework: the developmental rent-management analysis (DRMA). I developed the DRMA to examine the political economy factors that affect the process of technological upgrading and capacity building in developing countries (see Chapter 3). The DRMA provides an analytic framework to assess (1) how rent is created, destroyed, contested, and reallocated; (2) how rent seeking takes place; and (3) the outcomes from rent seeking. There are four steps in the DRMA framework.

Step 1 analyzes two separate issues regarding the political context of rent creation: (a) how political organizations are structured and (b) how political agents and forces interact to create, allocate, and manage rent.

Step 2 assesses the institutional structures that create and implement rent or rent policies.

Step 3 assesses the factors that characterize and drive an industry and its firms.

Step 4 assesses the development outcomes provided by the rent. There are three possible outcomes: (a) rent increases investments and technical upgrading resulting in long-term growth and development, (b) rent allocation boosts investment and revenues but does not improve firm competitiveness, and (c) rent is captured and redistributed to unproductive interests and thus not used productively. This step also assesses how rent outcomes shape the configuration of rent management, given the transformation of the firms and the industry. In some cases, a rent outcome can alter political context, institutions, and industry structure, thus modifying the configuration of rent management. In other cases, a new institutional structure (e.g., a preferential trade agreement) can change the context of the political economy and industrial strategy. Step 4 has a feedback loop to Steps 1, 2, and 3, which enables *dynamic analysis* of the DRMA.

DRMA is not meant to develop an analytically coherent development model or a new Asian development model, given the great variation in the contexts of each nation's political economy and industries. Rather, it aims to highlight the *connections* and *disconnections* among different agents and actors within a developing economy. The purpose is to identify *strengths* and *weaknesses* in the structure of incentives and pressures for technological upgrading and capacity expansion.

1.4.3 Qualitative research and analytical case studies

Economic development is a complex and multifaceted process. Understanding this process requires research methods that can capture intricate dynamics; characterize multiplex interplays among the state, the markets, and the firms; and support practical and effective policymaking. Given the book's objectives, I chose qualitative research and analytical case studies as the research methodologies for four reasons. First, statistical data is unreliable and often incomplete in Vietnam, especially in explaining the transformation of industrial sectors. In fact, there is no statistical data on rent-seeking activities except for scattered news reports. In addition, the state sectors are not required by law to report finances to the public. Second, qualitative research can help identify factors that are difficult to measure in quantitative analysis (Helper, 2000; Piore, 1979; Starr, 2014). For example, the incentives that motivate local firms to become more competitive are not easy to measure in the diverse and complex context of Vietnam's market economy with a socialist orientation. Third, case studies provide nuanced, qualitative evidence and analyses that are too complex to be captured in quantitative models. In this book, the case studies characterize how rent seeking takes place and how rent management operates in Vietnam's industrial manufacturing. These aspects are otherwise difficult to capture in quantitative research. Fourth, qualitative research offers rich and detailed accounts of how policies work in practice and how firms and industry develop. Given the constraints imposed by the inherently weak institutions and enforcement capacity of the state, these accounts are often convoluted, although, they provide important knowledge of the country's political economy.

More specifically, this book employs case-study analysis to assess how technical learning and capability building took place in Vietnam under the influence of rent creation and rent seeking. As noted above, three important industries are the subject of this analysis: telecommunications, textile and garment, and motorcycle. These industries were selected based on their distinct patterns of development and various successes in technology adoption. They also played varying crucial roles in aspects of Vietnam's development over the past four decades. For example, the textile and garment industry is the bedrock for Vietnam's participation in global trade and regional integration because it is one of the first industries that was opened to trade and foreign direct investment (FDI). The motorcycle industry is revitalizing the industrial sector in the contemporary period through its linkages with supporting industries in the production network. Finally, the telecommunication industry is providing crucial infrastructure and technology upgrading for Vietnam's economy.

1.5 Data collection

The empirical research in this book is based on data collected during four fieldwork sessions totaling 10 months: December 2010, April–October 2011, June 2012, and June–July 2016. I conducted 68 semi-structured interviews with government officials, firm owners, managers, suppliers, consumers, and industry experts. At the beginning of each interview, I asked a set of common questions written specifically for each industry. In addition, I prepared customized questions for each subject group, based on interviewee positions and expertise. For instance, I asked government officials to describe the rationale for their policies and how they were implemented among various agencies. Firm managers were asked to explain their company's business strategy and production operation, how technology was adopted, and how government policies helped remove constraints in business operations. The interviews were between one and three hours in length. Most interviews were conducted in Vietnamese and recorded with the interviewee permission. I transcribed and translated the interviews into English after each field visit. Given the sensitive nature of this research, the identities of all interviewees are strictly confidential. As per standard practice in qualitative research (Starr, 2014), data used in this book were carefully cross-checked for accuracy, consistency, validity, relevance, and completeness, either with other interviewees, news and government reports, or existing literature.

Because I am fluent in Vietnamese, I was able to access and read numerous official government documents, policy briefs, ministries' reports, and local newspapers. I was also a consultant for the World Bank Vietnam in September 2011 and July 2016, the Ministry of Planning and Investment from October 2011 to April 2012, and the United Nations Development Programme in Vietnam from September 2014 to July 2015. Together, these experiences provided invaluable information regarding donor agendas in promoting Vietnam's development, the government's policymaking process, and institutional settings of the Communist Party of Vietnam (CPV). These insights were critical for analyzing the mechanisms of rent management in the three industrial sectors.

My interviews with managers and workers in public, private, and foreign firms brought into focus the various constraints in firms' upgrading efforts and how technology adoption and learning takes place. In addition, interviews with a number of high-profile government officials and industry experts unraveled key aspects of the Vietnamese institutional structure, the internal political and economic arrangements among various interest groups, and the power struggles within key state apparatuses. Through networking, I also collected numerous secondary data from government offices, international organizations, and research think tanks. From this large data set, I was able to analyze eight case studies of industrial development in the telecommunications, textile and garment, and motorcycle industries.

1.6 Economic development in Vietnam, 1986–2018

1.6.1 Postwar reconstruction

The 30-Years War left Vietnam with heavy damage and an extremely impoverished economy. Immediately after losing the war in 1975, the United States imposed a trade embargo that cut off Vietnam from U.S. imports and exports, and prohibited trading with American allies. The World Bank, the International Monetary Fund, and the United Nations Educational, Scientific and Cultural Organization – influenced by the American government – all denied Vietnam aid (Davies, 2015). In addition, the Vietnamese government's central focus on heavy industry to revolutionize "the relations of production" largely led the government to ignore productions of the agriculture and consumer goods industries (Bui, 2000, p. 22). Farmers were also forced to hand over their crops in exchange for ration cards rather than cash. Without incentives to produce, agriculture production crashed. Annual food production was not enough to feed the people, and the average food per capita (measured in rice) reached only 300 kg per year (Bui, 2000). Thoburn (2013) points out that in the mid-1980s, "inflation was over 700 percent per year, exports were only half the value of imports and there were severe shortages of food and consumer goods" (p. 103). Consequently, the 10-year period following the end of the war and before economic reform was marked by poor quality of life; serious shortages of food, consumer goods, transportation, and health and education services; and high inflation. This prolonged period of stagnation and crisis pressured the Vietnamese government to move away from its central planning model of a strong focus on heavy industries. In the Sixth Party Congress in 1986, the Communist government announced the economic reform package known in Vietnamese as *Doi Moi*, which translates as *making changes toward modernization* (Bui, 2000).

In 1989, the revolutionary changes in eastern Europe, marked by the fall of the Berlin Wall and the collapse of the Union of Soviet Socialist Republics (USSR) two years later, created an additional economic shock and adjustment in Vietnam. First, the USSR's aid and trade with Vietnam fell sharply – 29 percent in the first six months of 1991 – causing a sharp decline in demand of Vietnamese goods (Elliott, 1992). The subsidized prices of goods and raw materials that benefited Vietnamese industries and consumers also disappeared with the USSR's collapse. However, by 1991, the economic reform begun in 1986 was underway, and Vietnam weathered external shocks much better than other former communist states, particularly Cuba (Weeks, 2001). Nonetheless, the discontinuation of trade links among communist countries pressured Vietnam to recommence trade relations with China in 1991, the European Union in 1992, Southeast Asia in 1995, and the United States in 2001. Elliott (1992) asserts that with the collapse of the USSR, political reform in Vietnam slowed, leading to both an increased crackdown on political dissent and a gradual economic openness through the 1990s. The demand shock from the fall of communism in eastern Europe affected Vietnam's textile and garment industry most, which was mainly organized as a collection of state-owned enterprises (SOEs). It was the search for new markets in major sectors that forced the Vietnamese government to liberalize some of its economy.

Vietnam's economy was hit hard in 1997 by the regional financial crisis, which slowed the country's growth by half from 1998 to 1999, as compared to 1995–1996 (Bui, 2000). Because of weak regional and global demands, Vietnam's economy deflated, and market access halted, leading to stagnation in production and consumer demands. Recovery was initially slow. Bui (2000) suggests that the slow pace of economic development in the years following the financial crisis was partly due to internal problems – a weak capital market, a lack of skilled labor, and an inadequate infrastructure. Communist leaders realized that the country needed deeper integration to expand its production and upgrade its industries. While the economy recovered in the early 2000s, Vietnam was well underway in its negotiation to become a member of the World Trade Organization (WTO).

As the government searched for options and ideas to reform the economy, the Communist Party leaders looked to the experiences of other successful Asian countries: Taiwan, South Korea, and especially China. Chinese economic reform, which had started a decade earlier, provided a useful model for Vietnam. It included a cautious and gradual opening up of the economy, while its SOEs continued to be primary players in important industries. Reform policies also focused on attracting FDI to promote technological change, exports, and industrialization. While the Vietnamese private sector was allowed to participate in a variety of economic activities, the public sector remained in charge of commissioning social and economic programs directed by the state. Consistently, the public sector has been the instrument for the state and the CPV to regulate the Vietnamese economy (Doan, 2012; Masina, 2006, p. 123).

From the end of the twentieth century and into the twenty-first, the Vietnamese government employed policies with extensive investment and credit expansion to achieve high gross domestic product (GDP), especially in the 1990s and the 2000s. During this period, Vietnam gained access to the WTO in 2007 and signed bilateral trade agreements with a number of strategic trade partners, such as the United States, the European Union, Japan, and several Southeast Asian countries. Before the global recession in 2008, Vietnam experienced a high growth rate, averaging 6.91 percent between 1986 and 2007 (World Development Indicators, 2018). However, while the global economy was falling fast into a deep recession in 2008, the Vietnamese economy entered a new phase of development and experienced a number of structural problems. This next section highlights important issues of Vietnam's economic development in the first two decades of the twenty-first century.

1.6.2 The economy: an overview

In 2018, Vietnam's population was 94.67 million people, with a population growth rate of 1.1 percent (Asian Development Bank, 2019). In the same year, the GDP at current prices was USD 241,272 billion, the highest value in the country's history (International Monetary Fund, 2019).[6] Estimated income per capita on a purchasing power parity basis was USD 7,510 in 2018, making Vietnam a middle-income country (International Monetary Fund, 2019). From the start of its economic reform in 1986, the country's growth rate has been impressive, averaging 6.53 percent between 1985 and 2018 (Figure 1.1). In both 2008 and 2012, the economy experienced a slowdown, as did other emerging

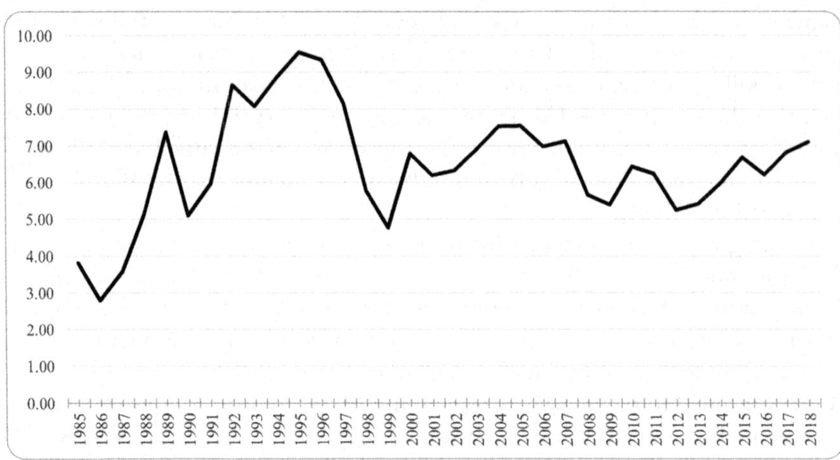

Figure 1.1 Vietnam's Growth Rate 1986–2018 (in percentage)

Source: Author's compilation based on data from World Bank (2019) and World Development Indicators (2018).

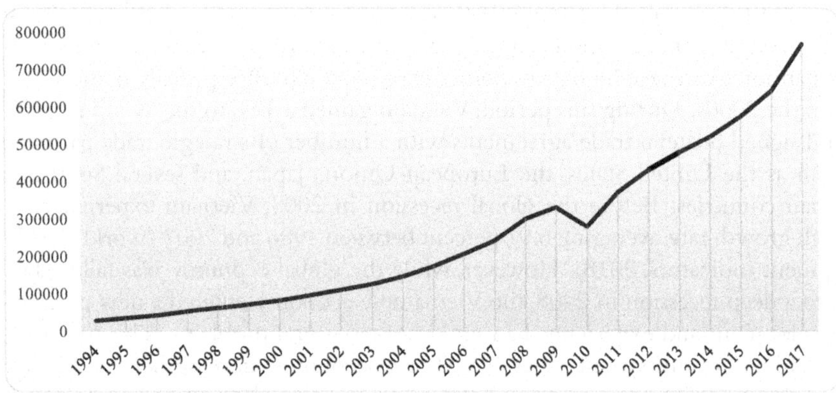

Figure 1.2 Manufacturing Output 1994–2017 (at current prices, in VND billion)

Source: Author's compilation, data retrieved from the Asian Development Bank (2013, 2018b).

economies. To stimulate the economy, the Vietnamese government devised a stimulus package that went into effect in 2012. As a consequence, Vietnam's economy recovered in 2013, and in 2018, the GDP growth was at its highest since 2007, at an estimated 7.1 percent (World Bank, 2019).

Parallel to the rapid growth rate in the GDP, Vietnam's manufacturing sector dramatically increased its output starting in the mid-1990s. Manufacturing output rose from USD 1.15 billion in 1994 to USD 33.36 billion in 2017 (Figure 1.2), a 28.8 times increase (Asian Development Bank, 2018b). The manufacturing sector has been the backbone of Vietnam's competitiveness and development thus far. It employed approximately 17 percent of the Vietnamese labor force (9.3 million workers) and contributed 15.3 percent to the GDP in 2017 (Asian Development Bank, 2018b).

Over the course of Vietnam's economic development, total production of agriculture, manufacturing, and mining outputs experienced a gradual increase from 1994 to 2007 and grew at a much faster pace after 2007 (Figure 1.3). The agriculture, forestry, and fishing sectors (listed as *agriculture* in the graph) have experienced spectacular growth since 2007, following a period of gradual increase starting in the 1990s. It is the largest industry group by employment, employing approximately 39.4 percent (21.6 million workers) of the labor force in 2017. The agriculture sector has outpaced both manufacturing and mining since 2008 and is now also the largest industry measured by total output (15.3 percent of the GDP).

Similarly, manufacturing output has risen since 1994 and picked up pace in 2010. Although manufacturing output outpaced agriculture between 1994 and 2005, it experienced a decline during the 2008 global economic crisis and only recovered in 2011. Vietnam's efforts to industrialize and modernize its economy achieved some success, and it continues to encourage agriculture production. The parallel growth of both key industries implies that industrial development did not crowd out agriculture. The mining industry also grew over the same period but has experienced a decline in output since 2014. The structural transformation of these three important industry groups – agriculture, manufacturing, and mining – from 1994 to 2017 is depicted in Figure 1.3.[7]

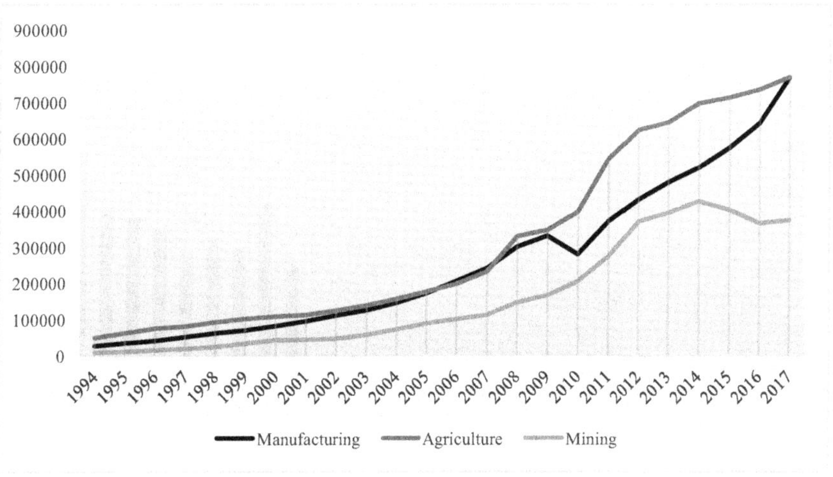

Figure 1.3 Output by Three Major Industries, 1994–2017 (at current prices, in VND billion)

Source: Author's compilation, data retrieved from the Asian Development Bank (2013, 2018b).

In the mid-1990s, FDI accounted for 30 percent of the total investments in Vietnam. However, the share of FDI fell to 20 percent in the wake of the Asian financial crisis (Asian Development Bank, 2013; Nguyen, Nguyen, Nguyen, & Nguyen, 2010). Vietnam's accession to the WTO in 2001 led to new inflows of FDI. This was due in part to reforms that Vietnam committed to in the trade treaty. The country relaxed rules restricting FDI, thus creating an expectation among international investors about the development prospects of the country. Since 2007, FDI has become the most important source of investment in Vietnam, and net inflows rose more than double: from USD 6.7 billion in 2007 to USD 14.1 billion in 2017 (Figure 1.4). Although Vietnam has succeeded in attracting FDI, the benefits from foreign investment have been mixed. Previous studies found little evidence of technical spillovers from FDI enterprises to local counterparts (Nguyen et al., 2008), and Vietnam has become heavily dependent on foreign capital as a source of economic growth since the mid-2000s (Nguyen et al., 2010). In 2017, net inflows of FDI as a percentage of the GDP was approximately 6.3 percent, the highest level since 2011 (World Development Indicators, 2018). The amount of FDI is shown in Figure 1.4.

International trade has been an important aspect of Vietnam's economic development. From the mid-1990s to the 2010s, Vietnam's export growth rate has stayed at 20 percent per year, on average, thanks to FDI. Export growth in the industrial sector has been especially high. However, the value added in final goods is insignificant since Vietnam relies heavily on imported intermediate inputs from abroad (Figure 1.5). Exports slowed slightly in 2009, due to a demand drop in the global market but increased rapidly starting only a

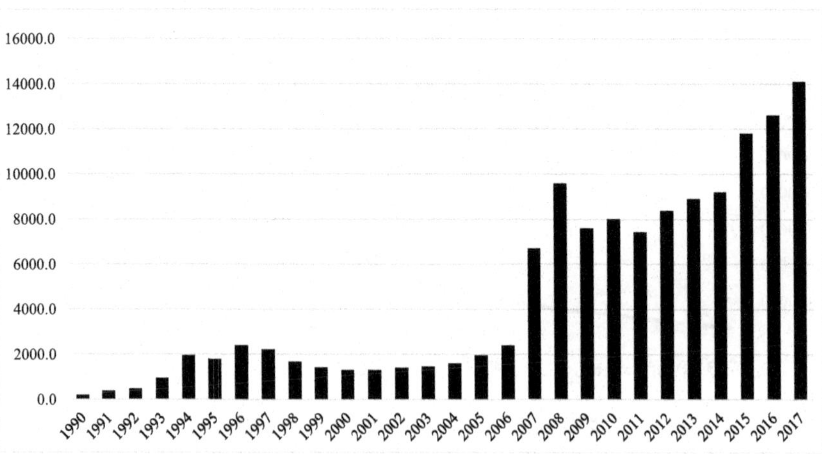

Figure 1.4 Foreign Direct Investment, Net Inflows 1990–2017 (in USD million)

Source: Author's compilation based on data from World Development Indicators (2018).

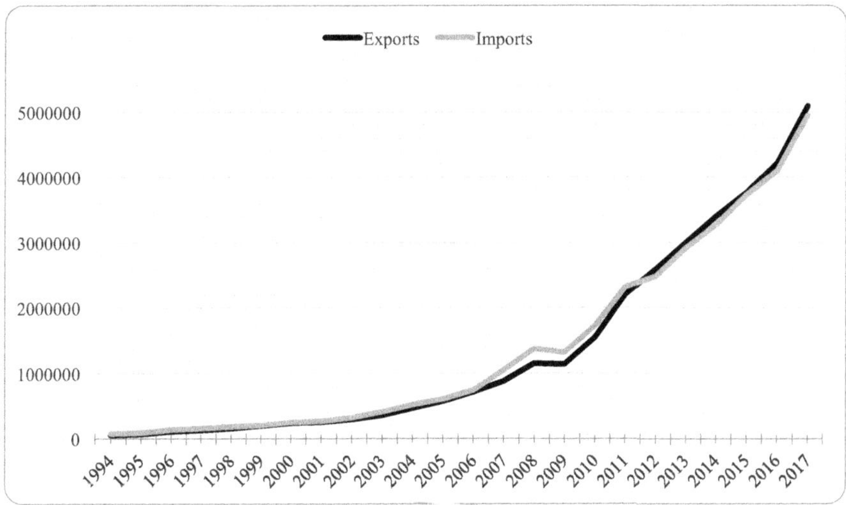

Figure 1.5 Imports and Exports of Goods and Services 1994–2017 (at current prices, in VND billion)

Source: Author's compilation, data retrieved from the Asian Development Bank (2013, 2018b).

year later. In 2017, the country exported USD 221 billion value in goods and services while importing USD 215 billion (Asian Development Bank, 2013, 2018b). Vietnam's imports value closely follows exports, implying that benefits from export surplus have been small and exports have not been the country's main source of revenue. More importantly, in the industrial sector, much of the value generated in exporting products, such as textiles and garments and electronics, involve assembling and low-skill manufacturing. Nevertheless, important learning and upgrading took place. Vietnamese exporters now engage in international trade, utilize new technology for higher productivity, and strive to be competitive. The history of imports and exports between 1994 and 2016 is captured in Figure 1.5.

Maintaining a stable macro environment, especially the inflation rate, has been a challenge for the Vietnamese government, as shown in Figure 1.6. Between 2004 and 2011, the high growth rate gave way to an unstable macroeconomic condition, when the inflation rate fluctuated between 7 and 23 percent. The instability severely undermined investor confidence in the country's long-term growth, and local firms struggled to weather the volatile costs of inputs during this period. Fortunately, the inflation rate declined beginning in 2012 and fell below 0 percent in 2015. It has been stable and below 5 percent in the late 2010s, landing at 3.5 percent in 2018 (Asian Development Bank, 2019).

Two important aspects of economic growth in an emerging economy are productivity growth and technological change, measured by the total factor

Figure 1.6 Vietnam's Inflation Rate, 1993–2018 (in percentage)

Source: Author's compilation based on data from World Development Indicators (2018) and Asian Development Bank (2019).

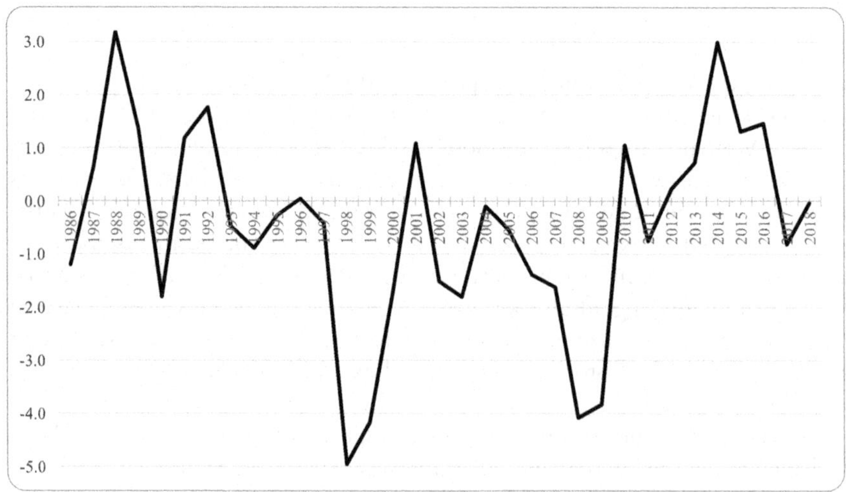

Figure 1.7 Growth of Total Factor Productivity, 1986–2018

Source: Author's compilation based on data from the Conference Board Total Economy Database (2019).

productivity (TFP). The TFP is an important indicator, as it demonstrates the level of industrialization and technology adoption that could be used to scale up capacity in all major sectors – industry, agriculture, and service. Vietnam's TFP was largely positive in the early period of economic reform (Figure 1.7).

The TFP, however, turned negative in a prolonged period between 1993 and 2010, but for a short spurt in 2001. This implies that much of Vietnam's growth during this period depended more on the increase of labor and capital and less on technological change, unlike the newly industrialized economies of South Korea, Singapore, and Taiwan. In the early 2010s, the TFP in Vietnam became largely positive again, varying between 1 and 3 percent; although, this only lasted until 2016. The generally positive TFP helps explain the rapid growth rate of industrial output and the sustained GDP growth rate during the 2010s. Now that Vietnam has achieved middle-income status, the quality and sustainability of its economic growth will very much depend on the economy staying productive and reducing reliance on capital and labor.

1.6.3 The state sector

Few topics elicit more fervent debate in Vietnam than state economic groups (SEGs) and state ownership. The state sector plays a pivotal role in the Vietnamese economy. According to the Ministry of Planning and Investment, in the early 2010s, Vietnamese SOEs held 70 percent of the total real property; accounted for 20 percent of investment capital throughout the economy; and devoured a staggering 60 percent of credit in the commercial banking system, 50 percent of state investment capital, and 70 percent of official development aid capital ("The unlearned lesson: Vinashin," 2012). Meanwhile, these same enterprises were responsible for only 25 percent of total sales revenues, 37 percent of pretax profits, and 20 percent of the value of national industrial output ("The unlearned lesson: Vinashin," 2012). Keen to emulate the experience of Japan's *Keiretsus*[8] and the Republic of Korea's *Chaebols*,[9] in 2005, Vietnam accelerated the process of creating general corporations (GCs) and SEGs – an alliance of several SOEs with similar business interests – before the country's accession to the WTO. As a result, the state sector was reduced in number, but its influence and market concentration remain intact. Furthermore, the 2005 reform allows the GCs and SEGs to hold tremendous market power and dominance: they have the highest market share in the sectors that they occupy. SEGs and GCs also enjoy privileged access to factor inputs, state capital, and a high level of operational autonomy from the state (Ngo & Tarko, 2018).

The GCs and SEGs initially did well following the 2005 reform, but their weaknesses were revealed in corruption scandals that erupted in the late 2000s. The state sector's failure was largely due to weak oversight and lack of transparency within the state system. The GCs and SEGs frequently expanded their operations into areas beyond their core competencies, mismanaged their finances, and concealed finance information from the government (World Bank, 2012). One of the biggest corruption cases involving a SEG was the Vietnam Shipbuilding Industry Group. The scandal caused public outrage in 2008, when one of its members, the state-owned shipbuilder Vinashin, failed to pay its international lenders, and the state inspectorate found widespread financial irregularities, embezzlement, and mismanagement in procurement and finances

(World Bank, 2012). According to a report by the World Bank (2012) at the time of the scandal, "the total Vinashin debt was reported to be US$ 4.4 billion in July 2010 – more than 200 percent of its annual sales and as much as 10 times its equity base" (p. 38). Vinashin's trial concluded in 2017, with two death sentences delivered to its former director general and sales manager. A life sentence was given to its former chief accountant. These three former officials were said to have embezzled USD 11.5 million in state assets ("Two executions," 2017).

In 2012, a mismanaged SEG again gained considerable public criticism, surrounding the case of Vinalines, Vietnam's largest state-owned shipping company and port operator. Vinalines was reported to have "defaulted on loans worth more than US$ 1.1 billion" and "nearly collapsed under some US$ 3 billion of debt" (*Agence France-Presse*, 2013). The chairman of the Ministry of Transport's Maritime Administration, Duong Chi Dung, and eight other Vinalines officials were prosecuted for embezzlement and mismanagement (*Agence France-Presse*, 2013). In one instance, Dung and Vinashin's chief executive officer, Mai Van Phuc, authorized the purchase of broken foreign floating docks, pocketing USD 1.6 million in government funds through the purchase (Lam, 2013). The broken docks "racked up enormous repair and maintenance bills" and thus opened the door for additional corruption and more wasted state resources (*Agence France-Presse*, 2013). Both Dung and Phuc received death sentences for their crimes, and the others each received life sentences.

Indeed, the 2005 reform was mixed with successes and failures since not all GCs and SEGs were barriers to economic development. Viettel Group, Vietnam National Textile and Garment Group (Vinatex), Saigon Alcohol Beer and Beverage Corporation (Sabeco), and Vietnam Dairy Products Joint Stock Co. (Vinamilk) are examples of high-performing GCs and SEGs. They contributed to state revenues, capacity building in the state sector, and forced fierce competition between the state and private sectors. For example, in 2017, Viettel Group, a GC operated under the Ministry of Defense and the most profitable firm in Vietnam, reported USD 1.94 billion in profit, a 12 percent increase from the previous year (Ha-Vy, 2018). Viettel contributed approximately USD 1.81 billion to the state budget in the same year, which was an increase of 2.3 percent on year (Ha-Vy, 2018). Similarly, in 2017, Vinamilk, Vietnam's state-owned producer of dairy products, earned USD 528.6 million in profit and contributed USD 185 million to the state budget ("Vinamilk eyes 51 trillion VND," 2017).

In 2017, the Vietnamese government once again came under intense pressure to privatize the state sector as part of its trade commitments with foreign partners. Internally, the government's decision to reduce the size of the public sector was also driven by a persistent fiscal deficit since 2009. The 2017 budget deficit was recorded at USD 7.58 billion – approximately 3.5 percent of GDP (Asian Development Bank, 2018a). As a result, in May 2017, "the government approved a blueprint for SOE restructuring in the 2016–2020 period, under which the government aims to equitize 137 more SOEs by 2020, most of which are large ones. It also stresses the plan to undertake divestments worth at least VND 250 trillion (US$ 11 billion) from equitized SOEs during this period"

(Le, 2017). The objectives are also to improve the performance of the SOEs, speed up Vietnam's commitment to liberalize its markets, and allow for more foreign investment in key sectors.

Despite the heavy push and commitments, the progress of this latest reform has been slow. By August 2018, out of 747 SOEs that completed initial public offerings in the earlier years, only 150 had floated shares on the local stock exchange. In Vietnam, initial public offerings and stock listings are distinct processes for most SOEs, and completion can take more than a decade. In addition, once equitized, many SOEs will remain at 65 percent state ownership ("Vietnam state company listings," 2018). This implies that the Vietnamese government will retain control of the major GCs in key industries, even while reducing the size of the state sector. Le Hong Hiep (2017) points out: "If the plan is successful, it may help improve Vietnam's long-term economic performance, attract a greater inflow of foreign investment, and contribute to Vietnam achieving emerging market status" (p. 1). The success and failure of managing the rent-seeking contest, resource allocation, and performance of the state will likely impact Vietnam's long-term growth and thus must be a priority of the country's development agenda in the coming decades.

1.7 Structure of the book

This book is organized into seven chapters. Chapter 2 surveys the literature on technology adoption, rents, and rent seeking in the context of development. The aim is to characterize the process of technological change and its links to economic performance in the presence of rents and rent-seeking activities in developing countries. From a theoretical viewpoint, the process of technological upgrade and capability building in a developing country is subject to a number of market failures that undermine firm and industry ability to optimize performance. As a result, appropriate rents and rent-management strategies are required to create the necessary incentives and pressures to solve the negative externalities, especially those that hinder technology adoption and innovation. Chapter 3 includes the framework for the analysis of rents and rent management: the DRMA framework, as mentioned previously. The central utilization of the DRMA framework is to observe how the three rent-management factors – politics, institutions, and industry organization – affect the structure of incentives and pressures that ensure firms' efforts toward technical learning, upgrading, and innovation. In addition, the DRMA enables a broader understanding of the various factors at play in the process of development, including a technological dimension. I then apply the DRMA framework to analyze Vietnam's industrial development.

Chapters 4, 5, and 6 assess the industrial development of the telecommunications, textile and garment, and motorcycle industries, respectively, from the 1990s to the 2010s. The qualitative analysis in these chapters covers eight case studies. I use a common structure for these three empirical chapters. Each starts with an overview of the respective industry's historical development before identifying the constraints that hinder domestic firms' efforts to achieve higher competitiveness. Following this, I apply the DRMA framework to the case study to discuss the rent-management mechanisms that determine the success or failure of the industry's development. These mechanisms involve rent creation and rent-seeking activities throughout the reform period. Each chapter concludes with observations and policy options for the industry to move forward. Chapter 7 synthesizes the empirical evidence and suggests three configurations of rent management that have driven Vietnam's industrial development since 1986. In addition, this chapter draws out lessons for other developing countries and contributions to development economics.

Notes

1 Economists often refer to the political economy approach as heterodox economics.
2 In this book, rent seeking and corruption are related processes, as both create rents. However, rent can also emerge from policymaking and market opportunities.
3 Rent-management mechanism and configuration of rent management are used interchangeably in this book.
4 Industry organization is defined as the structure of market competition and internal organization of firms affecting responses to different types of rent.
5 The industrial sector is defined broadly to include all modern productive activities.
6 USD 1 = VND 23,000 (exchange rate in July 2018).
7 Asian Development Bank's data for 2017 is considered to be estimated as of October 2018.
8 Keiretsus refers to a grouping of large Japanese financial and industrial corporations through historical associations and cross-shareholdings. In a keiretsu, each firm maintains its operational independence while retaining close commercial relationships with other firms in the group.
9 Chaebol refers to a South Korean form of business conglomerate. It typically comprises global multinationals that own numerous international enterprises; they are controlled by a chairman who oversees all chaebol operations.

References

Abegaz, B. (2013). Political parties in business: Rent seekers, developmentalists, or both? *Journal of Development Studies, 49*(11), 1467–1483. doi:10.1080/00220388.2013.822070

Acemoglu, D., & Verdier, T. (2000). The choice between market failure and corruption. *American Economic Review, 90*(1), 194–211.

Agence France-Presse. (2013, December 16). Vietnam hands out death sentences in Vinalines corruption case. *South China Morning Post*. Retrieved from www.scmp.com/news/asia/article/1382593/vietnam-hands-out-death-sentences-vinalines-corruption-case

Amsden, A. (1989). *Asia's next giant: South Korea and late industrialization*. New York: Oxford University Press.

Amsden, A. (2001). *The rise of "the rest": Challenges to the West from late-industrializing economies*. Oxford, England: Oxford University Press.

Amsden, A. H. (2009). Catch-up industrialization: The trajectory and prospects of East Asian economies. *Developing Economies*, 47(4), 488–491.

Asian Development Bank. (2013). *Basic statistics*. Retrieved from www.adb.org/publications/basic-statistics-2013

Asian Development Bank. (2018a). *Basic statistics*. Retrieved from www.adb.org/publications/basic-statistics-2018

Asian Development Bank. (2018b). *Vietnam, key indicators*. Retrieved from https://data.adb.org/dataset/viet-nam-key-indicators

Asian Development Bank. (2019). *Viet Nam: By the numbers.* Retrieved from https://data.adb.org/dashboard/viet-nam-numbers

Bardhan, P. (1999). *Political economy of development in India* (2nd ed.). Oxford, England: Oxford University Press.

Booth, D., & Golooba-Mutebi, F. (2011). *Developmental patrimonialism? The case of Rwanda* (Overseas Development Institute, Working Paper 16). Retrieved from Overseas Development Institute www.institutions-africa.org/filestream/20110321-appp-working-paper-16-developmental-patrimonialism-the-case-of-rwanda-by-david-booth-and-frederick-golooba-mutebi-march-2011

Booth, D., & Golooba-Mutebi, F. (2012). Developmental patrimonialism? The case of Rwanda. *African Affairs, 111*(444), 379–403.

Buchanan, J. M., Tollison, R. D., & Tullock, G. (1980). *Toward a theory of the rent-seeking society.* College Station, TX: Texas A&M University Press.

Bui, T. T. (2000). After the war: 25 years of economic development in Vietnam. *National Institute for Research Advancement (NIRA) Review, Spring*, 21–25.

Chang, H.-J. (1999). The economic theory of developmental state. In M. Woo-Cumings (Ed.), *The developmental state* (pp. 182–199). Cornell, NY: Cornell University Press.

Chang, H. J. (2000). State building and late development. *Studies in Comparative International Development, 35*(3), 133–135.

Chang, H. J., Cheema, A., & Mises, L. (2002). Conditions for successful technology policy in developing countries: Learning rents, state structures and institutions. *Economics of Innovation and New Technology, 11*(4–5), 369–398.

Cimoli, M., Dosi, G., & Stiglitz, J. E. (2009). *Industrial policy and development: The political economy of capabilities accumulation* (O. U. Press, Ed.). New York, NY: Oxford University Press.

Conference Board Total Economy Database. (2019). *Growth accounting and total factor productivity, 1990–2018.* Retrieved from www.conference-board.org/data/economydatabase/index.cfm?id=27762

Coolidge, J., & Rose-Ackerman, S. (1999). *High-level rent-seeking and corruption in African regimes: Theory and cases* (Policy Research Working Papers, Issue No. 1780). Retrieved from World Bank, Private Sector Development Department and Foreign Investment Advisory Service http://elibrary.worldbank.org/doi/book/10.1596/1813-9450-1780

Davies, N. (2015, April 22). Vietnam 40 years on: How a communist victory gave way to capitalist corruption. *The Guardian.* Retrieved from www.theguardian.com/news/2015/apr/22/vietnam-40-years-on-how-communist-victory-gave-way-to-capitalist-corruption

Doan, Q. (2012, November). *Reforming the SOEs in Vietnam: Does the new wave make any difference?* Paper presented at the Canberra Workshop, Canberra, Australia.

Elliott, J. (1992). The future of socialism: Vietnam, the way ahread? *Third World Quarterly, 13*(1), 131–142.

Fine, B. (1997). Industrial policy and South Africa: A strategic view. *Indicator South Africa, 14*(3), 49–54.

Fung, K. C. (1989). Unemployment, profit-sharing and Japan's economic success. *European Economic Review, 33*(4), 783–796.

Gray, H. (2015). The political economy of grand corruption in Tanzania. *African Affairs, 114*(456), 382–403.

Gray, H. (2018). *Turbulence and order in economic development: Economic transformation in Tanzania and Vietnam.* Oxford, England: Oxford University Press.

Gray, H., & Whitfield, L. (2014). *Reframing African political economy: Clientelism, rents and accumulation as drivers of capitalist transformation* (Working Paper Series, 159). Retrieved from London School of Economics http://eprints.lse.ac.uk/61252/

Hanousek, J., & Kochanova, A. (2016). Bribery environment and firm performance: Evidence from central and eastern European countries. *European Journal of Political Economy, 43*(C), 14–28.

Ha-Vy. (2018, March 1). Viettel reports massive revenue and profit. *Vietnam Investment Review*. Retrieved from www.vir.com.vn/viettel-reports-massive-revenue-and-profit-55245.html

Helper, S. (2000). Economists and field research: "You can observe a lot just by watching." *The American Economic Review, 90*(2), 228–232.

International Monetary Fund. (2019). *Report for selected countries and subjects*. Retrieved from www.imf.org/external/pubs/ft/weo/2019/01/weodata/weorept.aspx?pr.x=47&pr.y=3&sy=2017&ey=2021&scsm=1&ssd=1&sort=country&ds=.&br=1&c=582&s=NGDPD%2CPPPGDP%2CNGDPDPC%2CPPPPC%2CPCPIPCH&grp=0&a=

Khan, M. H. (2000). Rent-seeking as process. In M. H. Khan & K. S. Jomo (Eds.), *Rents, rent-seeking and economic development: Theory and evidence in Asia* (pp. 70–144). Cambridge, England: Cambridge University Press.

Khan, M. H., & Blankenburg, S. (2009). The political economy of industrial policy in Asia and Latin America. In G. Dosi, M. Cimoli, & J. E. Stiglitz (Eds.), *Industrial policy and development: The political economy of capabilities accumulation* (pp. 336–377). Oxford, England: Oxford University Press.

Khan, M. H., & Jomo, K. S. (2000a). Introduction. In M. H. Khan & K. S. Jomo (Eds.), *Rents, rent seeking and economic development: Theory and evidence in Asia* (pp. 1–20). Cambridge, England: Cambridge University Press.

Khan, M. H., & Jomo, K. S. (2000b). *Rents, rent-seeking and economic development: Theory and the Asian evidence*. Cambridge, England: Cambridge University Press.

Krueger, A. O. (1974). Political economy of the rent-seeking society. *American Economic Review, 64*(3), 291–303.

Krueger, A. O. (1998). Why trade liberalisation is good for growth. *The Economic Journal, 108*(450), 1513–1522.

Krueger, A. O. (2012). *Struggling with success: Challenges facing the international economy*. Hackensack, NJ: World Scientific Publishing Co.

Lall, S. (1992). Technological capability and industrialization. *World Development, 20*(2), 165–186.

Lall, S. (2004). *Reinventing industrial strategy: The role of government policy in building industrial competitiveness* (G24 Discussion Paper Series No. 28). UNCTAD, The Intergovernmental Group on Monetary Affairs and Development (G-24). Retrieved from http://unctad.org/en/Docs/gdsmdpbg2420044_en.pdf

Lam, M. (2013, December 17). Vietnam sentences top shipping execs to death for embezzlement. *Radio Free Asia*. Retrieved from www.rfa.org/english/news/vietnam/sentence-12172013171041.html

Le, H. H. (2017). Vietnam's new wave of SOE equitization: Drivers and implications. *Perspective, 57*.

Masina, P. P. (2006). *Vietnam's development strategies*. New York, NY: Routledge.

Mauro, P. (1997). *Why worry about corruption?* (Economic Issues No. 6). Retrieved from International Monetary Fund www.imf.org/external/pubs/ft/issues6/

Medema, S. G. (1991). Another look at the problem of rent seeking. *Journal of Economic Issues, 25*(4), 1049–1065.

Méndez, F., & Sepúlveda, F. (2006). Corruption, growth and political regimes: Cross country evidence. *European Journal of Political Economy, 22*(1), 82–98.

Ngo, C. N. (2016). Developmental rent management analysis: Learning, upgrading, and innovation. *Journal of Economic Issues, 50*(4), 1045–1068.

Ngo, C. N., & Tarko, V. (2018). Economic development in a rent-seeking society: Socialism, state capitalism and crony capitalism in Vietnam. *Canadian Journal of Development Studies, 39*(4), 481–499. doi:10.1080/02255189.2018.1467831

Nguyen, A. N., Nguyen, N. D., Nguyen, C. D., & Nguyen, T. (2010). *The global crisis and medium term growth prospects for developing countries: The case of Vietnam* (Working Paper Series No. 2010/08). Retrieved from Development and Policies Research Center https://pdfs.semanticscholar.org/6b55/ba798a4dc3e3d137b3f1441b504568adda51.pdf?_ga=2.244218373.1218768641.1566138497-2100227049.1566138497

Nguyen, A. N., Nguyen, T., Le, D. T., Pham, Q. N., Nguyen, D. C., & Nguye, D. N. (2008). *Foreign direct investment in Vietnam: Is there any evidence of technological spillover effects* (Working Paper Series No. 18). Retrieved from Development and Policies Research Center http://mpra.ub.uni-muenchen.de/7273/1/Vietnam_FDI_Spillover.pdf

North, D. C. (1990). *Institutions, institutonal change and economic performance.* Cambridge, England: Cambridge University Press.

North, D. C., Wallis, J. J., Webb, S. B., & Weingast, B. R. (2007). *Limited access orders in the developing world: A new approach to the problems of development* (Policy Research Working Paper No. 4359). Retrieved from World Bank http://elibrary.worldbank.org/content/workingpaper/10.1596/1813-9450-4359

Piore, M. (1979). Qualitative research techniques in economics. *Administrative Science Quarterly, 24*(4), 560–569.

Posner, R. A. (1975). The social costs of monopoly and regulation. *Journal of Political Economy, 83*(4), 807–827.

Rodrik, D. (2004). *Industrial policy for the twenty-first century.* Retrieved from Centre for Economic Policy Research http://econpapers.repec.org/paper/cprceprdp/4767.htm

Sachs, J., & Pistor, K. (1997). *The rule of law and economic reform in Russia.* Boulder, CO: Westview Press.

Samuels, W. J., & Mercuro, N. (1984). A critique of rent-seeking theory. In D. C. Colander (Ed.), *Neoclassical political economy: The analysis of rent-seeking and DUP activities* (pp. 55–70). Cambridge, MA: Ballinger.

Starr, M. (2014). Qualitative and mixed-methods research in economics: Surprising growth, promising future. *Journal of Economic Surveys, 28*(2), 238–264.

Stiglitz, J. E. (2013). Learning, growth and development. In J. Y. Lin & C. P. Sepulveda (Eds.), *Annual World Bank conference on development economics 2011: Development challenges in a post-crisis world.* Washington, DC: The World Bank Group.

Thoburn, J. (2013). Vietnam as a role model for development. In A. Fosu (Ed.), *Achieving development success* (pp. 1–23). New York: Oxford University Press.

Tullock, G. (1967). Welfare costs of tariffs, monopolies, and theft. *Western Economic Journal, 5*(3), 224–232.

Two executions, one life sentence in Vinashin case. (2017, February 23). *Viet Nam News.* Retrieved from https://vietnamnews.vn/politics-laws/351702/two-executions-one-life-sentence-in-vinashin-case.html#8S0s7HAEKiOmM4Q0.97

United Nations Conference on Trade and Development. (2018). *Trade and development report 2018: Powever, flatforms and the free trade delusion.* Geneva: United Nations.

The unlearned lesson: Vinashin, VinaLines, and other SOEs' inefficiencies. (2012, May 27). *American chamber of commerce in Vietnam.* Retrieved from www.amchamvietnam.com/the-unlearned-lesson-vinashin-vinalines-and-other-soes-inefficiencies/

Vietnam state company listings lose steam under stricter rules. (2018, August 8). *Nikkei Asian Review*. Retrieved from https://asia.nikkei.com/Business/Companies/Vietnam-state-company-listings-lose-steam-under-stricter-rules

Vinamilk eyes 51 trillion VND in revenue in 2017. (2017, September 22). *Bao Anh Vietnam*. Retrieved from https://vietnam.vnanet.vn/english/vinamilk-eyes-51-trillion-vnd-in-revenue-in-2017/332994.html

Wade, R. (1990). *Governing the market: Economic theory and the role of government in East Asian industrialization*. Princeton, NJ: Princeton University Press.

Weeks, J. (2001). A tale of two transitions: Cuba and Vietnam after the collapse of the Soviet Union. In C. Brundenius & J. Weeks (Eds.), *Globalisation and third world socialism: Cuba and Vietnam* (pp. 18–40). London, England: Palgrave Macmillan.

Whitfield, L., Therkildsen, O., Buur, L., & Kjaer, A. M. (2015). *The politics of African industrial policy*. New York, NY: Cambridge University Press.

World Bank. (1991). *World development report 1991: The challenge of development*. New York, NY: Oxford University Press.

World Bank. (2003). *Vietnam delivering on its promise* (Development Report 2003, Report No. 25050-VN). Retrieved from World Bank http://siteresources.worldbank.org/INTVIETNAM/Resources/VDR03.pdf

World Bank. (2008). *The growth report: Strategies for sustained growth and inclusive development*. Washington, DC: The World Bank Group.

World Bank. (2012). *Vietnam development report 2012: Market economy for a middle income Vietnam* (Joint Donor Report to the Vietnam Consultative Group Meeting). Retrieved from World Bank www-wds.worldbank.org/external/default/WDSContentServer/WDSP/IB/2011/12/13/000333037_20111213003843/Rendered/PDF/659800AR00PUBL0elopment0Report02012.pdf

World Bank. (2019). *The World Bank in Vietnam: Overview*. Retrieved from World Bank www.worldbank.org/en/country/vietnam/overview

World Development Indicators. (2018). *Vietnam*. Retrieved from The World Bank https://data.worldbank.org/country/vietnam?view=chart

2 Rethinking rent seeking for development and technological change

2.1 An evolutionary process within a rent-seeking economy

Economic development is an evolutionary process, with technological change as the core element and the primary driver of development and social change (Lall, 2004; Nelson, 2008). The cumulative acquisition of new technologies and the process of adapting them to the local environment allows for skills, knowledge, and production to gradually level up toward advanced countries. To the extent that it is possible, institutional structures, including the legal, political, and social environments, provide the framework for firms, workers, and entrepreneurs to thrive and catch up. From this perspective, "the co-evolution of technologies, firm and industry structures, and supporting and government institutions" as well as "the driving dynamics involve[d in] their interaction" critically shape the process of development in poor countries (Nelson, 2008, p. 13). However, it has become commonplace for economies in the early- or mid-stages of development to have vested interests that exploit the political and legal systems to secure as great a return as possible (Myrdal, 1979). Over time, the developmental state may be captured by political and economic interests and become the "soft state" as characterized by Myrdal (1968, 1979). In other words, a *rent-seeking society* is embedded in each developing economy (and to a lesser extent, advanced economies), which operates both formally and informally through political and economic structures. The extent to which rent seeking succeeds in producing economic growth depends upon its ability to enhance or hinder industrial upgrade and technological change (Khan & Jomo, 2000).

This chapter surveys the recent literature on technological change and rent seeking applied to economic development. It highlights the importance of rent creation and rent seeking for growth and development. The dual processes of technological change and rent seeking not only inform development theory and practice but also help developing countries understand themselves and their experiences. This theoretical survey suggests that the evolutionary process of economic development and industrialization must include rent management – a combination of incentives and conditions that promote development – to provide due attention to social, political, and economic factors influencing economic transformation.

2.1.1 *Preliminary definitions*

It is important to define, at least generally, some concepts that will be employed throughout. *Technological upgrade* is defined as any type of technical learning, including technology transfers, adoption, adaptation, and innovation. *Capability building* is the enhancement of organizational, technological, and managerial capabilities relevant for the development of new and higher quality products or more efficient production of existing products. As mentioned in Chapter 1, *rent* is defined as income higher than the next-best payment under an alternative structure of rights (Samuels & Mercuro, 1984).

The definitions and uses of *rent seeking* are more diverse. James Buchanan (1980b) identifies rent seeking as a means to "describe behavior in institutional settings where individual efforts to maximize value generate social waste rather than social surplus" (p. 4). Heterodox definitions include that of Steven Medema (1991), who offers an institutionalist understanding of the concept wherein legal institutions *create* and thus *alter existing* rights, which establish the bases for rents and the *reallocation* of rents.[1] In addition, Mushtaq Khan (2000a) identifies rent seeking as simply "the expenditure of resources and effort in creating, maintaining, or transferring rents" (p. 70). This book adopts the heterodox view of rent seeking defined by Medema (1991) and Khan (2000a). As illustrated in Figure 2.1, I argue that there are three different sources of rent: (1) from explicit rent-seeking activities, (2) via government policymaking, and (3) through opportunities arising from either market activities or the structure of industry. The conceptual framework of rent and rent seeking used in this book is applied both to the public and private sectors.

The literature on *rent management* "starts from the position that rents need to be created in order to channel investments into desirable sectors and is concerned with the conditions to make this happen" (Schmitz, Johnson, & Altenburg, 2013, p. 6). Thus, "rent management refers to the way governments create or withdraw policy rents and how they influence their allocation among different actors and for different purposes" (p. 7). The mechanism by which the process of rent management takes place has been elaborated elsewhere (Ngo, 2016a). There, rent management is understood as the interplay of politics, institutions, and market structures through which an industry or an entire economy are organized. It is

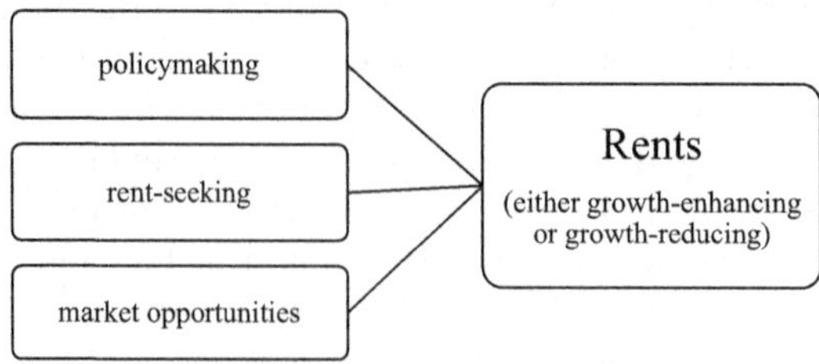

Figure 2.1 Sources of Rent Creation

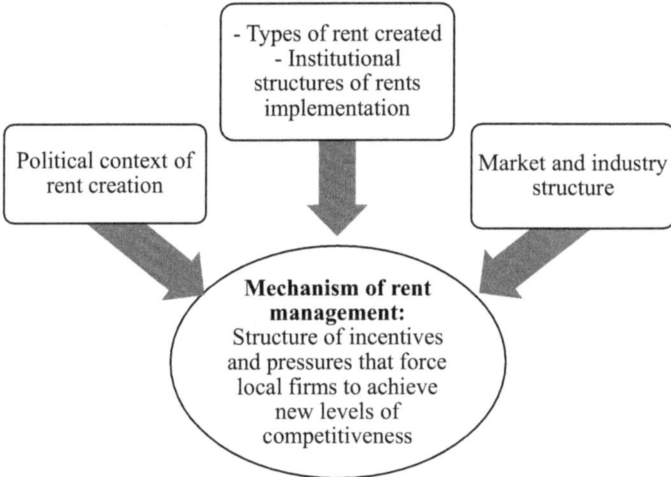

Figure 2.2 Mechanism of Rent Management

also the manner in which rent-receiving firms are incentivized or pressured to upgrade, or how the industrial structure of an economy is reconfigured. *Rent policy*, then, formalizes the processes through which rent management is most effective in achieving its desired goals; policy is explicitly designed to create rents for the express purpose of promoting development and oftentimes emerges from formal political and institutional structures. The factors contributing to a rent-management system are shown in Figure 2.2. The conceptual framework of this chart is detailed in Chapter 3.

An effective rent-management system establishes incentive structures that motivate the achievement of new technical learning, capability building, and competitiveness (Ngo, 2016a, p. 1046). These conditions are not limited to the formal political and institutional arrangements within a state, but are taken from a wider context of the interplay between politics, institutions, and the structure and interaction between the market and firms (Ngo, 2016a).

Finally, *industrial policy* is often referred to as technology policy, particularly if it aims to promote technological change, technology transfer, or innovation. Industrial policy is a subset of rent policy because it inherently creates rents for industries and firms. Rent seeking and corruption are related processes, as both create rents, although rent seeking is not always damaging, especially if it supports industrial development and growth. Nonetheless, rent can be created for purposes other than supporting industrial development (i.e., transfers for personal gain), and it can also emerge from market opportunities. The relationship between different rent policies is graphically demonstrated in Figure 2.3.

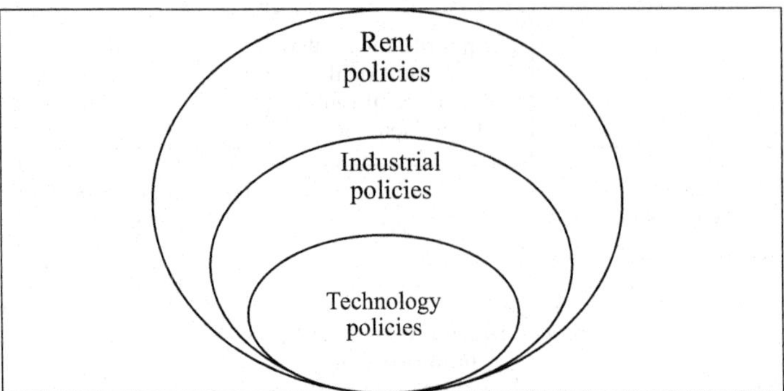

Figure 2.3 Relationships among Various Types of Rent Policy

2.1.2 Chapter organization

This chapter is organized into four sections. Section 2.2 assesses characteristics of technological change in a development context. It first reviews the neoclassical literature, focusing on the relationship between technology and growth. This view was largely derived from Solow's (1956, 1957) model on growth and technical change. Second, alternative approaches to technological transfers and appropriation of knowledge are presented. These approaches challenge Solow's and others' assumptions by pointing out that the appropriation of knowledge is neither automatic nor costless. It is in this context that the state's intervention in the forms of industrial policy is arguably essential for catching up. Section 2.3 surveys the market failures associated with technical learning. This section reviews three important aspects related to technical learning: the creation of a learning economy by Joseph Stiglitz (1989, 2013b), learning-by-discovery by Ricardo Hausmann and Dani Rodrik (2003; Hausmann, Rodrik, & Velasco, 2008), and a firm's organizational capability by Mushtaq Khan (2000a, 2000b, 2009, 2012).

Issues of rent seeking and rent management are explored in depth in the remaining parts of the chapter. Section 2.4 provides a review of the theoretical debates on rents and rent seeking with special attention to technological upgrading and capability building at the firm and industry levels. While the neoliberal approach suggests that the government should focus on eliminating rents and rent seeking entirely, heterodox economists assert that, under certain conditions, rents could be value enhancing (Chang, Cheema, & Mises, 2002; Khan, 2000b; North, Wallis, Webb, & Weingast, 2007), and thus, effective development strategies should take into consideration the creation and management of value-enhancing rents (Khan, 2000b; Ngo, 2016a; Whitfield, Therkildsen, Buur, & Kjaer, 2015). Finally, Section 2.5 considers the role of the political state and informal institutions in solving the critical twofold problem of development identified at the start of this chapter. The review focuses principally on the research of Hirschman (1957, 1958), Myrdal (1979), North and colleagues (2007, 2006), Ha-Joon Chang (1999), and Mushtaq Khan (1995, 2000a, 2012).

These myriad strands of literature do not constitute a unified school of thought. Nevertheless, they present strong analytical complementarities and share the common assertion that the analysis of technological change and capability building for developing countries should be based not only on economic theories on technology, growth, and development but also on a wider understanding of the formal and informal dynamics of rent seeking and rent-management processes. The literature provides useful insights in examining the determinants of technical upgrade and competitiveness in developing countries from a rent-management perspective.

2.2 Characteristics of technology adoption and growth in a development context

Economic and industrial development can largely be viewed as a process of technological "catch-up," in which firms in developing countries learn to master new technologies of production already in use in more advanced economies (Cimoli, Dosi, & Stiglitz, 2009a; Khan, 2013; Lall, 2004; List, 1984).[2] From this perspective, technological catch-up is the primary instrument that closes the technology gap between developing countries and the international technological frontier. By and large, this process could help domestic firms increase productivity and strengthen international competitiveness by supplying value-added goods and components across global value chains. This section reviews various strands of literature emphasizing the important process and contribution of technological change to economic growth and the role of the state in this process.

2.2.1 Classical and neoclassical positions on technology and growth

The leading roles of technology and technological progress for economic growth and development are widely discussed in economics literature. In "An Inquiry into the Nature and Causes of the Wealth of Nations," Adam Smith (1776/1998) identifies the gains to be made from the division of labor and production specialization. Smith highlights the benefits derived from a specific form of technological progress: specialization via organizational change. For Smith, specialization allows for economies of scale in production, increases efficiency, and ensures long-term technological progress through a crucial enabling factor: learning-by-doing (Van den Berg, 2016). Technological change is also central to Marx's (1859/1906) and in a somewhat similar way Schumpeter's (1942) analyses of the dynamics of capitalism, where innovation and competition drive processes of capitalist accumulation and growth. Similarly, it is instrumental in Kaldor's (1957, 1967) examination of industrial growth, capital accumulation, and economic development.

Between the 1960s and the 2000s, debate on technological change and industrialization in developing countries is largely dominated by neoclassical thinking on economic development, chiefly derived from (1) Robert Solow's (1956, 1957) growth model and (2) the Washington Consensus – a set of policies that John Williamson devised to address development problems in Latin America.[3] Solow's model includes several important neoclassical assumptions: diminishing returns to factors of production, constant returns to scale, savings equals investment, supply creates its own demand, and exogenous technological change. According to Solow, the only way an economy can enjoy long-term growth is through technology adoption or innovation that increases the productivity of labor. That is, technological change expands the production function, allowing for long-run growth in per capita output (Van den Berg, 2016, pp. 203–204). This approach to technological change has since been adopted in many economics textbooks and treated as standard economic analysis for development. Key policy and academic documents, such as the World Bank's "World Development Reports 1987: Industrialization and Foreign Trade" and "World Development Reports 1991: The Challenge of Development" or Anne Krueger's (1974, 1998) research on trade and development continue to provide the basic theme for neoclassical analysis on growth and development in poor countries.

With regard to the role of trade and international factor movements, neoclassical growth models presume that the most efficient and appropriate technologies from advanced countries are free and available for developing countries to adopt at each and every stage, given their relative factor endowments. It is thus expected that once developing countries purchase or transfer advanced technology from abroad, it is only a matter of time before developing countries catch up with more advanced economies in technological and economic terms (Warren, 2007). When it appears that different economies grow at different rates, inconsistent with the unconditional convergence theory, the inconsistency is attributed to distortions induced by industrial or interventionist policies (Fine & Jomo, 2006). In addition, differences in performance are regarded as the result of policy barriers, which slow technological trickle-down effects from technologically advanced countries to developing economies (Warren, 2007). In other words, government interventions deter the "automatic" transfer of technology from advanced to developed countries.

From this perspective, neoclassical thinking asserts that technological progress in developing countries is achieved by improving the channels and mechanisms[4] through which advanced technologies from developed economies reach developing economies. That is to say, developing countries should focus on improving incentives for the transfer of technologies. To achieve these objectives, neoclassical literature identifies four main mechanisms that promote technological catch-up and development: (1) trade openness, (2) deregulation that promotes competition, (3) foreign direct investment (FDI), and (4) macroeconomic stability. These mechanisms are largely reflected in the Washington Consensus agenda led by the World Bank and the International Monetary Fund during the 1980s–2000s period (Fine & Jomo, 2006).

The focus on these four mechanisms as avenues of technological upgrade for developing countries reflects the assumption that technology can be unconditionally transferred from abroad via trade and FDI. In addition, overregulation, interventionist policies, and macroeconomic instability are barriers to technological adoption because they deter investment and self-regulated activities of market forces. At the policy level, neoclassical views on the process of development, including its technological dimension, offer a theoretical basis for the implementation of structural adjustment and macroeconomic stabilization programs across the developing world. The Washington and Post-Washington Consensus were readily adopted in the World Bank's aid programs and the International Monetary Fund's financial reform package.

Critics of the neoclassical approach

Critics of neoclassical economics identify a number of shortcomings concerning technology and growth. First, neoclassical literature constructs and utilizes economic models that assume firms to be rational and optimizing agents with perfect information. Firms are understood to function in perfectly competitive market environments, including the market for technological goods, among others, with price signals accurately set by the market. In the absence of policy restrictions, technology is assumed to be freely available across borders and costless to apply within the firm. From a growth perspective, neoclassical thinking fails to "recognize the institutional complexities of modern market economies" (Nelson, 2008, p. 11). It is also unable to explain the evolutionary process of technological change and the diverse paths that poor countries took to converge toward more advanced economies (Van den Berg, 2016). These failures are severe in that neoclassical economics offers few insights, and thus policy suggestions, as to how poor countries might achieve the technological capacity crucial for catching up.

Second, the neoclassicals' primary concern with allocative efficiency is to the exclusion of other, and perhaps more important, types of efficiency. Neoclassical economics assumes that by construction, market mechanisms are efficient and nonmarket mechanisms are inefficient (Fine, 1997). This view is far from reality, especially in developing countries, where distorted price signals and market failures are much more pervasive and damaging than in developed countries (Fine, 1997; Khan, 2000b; Rodrik, 1995, 2004; Stiglitz, 1989, 1994). Third, neoclassical approaches largely focus on the allocation of resources in a competitive environment. Thus, they are unable to respond to a number of fundamental economic questions concerning: (1) how to mobilize and deploy new resources and create new capacities; (2) how finance, trade, employment, and the exchange and interest rates are associated with development strategy; and (3) how industrial policies fit with the development of the economy as a whole (Fine, 1997).

Additionally, transfers of technology from FDI are not voluntary and automatic. Amsden (2009) points out that most cases of accelerated accumulation of technological and managerial capabilities have historically occurred within domestic firms, not within subsidiaries of foreign-owned firms operating in a developing country. This is because "even when MNCs [multinational corporations] are an important source of capital investment, they often carry relatively limited technology transfer, with the most tacit forms of knowledge and a good deal of R&D activities being kept in developed countries" (Cimoli et al., 2009a, p. 8). Finally, new (endogenous) growth theory dismisses the standard neoclassical proposition in two fundamental ways. First, technology is endogenous and thus different firms, and countries may operate under significantly different technological conditions and costs (Van den Berg, 2016). Second, given the determinants of returns on capital, the direction of investment decisions is no longer solely determined by its relative scarcity but also by labor, education, and skills (Lall, 1992; Nelson, 2008).

Given the simplistic and unrealistic assumptions put forward by neoclassical growth models, policy agendas set by neoclassical thinking are both impractical and unachievable. More importantly, a partial move toward such policies advocated by the New Washington Consensus[5] can be damaging for countries, as it does not solve the pressing issues of development – that is, negative externalities and political, financial, and fiscal instabilities (Rodrik, 2004). In addressing these shortcomings, the heterodox view asserts that in real and historical contexts, technological change takes place in vastly different ways than the processes asserted by neoclassical literature.

2.2.2 *Alternative view: technological capability and the appropriation of knowledge*

The process of economic transformation is dynamic and evolutionary. Hence, as evolutionary economic literature emphasizes, "long-run economic change must be understood as involving the co-evolution of technologies in use and the institutional structures supporting and regulating these" (Nelson, 2008, p. 9). More specifically, this strand of literature maintains (1) "the significant differences in the rate of progress at any time across different technologies and industries," (2) "growth tends to be punctuated by 'eras' characterized by the development and diffusion of specific constellations of 'general purpose' technologies," and (3) "the evolutionary processes of economic growth are embedded in a rich structure of institutions" (Dosi & Nelson, 2009, pp. 56–57). These observations are amplified by the institutional view of technological change, suggesting that the most important challenge to technical progress in developing countries is not access to tools (or the technology itself) but the lack of indigenous tool-using capability (or technical capability) needed to develop competitive production capability in the global market (Ayres, 1944; Cimoli et al., 2009a; James, 1988; Khan, 2009). From this perspective, a critical problem is incorporating and adapting a technology to local production processes in order to achieve new competitiveness. Dilmus James (1988) is representative of this strand of literature. While technologies exist, it may be the case that political or other constraints prevent it from being available; the technologies "may be on display, but not for sale." Or perhaps:

> Other forms of knowledge cannot be obtained in the market. There is an irreducible component to know-how, often firm-specific, that cannot be acquired by means other than operating experience. Commonly known as "tacit knowledge," and almost universally assumed away by conventional economic analysis, its accumulation is crucial for the technological progress of a firm.
>
> (James, 1988, p. 342)

There is also an emphasis on local firms to acquire this tacit knowledge – a process that is not easy, free, or automatic. For domestic industries to gain new competitiveness, an approximate sequence of learning experiences by local firms includes,

> a growing talent for spotting a problem or opportunity with a technological dimension; learning to search, screen, select, and bargain for technology; acquiring the ability to modify imported equipment and production procedures to fit local conditions; developing the capability for making further innovative alterations of technology in response to changes in the economic environment; gaining mastery over designing equipment; and instigating organized research and development activities.
>
> (James, 1988, p. 340)

The heterodox literature emphasizes the idiosyncratic and context-dependent nature of firms' ability to acquire tacit knowledge (Lall, 1992; Nelson, 2008; Nelson & Winter, 1982). For example, Vietnamese component manufacturers frequently learn the trade from simpler Chinese technologies and machineries before they are able to upgrade and use more advanced technologies, such as Japan's, to produce higher-quality components for the international market (Ngo, 2016b). Furthermore, prevalent market failures exist in the development of key technological inputs – skills and capability – and in the diffusion and adaptation of new technology in the local context (Cimoli et al., 2009a; Hausmann & Rodrik, 2003; Khan, 2009; Stiglitz, 1989). As a result, there are high costs associated with the adoption and learning of advanced technologies because firms in poor countries frequently lack investment capital, skilled workers, technology-management knowledge, and international experiences (Cimoli et al., 2009b; Ngo & Chi, 2017). These constraints cannot simply be resolved by market forces and thus require an active government to correct them. More explicitly, development economists suggest that the state must play an active role in reducing the technology gap in developing countries through investment in skilled learning, acquisition of new technology, and systemic diffusion of technology, together with the necessary tacit knowledge (Chang et al., 2002; Hausmann & Rodrik, 2003; Khan, 2000b; Rodrik, 2007).

The rise of East Asian economies in the post-World War II era substantiates this view. During South Korea's industrialization, the Korean government protected domestic firms and assisted with industrialization using policies such as direct financing of technology transfers, tariffs, import licensing, and local content requirements. In Taiwan, the government directly purchased technology from abroad and adapted it in state-run labs. Once the state mastered the technology and adapted the technology to local demands and production, state agencies transferred the technology to Taiwanese small and medium enterprises. This process reduced the cost of technology investment for Taiwanese firms, cut short their learning period, and systematically helped local manufacturers across various sectors in the same period (Amsden, 1989; Wade, 1990). Together with effective exporting practices, the active East Asian governments transformed Taiwan and South Korea from a low-skilled, low-tech economy to an OECD country, with high-tech manufacturing and a leading trading hub in Southeast Asia (Amsden, 1989; James, 1988; Wade, 1990).

The East Asian experiences highlight a crucial empirical aspect of development: in a context where international comparative advantages are no longer determined only by factor endowments but also by the level of technological competence, local firms' ability to adopt and adapt new technologies is particularly significant for catch-up. In addition, development of technological capabilities in sectors associated with higher learning-by-doing, value addition, or complex manufacturing could contribute to greater industrial deepening, knowledge spillovers, and long-run growth (Stiglitz, 1989, 2013b). From this perspective, if not accompanied by efforts to upgrade local technological capabilities, across-the-board liberalization policies may lead to a situation where developing countries only reinforce existing advantages in simple, low-tech production, where they possess comparative advantages (Ngo, 2017). An increase in foreign competition within the domestic market has also been known to discourage local firms from investing time and capital into new technology. Instead, they opt to pursue low-cost production activities (Ngo, 2017; Ohno, 2008). Given the challenges associated with technology and capability development, development economists generally argue that developing countries must actively employ industrial policies to remove market externalities and support technological adoption and innovation that go beyond the policy framework put forward by neoclassical theories. The specific policy measures to effectively promote technological change in developing countries depend largely on the types of market failures experienced and local firms' ability to learn and adopt new technology into production. The market failures frequently associated with technology adoption and learning are surveyed in the next section.

2.3 Market failures associated with technical learning

The modern theory of market failures identifies important problems facing economic development. Market failure (or negative externality) is a general term to describe situations in which resources are not allocated in the most efficient manner, causing market outcomes to fall short of optimal efficiency. The argument here is that on its own, the market is not efficient in promoting growth and development. Market failures in technological adoption arise due to a number of supply-side constraints, such as technological externalities, information asymmetry, problems related to contracting throughout the learning process, insufficient access to financing by manufacturing firms, inadequate spillovers, and the uncertain nature of technological investment. In addition, they are the result of deficiencies in capital markets used to finance technological investments and learning. From the perspective of industrial capability building, the pervasiveness of market failures in the supply of technology-related inputs is particularly damaging because they deter the utilization of new technology in competitive production (Lall, 1992; Lall & Larsch, 1999). In addition to supply-side externalities, the market failures the literature identifies as demand side also constrain the process of technological accumulation among firms. These essentially refer to the lack of *incentive frameworks* for manufacturing firms to put forth serious effort into learning new technology, upgrading organizational capability, and innovating new ideas.

Central to the debate of market imperfections are the externalities that impact learning, described first by Arrow (1962) and then by Stiglitz (1989) and Khan (2000b) under the concept of learning-by-doing. Hausmann and Rodrik (2003) analyze learning externality from the perspective of learning-by-discovery. Finally, Khan (2009) points out the difficulty in learning to acquire effective organizational capability. These development economists use slightly different analyses. Together, they provide careful assessment of various aspects of failures in technical learning throughout the developing world.

2.3.1 Joseph Stiglitz: the creation of a learning economy

Joseph Stiglitz and Bruce Greenwald's development model emphasizes the creation of a "learning society" (Stiglitz & Greenwald, 2014). Using this model, Stiglitz (2016) identifies the "limitations of the market, the imperfections, for instance, of capital markets, the underinvestment that would occur in technology and education, and the importance of equality for maintaining social cohesion and trust" (p. 19). For Stiglitz, development policies must identify and correct negative externalities, especially market failures in technical learning. To explain market failures, Stiglitz (1989) employs the analysis of the first mover's positive externality. The first mover assumes risks of learning and discovery that the second and third movers do not want to take. As a result, businesses wait for the first mover to invest in new technology and technical learning. The risk is exacerbated, as once the high-cost learning is transformed into profitable tacit knowledge, first movers often do not have enough time to make a monopolistic profit because the second and third movers rapidly apply the new knowledge to their advantage. In developing countries where market failures in information, labor training, enforcement of contract, and capital markets are widespread, first-mover externalities may deter investments, especially in learning and innovation because risks and costs associated with being a first mover are so high (Stiglitz, 1989). As modern economies rely on knowledge and information to create additional comparative advantages, market failures in learning could severely impede development in poor countries. To correct this, Stiglitz (1989, 1994) argues that the government is responsible for financing technical learning, either directly through the education system or indirectly through subsidies at the firm level.

Stiglitz (1994) also points out that developing countries need active and dynamic industrial sectors to boost productivity growth and positive spillovers. The industrial sector maintains important advantages, such as high returns for technological change, economies of scale, and learning continuity. Most importantly, there are advantages from diffusion and spillovers to other sectors in the economy. From this perspective, a government needs to employ strategies that can lead to an expansion of its industrial sector. Stiglitz observes that nearly every successful country (including the United States) has had industrial policies wherein the government assisted the private sector in bringing new technologies to the marketplace (Stiglitz, 2013a). Industrial policies, defined as any policy affecting economic structures and industries, can help "correct" market failures in the form of subsidies (or rents). Such policies can also promote industrial activities that provide high returns and positive spillovers across sectors and segments of society. These policies also help poor countries to create learning societies and enable sustained development and growth. Stiglitz (2016) observes:

> Because development entails closing the knowledge gap that separates developing from developed economies, there are a broad range of *industrial policies* that governments can and should undertake to promote sectors and technologies with greater scope for learning and with greater spillovers for other sectors. While some of the standard wisdom (e.g. concerning protectionism) has been shown to be misguided, in other cases, it provides a further argument for the conventional prescriptions.
>
> (p. 35)

From this perspective, direct government subsidies alone are insufficient. Rather, Stiglitz argues for an all-encompassing set of active industrial or technology policies that addresses market failures to discourage the learning-by-doing process at large. This broad set of policies should include, at a minimum: cheaper and better technical training and education, credit for technology investment, enhanced rapid access to important market information, facilitated business opportunities with foreign buyers, and linkages and information sharing within and across sectors. The long-term policy objectives are to promote an active learning environment for firms, create new market opportunities, and strengthen investment and commitment to industrial production that advances local firm competitiveness.

2.3.2 Hausmann, Rodrik, and Velasco: learning-by-discovery

While observing the performance of developing countries throughout their reforms, Hausmann and Rodrik (2003) noticed that free-market followers, such as countries in Latin America, failed to perform despite successful adoption of foreign technologies; whereas, countries with initially weak market foundations and heavy state interventions, such as China, Taiwan, and South Korea, achieved phenomenal growth rates in the second half of the twentieth century. In their assessment, Hausmann and Rodrik (2003) highlight two major failures in the neoclassical approach: "There is too little investment and entrepreneurship ex ante, and too much production diversification ex post" (p. 603). They later describe this as market failure of self-discovery, or "the failure to develop non-traditional activities because of inadequate incentives to invest in learning what one is good at producing" (p. 614).

In modeling these externalities, Hausmann and Rodrik (2003) use a first-mover externality analysis that is similar to Stiglitz. Under a free-market system, the first entrepreneur often has less incentive to invest due to insufficient ex post profits. Moreover, it is uncertain when the second (or third) investor will enter the market to take advantage of the discovery, which in turn drives down monopoly profits. If the first inventor cannot guarantee profits from the investment ex ante, there will be very little pretext and motivation to invest in new learning. In the event that a lack of entrepreneurship in new discoveries and innovations becomes systemic in all industries, the country could suffer tremendous social and economic losses, technological backwardness, and delayed economic transformation (Hausmann & Rodrik, 2003).

In their model, Hausmann and Rodrik (2003) imply that every developing country has various comparative advantages, but investors do not have prior knowledge of these advantages. In other words, investors in developing countries need to learn crucially, "what one is good at producing" (p. 605). Although discovery of these advantages requires time and effort, knowledge does not always produce desirable outcomes. Even when profit is achieved, "the initial entrepreneur who makes the 'discovery' can capture only a small part of the social value that this knowledge generates . . . [as] other entrepreneurs can quickly emulate such discoveries" (p. 605). Hausmann and Rodrik's approach is distinct from the problem of learning in Stiglitz's (and others') model of externality in learning. By contrast, Stiglitz does not assume that developing countries have a number of hidden advantages – that is, "what a country will be good at producing" – that have yet to be discovered as do Hausmann and Rodrik (2003, p. 614).

To address learning-by-discovery externalities, Hausmann and Rodrik (2003) argue that "laissez-faire leads to under-provision of innovation and governments need to play a dual role in fostering industrial growth and transformation" (p. 629). More specifically: "They need to encourage entrepreneurship and investment in new activities ex ante, but push out unproductive firms and sectors ex post" (p. 629). Industrial policies, such as subsidies and preferential taxes, need to be selective and focused on the actual binding constraints in learning and discovery rather than tackle across-the-board reforms. Based on these propositions, Hausmann et al. (2008) advocate for cautious, experimental industrial policies. To successfully identify, prioritize, and implement growth policies, these three economists developed "growth diagnostics" – a framework to determine the most critical binding constraints on economic activities in poor countries:

> We start by asking what keeps growth low. Is it inadequate returns to investment, inadequate private appropriability of the returns, or inadequate access to finance? If it is a case of low returns, is that due to insufficient investment in complementary factors of production (such as human capital or infrastructure)? Or is it due to poor access to imported technologies? If it is a case of poor appropriability, is it due to high taxation, poor property rights and contract enforcement, labor-capital conflicts, or learning and coordination externalities? If it is a case of poor finance, are the problems with domestic financial markets or external ones?
>
> (Hausmann et al., 2008, p. 325)

Identifiable constraints that cause slow growth, which Hausmann et al. (2008) trace from low levels of private investment and entrepreneurship, are provided in a tree diagram (Figure 2.4). The authors emphasize that developing countries

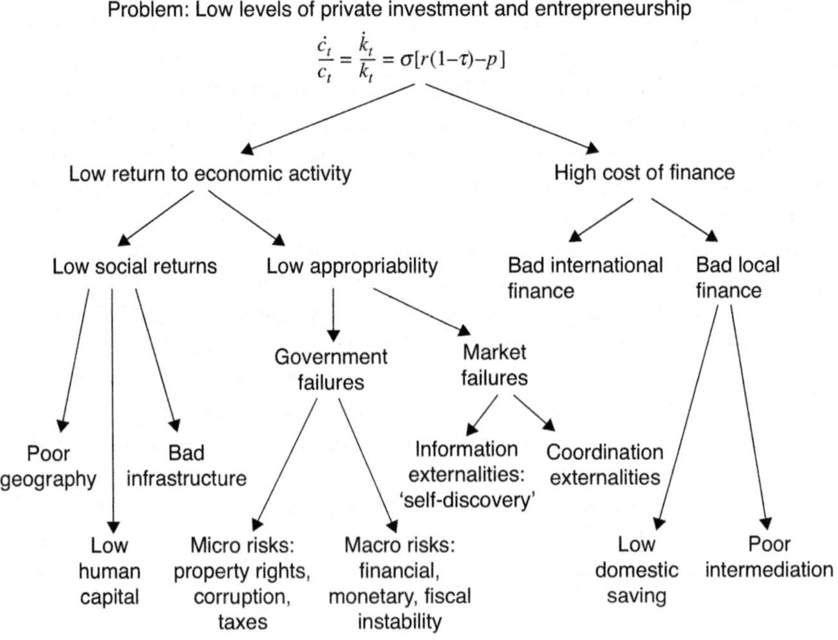

Figure 2.4 The Growth Diagnostic Framework

Source: Hausmann et al. (2008, p. 326).

must carefully assess empirical evidence within and across industries and tease out binding constraints *specific* to the context of the developing country.

Hausmann et al. (2008) further point out that growth diagnostics and policy responses require time, patience, and experimentation. They need to be institutionalized gradually. The government and its agencies must be ready to adjust their growth policies, given the dynamic responses in the economy. Otherwise, any short-term commitment to policies and adjustment may cause the reform process to fall apart (Hausmann et al., 2008). An important contribution of the growth diagnostic framework is that it underlines the local context and evidence from a specific developing country rather than suggesting a one-size-fits-all policy solution. The aim is to determine a policy agenda that is "likely to be considerably more effective than a laundry-list approach with a long list of institutional and governance reforms that may or may not be well-targeted on the most binding constraints to growth" (Hausmann et al., 2008, p. 355).

2.3.3 Mushtaq Khan: building organizational capability and ensuring high-level learning efforts

In contrast to Stiglitz, Hausmann, Rodrik, and Velasco, development economist Mushtaq Khan (2000, 2009, 2015) focuses on the development of *organizational* and *operational capabilities* within firms as necessary conditions for achieving significant competitiveness. The challenges of acquiring machinery and skills are not the most critical constraints; rather, it is organizational and operational capability that limit developing countries' ability to catch up (Khan, 2009). Organizational capability is defined as firms' ability to "coordinate and link together different parts of [production] operation from purchasing inputs to marketing, including communicating with trading partners, responding to feedback, improving store keeping, and so on, till an appropriate throughput of inputs and outputs is achieved" (p. 12). While some firms in developing countries may have the required number of skilled workers and new machinery, they are simply unable to produce products at the price and quality of firms in more advanced countries. The difference here lies in the acquisition of organizational and operational skills, as firms embed routines and tacit knowledge into their production. Without the cumulative tacit knowledge acquired through actual experience, local firms would not achieve the organizational capability and international competitiveness necessary for participation in the global value chain. Khan (2009) argues that the main problem of development is not the discovery of already existing comparative advantages but the creation of new comparative advantages through the development of the appropriate organizational and operational capabilities in the production process.

From this perspective, Khan's argument is distinguishable from that of Stiglitz, Hausmann, Rodrik, and Velasco. For Khan, subsidizing the first mover for discovery or for the positive externality does not guarantee that the first mover will be able to make something productively, especially if that first mover does not have the initial capacity to pursue the new discovery. This is because industrial upgrade is not only about bringing in new machinery and learning how to use it. Most importantly, it is about creating an entirely new production arrangement that is appropriate and effective in the local context, in order to produce products that are desirable in the domestic and foreign market (Khan, 2009). Therefore, unless local firms achieve organizational capability to create products that are outstanding in either quality or price, the approaches and policies proposed by Stiglitz and Greenwald (2014), Stiglitz (2016), or Hausmann et al. (2008) will not work.

Furthermore, achievement of organizational and operational capabilities through learning-by-doing requires a high level of effort by firms. In defining effort, Khan (2009) highlights the effort in learning to acquire tacit knowledge that improves a firm's organization of production. This is distinguished from the effort of workers in the regular work process. Khan's framework asserts that effort is required from both managers (who are often owners) and workers. Managers should apply significant efforts – time, thought, attention, and a can-do attitude – when experimenting with different organizational designs, internal management structures, inventory control systems, quality control systems, and so on, with the aim to reduce costs, improve quality, and increase productivity. These managerial efforts then translate to individual workers who need not only to acquire tacit knowledge on the production floor but also to continuously apply, fine-tune, and codify the new knowledge into production processes.

Khan (2009, 2015) contends that the problem in ensuring credible effort is twofold. First, external investors can only observe firm managers and worker efforts ex post. He points out: "The market failure that constrains economic development most seriously is that investors cannot be sure that they will be able to enforce the levels of *effort* that will make this investment [in learning] viable" (Khan, 2009, p. 1). Second, it is difficult to contract for high effort because of a large number of contingencies that can affect outcomes independent of effort. This is why private financing of significant new learning is rare in developing countries and needs to be distinguished from the first-mover problem. To address these constraints, Khan (2009) points out that there needs to be a mechanism for financing the learning-by-doing process, together with strong incentives and pressures for significant effort. He lists different kinds of mechanisms that historically have ensured such effort. In some countries, governments achieved needed effort by imposing severe penalties for the failure of learning ex post, as happened in South Korea from the 1960s through the 1980s. In other cases, as with India's automobile industry, successful learning was achieved when the government offered large conditional rents as ex post rewards, which ensured that the reward could only be captured if significant learning took place (Khan, 2009).

Khan's research on the market failure of organization capability is insightful and practical. It emphasizes that technical upgrade and learning is a complex process that involves numerous factors – technology, acquisition of tacit knowledge, and organization of production – as well individuals who must engage their skills, effort, and time into valuable and all-encompassing transformation, not just one or a few aspects of it. While he argues that the government should provide incentives to address market failure, the objective of industrial policy and its implementation should aim at achieving dynamic learning, interaction, and upgrade in the overall production process. Within this process, tacit knowledge must be created and diffused both on the manufacturing floor by the workers and through the necessary trials and errors in technology adoption and production organization by the managers.

2.3.4 Transformation of institutional and social relations

The previous sections survey major learning externalities in the literature as well as some forceful arguments for strategic and active state roles to correct them. An important aspect of government intervention through industrial policies is that technological changes and innovations transform institutions and social relations, not least in developing countries. Policies and subsequent technological progress create rents and redistribute rights and power among existing capital owners who have the means of production. This dynamic change inherently impacts social, economic, and political relations. As Simon Kuznets (1966) points out:

> The transformation of an underdeveloped into a developed country is not merely the mechanical addition of a stock of physical capital; it is a thoroughgoing revolution in patterns of life and a cardinal change in the relative power and position of various groups in the population . . . and must overcome the resistance of a whole complex of established interest and norms. (p. 30)

Karl Marx's (1847/1920) early observation offers similar insight: "In acquiring new productive forces men change their mode of production, and in changing their mode of production, their manner of gaining a living, they change all their social relations. The windmill gives you society with the feudal lord; the steam-mill, society with the industrial capitalist" (p. 119). Building on Marx's insight, Thorstein Veblen (1904) argues along much the same lines: "In a sense more intimate than the inventors of the phrase seem to have appreciated, the machine has become the master of the man who works with it and an arbiter in the cultural fortunes of the community into whose life it has entered" (pp. 322–323).[6]

Howsoever it may emerge, the processes of technological change and the industrial policies that support them reallocate rights and subsequently create rents for certain groups. The rate of technological progress challenges both the existing production structure and the interests of the current owners who have the means of production. Therefore, these owners resist any change and seek rents to protect their rights and benefits.[7] From this point of view, the analysis of rent seeking as a process becomes crucial to understanding market failures and institutional change that affect technical progress for development

(Khan, 2000a). The objective is to develop and to facilitate technological progress in productive activities that eliminate market failures and promote development. To do so, one needs to analyze the issue of rent seeking, which inhibits technical progress. This is compatible with institutionalist views of rents and rent seeking. Steven Medema (1991), for instance, quite correctly observes that "rents are inevitably created and reallocated through changes in the rights structure," and so one must be cognizant of "the impact of alternative rights/rents (that is, institutional) structures" (p. 1061). As rents are the *product* of institutional design of rights, duties, and the structure of social relations, an analytical framework analyzing the impact of such institutional designs is essential. From this point of view, analysis of rent creation and rent seeking is necessary to understand the evolutionary change that affects technical progress and development. The next section reviews conceptual foundations for the analysis of rents and rent seeking.

2.4 Rents and rent seeking in a development context

Rent-seeking activities between developed and developing countries are distinct in the characteristics of institution, political organization, and institutional structure. In developing countries, informal relationships between organizations and the state frequently take place behind formal institutional structures and relationships. Rents and rent seeking – damaging or not – are ubiquitous and widespread in poor countries (Khan, 2009). Policy, regulation, and legal change alter patterns of resource allocation and rights of individuals and groups in society, thus creating rent. Hence, once there is the possibility for change in legal and economic relations, rent seeking emerges (Medema, 1991). Similarly, technology policy that promotes technological change creates new rents and rights while also modifying and destroying existing ones. The government must not only ward off resistance from the losers, it must provide enough rents and time horizon for the creation of new technology and capacity. This section analyzes the issues of rent seeking, rent creation, and rent management in this context.

2.4.1 Theoretical approach to development: Ricardo, Marshall, and Schumpeter

Classical economists such as David Ricardo and Alfred Marshall, and their followers, most notably Joseph Schumpeter, characterize rents and rent seeking as major factors in economic development, either by enhancing the cumulative process of profit or by disrupting existing political and economic institutions to achieve higher growth. In Ricardo's theory, rent accumulated through ownership of land and development of the agriculture industry are the major drivers of economic development and the distribution of income in the economy. He defines rents as "that portion of the produce of the earth, which is paid to the landlord for the use of the original and indestructible powers of the soil" (Ricardo, 1817,

p. 33). He contrasts this with payment for *capital*, or the produce existing on the land. He criticizes Adam Smith for arguing that the demand for timber in southern Europe caused rent to be paid for Norwegian timber. Payment was not for the productive power of the land; rather, it was for the value of the existing resource (Ricardo, 1817, pp. 49–52).[8]

Alfred Marshall (1890) identifies rent from a producer and a consumer perspective. As the "gratification" the consumer gains from the purchase of a commodity "generally exceeds that which he gives up in paying away its price," he "derives from the purchase a surplus of pleasure" (p. 175). Marshall (1890) defines consumer rent as "[t]he excess of the price which he [the consumer] would be willing to pay rather than go without it, over that which he actually does pay" (p. 175). The time dimension is a factor in rent on capital. Interest in "old investments of capital" or "free" or "floating' capital" is termed by Marshall (1890) as quasi rent (p. viii). The income from land derived through an improvement in soil fertility, for example, may be regarded as quasi rent but, more accurately, Marshall (1890) notes, it should be regarded as a profit (p. 496). From this perspective, "quasi rents" represent a higher rate of return due to the short-term advantage of some firms that might have, for example, lower costs or favorable marketing conditions that allow them to charge a higher price. In the long run, Marshall argues that profits (or rents) would be competed away or capitalized in the value of the firm so that buyers of the firm's equity would get the same return as others in the industry.

For Schumpeter (1934/1983), the entrepreneur earns rent (or profit) during the period when the product is first introduced and when it is widely diffused and copied by other firms. He defines this entrepreneurial profit as "a surplus over costs," or "the difference between receipts and outlay in a business" (p. 128). While typically the outlays would include "all the disbursements which the entrepreneur must make directly or indirectly in production," an entrepreneurial wage must be included: "an appropriate rent for any land which may chance belong to him, and finally a premium for risk" (Schumpeter, 1934/1983, p. 128). The rent or additional profit provides the very incentive for the entrepreneur to innovate in the first place. New innovations disrupt the economic equilibrium of the market, replace old products and production processes with new ones, and thus drive the process of development. From this perspective, Schumpeter considers monopolist rent earned by the introduction of new innovation beneficial, as it drives greater economic efficiency and development. As with Marshall, Schumpeter argues that rent earned through innovating activities is temporary, as it would be competed away over time. Together, these economists share the common view that structural change within the economy generates rent. Thus, rent is a necessary part of the evolutionary process of development, both in the long and the short run because of its role in either capital accumulation or incentivizing entrepreneurs to invest in new innovation. In contrast to public choice and neoclassical economists theorizing on rents in the second half of the twentieth century, classical economists' view on rents is not inherently negative.

2.4.2 Public choice and neoclassical approaches and the agenda to eliminate rents

Beginning in the early 1970s, academic thinking on issues of rent takes a drastic turn, initially led by the public choice literature. This generation of rent-seeking models argues that, where damaging rents exist, the net effect is crippling because of high rent-seeking costs (Krueger, 1974; Posner, 1975; Buchanan et al., 1980, as cited in Khan, 2000a). This is because, as a state creates rents, economic actors devise means, such as bribery, to seek these rents. From the public choice point of view, such expenditures are wasteful, as they are not invested in productive economic activities. Hence, in the estimate of the total costs of rents, one needs to include costs associated with rent seeking. Subsequently, a cost combination model was developed that combines the established cost of monopolies with the high cost of rent seeking. The "father" of the concept, Gordon Tullock (1967, 1980), contends that in a competitive rent-seeking model, the aggregate resources devoted to pursuing redistribution of wealth ("transfers") can, in fact, equal the value of rents to be distributed. Furthermore, in using the *competitive* market model, this strand of literature demonstrates that a monopoly created and sustained through rents results in *lower* production output compared to the competitive market.[9] This result signals inefficient allocation of resources and creates a social cost in the loss of social benefit to society: the deadweight welfare loss. Broadly speaking, the public choice literature focuses on these negative consequences of rent seeking. James Buchanan's view is typical and influential:

> Rent seeking involves social waste. Resources that could otherwise be devoted to value-producing activity are engaged in competitive effort that determines nothing other than the distributive results. Rent seeking, as such, is totally without allocative value, although, of course, the initial institutional creation of an opportunity for rent seeking ensures a net destruction of economic value.
>
> (Buchanan, 1980a, p. 359)

Consistent with this perspective is the view of Kevin Murphy, Andrei Shleifer, and Robert Vishny (1993). Here, the authors distinguish between private and public rent-seeking activities and calculate their respective impacts on the economy.[10] Private rent seeking, equated with "theft, piracy, litigation, and other forms of transfer between private parties," negatively impacts production, as the target is "existing stocks of wealth" but has little, if any, effect on innovation. Public rent seeking, by contrast, is redistributive in nature, redirecting resources "from the private sector to the state" through taxation, or "from the private sector to the government bureaucrats who affect the fortunes of the private sector," as the state controls access to what becomes in essence "government-supplied goods, such as permits, licenses, import quotas, and so on" (Murphy et al., 1993, p. 412). The authors argue, however, that public rent seeking need not have a negative impact on innovation. For instance, if the state and its bureaucracies "can take an equity stake in innovative activities, so that they can effectively accept a bribe without demanding cash, turn innovators into insiders, reduce their own incentives for subsequent expropriation, and bear some of the risk," they may find it worthwhile to support innovative, entrepreneurial producers (Murphy et al., 1993, p. 413). It is equally plausible that the government would support established monopolies resistant to innovation, which, in turn, may *deter* innovation. In any event, rent-seeking activities, by their very nature, are viewed as having a deleterious effect on growth.

Interest in rent-seeking ideas is not unique to the public choice literature during this period. Neoliberal literature on international trade developed a formal model to estimate economic losses from rent seeking. In a seminal paper, Anne Krueger (1974) estimated that, in India, when individuals and businesses sought rents for the right to import, estimated rent-seeking costs were around 7.3 percent of the country's Gross National Product.[11] By associating "efficient" economic outcomes with growth and development, neoliberal economists suggest that rents and rent seeking are damaging for developing countries and should be strictly limited, if not totally eliminated (Krueger, 1974; Posner, 1975). From this point of view, the policy implication of avoiding rent creation involves a limited role for the state in market operation.

Starting in the 1980s, a later generation of the rent-seeking models reveal that, under different institutional structures, the cost of rent seeking could be substantially lower than previously estimated (Congleton, 1980; Rogerson, 1982). As a result, rent-seeking costs could fluctuate over a much wider range, so rent seeking would not necessarily be expensive. Models in this period also relax some assumptions, especially the ones that assume rent seeking always results in the creation of value-reducing rents. Asserting his theory of directly unproductive profit-seeking activities, or DUPs – that is, activities that "yield pecuniary returns but do not produce goods or services that enter a utility function directly or indirectly via increased production or availability to the economy of goods" – Jagdish Bhagwati (1982) points out that, to the extent these "activities use real resources, they result in a contraction of the availability set open to the economy" (p. 989). While the activities themselves may be "privately profitable," nonetheless, "their direct output is simply zero" (Bhagwati, 1982, pp. 989–990). Taking into account the second-best considerations, Bhagwati's model suggests that positive shadow prices[12] on resources used in rent seeking may not exist, thus "implying that individuals' quests to secure biddable rents need not always entail socially wasteful activity" (as cited in Hillman & Katz, 1984, p. 104).

2.4.3 *The heterodox approach and the potential of value-creating rents*

Heterodox economists, such as Samuels and Mercuro (1984), Medema (1991), and Khan and Jomo (2000), point to four inconsistencies in the public choice and neoliberal approaches to rent and rent seeking. First, they argue that these approaches assume the existing structure of rights within a society is perfect and thus any modification produces inefficient outcomes (Medema, 1991; Samuels &

Mercuro, 1984). Second, these approaches dismiss problems related to negative externalities that distort the functioning of competitive market mechanisms, and correcting these distortions requires an adjustment of rights, which creates rents. Third, because legal change involves the government transferring rights (and rents), the public choice and neoclassical approach would imply that all legal change is wasteful. This leads to the policy conclusion that, even in an imperfect market, the free market is better than government intervention – despite the possibility that the structure of rights within the society may be unjust or require modification. Finally, rent-seeking expenditures may not be entirely wasted if (1) recipients of these expenditures receive benefits that increase their utility and (2) the value created from the rent-seeking activity exceeds the value of outputs that could have been produced by rent-seeking expenditures (Khan, 2000a; Medema, 1991).

Development economists have since suggested broadening the analysis of rents and rent seeking (Abegaz, 2013; Chang et al., 2002; Khan & Jomo, 2000; Ngo, 2016a; North et al., 2007; Whitfield et al., 2015). Because rent seeking is ubiquitous, particularly in developing countries, it is as important to understand what happens *during* the rent-seeking process as it is to assess rent seeking by comparing the *before* and *after* costs (Rajagopalan, 1996). Mushtaq Khan (2000b) points out: "One problem in most of the rent-seeking literature has been that it has concentrated almost exclusively on the social costs of the resources *used up* in rent seeking and very little on the different types of rents and outcomes which rent seeking has *created* in different contexts" (p. 71). Therefore, the overall effect of rent seeking must be calculated using both the costs incurred and the rent outcomes created. More specifically, the analyses of rent and rent seeking could be broadened and seen as a *process* reflecting the interest-group power, with rents as the *outcome* of rent-seeking contests (Khan, 2000b).

The heterodox literature provides evidence that certain types of rents can be value enhancing and rent seeking can produce developmental outcomes (Abegaz, 2013; Kelsall, 2013; Khan & Jomo, 2000; Whitfield et al., 2015).[13] This assertion has gained momentum since the 1990s, particularly in light of the East Asian development model. Alice Amsden (1989) and Robert Wade (1990) suggest that, during their industrial development, both Taiwanese and Korean governments allocated subsidies to promote industrialization in socially beneficial manners.[14] In using rent and rent seeking as analytical tools, a growing body of heterodox literature provides significant empirical evidence and insights as to why and how poor countries developed, given substantial economic and institutional constraints. For instance, Kelsall (2013) shows that the Rwandan Patriotic Front regime retained a strong degree of control over rents and the polity. The regime dominated the private sector, allocated rents toward strategic industries, and oriented "rent management for the long term" (Kelsall, 2013, p. 142). As a result, Rwanda's economy has grown rapidly and poverty has been reduced.

In the mid-1990s, the public choice literature begins to suggest that rent seeking could lead to beneficial outcomes. Tyler Cowen, Amihai Glazer, and Henry McMillan (1994) maintain that "rent seeking can increase political effort and thereby increase social welfare" (p. 132). This is because, when some public policies generate rents for public officials who would otherwise have little incentive to spend time and effort proposing policies that benefit others, rent seeking can motivate political officials to provide public goods.[15] If the policies are beneficial to the public, their usefulness can compensate for the costs of rent seeking. Given such considerations, the authors argue that governments should, when deciding on policy, take into consideration "the need to develop rules of the game that motivate public officials to generate positive aggregate benefits" (Cowen et al., 1994, p. 142). As most heterodox literature working on the rent-seeking framework suggests some degree of state intervention, an important question at this juncture is whether the state should assume a leading role in the creation and management of value-enhancing rents and the extent to which state intervention is conducive for development. The next section reviews some of the literature on the role of the state in rent management.

2.5 The role of a political state in rent management

A common strand in discussions of technological change for development is the catalytic role of institutions and the developmental state in solving critical constraints faced by domestic firms, especially those associated with technical learning and upgrading. This section centers on the *extent* to which the state should create and implement the necessary policies (i.e., technology policies) to promote economic growth and development. Technology policy inherently creates rents and new opportunities for innovative firms while possibly disadvantaging stagnated ones. If technology policy is used as tool to promote industrial development, the role of the government and its institutions that coordinate rents and implement technology policy is critical for the success or failure of the policy. This section surveys the theoretical *linkages* between technology, institutions, and the role of the state in development.

2.5.1 Balanced versus unbalanced growth theory

Early literature on economic development associated with "Balanced Growth" or "Big Push" literature[16] (Rosenstein-Rodan, 1943; Scitovsky, 1954; Baran, 1957; Gerschenkron, 1962) asserts that economic development requires a developmental state capable of creating and regulating economic and political relationships in order to support sustained industrialization. Paul Rosenstein-Rodan (1961) argues that, with imperfect markets, the price mechanism fails to "provide the signals which guide a perfectly competitive economy towards an optimal position," and so it may be necessary to employ programming models as a means to introduce these missing "signals" (pp. 57–58). He thus advocates national industrial planning, through which "the whole of the industry to be created is to be treated and planned like one huge firm or trust" (Rosenstein-Rodan, 1943, p. 204). This would include expenditures for skill enhancement – "the best investment for the State" – and an emphasis on industrial complementarity – a focus on a multiplicity of industries instead of one or two (Rosenstein-Rodan, 1943, p. 205).

Tibor Scitovsky (1954) expands upon Rosenstein-Rodan's argument, phrasing it in terms of information coordination. In a decentralized, "perfectly" competitive market, prices serve as signals and so perform the function of coordination of plans, allowing the individual "to learn about the economic decisions of others and co-ordinate his decisions with theirs" (p. 150). However, Scitovsky (1954) observes, market prices merely "reflect the economic situation as it is and not as it will be"; thus, "they are more useful for co-ordinating current production decisions, which are immediately effective and guided by short-run considerations, than they are for co-ordinating investment decisions, which have a delayed effect and . . . should be governed not by what the present economic situation is but by what the future economic situation is expected to be" (p. 150). What is needed, Scitovsky (1954) concludes, is "a signaling device to transmit information about present plans and future conditions as they are determined by present plans," something the competitive market fails to provide (p. 150) – thus the "need either for centralized investment planning or for some additional communication system to supplement the pricing system as a signaling device" (Scitovsky, 1954, p. 150).

Taking a slightly different analytical view, Gunnar Myrdal (1979) advocates a role for the government in crucial institutional reforms – in land, health care, and education – that would transform developing countries. However, Myrdal also points out the close connection between government officials and business interests. He highlights that influences from vested interests, rent seeking, and corruption are features of a "soft" state that hinder development. Such a close connection leads to rent seeking and "a widespread disregard by public officials at various levels to rules and directives handed down to them, and often their collusion with powerful persons and groups of persons whose conduct it is their duty to regulate" (Myrdal, 1979, p. 37).

More importantly, Myrdal (1979) emphasizes the difficulty of such institutional reforms within the soft state, given the evolutionary and historical conditions leading to underdevelopment in the first place. Myrdal (1979) notes: "In colonial times there was a built-in mechanism that almost automatically led a metropolitan power to ally itself with the privileged groups in a colony and often to create such new groups. To support its rule, the colonial government would thus feel an interest in upholding and even strengthening the inherited social and economic structure in the colony" (p. 40). Considering the imperative need for institutional reform in developing countries, the soft state, and the history that reinforces it, Myrdal (1979) emphasizes the need to "record and analyze the actual situation in these countries and the political, social and economic forces that operate there" (p. 42). However, the economist falls short in explaining how the soft states achieve institutional reforms as they transition to a better social and economic structure, if at all.

Albert Hirschman addresses this policy concern. Hirschman (1957, 1958) emphasizes the role of the state, its institutions, and the economy to pick up the slack – "hidden" resources – available in the country to create the homegrown principles of development that work for the specific context of the country. He criticizes the "Big Push" approach for its requirement of large-scale organized state planning and the presumption of state capacity to design and implement institutional changes. Hirschman (1958) proposes an alternative approach, which he calls the principle of "Unbalanced Growth," which focuses on linkages and the internal pressures or problems in the development of a country. Unbalanced growth occurs because policy action has differential effects, and it produces weights and balance shifts over time. David Ellerman (2004) articulates Hirschman's alternative approach clearly:

> Not all problems can be attacked at once so attention is first focused on the small; on the sectors or localities where some of the preconditions are in place and where initiative is afoot on its own. The initial small successes will then create pressures through the forward and backward linkages to foster both learning and change that is nearby in sectors or locations – all of which might lead to a "growth pole" . . . or local industrial district. The successes when broadcast horizontally to those facing similar problems will start to break down the paralyzing beliefs that nothing can be done and will fuel broader initiatives that take the early wins as their bench-mark.
>
> (p. 317)

For Hirschman (1957), the role of government is to devise policy and institutional frameworks that "must be elastic and must regulate change rather than proscribe it" (p. 370). In addition, state planning must take the long view. Developmental change takes time as the effects of unbalanced growth policy transmit through firms, sectors, and the economy. From this perspective, Hirschman's unbalanced growth is consistent with the heterodox approach in that development is a "homegrown," cumulative, and dynamic process. Overall, the literature focusing on both balanced and unbalanced growth theories advocates for state involvement in industrial planning and development although they differ in scale and approach. More importantly, this literature provides conceptual and analytical foundations for subsequent scholarship centering on the role of the state in designing, coordinating, and implementing industrial and development policies.

2.5.2 North, Wallis, Webb, and Weingast: limited access order

In a series of publications, Douglass North, John Wallis, Steven Webb, and Barry Weingast elaborate a theory of order and violence through a historical perspective. North, Wallis, and Weingast (2006, 2009) develop the conceptual framework of limited access order (LAO) as a means by which to interpret recorded human history. LAOs are defined as orders "using the political system to limit economic entry to create rents, and then using the rents to stabilize the political system and limit violence" (North et al., 2006, p. 2). As "economics is politics by other means," in developing countries, political coalition often "successfully provides order when the political interests of coalition members are balanced by their economic stakes in the existing order" (North et al., 2009, p. 42).

The authors assert that each developing country is classified in one of the three forms of LAO: fragile, basic, or mature. As a country develops, it progresses from fragile to basic and finally to the mature form. According to North et al. (2007), to catch up to the developed world, the developing country must find ways to (1) reorganize itself, (2) improve control of violence, and (3) create a legal framework for regulating non-state organizations based on a rule of law. Under this framework, limiting violence and disorder are especially critical for progress along the LAO spectrum toward an open access order (the authors' description of advanced countries). Violence and conflict create instability, which directly impacts investment and production. In other words, North and his coauthors assert that violence imposes tremendous costs on institutions and undermines market activities and growth (Gray, 2015). Additionally, social order encourages agreements between elites with the understanding that violence reduces their access to rents:

> Powerful individuals possess privileges and rents, and since violence threatens or reduces those rents, the risk of losing the rents can make it in the interests of powerful individuals and groups to cooperate with the coalition in power rather than to fight. Privileged individuals have privileged access to social tools enabling them, and only them, to form powerful organizations. In limited access orders the political system manipulates the economy to create rents as a means of solving the problem of violence. Acknowledging this direct link between the creation of rents and maintenance of order enables us to integrate economic and political theory in a new way.
>
> (North et al., 2007, p. 3)

From this perspective, rent can be *functional* in the sense that rent creation and distribution by elites or the state could limit violence, prevent disorder, and intensify market activities. For North et al., the role of the state (a coalition between the elites and politicians) is to maintain social order and limit violence in order that developing countries move along the LAO spectrum to develop themselves into advanced countries. North and his associates consider state actions a manifestation of the dominant elites' interests, at least among fragile and basic states. Sustaining elites' interests through rent creation could ensure order and stability. Once poor countries reach the open access order, the mature state is expected to maintain social order by providing additional services such as enacting rule of law, enforcement of contracts, prevention of expropriation, and provision of public goods. By approaching development from this perspective, the access order model implicitly suggests that development requires reinforcing, rather than modifying existing power structures within the economy, so long as the goal of controlling violence is achieved.

In consequence, the LAO framework focuses more on issues of reducing violence in the context of economic development and less on how various economic agents are directly involved in production, accumulation, and catch-up (Gray, 2015). Therefore, the model presumes that as long as violence is under control and elites are satisfied by rents, economic development and movement along the access order will naturally occur. Given the unbalanced emphasis on violence reduction without consideration for possible social costs, Gray (2015) points out, "the Access Order approach could justify support for repressive and anti-democratic elites on the assumption that such support is necessary to achieve long-term developmental outcomes. The theory therefore serves to strip the progressive and transformatory potential out of development by ignoring accumulation and income distribution, by limiting politics to elite self-interest, by neglecting non-elite struggles and by remaining silent on how controlling violence may affect human capabilities, rights and freedom" (p. 72). The role of the state in rent creation and management from the North et al. framework is theoretically limited and would possibly undermine the socioeconomic transformation necessary for meaningful advancement and development of all people in poor countries.

2.5.3 Ha-Joon Chang: the autonomous developmental state

As part of the second generation of development economists, Chang et al. (2002) contend that "the presence of transaction costs imply that . . . market imperfections cannot be addressed through voluntary contracting among economic agents, thus lending further advantage to state mediation and arbitration" (p. 393). Their development model calls for an "activist technology policy" in which the state actively invests in creating dynamic efficiencies by using a combination of rents for technological upgrade; at the same time, the state manages rents by conditioning them upon specified performance criteria, such as export performance (Chang et al., 2002, p. 375).

To achieve this goal, Ha-Joon Chang (1999), countering what he describes as a neoliberal attack on developmental activism (i.e., an assault on the "Big Push" philosophy in vogue from the 1940s to the early 1970s), argues the need to reconstruct the notion of the developmental state. According to Chang (1999), a required feature is the state's ability to manage rent – a combination of rent creation for technology investment together with a disciplining mechanism for failing firms. While neoliberals contend that developmental activism "will inevitably lead to the 'corruption' of economic policymaking," nonetheless, "an explicitly 'political' management of the economy may be better in a world full of assets with limited mobility, as far as this is done with an eye to long-term 'developmental' goals" (Chang, 1999, p. 192). The essential *characteristics* of this reconstituted developmental state are autonomy, political management capability, and visionary leadership. According to Chang, the state must make the goals of long-term growth and structural change its primary ones. More importantly, it must "politically" manage the economy to ease conflicts inflicted by rent policies while keeping track of its longer-term goals. Finally, the state is to engage in institutional adaptation and innovation so as to achieve its developmental objectives (Chang, 1999). Chang (1999) proposes four specific functions that such a state must perform: coordination for change, provision of vision, institution building, and conflict management.

Implicitly, Chang's revised developmental state model requires benevolent, strong, and autonomous leadership, which would drive the Big Push forward and overcome resistance and contestation from elites who lose out in the reform process. His examples of "successful" developmental states include nineteenth-century Prussia, Meiji Japan, postwar France, and post-1949 Taiwan (Chang, 1999, 2011). Essentially, he proposes what the South Korean and Taiwanese states did during most of their industrial development from the 1960s to the 1980s, undertaking comprehensive programs designed to coordinate investment across sectors. However, this approach to development is difficult to achieve in most countries because it does not consider the possibility of intense political fragmentation and contestation among elites that are more severe than those constitutive of the South Korean and Taiwanese experiences. Converting a developing country's fragmented political arrangement into the East Asian state-led model will often require a major political and social shake-up that could be unachievable in many developing countries. For example, South Korea's development path initially involved a strong military dictatorship and military figure, Park Chung-Hee, who started the military coup in 1861, led the economic reform, and violently suppressed dissent in the first two decades of South Korean development from 1961 to 1979 (Chang, 1999, 2011). Furthermore, the East Asian state-led model is not the only one to produce growth and development. Historically, countries without South Korea's autonomous and integrated state did occasionally overcome market constraints and achieve growth, such as in some sectors in India and Thailand (see Khan, 2000a, 2009).

The role of the state depicted in Ha-Joon Chang's research is different from that of North and associates. Chang is more explicit in asserting that governments must be involved in both controlling conflict and violence and leading development using technology policy. Here, Chang's model speaks more to how the process of development takes place in the economic sphere, with explicit expectation that the state takes an activist role in driving industrial transformation. From this perspective, Chang's (1999) model of developmental state adds important empirical evidence of a development pathway that has proved successful and long lasting. However, the approach falls short in that it overlooks the diversity of different political arrangements and the difficulties in overcoming discord among political and economic interests in many developing countries.

2.5.4 Mushtaq Khan: managing the political settlement and rent seeking

Mushtaq Khan's research analyzing development of South Asian and East Asian economies adds significant dimension to economic development studies, especially from the political economy perspective. In agreement with Douglass North, Khan (2010) recognizes that, while some rents generated from informal institutions are indeed damaging to society, others, including "redistributive" rents, "may be essential for maintaining stability and preventing a descent into violence" (p. 31).[17] However, Khan (2010) asserts that other types of rent serve "a vital role in supporting the development of productive assets and technological capabilities" (p. 31). Khan (2013) clearly distinguishes redistributive rents created for the purpose of maintaining social order (political stabilization strategies) from rents created to support technical learning (technology strategies). However, he points out that value-enhancing rents in the economy may be created through a number of mechanisms *other* than through the LAO as suggested in North et al.'s framework. Implicitly, Khan's research not only broadens North et al.'s conceptual use of rents but also allows the state to play a larger role in development. Rents are not only an instrument for stabilizing social and political order, as North et al. (2007, 2009) suggest, but also function as the basis for policy options to stimulate technological change and industrial development directly and actively (Khan, 2013).

Khan maintains an important condition to this bold assertion that plays a central role in his framework. The creation of growth-enhancing rents for the purpose of industrial development must be *consistent* with the political configuration and the underlying distribution of power in society. According to Khan (2013), "The political settlement is relevant for understanding the likely outcomes of the policy because it describes the capability of organizations to challenge or distort the conditions of rent allocation implicit in the formal policy" (p. 25). To encourage learning and innovation, rent policies, first, *must be aligned with the interests that will produce the most efficient outcomes and must be shielded from the contestation of unproductive groups.* Second, rent policies must carefully embed credible *incentives* and *conditions* for improved technical learning and successful technology adoption (Khan, 2013). He writes:

> It is not enough to create rents to support learning, we have to be sure that these rents come with appropriate and enforceable conditions that create credible compulsion for effort. Here a background understanding of the current macro-level distribution of power across organizations (the political settlement) helps to identify the clusters of firms that are politically powerful and therefore likely to present the most serious challenges for effective rent management.
>
> (Khan, 2013, p. 29)

Khan's insight is highlighted by Schweinberger (2014), who points out that "[p]ublic-private networks in China are intrinsically tied to a highly developed patronage system which creates a variety of incentives for long-term commitments on the part of managers (which do not exist under liberal capitalism)" (pp. 176–177). Khan's inclusion of technology policies and political settlement to conceptualize the role of the developmental state is significant in that it provides an analytical and policy framework for development without the preconditions of a centralized, autonomous, disciplined, and visionary state, as suggested by Chang (1999) and Chang et al. (2002). Figure 2.5 depicts Khan's

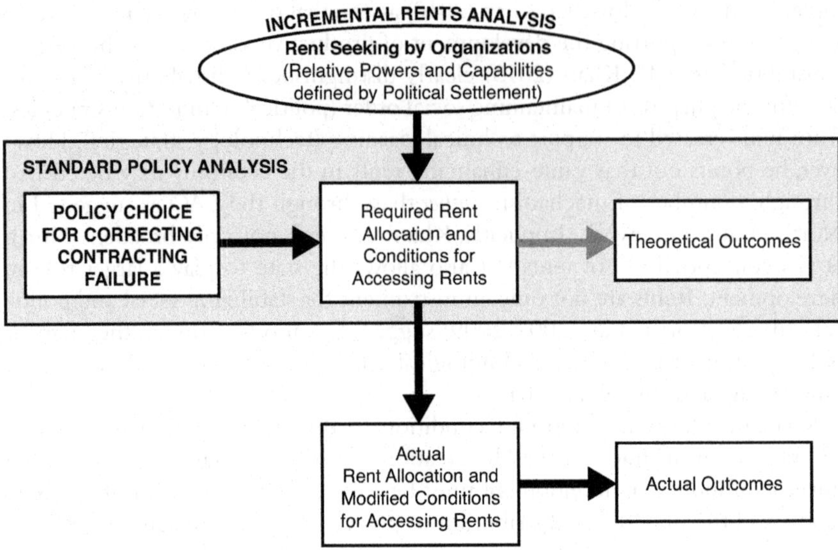

Figure 2.5 Incremental Rents Analysis versus Standard Policy Analysis

Source: Khan (2013, p. 9).

"incremental rent analysis" framework, which incorporates the importance of the political settlement into the success and failure of rent creation and allocation for development. Khan contrasts the depth of this framework with standard policy analysis, which ignores the dynamic process that transforms rent, its allocation, and the actual outcomes.

In contrast with the neoclassical literature on development, Khan (2000b) asserts that the government should not spend resources to *minimize* rents and rent seeking. In the context that rent seeking is ubiquitous in developing countries, the government should create institutions capable of *distributing* rents and *reconfiguring* the developmental rent-seeking process. For Khan, the role of the state, therefore, is to (1) have a thorough understanding of the political settlement crucial for effective (though incremental in some cases) creation and management of rents, (2) implement rent policies that provide incentive and condition for firms to build capability and transform the economy, and (3) manage rent seeking so that powerful interest groups do not block (and ideally support) the implementation of growth-enhancing rents. From this point of view, effective governance and sustained development require *understanding*, in a specific context, *how* rent seeking and rent creation take place and whether practical changes in political organizations and institutions can strengthen economic transformation in poor countries. The solution proposed is a revision to the mainstream analytical view of rent and rent seeking. He suggests that development analysis would benefit from treating rent seeking as a *process* and rent as the *outcome* of the rent-seeking process (Khan, 2000a, 2000b). The aim is to analyze the dynamic interaction and transformation from when rent seeking takes place, when rent creation and distribution occur, and the outcome(s) that rent produces. This dynamic analysis not only informs the underlying distribution of power (the political settlement) but the areas in which rent policy could be effective, by allocating rent(s) to the productive group of firms, protecting them from contestations of the unproductive group and imposing conditions for their performance using a clear set of discipline mechanisms.

Khan's call to analyze economic development, together with a practical expectation of the state that is intertwined with the existing power distribution among the political and economic elites provide a complex, dynamic, and all-encompassing framework for development analysis. He complements economic growth theories offered by North et al., Chang, and other development economists by adding the political dimension to development analysis in ways that are logical and do not compromise its complexity. The developmental rent-management analysis developed in the next chapter relies on Khan's theoretical foundation, incorporating both the political settlement analysis as well as his revisionist approach to rent and rent seeking.

2.5.5 Informality in rent management

Directly related to the challenge of managing political interests for development is the complexity of informality nested in the social, political, and economic structures of a state and its economy. Given the weakness of formal institutions in developing countries, informality is not only ubiquitous, it can also undermine or support implementation of development strategy in developing countries. While a great deal of the literature in institutions and development economics has focused on formal rules and institutions, North et al. (2007) maintain that institutions involve more than explicitly written rules: "They also include informal norms behavior, the mechanisms by which the rules are enforced, and individual beliefs and expectations about how the institution, and other individuals, will behave" (p. 25). This definition stresses the importance of informal institutions in the enforcement of rules and rent management in developing countries. In addition, the LAO framework gives equal emphasis to informal rules in that the limitations described in LAOs today are frequently informal. North and colleagues (2007) also observe that, in developing countries today, informal limitations to market entry and privileges are often achieved by using the formal institutions associated with the LAO in developed countries: political parties, legalized property rights, and corporate organizations. In other words, formal institutions are frequently used to create informal limitations for accessing rents in order to reinforce the power of the ruling elites (North et al., 2007).

Viewing informality from the perspective of social distribution of power, Khan employs a broad definition of informality. Informal institutions are patterns of behavior (enforced or otherwise) where the implicit enforcement mechanism does not involve enforcement by formal state organizations. Thus, informal institutions "include behaviour that is supported by habits, customs, cultures and values . . . [as well as] rules that may appear to be formal but are actually enforced by informal agencies like mafias and patron-client organisations" (Khan, 2012, p. 27). Thus, informal institutions include all institutions where enforcement does not involve the formal activities of the state. Even if enforcement is carried out by state organizations like the police, the institution can still be informal if the enforcement agencies are acting outside of rules or laws. This perspective suggests that some informal institutions can indeed be attributed to culture, but the focus on non-state enforcement means there are many other important areas of informality in developing countries. In the context of development, poor countries frequently encounter serious challenges in policymaking and implementation precisely because their political arrangements involve significant informal rent allocations that can weaken the enforcement of formal institutions. This implies that development strategies that rely primarily on the enforceability of formal institutions are not appropriate (and would not be entirely effective) as the primary response to correct negative market externality. In this context, development strategies need to account for the likelihood of informal institutions and political arrangements.

Informality plays a critical role in the analysis of rent management because it provides insights into the political and institutional mechanisms that determine the positive or negative outcomes of the rent. For instance, Schweinberger (2014) shows that, due to the existence of information asymmetries between government bureaucrats and the managers of state-owned enterprises, establishing trust is critical to creating greater efficiency within China's highly developed patronage system, as it "reduces (or even eliminates) the need for monitoring the performance of managers" (p. 177). In addition, powerful state and non-state organizations in developing countries that seek to create rents may not achieve their objectives through formal mechanisms alone and may significantly depend on informal mechanisms of rent creation and allocation. Therefore, informal institutions and their dynamics explain why and how rents informally operate in developing countries, separate from the formal structure of a country's politics and institutions. Similarly, informality also describes why rents are created, what rents are expected to achieve, and the actual outcomes associated with the rents.

The literature on informal institutions highlights a key observation: while a state may adopt formal industrial policies by creating rents and working steadily to improve its institutional structure so as to be capable of implementing rent policies, the effectiveness of these policies may be constrained by patterns of power outside formal political and institutional structures. As a result, successful rent-management strategies must account for both formal and informal political and institutional arrangements through which rents are sought, created, and managed. This is because much of the actual activities of creating and enforcing rents exist in informal relationships among organizations, members of interest groups, and other social groups. These informal dynamics are too often missing in the mainstream's economic analysis of development. Thus, it frequently reduces the ability of economic research to devise practical and effective development policy. As informality plays a critical role in development, the analysis of informality must be included in rent-management analysis. In Chapter 3, I discuss how this is done within the analytical framework of developmental rent-management analysis.

2.6 Toward an analytical framework for rent management

This chapter surveys recent literature on technological change, rents, and rent seeking applied to economic development. I argue that the analysis of rents and rent seeking is highly relevant for development analysis because it highlights interactions, change, and dynamics that occur during economic and social transformation. It is essential that development analysis assesses the mechanisms that underline political, institutional, and organizational arrangements among political and economic interests that create rents and impact technology policy and development outcomes. The analysis of rent management informs the creation and dynamics of these mechanisms. Two important questions are set out in this review: (1) *what are the most important aspects of technological change and industrial upgrade in poor countries?* and (2) *how are these problems solved in the face of weak state capacity and pervasive rent seeking?* To answer the first question, this chapter identifies important components of technological learning and upgrading. The literature presented supports the view that technological transformation in developing countries is a dynamic and cumulative process that involves interactions among various public and private actors. Furthermore, economic development involves the coevolution of technologies, firms, industries, and government institutions. Finally, the use of new technology to stimulate growth not only alters economic activities but also the rights and social relations among the state, entrepreneurs, financial institutions, workers, and consumers.

In response to the second question, this chapter assesses the debate respecting rents and rent seeking viewed from the classical, public choice, neoclassical, and political economy frameworks. The political economy approach adopts early observations made by classical economists. It emphasizes that while rent creation and rent seeking may lead to damaging outcomes, it may also be developmental if the subsequent outcomes offer more benefits to development than the costs used to seek rents. This alternative view suggests that, because rents and rent seeking are ubiquitous, particularly with respect to technological change, they should be managed and directed toward developmental objectives.

Given the need to manage rents and technology policy, this chapter surveys the development literature to highlight the role of the state in managing rent and rent seeking. The first generation of development theorists – Rosenstein-Rodan, Scitovsky, Myrdal, and Hirschman – emphasizes the role of the government in managing development processes, though the role varies greatly in scope and depth. North et al. (2007) point out the critical movement along the access order, with special attention to the limitations of violence and social disorder via rent creation. Chang (1999) and Chang et al. (2002)

assert the necessity of an autonomous developmental state, which is quite rare. Finally, Khan (2012) offers the political settlement analysis and a revision of the rent-seeking framework to analyze economic development from a political economy perspective.

The heterodox literature presented in this chapter suggests that, in the context of development via technological change, developing countries could achieve industrial upgrade not by eliminating rents, but by creating a rent-management system that enhances the acquisition of tacit knowledge and solves critical constraints that hinder capacity building and technology transfers. To this end, rent management should be viewed as constitutive of institutional, political, and market arrangements within an industry and an economy. It describes the process of organizational competition and institutional transformation. More specifically, the ways in which rent is managed affect the structure of incentives and pressures on the participants, which in turn determines whether they effectively use rent opportunities for learning, innovation, and investment. Therefore, the "management" of technology or rent policies does not necessarily take place from above by the central government or state agencies. Instead, developmental outcomes happen through the interplay of politics and institutions. This interaction could occur laterally at the firm level, among the entrepreneurs, the elites, and state institutions.

Implicitly, the heterodox literature broadens the conceptual framework of rent and rent seeking from the neoclassical literature and constructs not only alternative analytical tools but also a dynamic and evolutionary approach to growth and the political economy of development. The extension of this framework highlights the limitations of the mainstream approach to economic development, where the treatment of perfect market competition is static, unrealistic, and thus unfit for development analyses. Further, by broadening the conceptual framework of rents and rent seeking, this strand of literature helps explain the complexity and nuances of economic transformation crucial for policymaking and for understanding development processes.

The theoretical discussions in this chapter also establish that in order to achieve growth through technology adoption and capacity building, rent policies must not simply aim to remove constraints in the development process; rather, they must also consider the political and institutional conditions in that economy. In addition, these conditions cannot be limited to the formal political and institutional processes but must be taken from a wider context of informal political, institutional, and organizational arrangements among political and economic interests. From this perspective, the best approach to study economic development is to first analyze and map existing mechanisms of rent management (Figure 2.2). The objective is to examine the effects of these mechanisms on learning, technology adoption, and capacity building, given the political, institutional, and economic contexts of a specific country. This understanding allows for considerations of hands-on, practical, and meaningful policy reform, rather than choosing any single one-size-fits-all model.

Notes

1 This book uses the terms "heterodox" and "political economy" interchangeably. Both represent alternative approaches to the study of economic and social change, distinct from mainstream or neoliberal economics.
2 Friedrich List may also be considered an early promoter of state-led technological change and industrial policy. See his 1841 *Das nationale System der politischen Ökonomie* (*National System of Political Economy*; English edition 1856).
3 Williamson (2005) provides an assessment on the initial development and subsequent influence of the Washington Consensus. Serra and Stiglitz (2008) carefully assess and critique theoretical and empirical shortcomings of the Consensus.
4 The term "mechanism" describes the formal and informal processes that institutions implement and sustain.
5 Rodrik (2006) names it the "Augmented Washington Consensus."
6 Similarly, James Street (1987) concludes that, according to Veblen, the drive of technological change for development is possibly at odds with existing power structures that benefit from the status quo. This is because "the process of social change represented a running conflict between emerging techniques of production and the social institutions that tended to preserve existing power relationships and that, if sufficiently potent, could inhibit further technical progress" (p. 1864).
7 However, as Ha-Joon Chang (2011) observes, the refusal of a country to accept what he refers to as Global Standard Institutions – essentially, institutions identified by Western standards as superior to indigenous institutions – is not necessarily evidence of "irrational" decision-making; the country "may be following its own notion of rationality, efficiency and justice," and so it may be that "the path-dependence in the process of institutional evolution operates at a more fundamental level than we normally think" (p. 490).
8 "If all land had the same properties, if it were boundless in quantity, and uniform in quality, no charge could be made for its use, unless where it possessed peculiar advantages of situation. It is only then because land is of different qualities with respect to its productive powers, and because in the progress of population, land of an inferior quality, or less advantageously situated, is called into cultivation, that rent is ever paid for the use of it" (Ricardo, 1817, pp. 53–54).
9 An excellent introduction may be found in Mueller (1989, Ch.13).
10 Rent seeking *per se,* they define as "any redistributive activity that takes up resources" (Murphy et al., 1993, p. 409).
11 Krueger's (1974) seminal paper limited its concern to rents accruing from quotas.
12 Shadow prices indicate the highest price a producer could pay for the added resource without becoming worse off overall by adding the resource.
13 In defining rent seeking as a process and rent creation as an instrument for growth, the heterodox approach does not distinguish between rent policy (coming from either rent seeking or policymaking) and industrial policy because industrial policy inherently creates rents for industries and firms.
14 The policies implemented by the East Asian Tigers are frequently referred to as industrial policies, although Hausmann and Rodrik (2003) explicitly call them rents.
15 In making this assertion, Cowen, Glazer, and McMillan (1994) assume that public officials receive more rent as they promote public policies, and so long as the policies benefit the public, they increase social welfare.
16 The theory of the "Big Push" model emphasizes that developing countries require large investments to embark on the path of economic development from their present state of underdevelopment. This theory proposes that a "bit-by-bit" investment program will not impact the process of growth as much as is required for developing countries.
17 Khan (1995) defines and discusses the political settlement, and Khan (2000b) discusses redistributive rents and how they are essential for maintaining political stability.

References

Abegaz, B. (2013). Political parties in business: Rent seekers, developmentalists, or both? *Journal of Development Studies, 49*(11), 1467–1483. doi:10.1080/00220388.2013.822070

Amsden, A. (1989). *Asia's next giant: South Korea and late industrialization.* New York, NY: Oxford University Press.

Amsden, A. (2009). Nationality of firm ownership in developing countries: Who should "crowd out" whom in imperfect markets? In M. Cimoli, G. Dosi, & J. E. Stiglitz (Eds.), *Industrial policy and development: The political economy of capability accumulation* (pp. 409–423). Oxford, England: Oxford University Press.

Arrow, K. J. (1962). The economic implications of learning by doing. *Review of Economic Studies, 29*(80), 155–173.

Ayres, C. E. (1944). *The theory of economic progress.* Chapel Hill, NC: University of North Carolina Press.

Baran, P. (1957). *The political economy of growth.* New York, NY: Monthly Review Press.

Bhagwati, J. N. (1982). Directly unproductive, profit-seeking (DUP) activities. *Journal of Political Economy, 90*(5), 988–1002.

Buchanan, J. M. (1980a). Reform in the rent-seeking society. In J. M. Buchanan, R. D. Tollison, & G. Tullock (Eds.), *Toward a theory of the rent-seeking society.* College Station, TX: Texas A&M University Press.

Buchanan, J. M. (1980b). Rent seeking and profit seeking. In J. M. Buchanan, R. D. Tollison, & G. Tullock (Eds.), *Toward a theory of the rent-seeking society.* College Station, TX: Texas A&M University Press.

Chang, H. J. (1999). The economic theory of developmental state. In M. Woo-Cumings (Ed.), *The developmental state* (pp. 182–199). Cornell, NY: Cornell University Press.

Chang, H. J. (2011). Institutions and economic development: Theory, policy and history. *Journal of Institutional Economics,* 7(4), 473–498.

Chang, H. J., Cheema, A., & Mises, L. (2002). Conditions for successful technology policy in developing countries: Learning rents, state structures and institutions. *Economics of Innovation and New Technology, 11*(4–5), 369–398.

Cimoli, M., Dosi, G., & Stiglitz, J. E. (2009a). *Industrial policy and development: The political economy of capabilities accumulation* (O. U. Press, Ed.). New York, NY: Oxford University Press.

Cimoli, M., Dosi, G., & Stiglitz, J. E. (2009b). The political economy of capbilities accumulation: The past and future of policies for industrial development. In M. Cimoli, G. Dosi, & J. E. Stiglitz (Eds.), *Industrial policy and development: The political economy of capabilities accumulation* (pp. 1–18). New York, NY: Oxford University Press.

Congleton, R. (1980). Competitive process, competitive waste, and institutions. In J. M. Buchanan, R. D. Tollison, & G. Tullock (Eds.), *Towards a theory of the rent-seeking society* (pp. 153–179). College Station, TX: Texas A&M University Press.

Cowen, T., Glazer, A., & McMillan, H. (1994). Rent seeking can promote the provision of public good. *Economics and Politics, 6*(2), 131–145.

Dosi, G., & Nelson, R. (2009). *Technical change and industrial dynamics as evolutionary processes* (Working Paper). Retrieved from Laboratory of Economics and Management Sant' Anna School of Advanced Studies https://ideas.repec.org/p/ssa/lemwps/2009-07.html

Ellerman, D. (2004). Revisiting Hirschman on development assistance and unbalanced growth. *Eastern Economic Journal, 30*(2), 311–331.

Fine, B. (1997). Industrial policy and South Africa: A strategic view. *Indicator South Africa, 14*(3), 49–54.

Fine, B., & Jomo, K. S. (Eds.). (2006). *The new development economics: After the Washington consensus*. London, England: Zed Press.

Gerschenkron, A. (1962). *Economic backwardness in historical perspective*. Cambridge, MA: Harvard University Press.

Gray, H. (2015). Access orders and the "new" new institutional economics of development. *Development and Change*, *47*(1), 51–75.

Hausmann, R., & Rodrik, D. (2003). Economic development as self-discovery. *Journal of Development Economics*, *72*(2), 603–633.

Hausmann, R., Rodrik, D., & Velasco, A. (2008). Growth diagnostics. In N. Serra & J. E. Stiglitz (Eds.), *The Washington consensus reconsidered: Towards a new global governance* (pp. 324–355). New York, NY: Oxford University Press.

Hillman, A. L., & Katz, E. (1984). Risk-averse rent seekers and the social cost of monopoly power. *The Economic Journal*, *94*(373), 104–110.

Hirschman, A. (1957). Economic policy in underdeveloped countries. *Economic Development and Cultural Change*, *5*(4), 362–370.

Hirschman, A. (1958). *The strategy of economic development*. New Haven, CT: Yale University Press.

James, D. D. (1988). Accumulation and utilitzation of internal technological capabilities in the third world. *Journal of Economic Issues*, *33*(2), 338–353.

Kaldor, N. (1957). A model of economic-growth. *The Economic Journal*, *67*(268), 586–624.

Kaldor, N. (1967). *Strategic factors in economic development*. Ithaca, NY: New York State School of Industrial and Labor Relations, Cornell University.

Kelsall, T. (2013). *Business, politics and the state in Africa*. London, England: Zed Books.

Khan, M. H. (1995). State failure in weak states: A critique of new institutionalist explanations. In J. Harriss, J. Hunter, & C. M. Lewis (Eds.), *The new institutional economcis and third world development* (pp. 71–86). London, England: Routledge.

Khan, M. H. (2000a). Rent-seeking as process. In M. H. Khan & K. S. Jomo (Eds.), *Rents, rent-seeking and economic development: Theory and evidence in Asia* (pp. 70–144). Cambridge, England: Cambridge University Press.

Khan, M. H. (2000b). Rents, efficiency and growth. In M. H. Khan & K. S. Jomo (Eds.), *Rents, rent-seeking and economic development: Theory and evidence in Asia* (pp. 21–69). Cambridge, England: Cambridge University Press.

Khan, M. H. (2009). *Learning, technology acquisition and governance challenges in developing countries* (DFID Research Paper Series on Governance for Growth). Retrieved from School of Oriental and African Studies, University of London http://r4d.dfid.gov.uk/pdf/outputs/nem_misc/r8521-learning-and-technology-acquisition.pdf

Khan, M. H. (2010). *Political settlements and the governance of growth-enhancing institutions*. Retrieved from http://eprints.soas.ac.uk/9968/

Khan, M. H. (2012). The political economy of inclusive growth. In L. de Mello & M. A. Dutz (Eds.), *Promoting inclusive growth: Challenges and policy* (pp. 15–54). Paris, France: OECD Publishing.

Khan, M. H. (2013). Political settlements and the design of technology policy. In J. Stiglitz, J. Y. Lin, & E. Patel (Eds.), *The industrial policy revolution II: Africa in the twenty-first century* (pp. 243–280). London, England: Palgrave Macmillan.

Khan, M. H. (2015). *Supporting inclusive growth effective policy design for developing medium technology sectors* (Background Study for the 2015 National Human Development Report). Retrieved from UNDP Vietnam www.vn.undp.org/content/vietnam/en/home/library/poverty/Supporting-inclusive-growth-effective-policy-design/

Khan, M. H., & Jomo, K. S. (2000). *Rents, rent-seeking and economic development: Theory and the Asian evidence.* Cambridge, England: Cambridge University Press.

Krueger, A. O. (1974). Political economy of the rent-seeking society. *American Economic Review, 64*(3), 291–303.

Krueger, A. O. (1998). Why trade liberalisation is good for growth. *Economic Journal, 108*(450), 1513–1522.

Kuznets, S. (1966). *Economic growth and structure: Selected essays.* London, England: Heinemann.

Lall, S. (1992). Technological capability and industrialization. *World Development, 20*(2), 165–186.

Lall, S. (2004). *Reinventing industrial strategy: The role of government policy in building industrial competitiveness* (G24 Discussion Paper Series No. 28). UNCTAD, The Intergovernmental Group on Monetary Affairs and Development (G-24). Retrieved from http://unctad.org/en/Docs/gdsmdpbg2420044_en.pdf

Lall, S., & Larsch, W. W. (1999). Import liberalisation and industrial performance: Theory and evidence. In S. Lall (Ed.), *The technological response to import liberalization in Subsaharan Africa* (pp. 26–56). London, England: Palgrave Macmillan.

List, F. (1984). *The national systems of political economy.* London, England: Longmans, Green, and Co.

Marshall, A. (1890). *Principles of economics* (Vol. 1). London, England: Palgrave Macmillan.

Marx, K. (1906). *Capital: A critique of political economy.* New York, NY: The Modern Library.

Marx, K. (1920). *The poverty of philosophy: Being a translation of the misere de la philosophie.* Chicago, IL: Charles H. Kerr and Company.

Medema, S. G. (1991). Another look at the problem of rent seeking. *Journal of Economic Issues, 25*(4), 1049–1065.

Mueller, D. C. (1989). *Public choice II: A revised edition of public choice.* Cambridge, England: Cambridge University Press.

Murphy, K. M., Shleifer, A., & Vishny, R. W. (1993). Why is rent-seeking so costly to growth? *American Economic Review, 83*(2), 409–414.

Myrdal, G. (1968). *Asian drama: An inquiry into the poverty of nations.* New York, NY: Twentieth Century Fund.

Myrdal, G. (1979). Underdevelopment and the evolutionary imperative. *Third World Quarterly, 1*(2), 24–42.

Nelson, R. (2008). Economic development from the perspective of evolutionary economic theory. *Oxford Development Studies, 36*(1), 9–21.

Nelson, R. R., & Winter, S. G. (1982). *An evolutionary theory of economic change.* Cambridge, MA: Harvard University Press.

Ngo, C. N. (2016a). Developmental rent management analysis: Learning, upgrading, and innovation. *Journal of Economic Issues, 50*(4), 1045–1068.

Ngo, C. N. (2016b). Local value chain development in Vietnam: Motorcycles, technical learning and rents management. *Journal of Contemporary Asia, 47*(1), 1–26.

Ngo, C. N. (2017). Industrial development, liberalisation and impacts of Vietnam-China border trade. *European Journal of East Asian Studies, 16*(1), 154–184.

Ngo, C. N., & Chi, M. (2017). *Differentials in market constraints and value addition among micro, small, and medium enterprises in Viet Nam.* Retrieved from United Nations University World Institute for Development Economics Research www.wider.unu.edu/publication/differentials-market-constraints-and-value-addition-among-micro-small-and-medium

North, D. C., Wallis, J. J., Webb, S. B., & Weingast, B. R. (2007). *Limited access orders in the developing world: A new approach to the problems of development* (Policy Research Working

Paper No. 4359). Retrieved from World Bank http://elibrary.worldbank.org/content/workingpaper/10.1596/1813-9450-4359

North, D. C., Wallis, J. J., & Weingast, B. R. (2006). *A conceptual framework for interpreting recorded human history* (NBER Working Paper Series, Working Paper No. 12759). Retrieved from National Bureau of Economic Research www.nber.org/papers/w12795.pdf?new_window=1

North, D. C., Wallis, J. J., & Weingast, B. R. (2009). *Violence and social orders: A conceptual framework for interpreting recorded human history*. New York, NY: Cambridge University Press.

Ohno, K. (2008, August). *Vietnam-Japan Monozukuri partnership for supporting industries: For leveling up Vietnam's competitiveness in the age of deepening integration*. Paper presented at the Seminar on Action Plan for Development of Supporting Industry in Vietnam, Ha Noi. Retrieved from www.grips.ac.jp/vietnam/KOarchives/doc/EP23_monozukuri.pdf

Posner, R. A. (1975). The social costs of monopoly and regulation. *Journal of Political Economy, 83*(4), 807–827.

Rajagopalan, R. (1996). Rent-seeking: A selective survey of recent literature. *Vikalpa, 21*(1), 23–31.

Ricardo, D. (1817). *On the principles of political economy, and taxation*. London, England: John Murray.

Rodrik, D. (1995). Trade and industrial policy reform. In J. Behrman, H. Chenery, & T. N. Srinivasan (Eds.), *Handbook of development economics* (Vol. 3). Amsterdam, Netherlands: North-Holland.

Rodrik, D. (2004, October). *Rethinking economic growth in developing countries*. Paper presented at the Luca d'Agliano Lecture in Development Economics, Torino, Italy. Retrieved from www.dagliano.unimi.it/media/RodrikLecturePaper.pdf

Rodrik, D. (2006). Goodbye Washington consensus? Hello Washington confusion? A review of the World Bank's economic growth in the 1990s: Learning from a decade of reform. *Journal of Economic Literature, 44*(4), 973–987.

Rodrik, D. (2007). *One economics, many recipes: Globalization, institutions and economic growth*. Princeton, NJ: Princeton University Press.

Rogerson, W. P. (1982). The social costs of monopoly and regulation: A game-theoretic analysis. *Bell Journal of Economics, 13*(2), 391–401.

Rosenstein-Rodan, P. N. (1943, June–September). Problems of industrialization of eastern and south-eastern Europe. *The Economic Journal, 53*, 202–211.

Rosenstein-Rodan, P. N. (1961). Notes on the theory of the "big push." In H. S. Ellis & H. C. Wallich (Eds.), *Economic development for Latin America*. New York, NY: St. Martin's Press.

Samuels, W. J., & Mercuro, N. (1984). A critique of rent-seeking theory. In D. C. Colander (Ed.), *Neoclassical political economy: The analysis of rent-seeking and DUP activities* (pp. 55–70). Cambridge, MA: Ballinger.

Schmitz, H., Johnson, O., & Altenburg, T. (2013). *Rent management: The heart of green industrial policy*. Retrieved from Institute of Development Studies www.ids.ac.uk/publication/rent-management-the-heart-of-green-industrial-policy

Schumpeter, J. A. (1983). *The theory of economic development: An inquiry into profits, capital, credit, interest, and the business cycle*. London, England: Routledge. (Original work published 1934).

Schumpeter, J. A. (1942). *Capitalism, socialism and democracy*. New York, NY: Harper & Brothers.

Schweinberger, A. (2014). State capitalism, entrepreneurship, and networks: China's rise to a superpower. *Journal of Economic Issues, 48*(1), 169–180.

Scitovsky, T. (1954). Two concepts of external economics. *Journal of Political Economy, 62*(2), 143–151.

Serra, N., & Stiglitz, J. (2008). *The Washington consensus reconsidered: Towards a new global governance.* Oxford, England: Oxford University Press.

Smith, A. (1998). *An inquiry into the nature and causes of the wealth of nations.* Washington, DC: Regnery Publishing, Inc. (Original work published 1776).

Solow, R. M. (1956). A contribution to the theory of economic growth. *Quarterly Journal of Economics, 70,* 65–94.

Solow, R. M. (1957). Technical change and the aggregate production function: Review of economics and statistics. *Review of Economics and Statistics, 39*(3), 312–320.

Stiglitz, J., & Greenwald, B. (2014). *Creating a learning society: A new approach to growth development and social progress.* New York, NY: Columbia University Press.

Stiglitz, J. E. (1989). Markets, market failures, and development. *American Economic Review, 79*(2), 197–203.

Stiglitz, J. E. (1994). *Whither socialism?* Cambridge, MA: MIT Press.

Stiglitz, J. E. (2013a, January). *Creating a learning economy.* Paper presented at the Advanced Graduate Workshop, Bangalore, India.

Stiglitz, J. E. (2013b). Learning, growth and development. In J. Y. Lin & C. P. Sepulveda (Eds.), *Annual World Bank conference on development economics 2011: Development challenges in a post-crisis world.* Washington, DC: The World Bank Group.

Stiglitz, J. E. (2016, January). *The state, the market, and development.* Paper presented at Mapping the Future of Development Economics, Helsinki, Finland.

Street, J. H. (1987). The institutionalist theory of economic development. *Journal of Economic Issues, 21*(4), 1861–1887.

Tullock, G. (1967). Welfare costs of tariffs, monopolies, and theft. *Western Economic Journal, 5*(3), 224–232.

Tullock, G. (1980). Efficient rent seeking. In J. M. Buchanan, R. D. Tollison, & G. Tullock (Eds.), *Towards a theory of the rent seeking society* (pp. 97–112). College Station, TX: Texas A&M University Press.

Van den Berg, H. (2016). *Economic growth and development.* Singapore: World Scientific Publishing Co.

Veblen, T. B. (1904). *The theory of business enterprise.* New York: Charles Scribner's Sons.

Wade, R. (1990). *Governing the market: Economic theory and the role of government in East Asian industrialization.* Princeton, NJ: Princeton University Press.

Warren, A. N. (2007). *An exploration of factors shaping technological developments in the Mozambican manufacturing sector and their impact on enterprise performance* (Unpublished doctoral dissertation). School of Oriental and African Studies, University of London, London, England.

Whitfield, L., Therkildsen, O., Buur, L., & Kjaer, A. M. (2015). *The politics of African industrial policy.* New York, NY: Cambridge University Press.

Williamson, J. (2005). The strange history of the Washington consensus. *Journal of Post Keynesian Economics, 27*(2), 195–206.

World Bank. (1987). *World development report 1987: Industrialization and foreign trade.* Oxford, England: Oxford University Press.

World Bank. (1991). *World development report 1991: The challenge of development.* New York, NY: Oxford University Press.

3 Developmental rent-management analysis

Learning, upgrading, and innovation

3.1 Introduction

The previous chapter demonstrates that to achieve growth by enhancing the capacity of the industrial sectors, rent policies should not simply aim to remove constraints in the development process, but must create incentives and pressures for ensuring effort in technical learning and industrial upgrading. From this perspective, an analytical approach is needed to assess the interaction between rent policies, firm activities, and performance. This chapter constructs a conceptual and original analytical framework: the developmental rent-management analysis (DRMA) for the assessment of rents and rent management. This framework provides an analytical tool to examine the political, institutional, and organizational dynamics that drive economic development without the presumption of efficient markets, perfectly competitive firms, or an autonomous and capable guiding state.

Analytically, the DRMA is not meant to suggest a coherent or new development model, given the great variation in economic transformations of developing countries. Rather, it aims to highlight connections and disconnections among different agents within the political economy and industry. The purpose is to identify strengths and weaknesses in the structure of incentives and pressures for technological upgrading. In addition, the DRMA presumes that no single political or institutional arrangement provides exclusive access to successful rent management and developmental outcomes. A successful rent-management strategy is specific to the political and institutional contexts of a country and its political economy. From this conceptual dimension, an effective rent-management system is one that creates the *incentives* and *pressures* for local firms to achieve technical learning, capability building, and competitiveness. Finally, because the DRMA allows for a *systemic* analysis of economic transformation from political, institutional, and economic perspectives, the framework offers scholars, field researchers, and policymakers an alternative analytical approach to better understand the binding constraints of an industry, the complexity of a country's political economy, and policy solutions to promote developmental outcomes.

To this end, the rest of the chapter is organized into three sections. The next section provides a conceptual framework of the rent-management analysis.

Following this section, the DRMA framework is introduced and substantiated in detail. The final section highlights contributions of the DRMA and situates it within the literature of economic development. Because a major aspect of economic development involves industry development, the DRMA frequently refers to issues and concerns of technological adoption and industrial upgrade in analyzing economic development.

3.2 Conceptual approach of the developmental rent-management analysis

The drive to achieve sustained economic development in poor countries requires an understanding of how rent seeking and rent creation take place in the local context and whether feasible changes in political organizations and institutions can promote growth in these countries. Where rent is assessed as an *outcome* and rent seeking as a *process*, the overall management of rents and rent seeking (or rent management) depends on institutional, political, and market arrangements within an industry and an economy. Therefore, the analysis of rent management helps describe institutional, industrial, and economic transformations. This analysis not only explains the types of rent created through the rent-seeking process but also provides insights to effectively resolve binding constraints in development. The term "rent management" used in this context, and in the remaining analysis of this book, does not involve the exclusive control and monitoring of the state and its agencies. Instead, it denotes a *dynamic* configuration of the existing political arrangement, formal and informal institutions, and market structure that incentivizes and pressures firms' credible efforts to industrialize. From this perspective, rent-management analysis *contextualizes* the political economy of an industry or a specific aspect of economic development. The conceptual approach of developmental rent-management analysis is outlined in Figure 3.1.

Conceptually, the first analytical step is to map existing mechanisms of rent management. The analysis starts by asking: what is the configuration of rent management, given a specific development issue or industry within the country's political economy? The DRMA framework described below assists with the answer to this question. Once there is a clear understanding of the rent-management mechanism at work, the second step is to analyze *how* this structure of rent management influences firm incentives and pressures to upgrade their capacity via technology adoption. The examination of how rent-management factors affect firms' internal and external incentives and pressures is the most involved component of the DRMA. These incentives and pressures can influence firm industrial performance and, eventually, the outcomes associated with the rent. The incentives and pressures discussed here do not necessarily stem from state actions but could come from the configuration of a number of forces: for instance, market competition, the time horizon available to make a profit, and the balance of the supply and demand of the product. The incentives and pressures for performance are critical factors because if a rent is created without

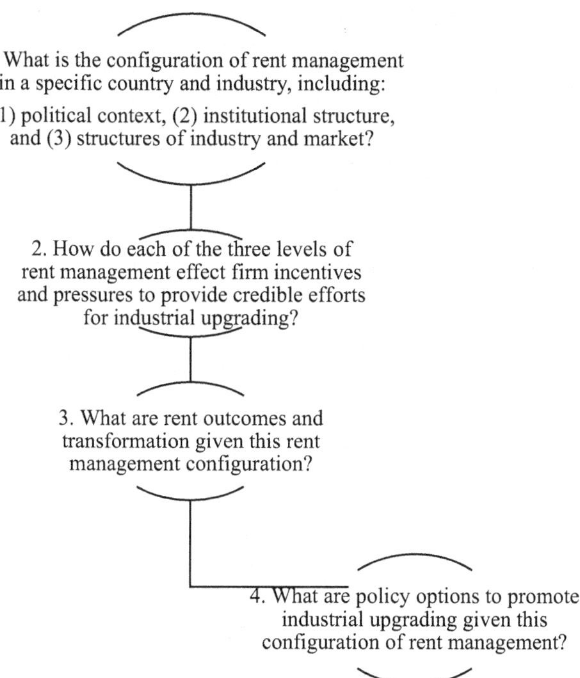

Figure 3.1 Conceptual Approach of the DRMA

effective incentives and compulsions for capability building, there is no guarantee that rent recipients will pursue high-effort strategies to acquire technical and organizational capabilities or engage in new innovation and production. Examples of incentives and pressures provided in the literature are shown in the third column of Table 3.1.

The third conceptual step is to *identify the rent outcomes* and *trace firm and industry transformations* over time and within the broader structure of rent management. For example, the successful development of the automobile industry in South Korea can be traced back to the government's persistence in financing the loss-making period – the time it took to acquire competitive production capacity – and policy promotions for automobile use in the domestic market (Amsden, 1989; Lee & Mah, 2017). It is important to note that the outcomes and transformations identified in Step 3 would subsequently modify the configuration of rent management (Step 1), either in the short term or the long term. Economic development is an evolutionary and dynamic process. The DRMA captures this evolutionary change and observes the interaction between different outcomes created by rents and their influence on the overall structure of rent management. Finally, once there is a clear

Table 3.1 Examples of Rents, Effects, and Outcomes

Rent Policies	*Effects*	*Incentives/Pressures*	*Outcomes*
1. Development grant 2. Access to land 3. Access to credit 4. Access to business licenses 5. Subsidies for domestic purchase of the product	**Positive** 1. Creating opportunity for effective learning 2. Incentivizing new innovation 3. Expanding production and productivity growth 4. Increasing production to achieve economies of scale 5. Learning new technology or technical skills **Negative** 1. Redistributing wealth and rents within and across interest groups 2. Raising entry barrier to reduce competition 3. Monopolizing market through political influence	**Internal Incentives** 1. Possibility of high profit that justifies new investments 2. Financial support for a loss-making period while new technical learning takes place 3. Access to new market abroad **External Pressures** 1. Market competition 2. Time horizon 3. Loss of rents and future opportunities **Internal Pressures** 1. Financial consequences of investment failure 2. Discipline by the state 3. Informal consequences such as shame, loss of social status, and relationships	1. Rent raises investment but does not produce long-term benefits (productivity is not increased) 2. Rent raises investment and productivity through learning and innovation leading to long-term growth 3. Rents captured or redistributed among interests causing no output expansion or productivity increase

understanding of a working rent-management system in a specific political economy, then the government could formulate industrial strategies to tackle political and institutional constraints as well as market failures that hinder development (Step 4).

The central utilization of the DRMA framework, therefore, is to help identify the types of rent being created, their roles in development, the critical binding constraints in the economy, and the policy space within the political economy to force a new round of change for growth and development. In Table 3.1, examples of factors in the DRMA are offered, including the types of rents created through government policies; effects of the rents on firms and industries; potential incentives and pressures for the firms, given the context of the industry and the wider economy; and, finally, possible outcomes assuming either success or failure of the rent effects.

The successful development of solar panel manufacturing in China helps elaborate Table 3.1. First, the Chinese government articulated a strategy and rent policies to lead the development of solar technology, in a number of legislations promulgated by the central and local governments, beginning in the early 2000s (Hua, Oliphant, & Hu, 2016). Chinese central and local governments initially provided local solar panel producers all four types of rent identified in Column 1 – development grant, access to land, discounted credit, and business license to manufacture solar panels in China (Mazzucato, 2015). Further, once the product became readily available, the government subsidized the cost of solar panels to boost domestic demand for energy-saving solar products (Bradsher, 2017). Here, the technology or Schumpeterian rent created the financial incentives for Chinese firms to learn the new technology and to manufacture solar panels, first for the local market, and later exported abroad (Hua et al., 2016). In addition, because solar panel installation was heavily subsidized in China and global market demand for alternative energy was growing, local firms saw a strong possibility of profits if the investments were successful (Column 2). There was also external pressure from the global market, as China faced intense competition with leading European and American manufacturers of solar technology (Column 3). The combination of government incentives and opportunity for profit, coupled with pressures from international competition and a limited time horizon forced local firms to put in real effort to transfer, learn, and adopt solar panel manufacturing technology (Column 4) (Bradsher, 2017; Hua et al., 2016; Mazzucato, 2015). The government's successful rent creation and management, along with the urgent need for alternative energy in the world market supported Chinese firms' development into global solar panel producers. It is a tale of successful developmental rent creation and management.

The next section explains the DRMA four-step approach for rent-management analysis in detail. The DRMA framework is based on the conceptual structure described in this section; however, the actual analysis is more nuanced. It observes dynamic rent management using both bottom-up *and* top-down factors.

3.3 The DRMA four-step approach

The DRMA provides an analytical tool to analyze the larger political, institutional, and organizational dynamics at work within an economy or a specific industry. The framework is designed for case-study analysis and is intended to be inductive through: (1) analyzing fundamental causes or factors of rent management, (2) determining development outcomes, and (3) observing the overall impacts of rent-management configuration within the political economy. In developing countries, statistical data is seldom available and scarcely credible even when it is available. Therefore, analytical case studies are nuanced in studying transformative events and development processes. The four steps are detailed in Figure 3.2. The next section describes the DRMA four-step approach in greater depth.

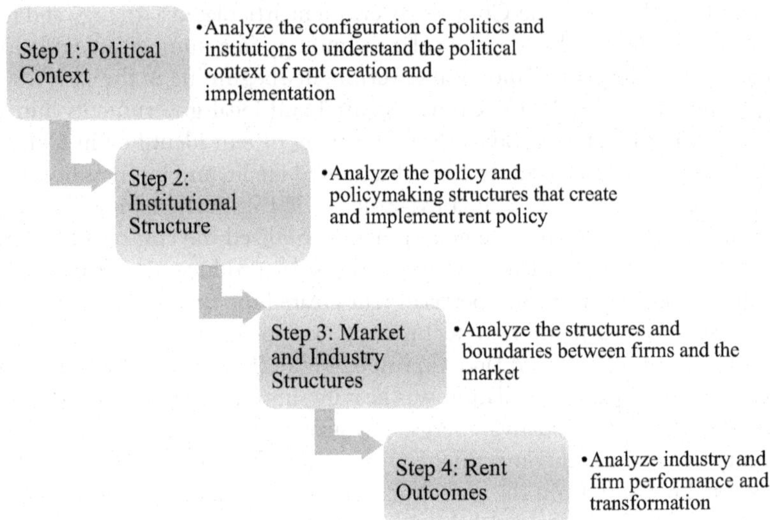

Figure 3.2 The DRMA Four-Step Approach

3.3.1 Step 1: political context of rent creation and management

Implicit and explicit in the DRMA is the central role of politics in rent management. Understanding the political context is critical for three reasons. First, it is through the political processes that economic institutions are modified, specific policies are selected, and performance is subsequently monitored (Moon & Prasad, 1998). Second, political organizations compete for rents or attempt to affect the management of rents by mobilizing and forming coalitions with powerful individuals and groups in society. Third, as institutions and politics shape rent policies and firm performance, the pressures created by rent seeking, policy choices, and firm performance can trigger political feedback, reshuffle political alliances, and induce new institutional design and rent policies or any combination therein.

Under Thaksin, Thailand provides a vivid example. While the political elites were under the influence of private interests, they were able to create rents not only for themselves and their cronies but also for small and medium firms and the poor population via proactive economic and social policies. Kevin Hewison (2006) provides a careful account of the transformation under Thaksin's tenure. The Asian financial crisis and neoliberal reform had severely aggravated poverty and the living conditions of the poor living in rural areas. Thaksin's Thai Rak Thai (TRT) party seized the moment and won the election by promoting a nationalist platform – one that would slow neoliberal reform and penetration by foreign firms while allowing domestic firms to gain rents, recover, and upgrade their competitiveness to compete with foreign investors once market liberalization policies resumed (Hewison, 2006). This was enacted through "a new social contract" (Hewison, 2006, p. 100). In exchange for electorate support, the TRT promised to reduce poverty through social programs, expand infrastructure, promote small and medium enterprises, and provide universal health care coverage. Thaksin fulfilled his promises after winning the election.

The new social contract was unprecedented: TRT became "a government that is representative of domestic capital [and yet] developed a social contract that delivers state-supported social protection at a level never before considered possible for Thailand" (Hewison, 2006, p. 101). In addition, big local businesses committed to cooperate with the party to carry out its social policies, as they were aware that political and social unrest would undermine economic recovery and opportunities. As a result, "the TRT government has presided over growth rates that increased to more than 6 percent in 2002" and was able to maintain a positive growth rate until 2006 (Hewison, 2006, p. 102). The TRT's political arrangement created a stable coalition between political elites, private businesses, and farmers that led to the creation of new institutions reinforcing the pact and managing rents.

Politics and institutions interact in a number of ways. First, the balance of political forces determines the ways in which formal and informal institutions operate to create and manage rents. Second, political mobilizations and struggles can also change the political order, which can transform the ways in which rent-managing institutions operate. For example, in Tanzania, given the intense contestation within ruling coalitions, industrial policies were supported only half-heartedly and thus were short lived (Whitfield, Therkildsen, Buur, & Kjaer, 2015, p. 294). Consequently, rent policies targeting the rice and manufacturing sectors, for example, did not have significant impacts on productivity growth among Tanzanian producers due to poor implementation (Whitfield et al., 2015, p. 231).

To the extent that information is accessible, it is instructive to understand two separate issues about the political context of a developing country and industry: (1) *how political organizations are structured formally and informally* and (2) *how political agents and forces interact to create, allocate, and manage rents.* These analytical steps together describe the political context of rent management and provide crucial understanding of the political dynamics embedded in the political economy of an industry and economy at large. The data could be collected through careful reading of political and economic history literature. More importantly, to understand the political forces at work, semi-structured interviews with relevant government officials and key figures among the elites, businesses, and community organizations are necessary. The interviews could provide intimate and nuanced accounts regarding the political actors and forces that shape rent decisions and implementation. It is crucial that interview data is carefully cross-checked across different interviewers and, when possible, the official documents, news reports, and statistical data.

3.3.2 Step 2: institutional structure of rent allocation and implementation

The second level of analysis is to understand the policy and policymaking structures that generate and enforce a particular rent. In this book, institutions are defined as rules that govern behaviors of individuals and groups within a given community. Institutions may be formal, such as legal codes and statutes that organize and structure the economy or the rules that allocate public resources to individuals and firms. Institutions can also be informal, such as social norms, culture, ideology, and group values. Informal institutions can influence economic and political performance because they affect customs and behaviors within a group. For example, elements of the Confucian tradition reflect deeply in many East Asian countries' cultures as well as social, economic, and political norms. Although the Confucian values are not often legally codified in the rule of law, they are informally enforced within the society. These values, however, play a decisive role in the speed of technical learning and development among East Asian countries, as they solve important market failures such as lack of trust, loyalty, work effort, and contract enforcement.

In a development context, many of the rules that compel actual behavior are informally agreed upon by individuals and groups based on a set of informal values. Therefore, informal institutions are critical, perhaps even more so than formal ones. For instance, Stellmacher (2007) shows that, in Ethiopia, the government failed to recognize the old feudal arrangement of land ownership and distribution that had historically governed local peasant communities. This led to the ineffectiveness of the *Derg* government's socialist-oriented land reform. More importantly, the combination of formal rules not being enforced, and local peasants' continued adoption of older schemes of land arrangement without legal recognition, led local peasants to engage in exploitative land use and unsustainable practices. As a result, in the past 100 years, Ethiopia's montane moist forests "have shrunk from approximately forty percent of the country's total area to less than three percent" (Stellmacher, 2007, p. 519).

For these reasons, the analysis of institutions in the DRMA framework assesses both formal and informal institutions, as they set the structure and context for rent creation and rent seeking. To the extent that data is available and credible, the analysis may include:

1 The overall formal and informal institutional structure of rent seeking at either the state or firm level
2 Policy instruments through which rents are created
3 Policies and regulations that allow the government to intervene in the credit market, land allocation, and technical training that promote industrialization; and the ways in which these policies create rents
4 The rules of rent allocation to recipients, the time horizon, and the institutional structure of rent management by the state

5 Informal structure and agreements between interest groups involved in the creation and implementation of particular rents
6 The ways informal structure and agreements come into place and how they operate in reality

Data regarding formal institutions can be collected through review of relevant statues, laws, or the government's official documents. In addition, qualitative data acquired through semi-structured interviews provides knowledge of the underlying informal institution at work, as well as how the government implement rents in reality. Finally, historical accounts, news reports, and statistical data on firms and industry performance help cross-check and illuminate the qualitative data or provide further context of the relevant institutions and institutional structures.

3.3.3 Step 3: market and industry structure

In the third step, the DRMA also requires industry analysis, defined as the structure and boundaries between firms and the markets that incentivize and compel local firms' high-level learning efforts. This third level of rent-management analysis includes assessing, among other factors, (1) market structures, (2) structures of firm ownership, (3) types of technology needed for industrialization, and (4) initial capability of local firms and workers in a sector, as it can determine the feasibility of learning particular technologies.

First, market structure matters because with any given rent allocation, the effort put into learning or innovation depends on the competitive environment in which a firm operates. Competitive environment involves factors such as size of the firm in relation to the market, the minimum efficient scale of production, market concentration,[1] uniqueness of the products,[2] entry barriers,[3] and degree of vertical integration.[4] Together, these factors determine the incentives and disciplining pressures of the market on firm performance. In addition, the level of competition in domestic and international markets could support or inhibit investments and efforts to achieve new technical skills and technology. Similarly, changes in international and domestic market structures – such as a supply shock for basic inputs – may provide new opportunities or constraints for industries. For example, the global financial crisis in 2008 caused a large-scale recession in the developed world, which severely slowed growth in the Asian economies because of weakened international demand for consumer goods. Therefore, strategies for investment and learning that may have been viable in a growing international market turned out to be unviable in the new context.

Second, an industry analysis has to consider the structure of firm ownership – that is, whether a firm is public, private, or jointly owned by public and private investors. In addition, whether a firm is domestic or foreign also matters in the rent-management analysis. This is because when a firm acquires a formal rent, it usually makes certain commitments for performance. The rent was most likely meant to help the firm overcome certain constraints in achieving new capabilities, upgrading, or innovation. The structure of firm ownership has important implications for the acquisition of rents as well as the capability and incentives of the firm to deliver on its commitments. For example, in the late 1990s, the Vietnamese government devised learning and technology rents mostly for large Vietnamese state-owned enterprises (SOEs), while very limited rents were created for the private sector (interviews, four government officers, Ha Noi; April–July 2011). In addition, the Vietnamese government was active in directing foreign contracts and joint ventures with foreign investors to large SOEs. In this case, the rent management involved the interaction between SOEs and foreign direct investment (FDI) in a state-led economy (interviews, four government officers, Ha Noi; April–July 2011). Hence, the type of firm ownership may be instrumental in the allocation, implementation, and management of a rent.

Finally, the type of technology required for upgrading and its level of sophistication also matter to local learning and productive efforts. As Lall (2004) points out, the process of gaining technological mastery in a new setting is not instantaneous, costless, or automatic, even if the technology is well diffused elsewhere:

> The learning process is highly technology specific since technologies differ in their learning requirements. Some technologies are more embodied in equipment while others have greater tacit elements . . . . Different technologies involve different breadth of skills and knowledge, some needing a narrow range of specialization and others a wide range.
>
> (p. 12)

From this perspective, it is crucial to assess the *technology gap* between the technology chosen for industrial upgrading and local capability. Are local firms operating in a targeted industry capable of learning, adopting, and adapting the advanced technology needed? For example, the production of automobiles requires a complex network of suppliers that provide components for automotive manufacturers. If local firms do not have component-manufacturing capability, rent policies that support the automotive industry would be ineffective, as the local industry could provide automobile assembly only based on low-cost labor and land, not on vertical integration within the supply chain.

Because technology transfers and upgrading require identification of technology gaps, the provision of rents must be accompanied by appropriate technology for local adoption and learning. Here, the selection of inappropriate technology may have economic and social costs, and it may slow the process of industrialization. For example, continuing use of a technology that is becoming outdated may cause a developing country to lose the advantage over its competitors. However, attempting to adapt a more sophisticated technology that does not match the learning capacity of the firms and workers could be wasteful. In sum, major tasks in the third step of DRMA are to identify the type of technology available in advanced countries, assess the level of technological capability of local firms, and analyze how such capability fits into the process of technological transfer and upgrading in the industrial sectors. This could be achieved with qualitative or fieldwork data coupled with statistical data from the government or firms. For example, interviews with managers at multinational corporations investing in a developing country could reveal areas where local capability falls short, as well as the skill level needed for a multinational corporation to invest in more advanced production techniques or a new line of manufacturing products. Statistical data could confirm some aspects of this observation and also the scale of the issue across industries.

3.3.4 Typology of rents

An important analysis in the first three DRMA steps is to identify the type of rent created, given the political context, institutional structure, and market or industry structures. Because DRMA is inductive and not intended to pick "winners of rent," identification of the type of rent created is analyzed ex post and is based on (1) the government's intended use of the rent and (2) the effects or actual outcomes once the rent is provided. Rents could be largely categorized into four types: learning, Schumpeterian or innovation, monopoly, and redistributive.[5]

Learning rents

Learning rents provide financing to enable learning-by-doing. Technical learning involves more than copying the operation of existing technologies; it requires adaptation of new technologies and innovations from advanced countries to local conditions. Learning has two important dimensions. The first is technical capability through learning-by-doing, and the second is organizational capability through restructuring the production processes. In practice, learning rents could be given ex ante to target learning and technological progress in a specific industry or sector, though it could, in principle, also be allocated ex post as a prize (Khan & Blankenburg, 2009). In some developmental states, South Korea for example, learning rents were allocated ex ante with conditions for specific achievements within a certain period of time. Together with the incentives provided by the rent, these conditions can create credible pressure on rent recipients to perform in order to retain rent or generate new rents. This combination of incentives and pressure by the state is arguably an essential mechanism for effective rent policies.

Learning rents can be intended or unintended. Policymakers create intended learning rents to induce new technological capability, including the adoption, adaptation, and transfer of advanced technology. Therefore, although the rent is created for learning, its outcome is not necessarily guaranteed. As such, whether this learning rent actually operates as rent for learning is an issue that must be analyzed and proven using empirical evidence. Unintended learning rents are also important because the learning effect can emerge from an accidental configuration of factors. For example, a rent may be created for redistributive purposes to assist individuals in a particular industry or for a particular group of firms. However, if the rent emerges from a configuration of factors that happens to induce recipients to enhance their organizational and technical capabilities, the result is unintended learning rents. To measure the success and effectiveness of learning, one could assess productive outcomes such as change in productivity growth or exports based on the development of new products or improvements in production organization.

Schumpeterian rents

Schumpeterian rents reward innovation, often in the form of tax breaks, subsidies, and patent protection. Innovating firms have an advantage over their competitors because they often develop better products or less expensive methods of manufacturing existing products that traditional firms cannot readily copy. Innovative firms can thus earn a generated rent because, with new innovations, firms will either have a cost or quality advantage over competitors. This allows them to earn a higher return as compared to the next-best alternative (Hausmann & Rodrik, 2003). If an innovation can be rapidly copied, thus becoming easily produced and sold, innovators can be discouraged from innovating.

There are three important properties of effective Schumpeterian rents. First, Schumpeterian rent signals the possibility of a significant prize for future innovators, providing incentives to innovate. To do this, the state may protect innovators through intellectual property rights that provide additional time for profit making. Second, the time horizon of protection is an important factor for ensuring desirable outcomes of Schumpeterian rents. Khan (2000) argues that because the process of innovation takes time, involves risk, and requires effort and investment, Schumpeterian rents should ensure sufficient superprofits to induce innovative activities; therefore, they should not be removed too quickly. On the other hand, Schumpeterian rents should not be given beyond the necessity of inducing further innovations, as their continuance has costs for consumers, and innovation rents can become indistinguishable from monopolistic or redistributive rents after a point (Khan, 2000). Third, Schumpeterian rents can either be ex post, such as patent-based rents, or ex ante, such as university research grants. The outcome depends on the characteristics of the innovation and the institutional context in which such rents are managed. Successful Schumpeterian rents may be assessed, for example, by the number of innovations created within firms, universities, and research institutions; by the positive impact in productivity and production; and by firm and industry export volumes.

Monopoly rents

Monopoly rents emerge as a result of entry barriers that allow firms operating in protected markets to charge higher prices for their products. Entry barriers can be natural, such as when the technology of production involves large economies of scale such that a single large producer can undercut newcomers.

Entry barriers can also be state made, by offering exclusive protective rights or licensing to a particular producer. In the neoclassical assertion, the creation of monopoly power leads to a general reduction in welfare (Abbott & Brady, 1991). Khan (2000), however, contends that "even in the extreme case of monopoly rents created by government protectionism to favor cronies, their dynamic effects are not always clear cut" (p. 31). In some cases, there may be genuine economies of scale in these industries, and superprofits may create incentives for greater investment. In other cases, monopoly rents may indeed signal lost output and growth opportunities (Khan, 2000). It may be difficult to distinguish Schumpeterian rents from monopoly rents because innovators often enjoy a temporary monopolistic position in the market for their innovation, which ends when protection is removed or the patent expires. Monopolists often try to justify their monopoly on grounds of innovation and economies of scale. As long as monopolistic power is monitored and temporary, monopoly rents can create incentives for technical progress and new innovation. As a result, the overall effects of monopolies vary case by case and depend on specific technologies, sectors, and firms.

Redistributive rents

Unlike learning or Schumpeterian rents, redistributive rents serve a number of diversified purposes such as to redistribute benefits, usually on political grounds. Redistributive rents can be an important tool for maintaining political stability and order. Khan (2000) points out that the economic effect of redistributive rents can have two negative components. The first is that redistribution may have adverse welfare implications because sectors are taxed due to transfers, and this can reduce firm incentives and investible resources for upgrading. The second is that rent seeking for redistributive rents can create political instability if the allocation of redistributive rents is continuously changing or vastly unequal. However, Khan (2000) also suggests that redistributive rents may positively provide the benefited individuals or groups with incentives and opportunities to use the rent for economically productive activities. For example, because investment decisions depend on political stability, redistribution of rents may be required to achieve stable political unity among interest groups. In some countries, transfers have been associated with rapid capital accumulation, development, and growth, such as in South Korea and Taiwan (Amsden, 1989; Wade, 1990). In other countries, conversely, the result has been large-scale theft and transfer of resources to foreign banks by cronies and politicians (Gray, 2018; Whitfield et al., 2015).

Because redistributive rents underpin both early capitalist accumulation and the political processes that maintain order and legitimacy, the implication of redistributive rents – negative or positive – is far more complex than the analyses offered within the neoclassical literature of rents and rent seeking. In addition, the pattern of redistribution can illustrate how well (or not) competing groups are organized and work together. As a result, rent-seeking activities that result in redistribution and transfers may explain why transfers can be growth enhancing rather than growth reducing. Consequently, for rent-management analysis, the pattern of economic and political distribution matters more than the fact that transfers take place.

In general, rents are value enhancing when they result in correcting certain market failures that developing countries encounter, especially failures that affect the process of technical learning and innovation. The East Asian miracle was partly attributed to rent policies that specifically targeted learning-by-doing in the form of low-interest loans, protected domestic markets, and export subsidies with enforceable conditions that ensured high levels of effort in raising competitiveness (Amsden, 1989; Lall, 2004; Wade, 1990). In a development context, learning and Schumpeterian rents are arguably the most important for economic development, while the effects of monopoly and redistributive rents can vary greatly depending on the circumstances.

3.3.5 International institutions and agreements

International institutions and a developing country's engagement in myriad preferential trade agreements play critical roles in rent management. While globalization opens unprecedented opportunities for countries to engage in the world economy, it also poses profound challenges to developing countries' rent strategies. For late developers, policy options for industrialization have been curtailed by various trade obligations that limit industrial strategies for learning and innovation. Commitment to global trade not only reduces the policy space for devising industrial or rent policies, it also raises the cost of policy implementation. For instance, intellectual property rights restrict the use of knowledge and thus, raise the cost of innovation (Stiglitz, 2008).

This is in contrast with the Asian Tigers' industrial experience in the previous period. From the 1960s through the 1980s, a number of East Asian countries used subsidies heavily to target new learning, and thus, technological upgrading was widespread (Amsden, 2001; Wade, 1990). Governments in countries such as Taiwan and South Korea targeted the development of certain industries and products. In Taiwan, this was accomplished through the Industrial Development Bureau, a unit of the Ministry of Economic Affairs; and in South Korea, it was through the Economic Planning Board. However, this use of subsidies is illegal today under the World Trade Organization (WTO). Similarly, before they became members of the WTO, the Vietnamese and Chinese governments used local-content policies to accelerate the integration of local firms to the foreign supply chain.[6] This is no longer a policy option for Vietnam and China as well as other developing countries. In response to limited policy space due to trade treaties, China succeeded in using its market power to force technology transfer from FDI to local businesses. Vietnam, however, largely failed to negotiate for technology transfer and know-how, and thus the benefits of FDI have been limited.

Conversely, time-bound preferential trade agreements with the least developing countries are important formal international mechanisms that both create rents and provide incentives and pressure for learning. For example, the Multifiber Arrangement (1974–1994) offered least developing countries either enumerated quotas or quota-free access for some lines of garments when relatively more advanced developing countries faced quota restrictions. The arrangement also offered preferential tariff rates to some least developing countries while advanced countries faced higher rates. Preferential treatment in the form of tariff- or quota-free market access were rents given to least developing countries. At the same time, the arrangement had an implicit time horizon, given its expiration date in 1994. The time horizon imposed pressures on least developing countries, as they understood that domestic firms only had a certain time window to achieve international competitiveness in the textile and garment industry. This combination of incentives and pressure has been effective to force learning and capacity building among garment manufacturers in least developing countries. In sum, international agreements can create rents and new institutional structures of rent management, which affect the overall outcome of technical learning and industrial upgrade.

3.3.6 Step 4: rent outcomes

In the fourth step of the DRMA, intended effects of rent are compared with actual outcomes. Step 4 also analyzes how these outcomes subsequently change the dynamics of the rent-management mechanism. There are three possible outcomes. In the first scenario, the rent allocation raises investment but does not produce long-term benefits because productivity does not increase. In other words, an initial boost in production is largely due to input expansion, not improvements in technical and organizational capabilities. This strategy does not usually result in long-term growth and development. In the second scenario, rent raises both investments and productivity through technical learning and upgrading, which results in long-term growth. This is known as a growth-enhancing outcome. In the third scenario, rents are captured or redistributed by unproductive interests and are used ineffectively. Here, there may not be growth at all, or there may be growth in damaging and speculative activities. The outcome in this scenario is regarded as a growth-reducing outcome. Because the DRMA framework is largely concerned with technological adoption and industrial capability building, it focuses particularly on whether rents operate as learning rents or as Schumpeterian rents in the end. In other words, did technical learning, technological change, and innovations influence increases in productivity, comparative advantage, export volume, and economic growth?

Because rent outcomes – whether growth enhancing or growth reducing – shape the configuration of rent management, one must assess whether and how such a dynamic occurs. How did the rent outcome(s) influence and redefine the configuration of rent management, given the transformation of firms and industry? In some cases, a rent outcome can alter the political context of institutions and industry structure, and thus modify the configuration of rent management. In other cases, new institutional structures, such as implementation of a preferential trade agreement combined with rent outcomes, can intervene and change

Table 3.2 Analytical Considerations for Each Step of the DRMA Framework

DRMA asks: How did the three levels of rent management incentivize and compel industrial upgrading of the local firms, and what were the outcomes?	
Step 1: Political Context	• Analyze the configuration of politics and institutions that describe the political context of rent creation and management • Identify the type of rent created: learning, Schumpeterian, monopoly, or redistributive
Step 2: Institutional Structure	• Identify and analyze the formal and informal institutions and institutional structures that implement rent policy • Assess the type of rent created: learning, Schumpeterian, monopoly, or redistributive
Step 3: Market and Industry Structures	• Analyze the industry's market structure, firm ownership, type of technology, and initial capability of the firm • Reassess and identify the type of rent created: learning, Schumpeterian, monopoly, or redistributive
Step 4: Rent Outcomes	• Identify rent outcomes • Analyze how outcomes emerge, given the configuration of rent management • Analyze how rent outcomes may reshape the configuration of rent management

the context embedding the rent-management mechanism. This is an important feedback loop from Step 4 to Steps 1, 2, and 3 and allows for a *dynamic* analysis of the rent-management framework. The analysis in each step of the DRMA framework is detailed in Table 3.2.

3.3.7 Examples of rent-management factors

The list below offers some important considerations in the rent-management analysis, particularly in the first three steps. In different combinations, these factors can incentivize and compel rent recipients to achieve new industrial competitiveness. The list provides a rough guideline but is by no means an exhaustive list of conditions.

Considerations

1 *Time horizon:* For rent to be effective in inducing learning effort, it has to be available over a sufficient time horizon, such that investors have enough time to invest in new machines, new organizational capabilities, and skills training to increase productivity and competitiveness. This factor is especially important if the investment requires time to master new technology. In principle, the time horizon should be neither too short nor too long, but sufficient for firms to achieve technical and organizational capability.
2 *Loss of rent and other future benefits*: If political and institutional configurations guarantee that firms will lose rents over time, it can create pressure

to achieve new learning and more quickly strengthen competitiveness. The loss of future rents or benefits must be sufficiently substantial that investors and firms are pressured to take advantage of current rents to acquire technical learning so as to sustain market power and profits.

3 *Initial capability*: Rent recipients must have initial technical and organizational capabilities sufficient to make development strategies viable, given the nature of the technology and the technology gap between local firms and global competitors. For example, to transfer a new dyeing technique to domestic textile manufacturers, local firms must have basic technical understanding about dyeing in order to absorb the new knowledge.

4 *Market competition*: Market competition increases pressure to upgrade if there will be a gradual opening of the market – that is, when a firm is pressured to learn while rents are temporarily available and before new entrants are allowed to enter the market. Gradual market liberalization can occur from formal institutions, such as signing a bilateral trade agreement with another country or a change in government policy (e.g., the government issues more licenses). Or, it could be an informal understanding with competing firms or agencies that the local market should have more foreign competitors. In essence, gradual competition can force firms or industries to raise productivity and competitiveness in order to survive. On the other hand, sudden substantial competition, especially with foreign firms, can destroy incentives for learning because the time horizon for increasing competitiveness may not be sufficient to make such a strategy viable.

5 *Informal pressures*: Some informal pressures are speculative, but it is critical for a rent-management analysis to investigate the types of informal compulsions or arrangements that may exist, such as:

- Holding power of the informal network within the political and economic system to which the firm belongs; this can determine a firm's perceived capability to protect its rents, and it can also affect the firm's strategies for productive effort
- Pressure on the firm from an informal network to maintain power by retaining existing rents and/or seeking new ones
- Personal and emotional incentives based on cultural and social values
- Informal rules of benefit sharing from rent outcomes among individuals or groups in the network; if firm managers are the residual claimants, they may have a greater incentive to put in effort than if they are involved in other types of surplus-sharing arrangements within the informal rent allocation network
- Corporate culture implications for efficient rent outcomes[7]
- A system of formal and informal checks and balances among rent seekers or interest groups, which may help prevent poor performers from permanently capturing rents and blocking efficient performers from achieving new capability; such a system can help rents to achieve better outcomes

The DRMA provides meaningful insight for policymaking. For historical, social, and political reasons, even if emerging economies cannot follow the model of South Korea and Taiwan as a developmental state (which required autonomous and strong state leadership), rents may still result in developmental outcomes, if there is a combination of factors that influence firms' incentives and pressures to invest in new technologies and capabilities when they receive rents. For instance, if domestic investors have a sufficient time horizon (condition 1), if there is appropriate initial technical capability (condition 3), if market competition is limited but growing while firms can reap benefits from investments in new learning and technology (condition 4), and if the bureaucrats and politicians who created the rent exert pressure for performance (conditions 2 and 5), then rents provided to the domestic firms and the corresponding sector are likely to achieve growth-enhancing outcomes.

In reality, however, most industries only satisfy some of these conditions. For example, a sector may have a sufficient time horizon (condition 1) but not enough pressure from elsewhere to boost learning and innovation (conditions 2, 4, and 5). Therefore, even as rents are provided through policies, investors may choose not to raise investments and productive effort. On the other hand, where there is a short time horizon (condition 1) but also a strong incentive to increase profits (conditions 4 and 5), the availability of rents for firms could result in speculative activities, especially in the real estate and financial markets. In that case, firms neither produce nor commit to long-term investment, as they will look only to capture short-term and speculative profits. As a result, these firms would be unlikely to achieve new industrial capability that may bear fruit in productivity and competitiveness in the long term.

3.4 Conclusion

Neoclassical literature on development, rents, and rent seeking asserts that to achieve growth and development, there should be no rents or rent seeking. In reality, rent seeking is ubiquitous in developing countries, and policymakers are under constant influence and pressure from rent seekers. In some cases, politicians even receive some of the rents they create and depend on them to maintain political stability. Even in cases of corruption, rent seeking does not necessarily produce unproductive outcomes, and the benefits of rent policy are not always obliterated. In this context, the real problem for development is not rent seeking per se; rather, it's when the interests of powerful groups run contrary to the collective interests of society and the economy, leading to conflict, underdevelopment, and unproductive use of resources. From this perspective, neoclassical literature is inadequate to confront the complex problems occurred in the transition period. Its policy suggestions focused on the removal of rents and rent seeking are too simplistic to solve the intricate and dynamic issues in development.

Economic development in a poor country can be achieved if policymakers and experts understand the existing rent-management mechanisms at work, especially the ones that undermine firm incentives to acquire industrial capability. The task is to tackle existing political arrangements, weak institutional structures, market imperfections, technology gaps, and the constraints faced by local firms in different sectors. It is unrealistic to expect these issues to be solved all at once over a defined period. The policy priority should be determined by the severity of each issue; available resources; feasibility for change, given the political and institutional constraints; and the positive spillovers across segments of the economy. The DRMA provides an analytical approach to understanding the interactions between these issues and influencing factors, with the aim of apprising policy priority in specific contexts. It provides the pathway for more informed industrial strategies in the developing world.

Notes

1 Market concentration is defined as the market power of firms measured by market share.
2 The uniqueness of products relates to the level of product differentiation.
3 Entry barriers are factors that discourage potential entrants by placing them at a disadvantage.
4 Vertical integration is the extent of the upstream-to-downstream integration of production.
5 For a comprehensive discussion on the typology of rents, see Khan (2000).
6 Local-content policy is a requirement that there must be a certain percentage of local content, or inputs, in a final industrial product. This requirement is in violation of the WTO's agreement.
7 For example, because of a military background in the largest mobile phone provider in Vietnam, the state-owned Viettel operates its business in an uncommonly disciplined working environment, much more so than other private and foreign businesses in Vietnam.

References

Abbott, A. F., & Brady, G. L. (1991). Welfare gains from innovation-induced rent seeking. *Cato Journal, 11*(1), 89–97.

Amsden, A. (1989). *Asia's next giant: South Korea and late industrialization.* New York, NY: Oxford University Press.

Amsden, A. (2001). *The rise of "the rest": Challenges to the West from late-industrializing economies.* Oxford, England: Oxford University Press.

Bradsher, K. (2017, April 8). When solar panels became job killers. *The New York Times.* Retrieved from www.nytimes.com

Gray, H. (2018). *Turbulence and order in economic development: Economic transformation in Tanzania and Vietnam.* Oxford, England: Oxford University Press.

Hausmann, R., & Rodrik, D. (2003). Economic development as self-discovery. *Journal of Development Economics*, *72*(2), 603–633.

Hewison, K. (2006). Thailand: Boom, bust and recovery. In G. Rodan, K. Hewison, & R. Robison (Eds.), *The political economy of Southeast Asia: Markets, power, and contestation* (pp. 74–109). Hong Kong, China: Oxford University Press.

Hua, Y., Oliphant, M., & Hu, E. J. (2016). Development of renewable energy in Australia and China: A comparison of policies and status. *Renewable Energy, 85*, 1044–1051. https://doi.org/10.1016/j.renene.2015.07.060

Khan, M. H. (2000). Rents, efficiency and growth. In M. H. Khan & K. S. Jomo (Eds.), *Rents, rent-seeking and economic development: Theory and evidence in Asia* (pp. 21–69). Cambridge, England: Cambridge University Press.

Khan, M. H., & Blankenburg, S. (2009). The political economy of industrial policy in Asia and Latin America. In G. Dosi, M. Cimoli, & J. E. Stiglitz (Eds.), *Industrial policy and development: The political economy of capabilities accumulation* (pp. 336–377). Oxford, England: Oxford University Press.

Lall, S. (2004). *Reinventing industrial strategy: The role of government policy in building industrial competitiveness* (G24 Discussion Paper Series No. 28). UNCTAD, The Intergovernmental Group on Monetary Affairs and Development (G-24). Retrieved from http://unctad.org/en/Docs/gdsmdpbg2420044_en.pdf

Lee, J., & Mah, J. (2017). The role of the government in the development of the automobile industry in Korea. *Progress in Development Studies*, *17*(3), 229–244. doi:10.1177/1464993417713269

Mazzucato, M. (2015). *The entrepreneurial state: Debunking public vs. private sector myths.* New York, NY: Anthem Press.

Moon, C. I., & Prasad, R. (1998). Networks, politics, and institutions. In S. Chan, C. Clark, & D. Lam (Eds.), *Beyond the developmental state: East Asia's political economies reconsidered* (pp. 9–24). New York, NY: St. Martin's Press.

Stellmacher, T. (2007). The historical development of local forest governance in Ethiopia: From imperial times to the military regime of the Derg. *Africa Spectrum*, *42*(3), 519–530.

Stiglitz, J. E. (2008). Economic foundations of intellectual property rights. *Duke Law Journal*, *57*(6), 1693–1724.

Wade, R. (1990). *Governing the market: Economic theory and the role of government in East Asian industrialization.* Princeton, NJ: Princeton University Press.

Whitfield, L., Therkildsen, O., Buur, L., & Kjaer, A. M. (2015). *The politics of African industrial policy.* New York, NY: Cambridge University Press.

4 The telecommunications industry

A leap of the giants

4.1 Introduction

The telecommunications industry offers a dynamic case study of industrial success due to its rapid technology adoption, growth, and transformation while largely under state control. Immediately after the war, the Vietnamese government identified the strategic importance of telecommunications in defense and development. Therefore, Vietnamese talents were sent to study telecommunications technology in Russia and East Germany. The foreign-trained engineers returned to Vietnam and took up leading positions within the government and major state-owned enterprises (SOEs). They made up the government intellectual and strategic vision for the industry in the postwar period. Led by the Ministry of Information and Communications (MIC) and the Ministry of Defense (MoD), the industry transformed from a monopolistic market dominated by one SOE to a competitive market with 11 major telecom operators in 2013 within just a decade and half (Ministry of Information and Communications, 2014, p. 59). After a period of expansion and consolidation, the industry had six major telecom providers by 2019.

The industry sustained an average growth rate of approximately 11.5 percent per year between 2006 and 2016 (Table 4.1). In 2019, Vietnamese state-owned telecom providers could produce 70 percent of telecom equipment needed for their own infrastructure and also export them to other developing countries (Thai-Khang & Van-Anh, 2019; Minh-Anh, 2019).[1] In a country with a population of 93.6 million, there are more than 128 million mobile subscribers (Ministry of Information and Communications, 2017). According to a government report, "Vietnam's fixed broadband Internet service charges were at the lowest level in the world with the first position among 139 nations" (Ministry of Information and Communications, 2017). The providers not only made communications and Internet services available throughout Vietnam, but provided services to 11 other developing countries.[2] Vietnam's largest telecom provider, Viettel Group (Viettel), alone earned nearly USD 1.8 billion in revenue in these foreign markets in 2017 (Nguyen, 2018).[3] The high rate of revenue growth in the telecom sector between 2006 and 2016 is illustrated in Table 4.1.[4] Revenue earning grew rapidly between 2006 and 2010. While it fell slightly starting in 2011, it nevertheless remained high through 2016.

Table 4.1 Total Revenue and Growth Rate in the Telecommunications Industry, 2006–2016

Year	*2006*	*2007*	*2008*	*2009*	*2010*	*2011*	*2012*	*2013*	*2015*	*2016*
Total Revenue	2,769	3,553	5,144	6,868	9,411	6,992	8,469	7,374	6,062	6,158
Growth by %	Base year	28	44	33	37	–27	21	–12.9	–21.64	1.58

Source: Author's compilation based on data from the (MIC, 2010, 2011, 2012, 2013, 2014, 2017).

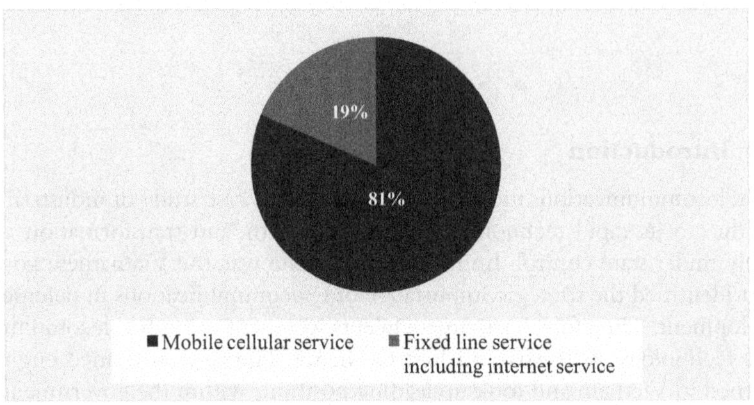

Figure 4.1 Market Share by Services in 2016 (measured in total revenue)
Source: Author's calculation based on data from the Ministry of Information and Communications, 2017.

An overview of the market share for each type of telecom service in the Vietnamese market is provided in Figure 4.1. Like many international users, most Vietnamese people use mobile phone service more than fixed telephone service. Therefore, the mobile phone market is the country's most dynamic niche in the telecom sector. It earned the largest total market share – 81 percent – with a total revenue of USD 5.01 billion in the same year. In addition, Internet service that empowers e-commerce and the Internet of Things has become widely available in Vietnam. In 2016, roughly 54 out of every 100 Vietnamese people, approximately 50.23 million users, had access to Internet service through fixed-line broadband (Ministry of Information and Communications, 2017). Among major telecom services, broadband Internet service experienced the fastest growth rate during the 2013–2016 period. Revenue for Internet service increased more than 100 percent year-on-year, from USD 474.7 million in 2012 to USD 965.4 million in 2013. In 2016, there were 36.2 million mobile broadband subscribers (wireless Internet access through a portable modem such as a USB modem) reaching 39 subscribers per 100 inhabitants (Ministry of Information and Communications, 2017).

To explain the industry's development, I divide development of the telecom industry into three stages (Figure 4.2). In the first stage, between 1975 and 1999,

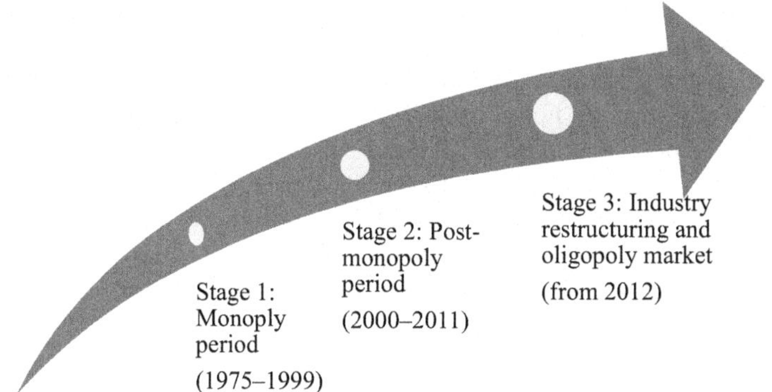

Figure 4.2 Three Stages of Vietnam's Telecom Industry Development

the industry consisted of just one state-owned provider: Vietnam Posts and Telecommunications Group (VNPT). Thus, it held a monopoly.[5] Case Study 1 reviews the industry development during this period. The second stage – the postmonopoly period – is marked by the launch of Viettel Group's long-distance service in 2000; this period lasted until 2011. Both, major developments and industrial upgrading took place during this period, which are analyzed in the second and third case studies. In the third stage, starting in 2012 and ongoing, the telecom industry started to experience some major shake-ups, including a merger between Electricity of Vietnam Telecom (EVN) and Viettel, the departure of Saigon Postel (another SOE), and the withdrawal of three (of four) foreign partners from Vietnam's mobile phone market.

This chapter draws on three case studies to analyze industrial development of the telecommunications industry. By applying the DRMA framework, it is possible to analyze and identify the configuration of rent management that drove industrial upgrading and capability building in this industry. It also allows an analysis of how the Vietnamese government's management of rents contributed to learning efforts and the rapid pace of industrialization in the sector. Rent-management analyses reveal that growth-enhancing industrial development is based on a number of factors. First, the government was determined to upgrade Vietnam's telecom infrastructure, as it was deemed necessary for industrialization. Second, the Viettel Group case study highlights the significant role of informality in rent creation and allocation that allows for rapid transfer and utilization of rents in the speedy installation of telecom infrastructure. Third, while market competition by itself could not help operators overcome market failures, especially in Stages 1 and 2, it was value enhancing in that it pressured operators to rapidly learn new technology and upgrade services. Finally, pressure of liberalization of the telecom market was an effective time horizon for Viettel

Group and VNPT to concentrate on learning and enhancing their services and competitiveness while the Vietnamese market was still relatively free from foreign competition.

The chapter outline is as follows. Section 4.2 identifies a number of sector constraints and explores how operators overcame them during the initial phase of their development. Section 4.3 illustrates Case Study 1 and analyzes VNPT's monopoly in the immediate period after the Vietnam War. Section 4.4 discusses Case Study 2 and assesses Viettel Group's entry into the sector and its efforts to upgrade telecom infrastructure, engage in telecom device manufacturing, lower prices, and generally boost the industry's overall service and capacity. In Section 4.5, Case Study 3 examines the adoption of third-generation (3G) technology in the Vietnamese market. The successful adoption of 3G technology marks a major milestone, as it provides data service in mobile devices and thus empowers users' connectivity, data access, and e-commerce. Section 4.6 reviews the changes that took place in Stage 3 of the industry's development. After a period of fierce competition, the industry structure took clearer shape, with three major state-owned telecom providers making up 95 percent of the market share and Viettel's ambitious global expansion. To wrap up the chapter, Section 4.7 offers implications for developmental rent-management strategy as well as options for the industry to move forward in its development.

4.2 Market constraints and solutions

This section reviews the market failures that constrained the telecommunications industry in the early periods. Given the government's strong support of the sector and its policies promoting learning and upgrading, a few operators, notably VNPT and Viettel Group, were able to overcome significant market failures to become major players in the market. However, as the industry emerged from a successful period of development and moved toward convergence with the information and communications technology (ICT) sector, many of these constraints resurfaced and now pose new challenges to Vietnam's telecommunications providers.

4.2.1 A capital-intensive industry in an underdeveloped credit market

The first two major investment issues in the telecom industry were the difficulties in accessing the credit market and extremely high initial fixed costs to set up an infrastructure, including transmission stations, trunk lines,[6] and backbone[7] networks. Setting up stations, lines, and networks requires a substantial amount of equipment and land, which remains difficult, if not impossible, to acquire in Vietnam. In addition, telecom equipment is much more capital intensive than equipment in other sectors, such as the garment manufacturing sector. Therefore, the cost to set up infrastructure across coverage areas and buy telecom technology from foreign providers requires considerable capital investment. Even in developed countries such as the United States, the United Kingdom, and

Germany, there are only a limited number of telecom providers, partly because of the high initial fixed costs in infrastructure and technology.

The Vietnamese credit market is inadequate to provide private investors access to credit for major investment projects, such as the telecom industry requires (interviews, two MoIT officials and Viettel manager, Ha Noi; April and June 2011). Consequently, lending for big investment projects often requires the government's guarantee for loans. This type of guarantee is mostly unavailable to private enterprises and traditionally offered only to a few state-owned telecom providers. Therefore, the lesson of how Vietnamese telecom providers overcame market failure in the credit market is particularly instructive. VNPT solved the problem by signing a business cooperation contract with Comvik in 1995. Over a 10-year period, this Swedish partner provided VNPT with capital, technology, and know-how to set up the first mobile phone network in Vietnam, through VNPT's legal entity and trademark MobiFone.[8] Later, other providers followed in VNPT's footsteps to set up business cooperation contracts with foreign partners; for example, Saigon Postel partnered with South Korea's SK Telecom in 2001; Hanoi Telecom signed up with Hong Kong's Hutchinson Telecom in 2005; and GTel Telecom joined with Russia's VimpelCom in 2008. Viettel Group is the exception to this, as it took advantage of the MoD's financial support and credit guarantee to solve its capital shortage. I explain how Viettel overcame this market failure in Case Study 2.

The Vietnamese government also played an important role in addressing the industry's constraints. First, during the early 2000s when Viettel and Saigon Postel first entered the market, the Vietnamese government attempted to rectify the infrastructure shortage by enforcing lending. Under Decision 58/2005/QD-TTg, issued by the prime minister in March 2005, the government instructed VNPT, the monopoly at the time, to lend its comprehensive infrastructure and network to newcomers, Viettel and Saigon Postel, so they could launch their own services. The decision specified that the lending rate would be reasonable and affordable. Second, the Vietnamese government permitted these upstart telecom providers to acquire foreign partners through business cooperation contracts, allowing them access to foreign capital and technology. Third, it backed the SOE's long-term loans, especially with state banks. These rent policies were sufficient to remove some capital constraints, so carriers could begin to develop new service and technical capabilities.

4.2.2 Lack of skilled labor, especially at the managerial level

Early in the telecom industry's development, shortages of both skilled technicians and managers severely constrained capability building and technology adoption, much as it did in other industrial sectors (interviews, five government officials and firm managers, Ha Noi; April–July 2011). However, during the 2000s, the Vietnamese government took major steps to resolve shortages by establishing higher education and technical training schools. Students and workers were eager to enroll in telecom technology training programs, as the perception was and remains that telecom is a growing industry with strong job potential and high salaries. According to the MIC (2017), at the tertiary training, Vietnam had 666 universities and colleges with approximately 1.75 million students studying at university and colleges. Of students enrolled in universities, 77 percent receive information technology, electronics, telecommunications, and information security training. Technical schools, of which there were few in the 1990s, numbered 220 in 2010 and 469 in 2016 (Ministry of Information and Communications, 2010, 2017). The number of students enrolled in vocational training schools increased from 30,350 in 2006 to 50,500 in 2010 to 238,655 in 2016 (Ministry of Information and Communications, 2010, 2017). Given the growing demand for telecom engineers and technicians, the number of universities offering degrees in telecommunications and ICT grew from 42 in 2001 to 206 in 2010 and to 250 in 2016. In 2016, there were 164 vocational training schools offering information technology, electronics, telecom, and information security training with 18,311 students per year studying in these fields (Ministry of Information and Communications, 2017).

Although Vietnamese workers were reputed to be fast learners, newly graduated workers still lacked tacit knowledge and hands-on training. A report from the Danish Federation of Small and Medium-Sized Enterprises and Axis Research (2006) points out that Vietnam's labor force supply for ICT is sufficient in quantity, but the quality of training still needs substantial improvement especially in regard to the application of technical skills, professional working attitudes, teamwork, and English competencies (pp. 3–4). Managers working for major telecom providers or supporting businesses in 2011 remarked in fieldwork interviews that both private and public businesses frequently had to train technicians and engineers on the job because their formal education was insufficient to meet requirements (interviews, three firm managers, Ha Noi; April–July 2011). As discussed in Chapter 2, acquiring tacit knowledge takes time and considerable effort. Oftentimes, employers incurred financial loss during training periods because of workers' inability to work effectively and their tendency to change employers (interviews, three firm managers, Ha Noi; April–July 2011).

These issues became more complex for industry development in the 2000s, particularly as labor costs rose rapidly in Vietnam, thus placing pressure on operational costs and investment expansion. In the 2000s, when the industry was rapidly developing, information technology (IT) professionals were in strong demand and salary levels were high by Vietnamese standards: USD 250–300 per month for entry-level positions, USD 400–500 for junior managers, and USD 550–900 for senior managers (Danish Federation of Small and Medium-Sized Enterprises & Axis Research, 2006). In 2013, Viettel Group raised salaries even higher than industry standards by paying senior engineers who had five or more years of experience approximately USD 1,500 per month (Thai-Khang, 2013). This wage rate more than doubled the average offered by VNPT and The Corporation for Financing and Promoting Technology (FPT, another IT conglomerate and a telecom provider) – two of the largest information technology companies in Vietnam (Thai-Khang, 2013). In 2017, the average salary for a Viettel worker (non-managerial positions) was reported to be USD 1,414 per month, one of the highest for an average worker in the country (Trung-Duc, 2018). As wages rose and graduates still required on-the-job training, providing extra technical and managerial training raised labor costs and squeezed operators' profits.

One interviewee, an upper-level manager at Viettel, explained that to overcome the labor shortages from the 1990s to the 2010s, Viettel's first approach was to recruit the best and most experienced engineers, either from within Vietnam or abroad, who could perform the technical tasks without much additional on-the-job training. For this, Viettel was willing to pay higher salaries. For technical and administrative employees, Viettel still provided on-the-job training. This occurred most often through senior staff coaching junior staff for one to three months, depending on the position. This approach offered a shorter training period because technicians and administrative staff could be brought up to speed relatively quickly. Viettel also organized training programs for its engineers and managers, so they could gradually take on more complex tasks and assume higher levels of responsibility (interview, Viettel manager, Ha Noi; April 2011). Through these practical approaches, Viettel temporarily overcame its skilled labor constraints. Other telecom operators used similar on-the-job training approaches, although on smaller scales and with less rigor.

The issue of technical training, however, continued to be critical, as the telecom industry was headed toward a convergence with the ICT industry, in order to provide greater mobile content in mobile phones.[9] Deepening the linkage between the ICT and telecom sectors was vital because the mobile phone market had reached its saturation point due to price competition. As a result, the shortage of experienced workers in software and hardware engineering held back the speed of development and convergence. One Viettel interviewee reported that despite paying higher salaries than other operators, Viettel continued to experience a shortage of senior engineers and midlevel managers, which affected the company's expansion plan (interviews, Viettel manager, Ha Noi; April and June 2011).

4.2.3 Dependence on foreign technology and equipment

Between the 1990s and the 2010s, telecom technology and machinery were frequently imported from Chinese or American telecom device suppliers, including Hutchinson, Nokia, Huawei, and ZTE. To some extent, all operators in Vietnam still currently use imported technology and components from foreign vendors, though Viettel and VNPT began to manufacture their own basic telecom equipment in the 2010s. From my fieldwork, it does not appear that learning to use foreign technology or components is a problem, as foreign vendors often set up the equipment and provide training to their Vietnamese buyers. Vietnam has a continuing dependence on foreign imports for telecom equipment and terminal devices as local demand for telecommunications increases. Between 2010 and 2015, net imports for telecom equipment nearly doubled, from USD 2,145 million to USD 4,205 million (United States Commercial Service, 2014). As the industry continued to engage in horizontal and vertical integrations, there were concerns that Vietnamese telecom providers were becoming dependent on imported equipment, including advanced handset components (interviews, four government officials and firm managers, Ha Noi and Ho Chi Minh City; April–June 2011 and June 2012). This reliance on imported equipment limited vertical linkages and confined the sector to service providence. It also reduced business profits and value addition in service packages providers offered to Vietnamese consumers. In addition, the increase in concerns of communications security raised the stakes for Vietnamese state-owned providers, as they also provided communication services for the Vietnamese government and defense networks.

Starting in the late 2000s, Vietnamese state-owned providers made long-term plans to solve the crucial constraints on the country's reliance on foreign telecom equipment. In 2009, Viettel management steered the company toward developing a new competitive advantage: it established its own research and development (R&D) institute to develop and produce operating software and simple components for its handsets and other telecom devices. It remains the largest and highest funded R&D research institute in the country. Following Viettel's lead, in 2011 VNPT also established an R&D center – VNPT Technology – with an initial capital investment of USD 25 million.[10] VNPT Technology specializes in electrical and telecom equipment R&D, IT and communications, digital content development, telecom and medical equipment imports and exports, landline services, and more (VNPT, 2011).

By the mid-2010s, the three major telecom providers – Viettel, VNPT, and FPT – led the industry in information and telecommunications technology by investing heavily in R&D for equipment manufacturing and services. In 2016, telecom providers boosted production in telecom devices and began exporting telecom equipment to other developing countries. VNPT alone earned USD 4 million revenue from its three largest export markets in 2016: Laos, Myanmar, and Indonesia (Huu-Tuan, 2017). In January 2019, the new Minister of MIC, Nguyen Manh Hung, announced in a public conference that Vietnam had the opportunity to become the fourth country in the world to manufacture and export all types of telecom equipment. He stressed that Vietnam must achieve this goal by 2020 (Thai-Khang & Van-Anh, 2019; Minh-Anh, 2019).

In the following sections, the successful development of the telecom industry is analyzed in three case studies using the DRMA framework. These cases illustrate rent-management mechanisms and their impact on the process of technical upgrading in the sector from 1990 to the mid-2010s.

4.3 Case study 1: failure of monopoly rent (1975–1999)

This first case study analyzes the telecommunications industry in the period immediately following the Vietnam War. Using the DRMA framework, the case study assesses the performance of the state-own monopolist, the VNPT Group by analyzing (1) the political context, (2) the institutional structure, and (3) the organization of the monopoly to explain the weak performance of the industry during this period.

4.3.1 Political context of the industry during the monopoly period

Between 1975 and 1993, telecommunications services in Vietnam were state run and involved price fixing, strict state regulations, and prohibition of entry into the industry. After the war ended in 1975, there was considerable political agreement among party leaders to retain state control of the telecom industry. This is reflected in Decree 390/CP, issued in 1979 by the government's Central Committee:

> The post and telecommunications [industry] is the communication and information instrument for the Party and government authorities at multiple levels. Meanwhile, it is an economic-technology sector of Vietnam's socialist economy, and thus it is to operate in accordance with the socialist approach.
>
> (Ministry of Information and Communication, 2019)

During this period, the state took charge of telecom regulations, operations, and pricing of telecom services. Two longtime government officials who worked in the industry explained that Vietnam's leaders asserted the need to retain complete control of the telecommunications industry in order to sustain the nation's security and social stability, which was primary to economic development (interviews, Ha Noi; June–July 2011).

4.3.2 Institutional structure of the monopoly

The telecommunications industry was organized based on a central planning model. In the beginning, the General Department of Post, Telephone, and Telegraph (PTT) was responsible for all aspects of postal service and telecommunications, including devising and implementing policies and providing services to government offices and Vietnamese consumers. During this period, the central government directly managed PPT, which was both the sole regulatory body and telecom provider in Vietnam. In 1990, Decree 224/NQ-HDNN transferred the management of PTT to the Ministry of Transportation and Posts. In the same year, Decree 115/HDBT transformed PTT into Vietnam Posts and Telecommunications (VNPT) – a general business corporation owned by the government. This decree effectively created a state-owned monopoly in the telecom industry. In 1992, Decree 91/TTG split the regulating body from VNPT and reinstituted the former name PTT for this regulatory unit. This decree officially separated VNPT's regulatory function and its service operation function. This move was in anticipation of competition in the telecommunications industry, as Vietnam deepened its economic reform and gradually integrated into regional and global economies. In 2002, PTT was upgraded from a general department to a ministry, and was again renamed, this time to the Ministry of Posts and Telecommunications. This was the predecessor of the present-day MIC.

As a government unit (and later a state-owned monopoly), VNPT had access to numerous state resources, such as subsidies to maintain the telecom network, public land, preferential credit, and tax exemption. Data regarding the exact volume of the rents given to VNPT is unavailable; however, all my interviewees agreed that the resources that VNPT received were more substantial than many other SOEs, given the strategic and pivotal role of telecommunications infrastructure (interviews, 11 government officials and managers of VNPT, Ha Noi and Ho Chi Minh City; April–July 2011). In the Vietnamese government's economic reform agenda, the telecommunications industry, defense, oil and gas, mining, and electricity were the few sectors considered most important to national defense and development.

4.3.3 Industry structure

As a state-owned conglomerate, perhaps the biggest rents that VNPT receives are the benefits and profits from being a monopoly that manages one of the most important and expansive infrastructures in both the public and the private sectors. It operates one of the two national telecommunications networks and provides services in all cities and 61 provinces.[11] In the summer of 2011, I interviewed the then chairman of VNPT as well as three directors at VNPT's regional offices in Ha Noi and Hue. Each recalled the important mission of managing the nation's key infrastructure. According to the four interviewees, VNPT was powerful, but its administrative structure was decentralized such that state resources and profits were dispersed widely among central, provincial, and local offices. In addition, state bureaucracy and the use of outdated technology also prevented efficiency and productivity within VNPT's complex organizational structure (interviews, Ha Noi and Ho Chi Minh City; April–June 2011). All four interviewees asserted that, during this period, VNPT's infrastructure was upgraded infrequently and used dated technologies set up during the war. They suggested that the complex organizational structure of VNPT made it difficult to introduce technological upgrade due to the time and costs involved in the process (interviews, Ha Noi and Ho Chi Minh City; April–June 2011). Throughout the 1990s, telecom and information technologies were advancing rapidly in the developed world. Meanwhile, Vietnamese state resources were largely used to maintain existing infrastructure, rather than to expand or upgrade. VNPT's monopolistic position also discouraged such a risky move. Consequently, services were slow, and tariff rates for civilian uses were so high that telecom services were largely unaffordable for most Vietnamese people.

The ex-chairman suggested that the industry's weak industrial upgrading during this period was also due to Vietnam's closed economy, which prevented VNPT from accessing modern technologies from abroad, as well as the lack of state resources to acquire them (interview, Ha Noi; June 2011). Indeed, the

United States did not lift the trade embargo on Vietnam until 1995, preventing much interaction with countries outside the communist bloc. The other VNPT directors agreed with this but also pointed out that VNPT lacked sufficient incentives and pressures from the state. These interviewees maintained that because the regulatory body and telecom provider were combined into one government unit between 1975 and 1992, there were major conflicts of interest in the state's regulation and monitoring of VNPT's performance (interviews, Ha Noi and Ho Chi Minh City; April–June 2011). In addition, VNPT was not under pressure to compete with capable rivals because market entry and licenses were restricted.

4.3.4 Rent outcomes

The failure of monopoly rent to industrialize VNPT meant Vietnamese consumers sufferred the high costs of tariffs and slow service. Meanwhile, the economy experienced a low penetration rate and weak infrastructure. For instance, in 1995, only four in 1,000 consumers had a telephone line, and there were only 23,500 mobile connections throughout Vietnam (Nguyen, Pham, & Gullish, 2005). The telecom network was described as "outdated," and the Internet was not available for residential use (Nguyen et al., 2005, p. 3). A consumer and a business owner in Ho Chi Minh City explained that it took VNPT up to one month to install a fixed phone line for a business or household in Ho Chi Minh City in the early 1990s (interviews, Ho Chi Minh City; May 2011). In addition, VNPT's tariff rates were high, making phone service too expensive for the majority of the population. In 2001, tariffs for international service in Vietnam were USD 2.00–2.30 per minute, more than twice the price of the same tariff in 2003 when Viettel offered international service at roughly 75 cents per minute using Voice over Internet Protocol (VoIP) technology (Nguyen et al., 2005). The rent-management analysis is summarized in Table 4.2.

Table 4.2 DRMA Summary of the Monopoly Period

Step 1: Political Context	• Government willingness to maintain the monopoly for security and defense reasons **Type of rent:** Monopoly rent based on the industry's historical context
Step 2: Institution Structure	• Lack of clear institutional mechanism to compel VNPT's performance and upgrading
Step 3: Market and Industry Structures	• Lack of market competition, limiting incentives to upgrade infrastructure and technical capabilities
Step 4: Rent Outcomes	• High tariff costs and slow service • Slow upgrading of infrastructure and technology • Unproductive capture of monopoly rents

The monopoly rents and resources provided to VNPT to help it industrialize failed due to (1) the decision to maintain a state-owned monopoly in the industry, (2) VNPT's institutional structure that complicated regulatory and operation functions, and (3) a complex and decentralized corporate structure. Together, these factors meant that there were insufficient incentives and pressures to upgrade. The outcome was VNPT's inability to use monopoly rents and resources to industrialize the telecom industry. Technological upgrading didn't begin until 1993, when VNPT received government permission to negotiate a cooperation contract with Swedish telecommunications provider, Comvik, to build the first mobile phone service network in Vietnam. VNPT subsequently signed the contract with Comvik in 1995. In addition, the government issued two new telecom licenses to two SOEs: Saigon Postel and Viettel. However, due to the long period of preparation, the new entrants did not begin offering telecom service until the end of the 1990s. From a rent-management perspective, the end of VNPT's monopoly in the late 1990s was important for developing the telecom sector because it introduced new foreign investment and competition. In addition, state-owned providers were forced to focus on technology adoption in order to gain competitive advantages and compete with VNPT. The next section analyzes the postmonopoly period, which was driven by an important market player: Viettel.

4.4 Case study 2: Viettel – the rise of a giant (2000–2014)

The precursor to Viettel was Sigelco, an SOE established in 1989 as an electronics information and equipment company under the MoD. The MoD commands the Vietnam People's Army (hereafter, the army). Sigelco provided services to the army via the military's own telecommunications network. In 1993, Sigelco became Military Electronics Telecommunications Corporation, under the trademark Viettel. When the government ended VNPT's monopoly status in 1993 by calling for more operators among the SOEs, Viettel applied for a license with the promise that it would not require government financial assistance to develop its new commercial telecom company (interview, senior Viettel manager, Ha Noi; April 2011). In 1995, Viettel was granted a license to provide local and long-distance landline services as well as mobile and Internet services, based on its experience working for the army (Cheshier, 2010).

After five years of preparation, Viettel officially joined Vietnam's telecom market in 2000, breaking VNPT's monopoly. The year 2000 thus marked a turning point in the industry's development. Initially, Viettel only offered long-distance service within Vietnam using VoIP technologies. In 2001, the service expanded to international destinations (Cheshier, 2010). In 2002, Viettel became an Internet service provider, and in 2004, it launched its mobile network under the same trademark. In 2009, the government issued Decree 2097/2009/QD-TTG, making Viettel a state-owned general corporation, and its name was changed to Viettel Group. Before Viettel, Saigon Postel had received a business license and launched its mobile phone service, but at that time VNPT owned a

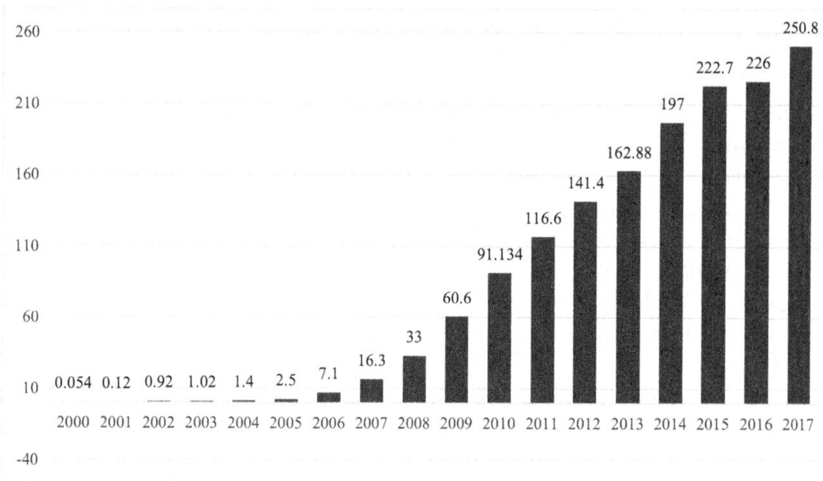

Figure 4.3 Viettel Revenue, 2000–2017 (in VND trillion)

Source: Author's compilation.

portion of Saigon Postel. Viettel's immense revenue growth between 2000 and 2017 is shown in Figure 4.3. In 2017, Viettel reported USD 11.94 billion in earnings; of that amount, USD 2.95 billion was profit. While financial information on state-owned business groups is not publicly available, news media reports indicate, "Viettel's profit made up 60 percent of the total profit of state-owned economic groups" (Ha-Vy, 2018). With considerable earnings, and contribution to state's revenue, Viettel became the largest and most powerful state-owned general corporation in the industry.

The success of Viettel raises many questions. Most importantly, how did this state-owned business group, in less than two decades, transform from a relatively small military telecom department into one of the country's largest conglomerates and overtake its most powerful rival, VNPT? In addition, how did Viettel overcome significant constraints in skilled labor, capital, and technology to grow and develop so quickly? This second case study explains Viettel's industrial development by analyzing how the three factors of rent management – political context, rent allocation mechanism, and industry structure – affected Viettel's incentives and pressures for learning, technology transfer, and upgrade.

4.4.1 *The political context of Viettel's development*

From the mid- to the late-1990s, the government issued a number of decrees that fundamentally changed the legal environment, with an understanding that industrial reform of the information and telecommunications industry was crucial to Vietnam's economic development.[12] After removing licensing barriers and allowing for new entries in 2001, the government published Vietnam's new strategy for the sector, highlighting key milestones and objectives through 2010 and a long-term vision through 2020 (Nguyen et al., 2005). Following up on this strategy, the MIC issued supporting ordinances and decrees that provided guidelines and implementation details. These events reflected the political will of the state to revamp the telecom industry, as Vietnam pushed its economic reform and integration into regional and global markets.

Within this background, Viettel's success involves three political components. First, when Viettel was initially given its business license, political support was provided with an *implicit condition* that Viettel would build a successful telecom venture that would not require direct subsidy or financial support from the central government (interviews, MIC official and Viettel senior manager, Ha Noi; April and June 2011). In opening competition within the state sector, the government, especially Prime Minister Vo Van Kiet, had to override VNPT's opposition. Viettel would have to prove that the friction between VNPT and the government was worthwhile, which it did by boosting development of the then sluggish industry. All business licenses must be renewed every 10–25 years depending on the type of service. If Viettel failed, political support from the government and its business licenses would be withdrawn and given to more capable local providers (interviews, MIC official and Viettel senior manager, Ha Noi; April and June 2011). This time horizon added pressure for Viettel to perform well in its new business venture.

Second, the MoD's political backing of Viettel's entry to the telecom market is consequential, as it is the supreme commander of the army and maintains tremendous political clout in the Communist Party of Vietnam (CPV).[13] In addition, it is an autonomous ministry, largely independent of the central government's monitoring and supervision (Thayer, 2012). The power underpinning Viettel comes from two institutional arrangements. First of all, the army holds significant political influence within the CPV. It permanently occupies one of 14 seats on the Politburo, which is the highest body in the CPV. Furthermore, since 2006, the army has had 10.6 percent representation (17 members) on the Central Committee, including chief of the general staff, director, and vice director of the General Political Department as well as deputy ministers (Thayer, 2012). This highlights the significant role of the MoD and the army within the ruling party. Consequently, the MoD can create and allocate any number of rents for Viettel without interference or authorization from the government (discussed in the next section).

Third, according to a Viettel senior manager, the MoD's strong political backing was conditioned on the promise that Viettel would run a successful telecom venture (interview, Ha Noi; June 2011). This same manager explained that the MoD owned a number of SOEs operating in various segments of defense activities in addition to Viettel, and it was only one of the technical units. When Viettel entered the commercial market, the MoD channeled political, financial, and physical resources into it, much of which was at the expense of other SOEs. Given the MoD's limited resources, if Viettel failed, the MoD would have reallocated its resources to other units (interview, Viettel senior manager, Ha Noi; June 2011). In effect, these conditions created effective pressures for Viettel to commit credible efforts not only to build a new successful business venture but also to revamp the telecom industry. Coupled with conditional supports from the government, the MoD's political and autonomous power offered Viettel a stable and dependable macropolitical environment, so much so that it could focus entirely on building the new commercial business.

4.4.2 Institutional mechanisms of rent allocation

The MoD provided Viettel with a number of rents in the form of land, labor, and access to finance and infrastructure. It also offered indirect financial support in the form of a credit guarantee.

Land, infrastructure, and labor

The telecommunications industry involves both significant fixed costs and economies of scale to build transmission stations and backbone networks. Therefore, a provider must either buy or lease land, hire labor to build the infrastructure, and adopt new technology. Because of these high fixed costs, most mobile phone providers initially rented VNPT's infrastructure, as building their own would have been prohibitively expensive. Viettel benefited from access to the army's land, backbone cables, and networks: the "military zones" that spread across the country and were readily available for usage. In addition, Viettel was initially able to use the army's transmission stations as well as backbone and trunk networks in many cities and provinces. Previously, these telecom infrastructures had been used for defense purposes only.

Viettel also avoided labor costs in building its infrastructure because the MoD deployed the army to build fiber cables, transmission stations, and other necessary infrastructures for Viettel's new networks (interviews, a Viettel manager and a Viettel supplier, Ha Noi and Ho Chi Minh City; April and May 2011). The Vietnamese army is highly disciplined, and Viettel benefited from a trained and hardworking workforce at no cost, saving considerable training time and resources. Viettel's infrastructure was faster and of higher quality than VNPT, since it was built later and incorporated newer inputs and technology (interview, Viettel manager, Ha Noi; April 2011). In summary, an important part of Viettel's success was the informal rents it received – not through official government policy, but as a result of the MoD's allocation of labor, infrastructure, and land.

Sources of financing

From the perspective of rents and rent seeking, Viettel also had access to three important financial sources as learning rents from the MoD: capital, loans from the military state bank, and credit guarantees. One of my interviewees was a Viettel senior manager ("Tuan"),[14] who had been working for Viettel for more than four years. Tuan had earned a doctorate in communications engineering and worked as a project manager at VNPT for a number of years before he joined Viettel. I interviewed Tuan in April and June 2011. Tuan was neutral, knowledgeable, and insightful in describing the business practices of both Viettel and VNPT. He explained that early on, the MoD provided Viettel with a small amount of initial capital, between USD 1–2 million, not including the military's labor and land. Along with this start-up capital, the MoD supplied loans through its own state bank, the Military Commercial Joint Stock Bank. Thayer (2012) points out that in 2003, the bank raised its charter capital, which allowed it to pledge additional credit for Viettel's large investment projects. Viettel benefited from better financing because lending costs with the Military Commercial Joint Stock Bank were substantially lower than with other commercial banks.

Perhaps the most effective financing strategy was that Viettel could delay payments to creditors and vendors by using the MoD's name. According to Tuan, Viettel convinced its vendors to allow delayed payments by using the MoD's reputation and implicit payment guarantee. Tuan explained that because the MoD provided a credit guarantee, foreign vendors agreed that Viettel could delay payments for up to two years after procurement. He said this delay was a privilege that other operators did not have. It allowed Viettel to expand its operations and recover the costs of investment even before payments started.

Financial data regarding rents provided to VNPT and Viettel are publicly unavailable because both corporations are 100 percent state owned. Therefore, it is difficult to compare the formal and informal rents they received. Resources provided to Viettel and VNPT are usually channeled through their managing ministries,[15] and the MoD is superior to the relatively new MIC in political power and resources. One can conclude that Viettel received many more resources – including military land and infrastructure, free and disciplined labor, and credit guarantees with foreign vendors – that helped it correct important market failures. Although both Viettel and VNPT had access to preferential credit through the general state banks, Viettel also had access to the Military Commercial Joint Stock Bank, which provided Viettel capital for large investment projects at low interest rates.

4.4.3 Structure of the telecom industry and Viettel

The structures of the telecom industry and internal management at Viettel highlight three important rent-management factors that affected growth-enhancing outcomes for Viettel and the telecom industry: management capability, market incentives, and pressure from international competition.

Management capability

Viettel's managerial and technological capability involved three important factors: knowledgeable and adaptable leaders, appropriate use of new technology, and effective business practices. First, Viettel's top two leaders at the time were trained in telecom technology and believed in the efficacy of technology and markets. General Manager Hoang Anh Xuan and Deputy General Manager Nguyen Manh Hung studied telecommunications engineering in Russia. Hung also earned two master's degrees: one in business management at the University of Sydney, and the other in economics at Vietnam National Economic University. It is generally agreed upon among the Viettel managers and business partners I interviewed that Xuan's skills in business operations and management balanced Hung's ability to devise successful investment strategies (interviews, Ha Noi and Ho Chi Minh City; April and July 2011). These include, for example, entering the overseas mobile phone service market, targeting low-income subscribers, and developing a 3G dongle to promote Viettel's 3G service.

Second, Xuan and Hung's strategic vision of greater market demand, coupled with development of new telecom devices, demonstrates their management capability. This combination proved an important factor in Viettel's early success. Tuan explained that when Viettel entered the mobile phone market, it chose GSM and VoIP technology, while Saigon Postel chose CDMA technology.[16] CDMA technology requires users to buy a new phone each time they change providers. In contrast, GSM technology uses SIM[17] chips, which allows subscribers to smoothly switch to different types of phones and providers. It also includes user-friendly data transfer. More importantly, VNPT (Viettel's major competitor) also uses GSM technology. Thus, VNPT subscribers were able to switch to the Viettel network without having to buy another mobile phone. This gave Viettel an immediate advantage over Saigon Postel.

According to Tuan, one of Viettel's effective business practices was its ability to reduce costs to the absolute minimum. Cost reduction remains one of Viettel's most successful business strategies. For Viettel's leaders, lower costs equaled higher profits and growth. Tuan explained that to reduce costs in its early years, Viettel's leaders selectively picked only basic service options when purchasing transmission stations and other transmitting devices from foreign vendors. For example, in the first years of mobile phone service in the early 2000s, Viettel avoided paying for options such as voice recording and text messaging.[18] This procurement strategy fit well with Viettel's business model, which targeted low-income subscribers who, at the time, would not use these features. In contrast, VNPT procured complete packages with all the special features and thus paid higher costs for equipment. Tuan indicated that, on average, Viettel spent half of what VNPT paid to build a transmitting station.

Market incentives

In the late 1990s, the telecom market in Vietnam experienced two crucial changes that further incentivized technological learning and upgrade. When Viettel entered the telecom market, there was limited competition (just VNPT), and tariffs for telecom service were high. In addition, the availability of VoIP technology (which depends much less on a backbone network, trunking, and transmitting cables) substantially reduced fixed costs for new entrants to the industry (interviews, two MIC officials, Ha Noi and Ho Chi Minh City; April and June 2011). With high consumer prices and lower setup costs, Viettel experienced an extremely high profit margin. Tuan explained that, because of VoIP technology, Viettel earned such high profits from its international phone service that it recovered its initial capital investment in one month. Both Tuan and an MIC official asserted that the high-profit margin in the early 2000s allowed Viettel to finance learning-by-doing, by experimenting with different strategies and making small business mistakes without jeopardizing the business venture (interviews, Ha Noi; April and June 2011). Finally, high-profit margins permitted Viettel to accumulate capital and aggressively expand its operation.[19]

The second important change in market structure was the reduced cost of mobile phones, starting in the early 2000s. Viettel began offering low-cost mobile phone service in 2004, as a major supply boom in affordable mobile phones was taking place in domestic and international markets, especially those imported from China.[20] For example, in 1998, the price of a mobile phone in Vietnam averaged USD 300. In 2004, a mobile phone cost USD 100 or less. By 2013, a Vietnamese consumer could buy a simple smartphone made in China or South Korea for USD 45.[21] Three interviewees confirmed that as mobile phones prices fell, Vietnamese consumer demand and mobile phone service usage rose, thus expanding the telecom market for providers (interviews, Ha Noi; April and June 2011). Viettel took advantage of this rapid demand expansion to make tremendous profits by offering low-cost services.

Pressure from international competition

An important factor that pressured Viettel to upgrade its capability was the opening of the Vietnamese telecom market to international investors. Vietnam signed two important trade agreements – one with the United States in 2001 and the other with the Word Trade Organization (WTO) in 2007. Both treaties included time schedules allowing foreign investment in Vietnam's telecom industry. According to the WTO schedule, starting in 2010, foreign investors could participate in a joint venture for up to 65 percent of total foreign ownership (and thus hold majority ownership) without any limitation on choice of partner (Russin & Vecchi, 2013). Potential competition from foreign providers pressured Viettel to enhance its competitiveness. Tuan explained that Viettel's leaders understood there was a limited horizon of protection for state-owned telecom providers before the forces of globalization obliged Vietnam to open up the industry. The leaders recognized that Viettel was a small telecom provider in the region and the world. As global investors invested in Vietnam's growing market, Viettel anticipated future competition with much more advanced and financially resourceful telecom operators worldwide.

In confronting pressure from domestic and foreign competition, Viettel strategically focused on technology upgrading. Tuan explained that Viettel's leaders felt they had no choice but to rapidly build comparative advantage by improving technological capability and market share, both in Vietnam and abroad. Pressure from international competition was one reason Viettel developed vertical linkages in telecom device manufacturing (to be more independent of inputs), expanded its international businesses, gained international recognition, and built international expertise.

4.4.4 Rent outcomes: Viettel's success and the industry's transformation

This section discusses Viettel's efforts to gain comparative advantage in domestic and international markets as well as some of its technological achievements. Essentially, Viettel forced the industry's transformation.

Research and development and telecom device manufacturing

Once successful in becoming one of the largest telecom providers in the domestic market, Viettel reoriented its business strategy to be a high-tech enterprise – a manufacturer of advanced telecom equipment. It began preparation for strategic investment in research and development (R&D) and telecom device manufacturing in the late 2000s. In 2009, Viettel established an R&D institute to focus on adopting, adapting, and developing new telecom devices. In 2010, it invested USD 9.3 million to build its first manufacturing plant to produce telecom equipment and other hardware devices. According to Tuan, in 2011, Viettel had roughly 300 engineers working intensively at the research institute to design and develop various telecom devices. *Tuoi Tre News* reported that the plant was one of the most modern in Southeast Asia, capable of producing numerous telecom devices – including mobile phones, tablets, all-in-one computers, and its own branded smartphones as well as network infrastructure devices and military information equipment ("Viettel expands," 2011). Nguyen Dinh Chien, then director of the R&D institute, reported that, in 2012, Viettel "succeeded in designing and manufacturing 16 sample products for military and civil purposes among 22 products that the institute has been developing" (Van-Oanh, 2012).

One of Viettel's earliest learning experiences in telecom device manufacturing was the successful development of a 3G dongle – a portable device that enables a personal computer to connect to a 3G network. According to Tuan, after making a substantial investment to develop the 3G network in 2010, Viettel realized it needed to boost demand for 3G service to recover its investment. The strategic plan was to develop and manufacture a Viettel dongle to provide 3G service at cheaper prices than competitors, while simultaneously boosting demand for Viettel products and services. This was a vital part of Viettel's attempt to integrate vertically within the telecom industry. In 2010, Tuan was the team leader of the 3G dongle project. He explained that the R&D institute developed and manufactured the first Viettel 3G dongle at its own Vietnamese plant within eight months. The dongle is 100 percent Vietnamese made, using Viettel hardware. When asked how Viettel learned to make the dongle, Tuan explained that Viettel had to buy the rights to use Qualcomm (a global telecom device company) technology to produce the chipset at its Vietnamese plant.

With the license, Qualcomm transferred the technology by providing instruction and technical assistance to help Viettel's engineers design and manufacture the chipset for the dongle. During the R&D phase, Qualcomm provided technical advice and support to Viettel engineers to ensure product development success ("Thiet Bi Di Dong," 2012). The Viettel R&D team then developed each component of the 3G device step by step using Qualcomm's specifications. Tuan explained that there were approximately 50 engineers at the R&D institute working under his direction in the eight-month period.

Tuan pointed out that the most difficult learning curve for his team was developing the software, or the operating system, for the dongle. It could not be copied or purchased from elsewhere, so Viettel had to develop its own propriety software. He explained that a generic dongle sold by other 3G providers did not have customized features. His team designed the software to include Viettel dongle functions available only to Viettel customers. For example, Viettel's 3G dongle only worked on the Viettel 3G network, which prevented Viettel customers from using its propriety dongle on VNPT's 3G network. At the time of my fieldwork in 2011, Tuan told me that the cost of making the Viettel dongle was equivalent to buying a similar dongle from Chinese manufacturers.

After eight years of developing, testing, and producing telecom equipment for the Vietnamese market, Viettel began to export telecom equipment in 2017 to countries where it had been providing telecom services, including Laos and East Timor. Looking ahead, the company aims to manufacture 80 percent of all telecom equipment used for its infrastructure both in Vietnam and abroad by 2020. It is also developing sample chipsets and 5G transmitting stations in preparation for commercial deployment of 5G technology in Vietnam in 2021. In 2019, the Viettel deputy general manager stated in an interview that Viettel has entered a new phase of its business development: to become a technology business group with international reach (Thai-Khang & Van-Anh, 2019). Thus, its R&D arm is currently focused on development in three strategic technology areas: high-tech defense, electronic and telecommunications devices including smart home and smart business solutions, and Internet security (Thai-Khang & Van-Anh, 2019). In summary, Viettel successfully transformed itself to become a leading telecom provider in Vietnam and abroad. More importantly, the state-owned corporation upgraded its technology and developed other innovations with an aim to become not only a service provider but also a technology leader in the global marketplace.

Industry's transformation and benefits to the economy

Viettel's success took place in conjunction with the industrialization of the telecommunications industry. It introduced improvements ranging from the extension of backbone networks connecting Vietnam from the north to the south to the development of Vietnamese-branded smartphones and the 3G dongle to the opening of high-tech production plants and R&D centers. Viettel's accomplishment not only benefited itself; it drove competition, reduced tariffs, and contributed to the overall transformation of the industry and the Vietnamese

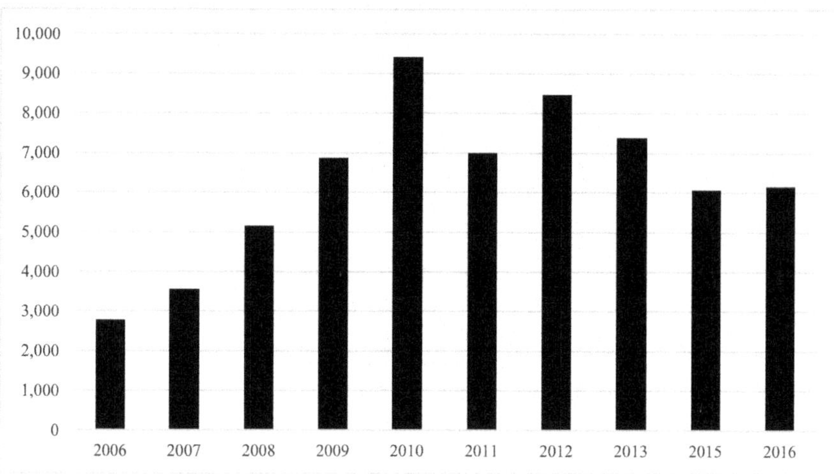

Figure 4.4 Total Revenue of the Telecom Sector in Vietnam between 2006 and 2016 (in USD million)

Source: Author's compilation using data from the Ministry of Information and Communications (2010, 2011, 2012, 2013, 2014, 2017).

economy. The impressive growth in revenue in the Vietnamese telecom sector since 2006 is shown in Figure 4.4.[22]

Between 1995 and 2009, the number of main telephone lines grew 500 percent, from four per 100 inhabitants in 1995 to 20 in 100 in 2009 (Ministry of Information and Communications, 2014; Nguyen et al., 2005). The growth of mobile phone use in Vietnam in the following period is more significant than fixed phone lines. It contributed significantly to Vietnam's gross domestic product (GDP) growth. According to research by Deloitte (2012), "A doubling of mobile data use leads to increase in GDP per capita growth of 0.5 percentage points" (p. 7). In the seven-year period between 2009 and 2016, subscription services for 3G phones increased by 5.15 times in Vietnam. This implies that, by itself, 3G growth in the telecom industry contributed approximately 2.5 percentage points to Vietnam's per capita growth in this period.[23] Furthermore, the industry's rapid growth created new employment in the technology sector. According to the Ministry of Information and Communications (2014), the number of employees in telecommunications increased from 79,799 in 2011 to 83,691 in 2013, a 4.8 percent gain in two years. In addition, the industry provides a higher salary and salary growth compared to other industries (First Alliances, 2016). In 2015, Vietnam per capita income was USD 1,684 (Trading Economics, 2017), or approximately USD 140 per month. However, the gross salary paid to an information technology engineer with two to five years of experience in Ha Noi ranges from USD 800–1,500 per month (First Alliances, 2016). Finally, in telecommunications, Vietnam went from a technology receiver before 2000, to a

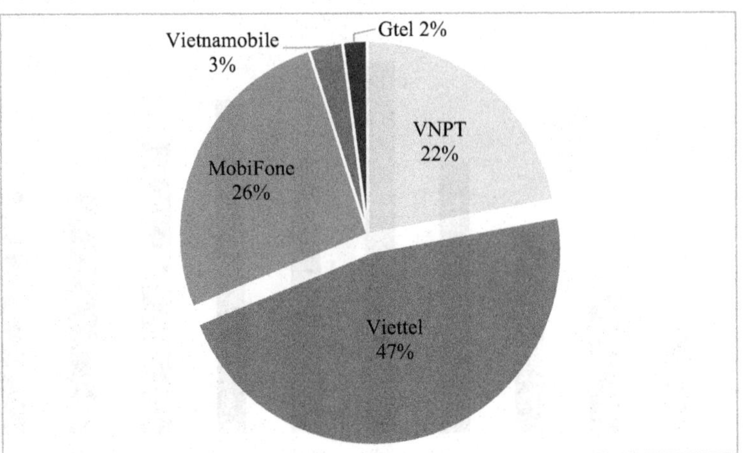

Figure 4.5 Market Shares of Mobile Phone Service Providers by Subscribers in 2016

Source: Author's compilation based on data from Vietnam Ministry of Information and Communications (2017).

service and equipment exporter in the 2010s. Between 2010 and 2012, Vietnam's export revenue from telecom services increased approximately 38 percent, from USD 576 million to USD 794 million (United States Commercial Service, 2012). Furthermore, export revenue of telecom equipment increased by 94 percent from 2010 to 2015 (United States Commercial Service, 2014).

Viettel drove much of this export growth because it was the first provider and manufacturer to export telecom services and equipment abroad. Viettel's rapid success pressured VNPT and other telecom providers to follow in Viettel's footsteps and establish R&D institutes to develop and manufacture telecom devices for their own network beginning in the early 2010s. At the end of 2016, VNPT exported USD 4 million telecom devices to other developing countries. In the same year, it also built the second manufacturing plant in Hoa Lac High-Tech Industrial Park, where Viettel also has its largest production plant (Huu-Tuan, 2017). By early 2010, Viettel and VNPT formed a duopoly market in mobile phone service. In 2014, MobiFone was separated from VNPT to become an independent state-owned provider. The separation, in effect, created an oligopoly market in the telecom industry, with Viettel now the largest provider in the country. The market structure of the industry in 2016 is illustrated in Figure 4.5.

4.4.5 The industrial transformation of VNPT and Viettel: a comparative note

The VNPT and Viettel case studies illustrate two different rent-management mechanisms in two periods, explaining distinct episodes of industrial transformation in the telecommunications industry. In the first case study, the

Vietnamese government created monopoly rents for VNPT but offered insufficient incentives and pressures for credible effort and performance. This is because the monopoly rent was granted without condition and without a disciplining mechanism linked to outcomes. There was also no market competition to pressure VNPT to scale up its capability. With little pressure to learn, the outcome was rent capture and a loss of development opportunities.

The second case study is notably different. The DRMA is summarized in Table 4.3. In the case of Viettel, all three factors of rent management (political context, rent allocation mechanism, and structure of the industry) provided incentives and pressures for capacity building and technology acquisition. Even if each factor did not work perfectly by itself, an effective mechanism of rent management emerged. Viettel's case is perhaps the closest to the growth-enhancing rent management that supports industrial learning and development. Political will from the government and the army supported development of the industry through Viettel. In addition, informal and formal learning rents were provided to Viettel, with implicit conditions for performance. Finally, Viettel's leaders and managers took advantage of (1) market opportunities, (2) favorable and inexpensive technologies that fueled market demand for telecom devices and services, and (3) pressure from competition with local and foreign providers. This combination of factors created an effective rent-management mechanism for Viettel and for the industry to industrialize and develop.

These two case studies provide empirical support for the institutional and development economists' approach to rent and rent seeking. When coupled with credible competitive market pressure, rents that provide needed resources

Table 4.3 DRMA Summary of the Postmonopoly Period

Step 1: Political Context	• Conditional political support from the MoD and the Vietnamese government **Type of rents:** Informal learning rents based on privileged access to the army's land, labor, infrastructure, finance, and credit guarantees
Step 2: Institution Structure	• Effective institutional arrangements for rent allocation from the MoD, including informal mechanisms for allocating land, infrastructure, labor, capital, and credit guarantees to Viettel
Step 3: Market and Industry Structures	• Capable leadership and managers • Market incentives from high-profit margins, advanced technologies and cheap handsets • Pressure from international competition with the opening of the Vietnamese market
Step 4: Rent Outcomes	• Development of 3G dongle and numerous Viettel-made handsets and telecom devices • Industry's successful upgrading in infrastructure and services • Rapid expansion to foreign markets as service and technology exporters • Creation of an oligopoly market

give firms the incentive to choose innovative responses. In consequence, it is innovative efforts, not optimizing solutions, that allow firms to become competitive (Lazonick, 2013). Second, rent-management analysis provides a more nuanced understanding of the political economy of an industry and how local firms develop new capabilities using formal and informal rents. The two case studies also suggest that firms could use rents to subsidize high-cost production (i.e., VNPT) and optimize but not innovate, or firms could employ rents to finance investment in technology and innovation to improve productivity and competitive advantage (i.e., Viettel). Third, Viettel defies the theory of market competition by illustrating that industrial development driven by SOEs can be successful. Where pervasive rent seeking coexists with credible conditions and competition, even in the state sector, local firms can have sufficient incentives and pressures to improve performance.

Finally, the rent-management analysis provides additional insights ignored in neoclassical rent-seeking literature. For example, the privileges or rents that Viettel and VNPT received did not come from rent-seeking activities but through historical, political, and institutional contexts of a socialist economy. Thus, the DRMA framework helps explain aspects of development where rents may not necessarily derive from corruption, but from the mechanisms of a country's political economy and market opportunities. In addition, where rent seeking does take place, it does not necessarily lead to waste and redistribution, as asserted by public choice and neoliberal scholars; rather, rents or resources could be used for productive activities. For example, despite receiving rents from the MoD, Viettel was under pressure to perform in the second period and utilized the resources available to rapidly achieve new industrial upgrading. Finally, Viettel provided useful lessons of how it resolved specific market failures in land, labor, technology, and financing; was offered opportunities and incentives; and succeeded in becoming a global telecom provider. From this perspective, DRMA could help explain the development of industries, especially where a state-industry rent-seeking nexus exists (such as the *Chaebols* in South Korea).

4.5 Case study 3: third-generation technology adoption in Vietnam

In August 2009, the MIC granted four 3G technology licenses to Viettel, MobiFone, VinaPhone, and a joint venture between EVN Telecom (a subsidiary of Vietnam Power Group) and Vietnamobile,[24] based on six applications submitted for the 3G licenses. At that time, both MobiFone and VinaPhone were owned by VNPT. The four licenses, which took effect in September 2009, permitted these operators to provide 3G technology service to Vietnamese consumers, including high-speed data access via mobile phone and features such as videophone, online video streaming, and music downloads. During my fieldwork in Vietnam in 2011, interviewees repeatedly identified the adoption of 3G technology[25] (starting with the granting of these four licenses) as an example of the adverse effects of rent seeking and redistribution on Vietnam. One of the analytical questions

I raised in my interviews was: were the rents associated with the allocation of the 3G licenses truly intended as value-enhancing rents or as redistributive rents offered to enhance political stability and private profits? Also, regardless of the government's intentions behind the allocation of these rents, did the rents indeed produce value-enhancing outcomes? If they did, what was the structure of rent management that underpinned the adoption of 3G technology in Vietnam?

4.5.1 Conflicting accounts of the political context

In November 2008, the MIC provided details of its tender and announced it would issue four 3G licenses to local providers. Six of the seven then active mobile phone providers submitted their applications as part of what was informally called the "beauty contest" ("Vietnam plans to award," 2008). To enter the contest, applicants had to submit detailed business plans of the different stages in developing their 3G networks. Once selected, licensees had to deposit the projected capital into a state-owned bank. If an operator did not fulfill the promised commitments, it would be subjected to a significant fine (Vietnam Financial Review, 2009).

The rent distribution argument

There is conflicting evidence about the political context that drove the creation and allocation of the licenses, which was a form of rent for local providers. The industry insiders that I interviewed argued that the contest's process (*co che xin cho*, or application-granting mechanism) was a form of inefficient rent distribution and that the MIC had thereby created and allocated value-reducing rents. A director of a research institute at the MIC argued that the process of granting licenses through a contest instead of through bidding or auctioning was an example of politically connected Vietnamese SOEs capturing national resources for corporate profits. He pointed out that because the 3G licenses would inflate the market value of the providers if they became privatized, the government should have charged market prices for the valuable commercial licenses (interview, MIC director, Ha Noi; April 2011).

Many countries indeed have auctioned their spectrum.[26] For example, the U.S. government, in its 700 MHz spectrum auction in 2008, earned USD 16 billion when Verizon paid USD 9.4 billion and AT&T paid USD 6.6 billion for sections of the spectrum (Gardiner, 2008). In France, Free Telecom obtained the fourth and final 20-year 3G license for nearly USD 799 million (EUR 619 million). These licensees not only paid substantial prices but also had to make all payments to their respective governments within the first year of licensure (Nguyen, 2007). In Vietnam's contest, the government collected only a small fraction of the tangible and intangible benefits each telecom provider would receive (Nguyen, 2007). Although the official license fee was not published, it was reported that the MIC expected to collect a total of USD 100–150 million from the licensees – a small amount compared to the

United States and France – over the 15-year life of the licenses (Nguyen, 2007; Thai-Khang, 2008).

When I asked an MIC official critical to the beauty contest to explain the contest's mechanism and rationale, he explained that the Vietnamese government had a tendency to grant licenses to state-owned companies without realizing that it needed to treat commercial licenses as profit-making opportunities for the country and that these licenses should be charged at the market price. He indicated that this customary practice is derived from Vietnam's socialist history and that the government manages various interest groups by dividing rents – in this case, the commercial opportunity – to maintain political coherence and stability. In other words, the state uses rent distribution as a means to reduce conflicts among interest groups. The MIC official argued that the government is more concerned with taming conflicts than with the actual commercial or development outcomes of rent. By offering business opportunities to various interest groups inside the government, benefits trickle down only to the extent that the interest groups behind the enterprises do not object to or resist the government. Effectively, this is a system of benefit sharing that reinforces political legitimacy and stability (interview, MIC director, Ha Noi; April 2011).

Both the MIC director and a former chair of the Vietnam Chamber of Commerce and Industry underscored that charging an appropriate fee for the 3G licenses would have provided the MIC with financial resources it could have used to enhance institutional capacity and efficiency in monitoring and supervising the sector's activity (interviews, Ha Noi and Ho Chi Minh City; April and May 2011). The MIC's failure to properly auction its four 3G licenses highlights the government's preference to redistribute rents in return for control of the economy as well as social and political stability. This, however, means that the MIC overlooked the considerable financial benefits the licenses could have generated had they been auctioned at fair market value.

The MIC's position for rent creation

The MIC official and architect behind the beauty contest offered a different explanation when I interviewed him in Ha Noi in June and July 2011. He pointed out that most major telecom providers in Vietnam are state owned. They are small in comparison to global telecom providers and thus do not have the capital readily available for investment in new technologies such as 3G. This particular technology required considerable fixed costs to build new networks and infrastructure; therefore, it would have been risky to hold an auction for the 3G licenses. A high license fee, for example, would have negatively affected the investment speed and effectiveness of the providers to implement the new technology. This is why one criterion of the contest was a provider's financial commitment to developing 3G networks, as demonstrated by depositing the projected capital into a state-owned bank and earmarking it for implementation.

Pham Hong Hai, then director general of the MIC's Authority of Telecommunications, pointed out in the media that the MIC had learned from other countries' experiences that many mobile phone providers came close to bankruptcy after successfully bidding for a 3G license due to the cost of the license and the slow technology uptake from local consumers. Therefore, paying a high license fee might be a burden to businesses and possibly slow down their technological adoption and success (Thai-Khang, 2008). Using a similar argument, the MIC official who designed the contest explained that these foreign lessons proved that auctioning 3G licenses could cause telecom providers to bid aggressively so as to not lose the opportunity to gain a license. As a result, many companies outbid each other, subsequently stretching themselves too thin. So even if they won the bidding war, they might lack the capital to develop adequate 3G technology, thus losing potential subscribers and risking bankruptcy. He asserted that the government was more concerned with the successful development and adoption of technology than with collecting fees from its own SOEs (interviews, MIC official, Ha Noi; June and July 2011).

He maintained that under the contest model, rather than spending money in auctioning for a license, telecom providers who won licenses could use their financial resources to invest in new networks and develop new services. Hence, consumers – not just operators – could benefit from the upgraded service (interviews, MIC official, Ha Noi; June and July 2011). From a rent-management perspective, this is the argument for the creation of a value-enhancing rent. In essence, granting 3G licenses at low prices was a form of *learning rent*, with which the Vietnamese government aimed to encourage the rapid development and adoption of 3G technology. This is a plausible argument, but only if the institutional and market conditions were sufficient that providers could deliver the fastest technology and productivity improvements to consumers as the government intended.

4.5.2 Beauty contest structure and implementation

The second level of the DRMA involves the institutional structure of the beauty contest and the rules for allocating the rents in question. To enter the contest, as noted above, the MIC asked applicants to submit detailed, step-by-step business plans of how they planned to develop their 3G networks and the different stages of implementation. Applicants also had to prove their financial commitment by depositing the project capital into a state-owned bank. The four winning contestants deposited a total of approximately USD 455 million (Vietnam Financial Review, 2009).[27] After granting the licenses, the ministry issued regulations to supervise the 3G deployment. If a licensee failed during this first competition phase, it would most likely be allowed to supply 3G service but at a different frequency band or join with another 3G license winner to provide services via roaming or sharing network infrastructure ("Vietnam announces," 2009).

From a rent-management perspective and compared to examples of rent policies in other Vietnamese industries, the institutional structure of the beauty contest was relatively transparent. The MIC clearly set up the legal and policy frameworks for the allocation of the 3G licenses and the subsequent monitoring of conditions. Although the Vietnamese industrial experience usually shows little transparency between managing ministries and their SOEs, the policy framework and the implementation of the 3G technology was considered more open (interviews, two managers of telecom providers and two industry experts, Ha Noi and Ho Chi Minh City; April–July 2011). Perhaps one reason for this was the severe competition among providers and the wide press coverage of the beauty contest. This is not to suggest that mismanagement and favoritism did not take place; my qualitative data is inconclusive on this point. However, the overall structure of rent allocation and monitoring of 3G technology deployment reflected the MIC's goals and expectations.

4.5.3 Industrial transformation and rent outcomes

In the first three years after launching their 3G service networks – 2009, 2010, and 2011 – consumer uptake of 3G technology was slow, and service networks experienced occasional interruptions (interviews, five 3G subscribers, Ha Noi and Ho Chi Minh City; June and August 2011). Data collected from the Nielsen Company show that six months after 3G service was launched in 2009, just under half (48 percent) of Vietnamese mobile users were even aware of it. A mere 3 percent had subscribed, and that rose only to 11 percent by 2010 (Panganiban, 2010). By the middle of 2011, the four operators had built more than 30,000 3G base transceiver stations nationwide, which provided network coverage to most of the country's towns and cities (Dewar, 2012). However, the quality of the networks was said to be poor, and an MIC official observed that a lack of awareness of 3G services remained a major challenge for consumer adoption of 3G service (interview, Ha Noi; May 2011). The slow uptake was partly due to both an absence of third-party content providers and the relatively high cost of switching to smartphones.

Starting in 2012, service quality and revenue from 3G technology began to improve, thanks to a rapid increase in subscribers. Viettel, MobiFone, and VinaPhone upgraded their access speed from 21.6 to 42 megabits per second, significantly improving service quality in 2014 and 2015. According to government statistics, the number of 3G subscribers increased from roughly 7 million in 2009 to 36.19 million in 2016, a fivefold increase in subscription. The rapid increase in subscriptions, hence, adoption of 3G technology, is shown in Figure 4.6. After a slow period of consumer uptake between 2008 and 2009, the number of 3G users increased swiftly, especially after 2012.

In general, Vietnam's overall adoption of the 3G technology was considered a success (interviews, four Vietnamese consumers and three industry experts, Ha Noi and Ho Chi Minh City; April–July 2011). 3G adoption offered new learning opportunities for providers and contributed to the larger industry transformation. Furthermore, this new technology provided a better telecommunications infrastructure for consumers and businesses in Vietnam, and it continues to enhance overall development of the economy. The market structure for 3G services as of 2016 is shown in Figure 4.7.[28]

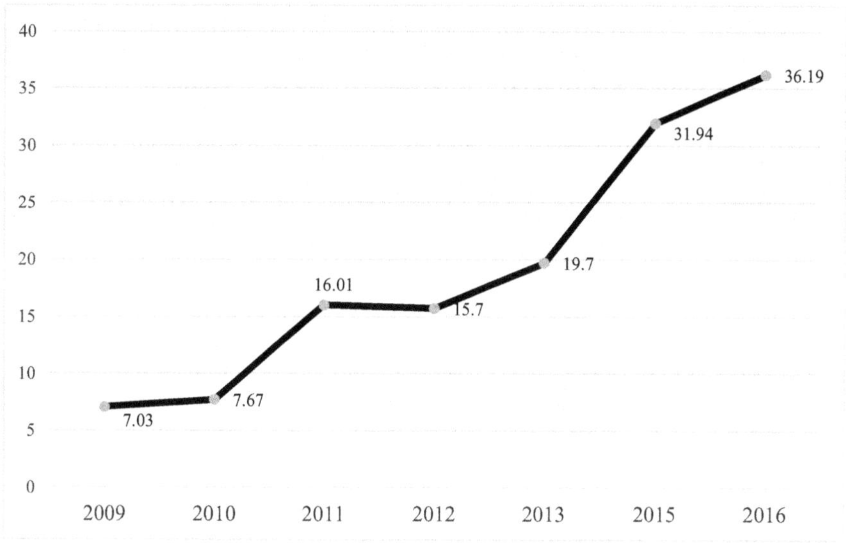

Figure 4.6 Number of 3G Mobile Phone Subscribers (in millions)

Source: Author's compilation using data from the Ministry of Information and Communications (2010, 2011, 2012, 2013, 2014, 2017).

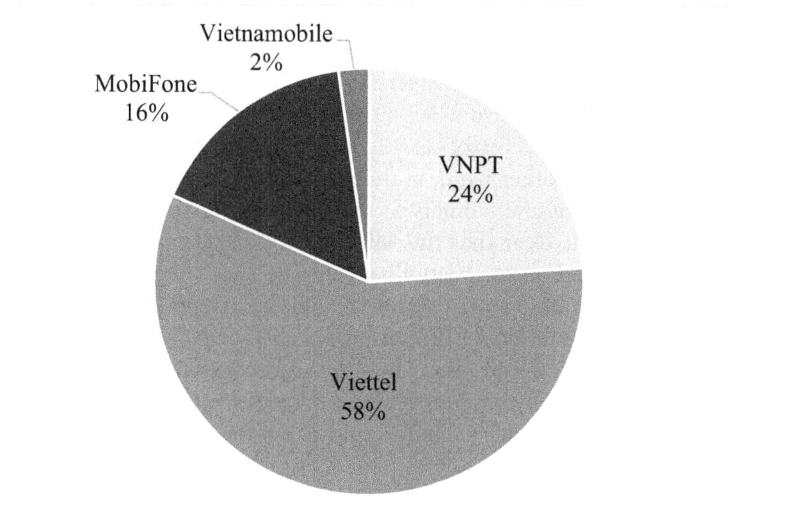

Figure 4.7 Market Share of 3G Mobile Service by Subscribers in 2016

Source: Author's compilation based on data from Ministry of Information and Communications (2017).

In 2011, EVN Telecom, one of two members of the 3G consortium that received a 3G license (with Vietnamobile) went out of business. The government arranged for EVN to merge with Viettel, whereby Viettel assumed all its assets and debts. My 2012 fieldwork data suggest that EVN Telecom's high-profile bankruptcy was arguably due to its aggressive investment in the 3G network, which resulted in limited subscribers and financial losses (interviews, two government officials and an expert, Ha Noi; June 2012). In retrospect, the MIC's concern that telecom providers who aggressively bid for a 3G license would fail, given the cost of investment and the lack of expertise, came true in EVN Telecom's case. When EVN Telecom gave up its license, the MIC allowed Vietnamobile to keep the 3G license possibly to prevent a duopoly market structure between Viettel and VNPT. However, EVN Telecom's merger with Viettel enhanced Viettel's market share and market power. In Figure 4.7, the data show that, by 2016, Viettel took up almost two-thirds of the 3G mobile phone service and was the market leader in this field.

4.5.4 *Vietnam's adoption of 3G technology: observations*

This case study demonstrates an example of a relatively effective system of rent distribution, which led to successful technological adoption and developmental outcomes. Despite contradictory arguments for and against the 3G license contest, the political economy of Vietnam suggests that these arguments may actually have been complementary because both may have motivated the government in its rent allocation rules. On the one hand, the pro-contest view is credible in that, while 3G licenses provided a long-term boost to the equity value of the licensees, MobiFone, VinaPhone, and Viettel are all 100 percent state owned; therefore, much of the upgraded value benefits the state. Furthermore, it took the providers more than three years to make back their investments due to slow consumer uptake of the new technology. This supports the MIC's assessment that making a profit from 3G technology would not be as easy as many predicted, and the high cost of an auctioned license could lead providers to go bankrupt. On the other hand, in the anti-contest view, it is no coincidence that three of four contest winners are SOEs (only Vietnamobile is a private company), making it clear that the MIC favored government-run businesses. For example, as noted above, Viettel is owned by the powerful MoD, which is a managing body of the People's Army of Vietnam. Rents created through the 3G license allocations no doubt supported the state-owned providers' economic and market power in the industry. Thus, the argument of rent seeking and rent redistribution among powerful state-owned conglomerates for the sake of political stability is also plausible. Table 4.4 summarizes the DRMA analysis in this third case study.

From a rent-management analysis perspective, a number of factors affected the rent-management mechanism, resulting in a moderate value-enhancing outcome. These included both a clear government rationale for creating the rent and an institutional framework to enforce the requisite investment conditions.

Table 4.4 DRMA Summary of the "Beauty Contest" and Adoption of 3G Technology

Step 1: Political Context	• Political will to create rent specifically for accelerated adoption of 3G technology • Possible political motives to allocate licenses among SOEs to maintain political stability **Type of rent:** Learning rents allocated by 3G licenses with possible redistributive purpose
Step 2: Institution Structure	• Clear and effective formal rules of allocating rents according to the "beauty contest" structure • Effective monitoring and enforcement of technology implementation
Step 3: Market and Industry Structures	• Severe competition among licensees • Short time horizon, creating major pressure for effort • Sufficient initial capability to manage 3G network and service • No technology gap in the adoption of the 3G technology
Step 4: Rent Outcomes	• Rapid investments and implementation of the technology • Improvements in telecom infrastructure and economic development • Competitive pricing that benefited users

However, it took more than just political context and the government's enforcement of the rent conditions to make this rent policy successful. Relevant factors include the initial capability of the operators to adopt the technology, the short time horizon of the adoption timetable, incentives to gain more market power, and the pressure of market competition among the licensees. Together, these factors ensured high levels of effort, investment, and competitive pricing, such that the outcomes of the rent have been largely positive. Profit and service quality improved as demand rose, and the MIC's rent policy enhanced Vietnam's technological level and infrastructure. It also benefited individual consumers and businesses, whose activities and efficiency improved, thanks to data access via telecom service. Finally, the successful development of a 3G network was crucial in leading the way for Vietnam's adoption of 4G technology starting in 2017.

4.6 Industry restructuring and the emergence of an oligopoly market

In 2012, the Vietnamese telecom industry entered its third phase of development (Figure 4.2), which involved a major organizational restructuring of the market. Between 2012 and 2014, there were three major events. The first occurred in January 2012 when EVN Telecom successfully merged with Viettel, after EVN Telecom suffered considerable losses and heavy debts. The prime minister's decision for the EVN-Viettel merger was considered political and reflected Viettel's strong influence on the government and its close relationship with political leaders. During the run up to the merger, Hanoi Telecom (owner of Vietnamobile Network) had also wanted to buy EVN and its 3G license, as it had been renting

EVN's infrastructure and sharing its 3G license. Hanoi Telecom also feared that if Viettel and EVN merged, Viettel would drive up rental prices and force it out of the market. Despite Hanoi Telecom's numerous inquiries and letters to the MIC and the prime minister, the merger was allowed. Although Hanoi Telecom was able to retain the 3G license, its concerns were well founded. In March and April 2012, three months after the merger, VNPT and Viettel raised their network rental price by more than 200 percent (Tran, 2012).

The second event was the departure of VimpelCom. As briefly noted earlier in this chapter, GTel Mobile (which did not win a 3G license) set up a business cooperation contract with Russia's VimpelCom in 2009. However, VimpelCom abandoned this joint venture after three years, in April 2012, suffering an investment loss of more than USD 400 million in the process (Frolov & Staples, 2012). VimpelCom's departure forced GTel Mobile to stand alone, and it renamed its telecom network Gmobile. VimpelCom was the third foreign venture in Vietnam's telecom market to leave: Sweden's Comvik left in 2005, and South Korea's SK Telecom left in 2010. Hong Kong's Hutchinson Telecom, associated with Hanoi Telecom, is the only foreign company still operating in Vietnam. Why did these foreign companies leave Vietnam's telecom market? My fieldwork data and secondary literature suggest that it was due to market competition and tariff rates that were too low to make a profit. In other words, foreign firms could not compete with Viettel and VNPT and thus could not make a profit in Vietnam's mobile phone market. Like VimpelCom, SK Telecom also lost a significant portion of its investments. This is said to have discouraged other foreign investors from entering the Vietnamese telecom market (interviews, two MIC officials and a Viettel manager, Ha Noi; April–June 2011).

The third event was multipronged. For one, Saigon Postel went out of business in March 2014, after it failed to find another foreign partner after SK Telecom left Vietnam in 2010. In 2012 and 2013, media reported that Saigon Postel was heavily indebted, and it had stopped paying its employees at the end of 2012 (Anh-Quan, 2014). For another, in 2012, Indochina Telecom, a new telecom operator, had its license revoked due to slow implementation of mobile services. Finally, in June 2014, the prime minister approved the separation of the MobiFone network from VNPT, allowing MobiFone to become an independent state-owned provider. This decision left VNPT with only one mobile phone network: VinaPhone. MobiFone has been placed under direct management of the MIC until it can be equitized, although the government has asserted that it will continue to hold majority ownership even after that ("PM gives go-ahead," 2014). As a result, in 2014 the mobile phone market had only five major players: VNPT, Viettel, MobiFone, Hanoi Telecom (or Vietnamobile), and GTel Mobile (or Gmobile). Together, in 2016, VNPT, Viettel, and MobiFone owned more than 90 percent of the market share in all major service areas, including fixed phone, mobile phone, and Internet services (Figure 4.8). After MobiFone was split from VNPT, Viettel has been holding the largest market share and thus assumed a market leadership position in the industry.

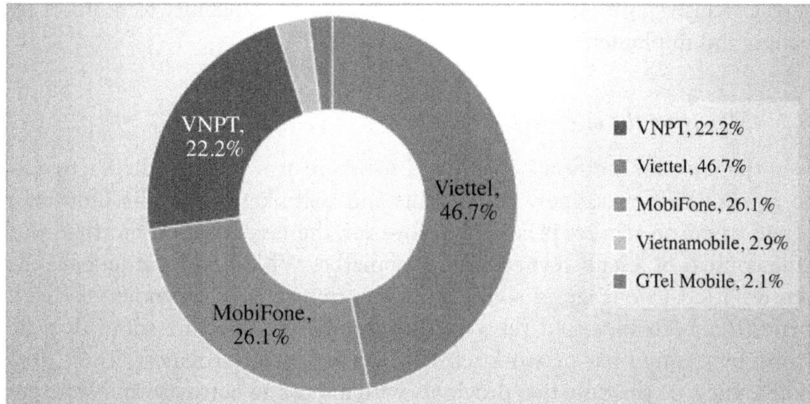

Figure 4.8 Market Share of Mobile Phone Service Providers, 2016 (by subscribers)

Source: Author's compilation based on data from Ministry of Information and Communications (2017).

4.7 New challenges and policy considerations

In this chapter, three case studies illustrate the industrial development of Vietnam's telecommunications industry using the DRMA framework. The telecom industry's success is based on a number of rent-management factors that offered domestic providers effective incentives and pressures to rapidly upgrade their investments and capabilities. Operators had to overcome market failures in land, infrastructure, labor, capital, and technology that constrained the development of the industry, especially in its early stages. However, market competition, even within the state sector, was value enhancing in that it increased the operators' drive to succeed. The case study of Viettel highlights the roles of informal rent creation and allocation, given that the MoD provided military resources to Viettel as rents. In addition, technological upgrade, research, and development were all important in helping Viettel's leaders catch up with VNPT. Furthermore, the pressure of liberalization in the telecom market set an effective time horizon for Viettel and VNPT to achieve global competitiveness. In developing and adopting 3G technology, the Vietnamese government succeeded in allocating rents, in the form of 3G licenses, to speed up the development of the new technology. Although there was a possible redistribution aspect of rent allocation, telecom providers successfully built 3G infrastructure, made the service available, and have so far recovered from their initial investment. This case study demonstrates that a rent can have learning, Schumpeterian, and redistributive characteristics. However, in spite of its redistributive nature, the design and implementation of the rent was effective in forcing new development in the telecom industry.

The rent-management analyses in all three case studies suggest four policy considerations: (1) manage the oligopolies from damaging rent seeking and anti-consumer behaviors, (2) promote capacity building in new technological innovations and manufacturing, (3) expand value added through mergers with the ICT industry, and (4) develop strong enforcement capability to monitor rent creation and implementation.

4.7.1 *Managing the oligopoly*

Given the telecom industry's established structure, it is unlikely the Vietnamese government will create new major rents and will likely allow the industry to operate based on market principles. However, the task is easier said than done in the context of a state-owned oligopoly market. VNPT and Viettel have each been reported to engage in some monopolistic practices. As noted earlier, in April 2012, both increased the cost of telecom infrastructure more than 200 percent by raising their network rental prices to smaller providers (Tran, 2012). Because they are the only two providers with backbone networks and large coverage of base transceiver stations, which are the main infrastructure for mobile phone services, small operators such as GTel Mobile and Vietnamobile have not only struggled to keep up with rising infrastructure costs but also with the tariff war to stay in business at all. As analyzed in the case studies, competition among the providers ensured the highest learning effort, not least among the SOEs. However, this is becoming increasingly difficult because three providers jointly hold the majority of the market share. The challenge for the MIC and the Vietnamese government is to maintain a competitive environment and disallow these conglomerates from forming a cartel against consumers and the two smaller operators.

Will new foreign entry offer additional capital, technology, and pressure for high effort? My interviewees from the MIC and Viettel observed that making a profit in telecom service is harder now because the mobile phone market has reached saturation and the landline business is declining. The Internet market is still expanding rapidly, but there are already a number of established providers charging relatively low tariffs. Unless foreign providers have a clear strategy to either cooperate or compete with Viettel, MobiFone, and VNPT, new ventures in Vietnam will face severe difficulties (interviews, two MIC officials and a Viettel manager, Ha Noi; April–July 2011). From a rent-management perspective, foreign entry is a possible strategic policy option for the telecommunications industry, especially by 100 percent foreign-owned enterprises. Pressure from foreign competitors could compel credible learning efforts to upgrade technology and infrastructure as well as provide better service to Vietnamese consumers.

The focal point of a developmental rent-management strategy must be to monitor the three major providers for damaging rent seeking and anticompetitive activities. This would benefit both the consumers and the development of the industry as a whole. Although the MIC was less assertive in monitoring and penalizing anticompetitive behaviors during the second phase of the industry's development, it is now critical to regulate Viettel, VNPT, and MobiFone to prevent anticompetitive practices. The prime minister and the minister of MIC, in particular, must understand the potential economic and social consequences of damaging rent captures and communicate their willingness to discipline those behaviors to discourage growth-reducing rent seeking and ensure further development of the industry.

4.7.2 Maintaining the speed of industrial upgrading and merging with ICT

The future of the Vietnamese telecom industry depends on successful and continuous technological upgrading as well as research and development for new innovations. This is because the industry is no longer limited to connecting people via telephone, as it used to be. Fortunately, the industry leaders are acutely aware of this. They identified two directions where upgrading could take place: (1) high-tech manufacturing for all telecom equipment and (2) becoming information-content providers in the ICT sector.

In 2018, Nguyen Manh Hung, the general manager of Viettel, was promoted to minister of the MIC after a corruption scandal involving two of MIC's ex-ministers. Hung envisioned that the next opportunity for Vietnamese operators would be to design and produce not only all-in-one smartphones, telecom equipment, and devices but also mobile phone applications. In January 2019, Hung projected that Vietnam could become the fifth largest telecom device manufacturer in the world after Ericsson, Nokia, Huawei, and ZTE, especially if it succeeds in its experiment with 5G technology in 2019 (Thai-Khang & Van-Anh, 2019; Minh-Anh, 2019). Vietnamese providers are currently manufacturing approximately 70 percent of telecom devices and are pushing to export them to other low- and middle-income countries such as Indonesia and Malaysia. The government has urged Vietnamese firms to use telecom devices made by Vietnamese providers, as they would save costs and ensure information security, an issue that has been raised by the MIC numerous times in recent years. Hung asserts that since Vietnam had a strong start in network equipment and smart device manufacturing, it is entirely possible that operators could ramp up their R&D in producing devices at global market prices, especially if they position themselves to be alternative producers to Chinese devices.

Second, the MIC minister points out that the telecom infrastructure of the future must not only include information and communications networks but also the infrastructure for digital economy, digital society, and infrastructure for the Internet of Things (Thai-Khang & Van-Anh, 2019; Minh-Anh, 2019). Given the rapid development of digital technology through telecom devices, the future of the sector lies in the *integration* of telecommunications, computers, and smart devices as well as the necessary software such as smart applications; storage such as cloud technology; and audiovisual systems such as web streaming, video conferencing, and live broadcast services. In this meta-integration, users are enabled to access, store, edit, and communicate information (with sound and visual components) through a wide array of digital platforms. The integration of telecommunications with ICT will create tremendous new added value for users and businesses. It would certainly enable application of innovative ideas and development of new products that serve other industries and firms as well as the development of the economy.

As VNPT, MobiFone, and Viettel expand the scope of their businesses to include ICT services, they substantially affect and change the structure of the ICT industry. Unlike telecom services, the ICT industry involves a number of small and medium enterprises (SMEs) working in many niche areas. The government has to be careful that large telecom providers do not crowd out or unfairly compete with the numerous smaller firms in the industry. In my interviews with two information technology companies in Ha Noi, the SMEs raised urgent concerns that Viettel and VNPT had unfairly leveraged their financial strength and political support to compete ruthlessly with the SMEs, effectively driving them out of new development in the ICT sector (interviews, CEOs of two IT companies, Ha Noi; April and June 2011). One IT company owner claimed Viettel misled his engineering team into revealing the company's new development ideas and then took the ideas and developed their own products instead of collaborating with his company (interview, owner and CEO of an IT company, Ha Noi; April 2011).

Once again, the assurance that all players will compete fairly is critical to ensure sustainable growth for both the telecommunications and the ICT industries. The next challenge for the MIC is to regulate the possible anticompetitive patterns of the oligopolies in the ICT industry. It is crucial that new value generated by the telecom providers in the ICT industry supports, not discourages, the development of the industry overall. One possible solution is to promote a local value chain, allowing connectivity and cooperation between small and innovative firms with large and resourceful telecom providers. This requires the willingness of telecom providers Viettel, VNPT, and MobiFone to work with ICT firms rather than drive them out of businesses as they did in the telecom industry a decade ago. This is difficult, given an oligopoly's tendencies to accumulate and concentrate market power. However, with clear guidance from the government and industry leaders, perhaps the state-owned firms could once again lead and provide additional opportunities for inclusive development and integration between telecommunications and ICT rather than adopt a winner-take-all approach.

4.7.3 Development strategy reconsidered

The three case studies highlight how the relative bargaining power within and between the CPV, state bodies, and SOEs can influence the types of rents created and the terms under which they are managed. Viettel's experience, the 3G beauty contest, and the political dynamics analyzed underline the validity and possibility of growth-enhancing rents, even in the presence of rent seeking within the state apparatus. The key to developmental outcomes is much less about eliminating rent seeking but more about using rents for development purposes, together with credible effort and a commitment to technical and capacity building. Rent creation and implementation are gradual and changing processes of bargaining, policymaking, and enforcement of commitments within and across political and economic interests. For example, when Viettel was given permission to break VNPT's monopoly, political support was provided *in exchange* for Viettel's commitment to build a successful telecom company without any direct subsidy or financial support from the government. This bargain was highly advantageous for the Vietnamese government, even though it required the government, especially Prime Minister Vo Van Kiet and the MIC to override VNPT's opposition in order to introduce competition within the state sector and the development of the industry.

The research presented here suggests that Vietnamese policymakers and business leaders understand *the nature* of bargaining power among various interest groups. However, they lack an understanding of the available *policy options* that not only satisfy the interests of these groups but ensure that vital rent allocation and management decisions are not left to arbitrary internal forces. In fact, these decisions must be oriented toward growth-enhancing industrial development (interviews, three government officials, three economic experts, and two CEOs, Ha Noi and Ho Chi Minh City; April–July 2011 and June 2012). This is an area where the DRMA could provide nuanced analyses and insights. If learning and Schumpeterian rents are to be devised, allocated, and managed based on value-enhancing criteria, it must be done with careful consideration of Vietnam's political and institutional realities. In other words, development policies must also be consistent with the internal politics of the country in order to promote growth and development. The telecom industry and the rent-management analyses presented in this chapter provide an example of how political bargaining, institutional arrangement, and market conditions encourage high levels of coordination between the state and the firms as well as investment in technology, learning, and R&D. This successful development story offers valuable lessons for the development of other industries in Vietnam and in the developing world.

Notes

1 In 2016, the second largest telecom provider, VNPT reported earnings of "4 million US dollars from equipment exports" (Xuxin, 2017).

2 Some notable destinations where Vietnamese telecom provided service are Cambodia, Laos, Timor Leste, Haiti, Mozambique, Peru, Tanzania, Burundi, and Cameroon.

3 If the data source or newspaper provided the data in USD, I reported the same value as shown in the source. However, if VND was used in the data or in interviews, I converted the value to USD using the exchange rate of USD 1 = VND 21,000.

4 MIC calculates the revenue using current prices and the current exchange rate. The government did not release data for 2014.

5 Although the first period is marked as ending in 1999, Vietnam's government move to expand the sector beyond a monopoly started in 1993. However, because of the long preparation time it took other providers to establish services, the second period did not begin until 2000. This is discussed in Case Study 2.

6 A trunk is a line or link designed to handle many signals simultaneously that connects major switching centers in a communications system. The transmitted data can be voice (as in the conventional telephone system), data, computer programs, images, video, or control signals.

7 A backbone is a larger transmission line that carries data gathered from smaller lines that interconnect with it. At the local level, a backbone is a line or set of lines that local area networks (LANs) connect to for a wide-area network connection or within a LAN to span distances efficiently (e.g., between buildings). On the Internet or other wide-area networks, a backbone is a set of paths that local or regional networks connect to for long-distance interconnection.
8 Comvik owned 45 percent of VNPT from 1995 to 2005. After a period of successful development, the government separated MobiFone from VNPT in 2014, creating an independent telecom provider under the same trademark.
9 Mobile content is any type of electronic media that can be viewed or used on mobile phones, such as ringtones, graphics, discount offers, games, movies, and GPS navigation.
10 Unlike Viettel, which owns 100 percent of its R&D institute, VNPT only holds 51 percent of VNPT Technology (VNPT, 2011).
11 The second network is operated and controlled by the Vietnam People's Army under the Ministry of Defense.
12 Russin and Vecchi (2013) describe this in detail.
13 Thayer (2012) argues that key military leaders in the Vietnam People's Army are actively involved in internal factional politics within the Communist Party of Vietnam.
14 Tuan is not the real name of this Viettel manager. The identity of this interviewee is kept confidential per the interviewee's request.
15 The MoD manages Viettel while the MIC oversees VNPT.
16 GSM is global system for mobile communications; CDMA is code division multiple access.
17 SIM is subscriber identity module.
18 Viettel later added text-messaging options, as it moved to target higher-income subscribers and promote its 3G service.
19 Viettel had to pay dividends to the MoD and taxes to the government, but it was allowed to retain much of its profits for reinvestment (interview, senior Viettel manager, Ha Noi; April 2011).
20 The improvement in mobile phone and telecommunications technology, which led to growth in revenue and subscriptions, occurred in Vietnam as well as in other developing countries.
21 This is the comparable price in the international market.
22 The MIC did not release data for 2014
23 According to the MIC (2017), the number of 3G service subscribers increased from just over 7 million in 2009 to a little more than 36.1 million in 2016.
24 Vietnamobile is privately owned, and EVN Telecom was a state-owned telecom provider.
25 In 2009, 3G technology had been used in developed countries but had yet to be introduced in Vietnam. To introduce the technology to domestic consumers, telecom providers must acquire a license from the Vietnamese government in order to "adopt" the technology – purchasing the technology and equipment from foreign suppliers and adapting them to the Vietnamese telecom networks.
26 A spectrum auction is a process whereby a government uses an auction to sell the rights (licenses) to transmit signals over specific bands of the electromagnetic spectrum and to assign scarce spectrum resources. With a well-designed auction, resources are allocated efficiently to the parties that value them the most, and the government secures revenue in the process.
27 These deposits were in addition to the license fees paid to the government.
28 Both VinaPhone and MobiFone were owned by VNPT until June 2014. Hanoi Telecom owns Vietnamobile.

References

Anh-Quan. (2014, March 16). SFone nguy cơ' bị thu hồi băng tần [S-Fone is at risk of losing its telecom frequency]. *VNExpress*. Retrieved from https://vnexpress.net/kinh-doanh/s-fone-nguy-co-bi-thu-hoi-bang-tan-2963678.html

Cheshier, S. (2010). *The new class in Vietnam* (Ph.D. Thesis). Queen Mary, University of London, London, England. Retrieved from https://pdfs.semanticscholar.org/db6e/e991b71b82b97804a2d0a094e0171a4b2390.pdf

Danish Federation of Small and Medium-Sized Enterprises, & Axis Research. (2006, December). *Business opportunitiy study within the IT and telecommunication industry in Vietnam.* Copenhagen: Ministry of Foreign Affairs of Denmark (Danida).

Deloitte. (2012, November). What is the impact of mobile telephony on economic growth? *A Report for the GSM Association.* Retrieved from www.gsma.com/publicpolicy/wp-content/uploads/2012/11/gsma-deloitte-impact-mobile-telephony-economic-growth.pdf

Dewar, C. (2012, April 19). 3G growth stalls in Vietnam. *Wireless Intelligence.* Retrieved from www.wirelessintelligence.com/analysis/2012/04/3g-growth-stalls-in-vietnam/

First Alliances. (2016, August 1). Vietnam 2016 salary guide. *Vietnam Advisors.* Retrieved from www.vietnamadvisors.com/vietnam-2016-salary-guide/

Frolov, A., & Staples, D. (2012, April 25). VimpelCom's sale of Vietnamese business credit positive. *Moody's Investor Service.* Retrieved from www.moodys.com/research/Moodys-VimpelComs-sale-of-Vietnamese-business-credit-positive-PR_244255

Gardiner, B. (2008, March 20). In spectrum auction, winners are AT&T, Verizon and openness. *Wired.* Retrieved from www.wired.com/epicenter/2008/03/fcc-releases-70/

Ha-Vy. (2018, January 3). Viettel reports massive revenue and profit. *Vietnam Investment Review.* Retrieved from www.vir.com.vn/viettel-reports-massive-revenue-and-profit-55245.html

Huu-Tuan. (2017, February 24). Nhà mạng đua xuất khẩu thiết bị viễn thông [Providers race to export telecom device]. *Bao Dau Tu.* Retrieved from https://baodautu.vn/nha-mang-dua-xuat-khau-thiet-bi-vien-thong-d59275.html

Lazonick, W. (2013). The theory of innovative enterprise: A foundation of economic analysis. *The Academic-Industry Research Network* (Working Paper #13–0201). University of Massachusetts. Retrieved from www.theairnet.org/v3/backbone/uploads/2015/08/Lazonick.TIE-Foundations_AIR-WP13.0201.pdf

Minh-Anh. (2019, January 17). Việt Nam có thể vào Top 4 thế giới về sản xuất thiết bị viễn thông? [Can Vietnam become top 4 in telecommunications device manufacturing?]. *VNMedia.* Retrieved from www.vnmedia.vn/cong-nghe/201901/viet-nam-co-the-vao-top-4-the-gioi-ve-san-xuat-thiet-bi-vien-thong-624933/

Ministry of Information and Communications. (2010). *White book 2010: Vietnam information and communication technology.* Ha Noi: Information and Communications Publishing House.

Ministry of Information and Communications. (2011). *White book 2011: Vietnam information and communication technology.* Ha Noi: Information and Communications Publishing House.

Ministry of Information and Communications. (2012). *White book 2012: Vietnam information and communication technology.* Ha Noi: Information and Communications Publishing House.

Ministry of Information and Communications. (2013). *White book 2013: Vietnam information and communication technology.* Ha Noi: Information and Communications Publishing House.

Ministry of Information and Communications. (2014). *White book 2014: Vietnam information and communication technology.* Ha Noi: Information and Communications Publishing House.

Ministry of Information and Communications. (2017). *White book of Vietnam information and communication technology: Information and statistical data.* Ha Noi: Information and Communications Publishing House.

Ministry of Information and Communications. (2019). Lịch Sử Ngành Thông Tin Truyền thông Việt Nam [History of the information and communications industry]. *Ministry of Information and Communications.* Retrieved from http://mic.gov.vn/pages/thongtin/97878/lich-su-phat-trien.html

Nguyen, H. T. (2018, May 4). Doanh thu 2017 của Viettel ở nước ngoài tăng 38% [Viettel's 2017 revenue grows 38%]. *VNExpress.* Retrieved from https://vnexpress.net/kinh-doanh/doanh-thu-2017-cua-viettel-o-nuoc-ngoai-tang-38-3744727.html

Nguyen, H. T., Pham, T. Q., & Gullish, J. (2005). *Competition review of the Vietnamese telecom sector* (Vietnam Competitiveness Initiative Policy Paper #3). Development Alternatives Inc. Retrieved from http://pdf.usaid.gov/pdf_docs/Pnade784.pdf

Nguyen, N. (2007, September 9). Cấp phép mạng 3G, những điều đáng suy nghĩ! [3G license: Issues worthy of consideration]. *Thong Tin Cong Nghe*. Retrieved from www.thongtincongnghe.com/article/1069

Panganiban, M. (2010, December 17). A year of 3G in Vietnam: How attracting the young can accelerate growth. *Nielsen*. Retrieved from www.nielsen.com/us/en/insights/article/2010/a-year-of-3g-in-vietnam-how-attracting-the-young-can-accelerate-growth/

PM gives go-ahead for MobiFone, VNPT split. (2014, June 13). *VietnamNet*. Retrieved from http://english.vietnamnet.vn/fms/science-it/104907/pm-gives-go-ahead-for-mobifone-vnpt-split.html

Russin, J., & Vecchi, S. (2013, November). Telecommunications in Vietnam. *Russin and Vecchi International Legal Counselors*. Retrieved from www.amchamhanoi.com/wp-content/uploads/2014/02/Telecommunications.pdf

Thai-Khang. (2008, October 24). Thi tuyển 3G: Giờ G đã điểm [3G competition: The G hour struck]. *ICT News*. Retrieved from http://ictnews.vn/home/Vien-thong/5/Thi-tuyen-3G-Gio-G-da-diem/13445/index.ict

Thai-Khang. (2013, March 18). Thu nhập bình quân nhân viên Viettel là 18 triệu đồng/tháng [Average salary of Viettel's employee is VND 18 million per month]. *ICT News*. Retrieved from https://ictnews.vn/kinh-doanh/doanh-nghiep/thu-nhap-binh-quan-cua-can-bo-nhan-vien-vnpt-la-18-trieu-dong-thang-150498.ict

Thai-Khang, & Van-Anh. (2019, January 21). Người Việt đủ khả năng nghiên cứu sản xuất thiết bị hạ tầng viễn thông [Vietnam is capable enough to manufacture telecommunications equipment]. *ICT News*. Retrieved from https://ictnews.vn/cntt/chuyen-doi-so/nguoi-viet-du-kha-nang-nghien-cuu-san-xuat-thiet-bi-ha-tang-vien-thong-178018.ict

Thayer, C. A. (2012, March). *The political role of the Vietnam People's Army: Corporate interests and military professionalism*. Paper presented at the Association of Asian Studies Annual Conference, Toronto, Canada.

Thiet bi di dong 3G do Viettel san xuat se dung chip Qualcomm [Mobile phone equipment 3G produced by Viettel will use Qualcomm chip]. (2012, March 30). *ICT News*. Retrieved from http://ictnews.vn/home/Vien-thong/5/Thiet-bi-di-dong-3G-do-Viettel-san-xuat-se-dung-chip-Qualcomm/101607/index.ict

Trading Economics. (2017). Vietnam GDP per capita. Retrieved from www.tradingeconomics.com/vietnam/gdp-per-capita

Tran, F. (2012, July 13). Vietnam's big guys accused of monopoly. *Telecom Asia*. Retrieved from www.telecomasia.net/content/vietnams-big-guys-accused-monopoly

Trung-Duc. (2018, November 5). Thu nhập nhân viên Viettel đạt 29,7 triệu đồng/tháng [Salary at Viettel reached VND 29,7 million per month]. *The Gioi Tiep Thi*. Retrieved from https://thegioitiepthi.vn/thu-nhap-nhan-vien-viettel-dat-29-7-trieu-dong-thang-141783.html

United States Commercial Service. (2012, March). *Vietnam market for telecommunications equipment and services*. United States of America Department of Commerce. Retrieved from www.export.gov/

United States Commercial Service. (2014, June). *Vietnam market for telecommunications equipment and services*. United States of America Department of Commerce. Retrieved from www.export.gov/vietnam/build/groups/public/@eg_vn/documents/webcontent/eg_vn_076819.pdf

Van-Oanh. (2012, March 31). Viettel pins hopes on R&D revenue. *The Saigon Times*. Retrieved from https://english.thesaigontimes.vn/22698/Viettel-pins-hopes-on-RD-revenue.html

Vietnam announces four 3G licence winners. (2009, April 3). *IHS Markit*. Retrieved from www.ihs.com/products/global-insight/industry-economic-report.aspx?id=106595677

Vietnam Financial Review. (2009, October 22). *Vietnam's telecommunications update*. Retrieved from www.vtcomtech.com/

Vietnam plans to award 3G licenses in Q2 2009. (2008, November 11). *Institute of information and communications technology planning and evaluation*. Retrieved from www.iitp.kr/en/2/notice/globalNews/view.it?identifier=0000769343

Viettel expands into telecom device manufacture. (2011). *Vietnam Business News*. Retrieved from www.vnbusinessreg.com/viettel-expands-telecom-device-manufacture/

VNPT. (2011, April 14). *VNPT technology to be established*. Retrieved from www.vnpt.vn/en/News/IntCop/View/tabid/235/newsid/13891/seo/VNPT-Technology-to-be-established/Default.aspx

Xuxin. (2017, February 24). Vietnamese telecom giants on race of exporting telecom equipments. *Xinhuanet*. Retrieved from www.xinhuanet.com//english/2017-02/24/c_136082932.htm

5 The textile and garment industry in the value chain and industrial transformation

5.1 Introduction

The contemporary development of Vietnam's textile and garment (T&G) industry started in the early 1980s in the framework of cooperative agreements with other communist countries. The industry's main advantage was cheap labor. During this period, state-owned enterprises (SOEs) benefited from guaranteed market shares and thus had little incentive for innovation, industrial upgrade, or market development. In the wake of government economic reform in the late 1980s, communist-style economic cooperation was replaced with low value-added garment manufacturing set up by foreign investors, especially from Taiwan and South Korea. Foreign investors built manufacturing facilities in Vietnam and exported goods back to their home countries, and subsequently to international buyers. These developments were prompted by a number of trade treaties signed between Vietnam and its key trade partners beginning in the early 1990s (Ngo, 2017).

Throughout the 1980s and 1990s, Vietnamese private and public T&G enterprises had limited success at direct exporting to foreign buyers, as the large export shares were organized and controlled through foreign trading houses (IBM Belgium, DMI, Ticon, & TAC, 2009). Compared to major apparel producers in China, India, and Sri Lanka, Vietnam's T&G industry developed late, first achieving critical and world competitive mass in the 2000s. The sector's relative immaturity was reflective of the limitations of its skilled labor; technology; production organization; and management skills in logistics, design, marketing, and branding (IBM Belgium et al., 2009). When Vietnam became a member of the World Trade Organization (WTO) in 2007, the T&G industry finally became integrated into the global value chain, particularly in garment production, with major export markets in the United States, Europe, and Japan. Industry growth has been impressive. On average, export revenue in T&G grew 15 percent each year between 2005 and 2017 (Figure 5.2), and Vietnam ranked third in the world as a garment exporter, trailing only China and Bangladesh (Akter, 2018). In 2017, the industry exported USD 30.17 billion of yarn, textiles, and garments, accounting for 14 percent of the country's total exports (General Department of Vietnam Customs, 2018).[1] Despite considerable export revenue and growth, the industry's export growth has only been in volume expansion, but not value added, because Vietnamese suppliers have been slow to move up the value chain.

The Vietnamese T&G industry offers a unique study of economic development because of its particular characteristics and paths to industrialization.[2] It was one of the first industries to be liberalized under the government's reform agenda as early as the late 1980s. In addition, trade liberalization and foreign direct investment (FDI) are driving forces of industry development and thus make up a distinct configuration for rent management in both the public and private sectors. It is an example of a low value-added industry, where trade liberalization created enormous trade volume; however, the value added in production was limited.

This chapter analyzes the industrial development of Vietnam's textile and garment industry from 1990 to the early 2010s, using the developmental rent-management analysis (DRMA). It identifies key areas of industrial capability building and how different rent-management factors contributed to technical learning and upgrading efforts. Three analytical case studies assess the development of the industry: during the quota period from 2001 to 2006 (Case Study 1), in relation to the Vietnam-China border trade from 1990 to the 2010s (Case Study 2), and among SOEs during the 1990–2010s period (Case Study 3). A major focus of the chapter is to analyze rent-management mechanisms that hindered the industrialization of the T&G industry, especially explaining why vertical integration between the textile and garment sectors failed between 1990 and the 2010s. This apparent failure had tremendous consequences: the industry was slow to move up the value chain, achieved limited industrial upgrade, relied on price competition as its main source of competitiveness, and thus became more susceptible to demand shocks in the world market. Without this failure, T&G could have offered more productive value and spillovers not only for domestic firms and their own industry but also for the economy overall.

The case studies and rent-management analyses offer five major observations. First, while there was political will to boost growth in the T&G industry, market failures affected the acquisition of land and capital and constrained business coordination, management, and learning. Second, the weakness of upstream subsectors created significant bottlenecks for industrial capability building and undermined vertical integration of the industry within the value chain. The government attempted to address some externalities using quotas to support export promotion (Case Study 1) and by implementing industrial policies to accelerate the development of the textile sector (Case Study 3). Unfortunately, neither measure was quite successful. Third, the government has so far failed to prevent illegal imports of garments and textiles through the China-Vietnam border (Case Study 2), thus reducing market demand for Vietnamese inputs. Vietnamese firms, therefore, missed the opportunity to acquire technical learnings necessary for industrial upgrade (Case Study 3). Fourth, while FDI has been an important source of capital and technology transfer in a number of sectors, in the textile sector, it offered only limited knowledge transfer – nothing beyond basic production and low-skill technical training. Finally, the industry's limited success occurred in an ad hoc and spontaneous manner. Public firms were able to use rents – which were largely unavailable to the private sector – to improve their productivity and competitiveness. The case studies offer important insights to address the industry's pivotal failures through more informed rent-management policies and practices.

Section 5.2 provides an overview of the industry's growth, structure, and standing in the global value chain. Section 5.3 offers a review of the market failures faced by the industry in the 1980–2010s period. Sections 5.4, 5.5, and 5.6 each analyze one case study using the DRMA framework. Finally, Section 5.7 offers observations and possible policy options to strengthen the industry.

5.2 Industry structure

5.2.1 Key organizational features of the industry

There are various ownership structures within the T&G industry, including SOEs, private enterprises, and foreign-owned enterprises with up to 100 percent foreign capital and joint ventures. The T&G industry is structured so that a large portion of state-owned firms are grouped under the Vietnam National Textile and Garment Group (Vinatex), a state-owned general corporation. Until the mid-2010s, centrally controlled SOEs accounted for a significant amount of production output and were much better capitalized than smaller, locally controlled SOEs.[3] However, the government has been slowly equitizing state-owned firms as part of its commitment to the WTO. Therefore, their number is decreasing. Currently, Vinatex is the largest public shareholding company in the sector.[4]

There are two active associations in the T&G industry: the Vietnam Textile and Apparel Association (VITAS) and the Association for Garment Textile Embroidery Knitting (AGTEK). According to separate sources, these two organizations are somewhat disconnected from each other (interviews, four officials at VITAS and AGTEK, Ha Noi and Ho Chi Minh City; April–October 2011). The government originally established VITAS to act as the industry's watchdog. It has 15 branches and 683 members, that together account for 70 percent of the total production capacity of the industry (Fair Wear Foundation, 2015). VITAS advises state agencies on policies and mechanisms relating to the development of the industry. In addition, it represents the industry when dealing with international buyers by facilitating contracts between domestic enterprises and foreign investors. An interviewee, whose firm is a member of VITAS, explained that because of VITAS's close connection with state agencies and SOEs, it is largely a lobbyist for SOEs, not for private or foreign enterprises (interview, Ho Chi Minh City; June 2011). By contrast, AGTEK largely represents small and medium firms in southern Vietnam, which constitute approximately 62 percent of total businesses in the sector. It has fewer connections with the central government than VITAS. However, it is active in promoting business and trade opportunities among members and international buyers.

In 2018, there were approximately 6,000 enterprises operating in the T&G industry, employing roughly 2.5 million workers (Akter, 2018). Garment production comprised approximately 70 percent of the total share measured by number of enterprises. The textile sector made up 27 percent, and the remaining 3 percent involved accessories such as buttons, decorative pieces, and so on. The textile sector is further divided into three subsectors or stages: spinning, which produces yarn; weaving, which produces fabrics; and dyeing and finishing, which produce the final textile used to make garments (Le, 2011). Vietnam has a relatively small spinning subsector that produces yarn (or *soi* in Vietnamese), approximately 6 percent of enterprises (Le, 2011). Nevertheless, yarn production is perceived as an area where Vietnam has a comparative advantage in addition to garment production. Between 2013 and 2017, yarn production increased by almost threefold from 720,000 metric tons to 2,050,000 metric tons (Vo & Francic, 2018). In 2017, 66 percent of the production was exported to textile producing countries – China, South Korea, and Turkey (Vo & Francic, 2018). Weaving comprised 17 percent of enterprises, with a small dyeing subsector of about 4 percent that produced final textile products mostly for domestic use (Le, 2011).

A VITAS senior representative explained that high-capacity weaving and quality dyeing require advanced technology and techniques, which are lacking in the industry. In addition, to be competitive, these two subsectors require sophisticated technology, but a significant proportion of the machines and techniques used in Vietnam are outdated (interview, Ha Noi; June 2011). Interviewees in the garment sector explained that while it is more labor intensive, garment work requires less capital investment, simpler technology, and a shorter learning period as compared with the textile sector (interviews, six experts and firm managers, Ha Noi and Ho Chi Minh City; April–September 2011).

5.2.2 The textile and garment industry in the value chain

There are five stages of T&G production, from the production of raw materials to retail. A quick overview of these stages is provided in Table 5.1.

Concerning Stage 1, prior to 2000, Vietnam was an exporter of cotton and wool as raw materials. However, during the first decade of 2000, Vietnam

Table 5.1 Stages of Vietnam's T&G Value Chain

Stages	*1. Raw Materials*	*2. Textile Companies*	*3. Garment Manufacturers*	*4. Wholesalers and Exporters*	*5. Retailers*
Natural fibers	Cotton, wool, silk, hemp	Thread (or yarn), fabric, textile	Designing, cutting, sewing, assembling, finishing	Labeling, packaging, shipping	Branding, marketing, sales
Synthetic fibers	Oil, natural gas	Polymer, synthetic, fiber, cloth			

Source: Modified from Martin (2008, p. 30).

became an importer, when domestic production of both materials shrank dramatically from 32,267 hectares in 2003 to less than 2,000 hectares in 2015 (Ha, 2012; Vo, 2015). In the early 2010s, cotton prices in international markets fluctuated greatly, causing additional difficulty for Vietnamese textile manufacturers. A former textile executive observed that since Vietnam no longer has a comparative advantage in cotton production, it should focus on producing textiles from silk or synthetic fibers (interview, former vice president of the Thanh Cong Textile Garment Company, Ho Chi Minh City; May 2011). The executive further pointed out that because Vietnam has large oil reserves – an important input for polyester fiber – the country could achieve competitiveness in synthetic fibers. However, he also believed that Vietnam had yet to fully exploit this advantage in natural resources. Indeed, by the mid-2010s, the government and two large state-owned conglomerates, Petro Vietnam and Vinatex, joined forces to exploit opportunities in synthetic textile production. I analyze this failed attempt in Case Study 3.

Stage 2 is the production of textiles and fabrics, which are mostly manufactured by SOEs and some foreign firms in Vietnam. Vietnamese textile factories do not have competitiveness in textile production due to low quality, lack of diversity, and price. According to the General Department of Vietnam Customs (2018), while Vietnam is an exporter of fiber and yarn, selling USD 3.59 billion to international markets in 2017, it is an importer of textile and fabric. My compilation and calculation show that between 2005 and 2017, textile imports increased almost fivefold, from USD 2.39 billion to USD 11.38 billion (see also Figure 5.1).

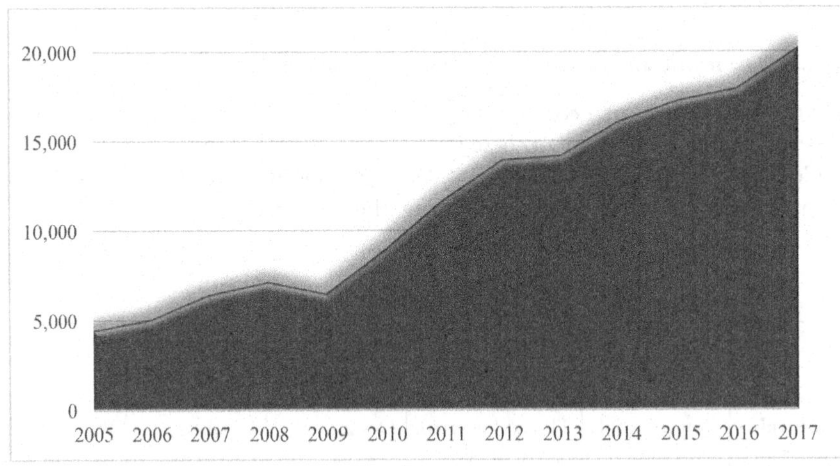

Figure 5.1 Vietnam's Estimated Imports of Inputs for Garment Production, 2005–2017 (in USD million)

Source: Author's compilation and calculation, data from government reports and the General Department of Vietnam Customs (2012, 2013, 2014, 2017, 2018).

A senior representative of VITAS explained his disappointment in this balance: Vietnamese enterprises failed to capitalize on the industry's comparative advantage in fiber production to increase production of textiles and fabrics. The textile sector is especially weak in dyeing and finishing and thus cannot manufacture high-quality textiles. He said:

> We import cotton to produce yarns, then export our yarns, but import fabrics and textiles for garment production. If we could develop additional capacity in dyeing and finishing and thus produce fabrics and textile domestically, we would import fewer foreign textiles and increase local content and value of our garment production.
>
> (interview, VITAS official, Ha Noi; June 2011)

My fieldwork data suggest that state-owned Vietnamese textile companies do not make a profit from textile production. The same former vice president of Thanh Cong Textile Garment Company, cited earlier, notes that despite Thanh Cong being known as a successful textile producer, the company actually incurred losses in textile manufacturing. As a result, it used garment production to cover financial losses from textile production. He explained that Thanh Cong maintained textile production to avoid laying off workers, to sustain the reputation of the company, and in hopes that it would eventually produce its own high-quality fabrics (interview, Ho Chi Minh City; May 2011).

Vietnam's comparative advantage is mostly seen in Stage 3: garment manufacturing. This competitiveness is owed to a large and young labor force, with limited technical skills and a willingness to work for cheap. As mentioned, the start-up cost in garment production is low, allowing for quick and relatively easy entry to the sector. Over time and thanks to the Vietnamese government's "open-door" policies, garment producers quickly learned the trade and became global exporters. By the late 2010s, exporters demonstrated their global competitiveness through special attention to quality control, effective management of inventory, and capacity to reliably deliver outputs on time (interviews, two garment producers, Ho Chi Minh City; June 2016). In consequence, there has been a rapid rise of revenue from garment exports since the early 2000s. For example, from 2005 to 2017, T&G export revenue increased sevenfold, from USD 4.83 billion to USD 26.1 billion (Figure 5.2).[5] Phi, Tran, and Trinh (2014) report that more than 60 percent of garment exports are shirts, trousers, jackets, sporting clothes, sweaters, polo shirts, and dresses.

The imbalance between textile and garment sectors

The disparity in development between the textile (Stage 2) and garment (Stage 3) sectors is arguably due to their historical and technical composition. Before Vietnam's economic reforms, the government oriented the economy toward production in "heavy" industries (vs. "light" industrial manufacturing), and thus, the textile sector was larger than the garment sector. Following

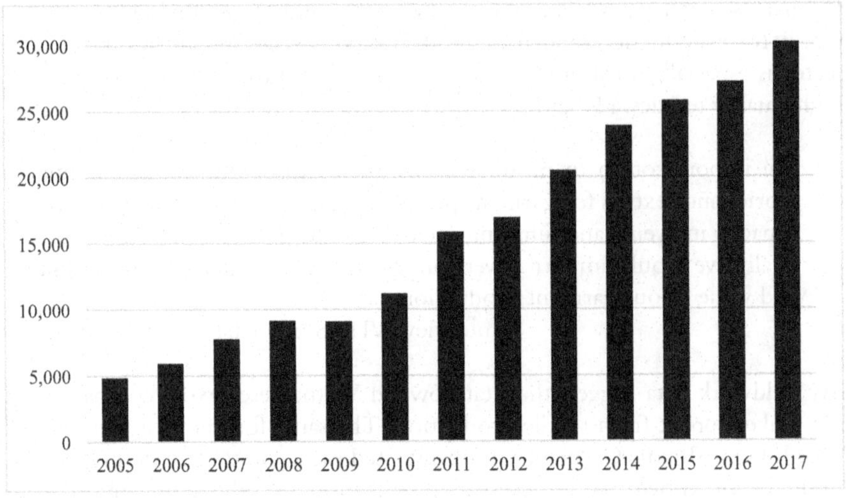

Figure 5.2 Total Revenue in T&G Exports (in USD million)

Source: Author's compilation and calculation using data from the General Department of Vietnam Customs (2012, 2013, 2014, 2017, 2018).

economic reform in 1986 and the state's partial withdrawal from complete control of the economy, garment production rose to prominence, while textile production fell behind and continued to shrink (interview, former chairman of VITAS, Ho Chi Minh City; October 2011). Hill (1998) provides two historical explanations for the contemporary ailing textile sector. The first is that the collapse of Russian and eastern European markets disrupted the sector's main export markets, causing considerable decline in demand and output. The second is that economic reforms in 1986 led to a major "shake out" of the industry, especially for SOEs. In the context of gradual market liberalization and the government's incremental withdrawal of subsidies – while SOEs' technical and production capabilities were still inadequate – state-owned textile factories scrambled to compete with foreign entrants (Hill, 1998). This observation was confirmed in my fieldwork in 2011, when four officials and industry experts expressed similar opinions (interviews, Ho Chi Minh and Ha Noi; May–October 2011). Vietnam's low-quality textiles lost ground to higher-quality foreign products; thus, domestic textile producers only supplied to the local market.

As noted earlier, the technology and capital requirements of the two sectors are distinct (Table 5.2). The textile sector is capital intensive and dependent on both economies of scale and technology management. Vietnamese producers are weak on these criteria (interviews, two managers of textile companies, Ho Chi Minh City; May 2011). In addition, dyeing and finishing require skilled labor and advanced techniques often considered trade secrets among producers. The garment sector, on the other hand, is consumer oriented and requires simpler technology and less start-up costs. More importantly, beginning in the 1990s, garment producers had access to international markets, allowing them to learn the trade and develop over time. There is also no labor constraint in the garment sector because training requires less time and effort; thus, it is easier to hire and train new workers. An owner of a garment factory in Ho Chi Minh City explained that her senior employees commonly trained new employees, with roughly two to three months required for a new worker to become fully productive (interview, Ho Chi Minh City; April 2011). In Table 5.2, distinct characteristics of the two sectors are summarized. The table shows that it is much easier for Vietnamese producers to quickly develop capability in garment manufacturing, which requires less skills, technology management, and investment capital compared to the textile sector.

In Stages 4 and 5, Vietnamese exporters do not have international competitiveness in either global wholesale or retail markets. To change this, Vietnamese T&G firms must move from reliance on buyer inputs (cut, make, trim) to independently sourced inputs (free on board). Another senior representative at VITAS indicates that as much as 70 percent of Vietnamese producers did not have access to independent input sources (interview, Ha Noi; June 2011). Vietnamese garment producers must also break into steady relationships between brand names and suppliers, some of which are established global and regional trading houses. Tran (2012) posits that 70 percent of garment inputs used by domestic producers are provided by foreign suppliers or brand names. These observations are consistent with my calculation using data from the General Department of Vietnam Customs published from 2012 to 2018, and VITAS's industry report: local content ratio of garment manufacturing was roughly 26 percent in 2011 when the interviews took place. The local content ratio only slightly improved to 33 percent in 2017 (Table 5.3). The data suggests that Vietnamese garment

Table 5.2 Key Distinctions between the Textile and Garment Sectors in Vietnam

Characteristics	*Textile*	*Garment*
Intensity	Capital intensive	Labor intensive
Scale of economies	More important	Less important
Ownership	SOEs and foreign firms	SOEs and foreign and Vietnamese private firms
Vertical integration	Common to have integration with spinning, weaving, dyeing, and finishing	Some integration during the central planning period but less so as garment exports increase
Size	Mostly large firms	Mostly small- and medium-sized firms
Market	Mostly domestic (except for unfinished fiber)	Mostly foreign (especially European Union countries, Japan, and United States)

Source: Adapted from Hill (1998).

Table 5.3 Estimated Local Content Ratio, 2005–2017 (in USD million)

Year	*2005*	*2006*	*2007*	*2008*	*2009*	*2010*	*2011*	*2012*	*2013*	*2014*	*2015*	*2016*	*2017*
Total exports revenue	4,838	5,927	7,780	9,130	9,084	11,210	15,833	16,930	20,480	23,909	25,777	27,169	30,171
Estimated imported inputs	4,365	4,992	6,356	7,064	6,422	8,912	11,720	13,919	14,147	16,063	17,219	17,889	20,157
Local content ratio (%)	9.78	15.78	18.30	22.63	29.30	20.50	25.98	17.79	30.92	32.82	33.20	34.16	33.19

Source: Author's compilation and calculation.

producers relied heavily on imported inputs for their production, constraining them from moving up the global value chain.

An important observation from this value-chain analysis is that by the early 2010s, the industry's development was limited by low value-added production due to weak linkages in the value chain. To increase value addition, profit, and industrial competitiveness, Vietnamese producers have three options: (1) develop a larger base for textile production to increase value added in garment production (Stage 3); (2) actively take control of logistics as wholesalers and thus become global trading houses (Stage 4); or (3) move to create their own brands in the international market (Stage 5). The first option could be viable, as Vietnam's tradition of textile production dates back to the postcolonial period, and the country has large crude oil reserves. However, so far, the government's effort to explore this option has been unsuccessful (Case Study 3). In 2016, when I conducted field research in the industry, garment producers appeared to focus on option 2 – they became more actively involved in managing their own logistics and inputs and in producing at high volume for international retailers and trading houses (interviews, two garment producers and an industry expert, Ho Chi Minh City; June 2016).

Option 3, selling Vietnam-branded products in foreign markets, is challenging because Vietnamese producers and designers have neither the experience in international marketing nor a reputation with consumers in foreign markets. Nevertheless, while it has been difficult for domestic producers to promote their own brands in the international market, by 2016, garment producers and designers made tremendous progress in the domestic market, incorporating Vietnamese culture and characteristics in their designs and setting fashion trends among local consumers (interviews, two garment producers and an industry expert, Ho Chi Minh City; June 2016). In the process, they accumulated crucial experience preparing to penetrate Stage 5 of the global value chain. Overall, the industry development in the late 2010s suggests that T&G producers are moving toward servicing and branding, rather than manufacturing ("Garment and textile industry on course," 2019).

5.3 Constraints in the textile and garment industry

5.3.1 Lack of skilled labor

In the early 2010s, researchers in the field disputed the significance of skilled labor shortages in the T&G industry. Some investigators maintained that Vietnamese workers have certain comparative advantages over China, including proficiency in embroidery and needlework skills (Nieuwoudt, 2009). However, if the T&G sector is split into upstream (textile) and downstream (garment) production, most of the skilled workforce is located in the garment sector, where, as previously noted, skills are basic and easy to learn on the job. The textile sector, however, faces a substantial shortage of technicians and engineers, especially in the fields of spinning, weaving, and dyeing.

Interviewees at both VITAS and AGTEK point out that labor shortages have been a major inhibitor to the textile sector for two reasons. First, engineering students tend to study subjects conducive to careers in high-tech industries, such as computer science, mechanical engineering, and telecommunications. They do not want to work in the textile sector because of negative images carried over from when textile producers were state-owned and perceived as bureaucratic and inefficient. The second reason is low wages. In Ho Chi Minh City, for example, I was told that salaries for textile technicians and engineers were approximately USD 150 per month (interview, an engineer who worked at a state-owned textile factory, Ho Chi Minh City; April 2011). For comparison, engineers with similar years of experience (two to five years) in Vietnam's telecommunications industry made between USD 250–500 per month in 2011. The same engineer explained that the only reason he did not switch to another field was because he liked his job and was reluctant to risk changing careers. He reported further that few young workers are interested in textiles and his company has had trouble hiring.

The Vietnamese government is aware of this skilled labor shortage. To address this problem, over the past two decades, state-owned conglomerate Vinatex has been assigned by the government to open training campuses in both the north and south. In 2019, Vinatex had three universities and colleges with more than five campuses that specialize in technical training for the textile sector, including associate degrees in mechanical engineering, sewing technology, and fashion design.

5.3.2 Shortage of capital and land

In Vietnam, land is not considered private property; hence, enterprise owners either rent land or obtain land-use rights (the so-called red books). Renting is relatively expensive and also insecure. The red books can be obtained in two ways: through transfer or government lease. Obtaining land-use rights through lease is a lengthy and costly process. As a result, an estimated 70 percent of all transactions in red books take place in the vibrant, yet unofficial, market through which private businesses mainly lease plots of land from SOEs or farmers (Buisman & Wielenga, 2008, p. 39).

Throughout the 1990s and into the early 2000s, major Vietnamese commercial banks made it extremely difficult to obtain loans at low interest rates, especially for private enterprises (Hill, 1998; Thomsen, 2007). The thinking was that "since private enterprise owners generally lack ownership rights over land and buildings, they have few possibilities to offer collateral against loans from the official banking system" (Thomsen, 2007, pp. 761–762). Market constraints related to capital and land shortage were less severe in the state sector because SOEs were privileged with easier access to credit through state-owned banks. During the central planning period, the government also gave SOEs large areas of land to use as collateral for loans on large development projects. Unlike SOEs, the constrained private domestic enterprises were hindered in their ability to borrow and thus faced difficulties in acquiring new technologies and expanding productive capability (Ngo & Chi, 2017). Given the high start-up costs, this problem is especially severe in the textile sector and explains why textile production is dominated by SOEs.

Lack of capital and access to credit are particular obstacles for Vietnamese producers trying to achieve higher value-added production. First, working capital is needed to pay for stock, fabric, and accessories and to produce on what are usually 90-day payment terms. Second, foreign buyers are increasingly reluctant to accept contracts based on Letters of Credit that guarantee that the producers will be able to fulfill the contract.[6] Third, readily available capital is required for wages and salaries, because even if there is a gap of time between orders, workers still have to be paid (Thomsen, 2007). In the early 2010s, the government made changes to allow more private enterprises access to domestic capital through bank loans. However, in 2011, for example, the interest rate was a staggering 16.94 percent (World Bank, 2013); thus loans remained impossible for small- and medium-sized enterprises during the early 2010s.[7] Shortages of capital and credit help explain why private and domestic producers prefer garment manufacturing to textiles. As a result, SOEs with state financing and foreign investors with ready investment capital dominate textile production. In addition, nearly all textile production by foreign firms in Vietnam is used either for direct or indirect exporting.[8] Therefore, textiles produced by foreign investors have been largely unavailable for local garment producers. All these problems together caused severe shortage of high-quality textile in the domestic market.

5.3.3 Weak coordination

The T&G industry also suffers from weak coordination at the ministry and association levels, which inhibits development. At the state level, there are nearly no close exchanges between the state and private firms: "Channels of communication between the industry and the government do not appear to be well developed" (Hill, 1998, p. 54). At the ministry level, the belief is that "senior government officials have great background knowledge of the industry and its historical development" (Hill, 1998, p. 53). Private firms, however, feel the opposite: the government knows little about their business activities, is not interested in their problems, and offers an unfriendly regulatory environment (Hill, 1998). My fieldwork in 2011 and 2016 confirmed this latter observation. Small business owners felt largely detached from the industry or were unaware of the policy agenda in Ha Noi (interviews, four private garment and textile producers, Ho Chi Minh City and Ha Noi; April–September 2011). A small domestic garment producer in Ho Chi Minh City told me that, on the whole, she would prefer the government to stop interfering in her business through administrative and tax harassments and "leave [her] alone to run the business" (interview, Ho Chi Minh City; April 2011).

At the association level, private garment producers felt no connection with major associations such as VITAS and AGTEK to explore business relationships with foreign investors. According to managing members of AGTEK and VITAS, these two associations maintain only loose and informal contact with each other, and they do not channel information or facilitate business opportunities with foreign buyers across members of each association (interviews, VITAS and AGTEK representatives, Ha Noi and Ho Chi Minh City; May–June 2011). This lack of communication may be due to the fact that these associations were created for different purposes and serve different types of members. Until the mid-2010s, government watchdog VITAS had always been headed by the chairman of Vinatex, who is a government appointee and known to be supportive of SOEs. On the other hand, AGTEK, created by businessmen of Chinese Vietnamese descent, is mostly self-governed by its members and is said to have a weak relationship with its managing ministry, the Ministry of Industry and Trade (MoIT). Therefore, AGTEK has weak lobbying capabilities. It largely focuses on providing information, training, and business opportunities among southern textile and garment producers (interview, AGTEK senior representative, Ho Chi Minh City; June 2011). With a lack of coordination at the ministry and association levels, businesses often have to find their own sources of information, supplier networks, and business contracts. As a result, these small and medium producers have limited competitiveness and are slow in acquiring new technical and management capacities, though they match each other in the ability to lower prices and squeeze wages.

5.3.4 Machinery, equipment, and technical upgrading

Hill (1998) found in his Vietnamese T&G industry fieldwork in the late 1990s that equipment in many businesses was antiquated and also noted, "most firms appear to have an unusually wide range of machinery, some of which has reportedly been delivered on an ad hoc basis to firms as part of aid programs and without any integrated production operating plan" (p. 46). Starting in the mid-2000s, SOEs in joint ventures with foreign partners benefited from foreign technology, management, and marketing skills. But even here, there have been mixed results. Between 2007 and 2012, there were 485 FDI projects in the T&G industry, with a total registered capital of more than USD 2 billion. Foreign investment continued to increase rapidly in the late 2010s, especially due to Vietnam's participation in the Comprehensive and Progressive Agreement for the Trans-Pacific Partnership in 2019. In 2018, VITAS reported that "a total of nearly US$ 15.9 billion in FDI had been injected into more than 2,090 textile and garment projects in Việt Nam" ("FDI firms expand in local textile-garment sector," 2018). According to a representative at AGTEK, firms that were in joint ventures with foreign investors outperformed domestic firms in technological adoption and capability (interview, Ho Chi Minh City; June 2011). However, there were limited spillovers from foreign investment into the domestic labor force and firms because foreign investors actively hid trade secrets and technical expertise (such as dyeing techniques) from local employees and partners (interview, AGTEK representative, Ho Chi Minh City; June 2011).

During the 2000s, additional investments were made to improve equipment and machinery throughout the industry. However, researchers observed that they were too little and could not satisfy the demand for expansion and upgrading needed to increase outputs' production and quality (IBM Belgium et al., 2009). Specific data on technology investment is limited for this sector, although there is some evidence of investment in modern machinery. For example, in a report to the U.S. government, Vo and Francic (2018) report that the industry's total number of spindles increased from 6 million units in 2013, to an estimated 7.5 million units in 2017. The industry also utilized 103,000 rotors in 2017. Together, they added 1.3 million tons of yarn production for the spinning sector, from 720,000 tons in 2013 to 2.05 million tons in 2017 (Vo & Francic, 2018).

During my fieldwork in 2011, representatives at VITAS and AGTEK each pointed out that it would be misleading to think that Vietnamese producers do not have advanced machinery in both textile and garment production. They explained that the problem was in learning how to use the machines to improve production and output quality, to which Vietnamese producers do not give due attention. Speaking for state-owned firms, a senior VITAS representative told me that SOEs often spend large capital investments to buy new equipment but do not buy the "know-how," showing the different aspects of the machines' functions and capability (interview, Ha Noi; June 2011). These SOE managers thought that their workers could learn how to use the machines by reading the manual, or through learning-by-doing, rather than through training provided by foreign sellers or from a software. However, on the manufacturing floor, the engineers were afraid of damaging the new machines, so they avoided operating and, thus, learning them. The same VITAS representative explained that when SOEs did use upgrades, it was to produce traditional low-quality products: "When it comes to technological upgrading, textile managers are slow in learning and integrating new technology to their operation" (interview, Ha Noi; June 2011). The T&G industry thus faced serious constraints in advancing technological adoption to boost productivity, especially among domestic producers, because the new equipment and technology required considerable effort in learning, experimenting, and developing tacit knowledge. Even when new machines were available, domestic producers failed to acquire knowledge on how to use them to achieve new productive capability and thus to become more competitive in the global value chain.

The next three sections present case studies that together offer a detailed picture of the rent-seeking and rent-management configurations within the T&G industry and how they influenced development of the industry as a whole. The purpose of these three case studies is to assess the mix of political, institutional, market, and industry factors that explain why there were high or low levels of effort put forth in the development of firms and the overall industrialization of the industry.

5.4 Case study 1: the quota period (2001–2006)

In 2001, with the signing of the U.S.-Vietnam Bilateral Trade Agreement, Vietnam officially gained access to the U.S. market with garments as the primary export product. To put a cap on apparel imports, the U.S. imposed export quotas for Vietnamese garments under the framework of the so-called American Multifiber Arrangement (MFA). The agreement gave Vietnam's T&G industry a short grace (or quota-free) period from 2001 to 2002, followed by export quota imposition starting in January 2003 (Thoburn, 2007). This case study largely details quota distribution for exports to the United States between 2001 and 2006 when the American MFA quota officially ended, preceding Vietnam's membership into the WTO in January 2007.[9] The case study especially focuses on 2003 and 2004 when mismanagement of quota distribution reached its height. It employs the DRMA framework to analyze rent-seeking processes and outcomes, given the industry's configuration of rent management.

5.4.1 Political context and the rules of quota distribution

Although quotas are often viewed as restrictions to trade, it was a benefit for Vietnamese garment producers. Vietnamese producers had no U.S. market access before the opening of trade. Once the trade agreement opened the U.S. market, they benefited from large market demand for clothing abroad, allowing for production expansion and higher profits. From this perspective, an export quota imposed by an external actor such as the United States creates rents for T&G producers, who can export at world market prices that are higher than domestic prices, if they receive quota allocations. The U.S. MFA quota generated two potential incentives for Vietnamese producers, one positive and one negative. The former was for firms to acquire technology and coordinate different production linkages in order to expand production and exports, given the large market potential in the United States. The latter was that firms could capture redistributive rents by bribing corrupt government officials for quotas.

Officially, the Vietnamese government was concerned with the potential corruption and rent seeking associated with quota allocation. When the government assigned the distribution responsibility to the Ministry of Commerce and the Ministry of Industry,[10] the managing ministries for the T&G industry at the time, Deputy Prime Minister Vu Khoan issued Document 669/CP-KTTH (hereafter, Document 669) on May 21, 2003. It stated:

> There must be a mechanism to ensure that there will not be any *selling*, *buying*, or *transferring* of quotas. Under no circumstances should the Inter-ministerial Managing Group grant quotas to enterprises that *do not* have a production line. Investigate thoroughly any commercial fraudulence. Those who violate the law should not receive any further quotas.
>
> (Hai, 2004; emphasis added)[11]

Document 669 instructs the designated ministries to closely monitor the distribution process. It clearly shows that the government was aware of the potential for corruption. More importantly, it demonstrates that top political leaders were at least formally committed to make learning rents work for the development of the industry.

I interviewed government officials during this period on what they thought the *informal* political intentions were behind the allocation of rents, but the inquiries yielded little information; I suspect those who did not want to answer were involved, in some capacity, in rent-seeking themselves (i.e., buying and selling of quotas). A manager at a large garment factory who was actively involved in quota trading during this period pointed out, "Perhaps not directly, but the family and relatives of those officials may be in the trade, and they could informally give orders to allocate quotas to their close connections" (interview, Ho Chi Minh City; September 2011).

5.4.2 Policy and institutional structure of quota allocation

Following Document 669, the ministries subsequently moved the quota-distribution responsibilities to the Inter-ministerial Managing Group (hereafter, the Managing Group), still comprising representatives from the Ministry of Commerce and Ministry of Industry but adding VITAS as a third arm. Bui Xuan Khu and Mai Van Dau, both deputy ministers of the Ministry of Commerce, and Le Van Thang, deputy director general of the Import-Export Department of the Ministry of Industry, helmed the Managing Group. According to *VietnamNet* (2004), quota allocation was primarily based on the following criteria:

1 Prior year's performance or previous production capacity
2 New investment in machinery
3 Percentage of local content, especially local textiles in garment exports
4 Export relationship with large U.S. importers and distributors
5 Priority given to garment producers in poor provinces

Procedurally, a garment manufacturer had to submit an application for quota, along with documentation – such as advanced contracts with foreign buyers – proving it had met the criteria for quota allocation. If the Managing Group approved this application, a quota was granted, and the applicant paid a *gia cong* (small administrative fee or official price) to receive quota documentation. If the official criteria listed above had been carefully enforced, quota allocation would have rewarded investment in exporting, production capacity and equipment, and addressed regional inequalities.

Elements of the allocation mechanism could therefore be interpreted as providing *learning rents* for both the garment and the textile sectors. First, the criterion of enterprise performance in the prior year targeted technical and organizational capability building. That is, the more an enterprise improved its industrial capability based on the previous year's performance, the more likely the enterprise would be to receive a quota the following year. Second, the criterion of local content was intended to promote the use of local materials (textiles and accessories) in garment exports, thus providing a market for the textile sector to expand production and potentially upgrade their quality, given the large demand from the garments exporters. Finally, the criterion of rewarding new investment in machinery and facilities was to encourage T&G producers to update technical capabilities and equipment so as to boost quality and productivity.

Although the government intentions manifested in the allocation criteria and the three-arm structure of the Managing Group, quota allocation was neither monitored nor supervised by higher levels of the government (i.e., the minister or the prime minister) nor by an independent agency. In addition, if the Managing Group wrongly denied applications, garment manufacturers did not have the benefit of a procedural appeal. Consequently, the *co che xin cho* (application-granting mechanism) set up by the Managing Group did not create real pressure for productive outcomes. In reality, it encouraged rent seeking that distributed quota benefits to connected firms and individuals. One interviewee, who had worked as an SOE manager in 2004 and thus had regular contacts with members of the Managing Group, asserted that the Managing Group was not interested in boosting industrial capability, improving local content, or developing upstream industries for garment exports. In his opinion, despite the formal criteria for quota applications, government officials in charge of the allocations were actively engaged in capturing rents or financial benefits from quota redistribution (interview, Ho Chi Minh City; September 2011). Indeed, during this period, rent-seeking activities were widespread because public, private, and foreign firms operating in Vietnam were incentivized to seek quotas through bribery. The corrupt firms either gained access to the U.S. market or resold quotas on the black market for tremendous profits.

5.4.3 Industry organization during the quota period

Another factor affecting operation of the rent-management system during the quota period was the organization of the industry itself. In this case, industry structure neither supported productive rent management nor discouraged redistribution of quota rents. As noted earlier, VITAS was largely created as a government watchdog, and a de facto think tank for the ministry, rather than as the actual representative for T&G manufacturers. During the quota period, VITAS neither monitored nor complained about illegal quota trading and bribery for quota allocation. The political and organizational weaknesses of these associations explain firms' lack of power over corrupted officials. In essence, although the quota rents were not created by the Vietnamese government, their allocation was entirely state led. Furthermore, Vietnamese firms could not prevent the government from extracting rents from the industry in the form of bribes. As a result, public, private, and foreign firms operating in Vietnam were incentivized to seek quotas through bribery in order to gain access to the U.S. market or to resell them on the black market for short-term profits.

Dynamics of rent seeking

The rent-seeking activities during the quota period took two forms. In the first, as just described, firms bribed government officials to receive quotas from the Managing Group, even though they had weak productive capacity or made false claims of meeting the allocation criteria. The second form involved quota exchanges on the black market. Initially, the government announced that quota exchanges were illegal. The law made clear that an enterprise that could not fulfill its quota must return it to the Managing Group for reallocation. However, between 2003 and 2004, then deputy minister of the Ministry of Commerce, Mai Van Dau signed three official documents that permitted enterprises to *chuyen nhuong* (exchange) quota allocations amongst themselves (Cong-Minh, 2006). These official documents thus created a market for quota exchange, which immediately caused quota overvaluation and even led to speculative trading. A "quota broker" indicated that in early 2004, the unofficial sale price of quotas on the black market was many times higher than its initial purchase price, including the cost of bribery (interview, Ho Chi Minh City; September 2011). In fact, Van-Thanh (2004) reported that the quota price on the black market was possibly 20 times higher than the official fee in some high-demand categories, such as T-shirts.

In one scenario, there might be two garment producers – one who received quotas from the government but was either unwilling or unable to produce garments for exports (GP1) and one who did not receive the quota allocation but had productive capacity (GP2). In this case, GP2 could buy the quota from GP1 in order to produce and sell their garments to U.S. buyers. Under this rent-seeking system, all parties made a profit from the quota exchange. The government official (GO) received bribes; GP1 received rents from the difference between the bribe it paid to the GO and the payment it received from GP2; and GP2 earned profits from selling garments to American buyers. However, GP2's profit was much less, if it had to buy its quota from GP1 instead of being allocated its quota through the official system, which only required a small administrative fee. According to research conducted by Van-Thanh (2004), the unofficial payment for quotas on the black market often cost approximately one-third of the total value of the contract between Vietnamese producers and U.S. buyers. For example, a contractual price with foreign buyers for the jacket category was approximately USD 4 per piece, but the illegal quota price on the black market fluctuated between USD 1 and 1.5 per piece. In order to maintain its competitiveness, a GP2 firm likely made up for the cost by squeezing worker salaries instead of transferring the cost of its rent seeking to American customers by increasing the selling price (Van-Thanh, 2004).

In addition to unregulated trades of quotas, there were other common problems in the allocation system. Van-Thanh (2004) also reported the following prevalent scenarios. For example, Company A, which could produce to capacity, would apply and receive a promise from the Managing Group that it had a quota allocation (e.g., for 20,000 dozen garment pieces). However, by the time the garments were made and ready to be sent to a U.S. buyer, Company A would have received only one-third of its promised quota, despite the government promise and the fact that it met all allocation criteria. This forced Company A to scramble and purchase quotas on the black market, regardless of price, in order to ship their garments to the U.S. buyer. In a different scenario, Company B, which did not have a factory, workers, or equipment, or was specialized only in import-export (not manufacturing), could bribe officials to receive a quota for 1 million dozen garment pieces. The company would then sell the quota on the black market, and make a handsome profit, despite the fact that it did not produce or export a single garment (Van-Thanh, 2004). During the quota period, both scenarios were widespread (interview, manager of a garment company, Ho Chi Minh City; September 2019). The quota broker said in an interview that garment companies commonly obtained fake contracts with textile firms to report high local content percentage or submitted false reports of previous performance to justify large quota allocations (interview, Ho Chi Minh City; September 2011).

Rent-seeking activities during the quota period came under public scrutiny in 2004. Vietnamese newspaper, *Vietbao* reported on a corruption scandal that involved A Chau, a local garment manufacturer. In its application for the quota, A Chau falsely reported that it had bought textiles from local producers, and a high-ranking member of the Managing Group, Le Van Thang, signed the quota authorization knowing full well the claim was false (Tung-Duy, 2004). Thang received a large sum of money from A Chau. However, his quota approval did not go through, as officials of the Managing Group signed off for more quota allowance than the quantity set by the United States. A Chau – which had then produced a large quantity of garments for a foreign buyer but could not export it – reported the case to law enforcement authorities to recover financial losses. A Chau's initial claim led to the discovery of a large number of bribes and exchanges of quotas on the black market at both the ministry and firm levels, which until then, took place either under the table, behind closed doors, or on the black market.

5.4.4 Rent outcomes from the quota period

After A Chau's scandal became public, a number of similar scandals were subsequently reported in the media, creating public outrage over government corruption. Truong Dinh Tuyen, the then minister of commerce, testified to the Party Congress that the financial stakes were too high, so rent seeking to obtain quotas was unavoidable. "Where there is a distribution mechanism, there will be wrongdoings," he said (Phuoc-Vinh, 2004). In addition, he admitted that the Managing Group's allocation mechanism was largely flawed because it lacked independent monitoring and supervision from a higher authority or agency ("Đứng Đầu Bộ Thương Mại," 2004). In responding to questions by the Party Congress, Tuyen claimed he knew about the scandal only from the media (Phuoc-Vinh, 2004). He said he had heard rumors about corrupt activities, but without evidence, he was not in a position to discipline his associates. This testimony was contradictory to his role as the minister of commerce – he was to supervise his deputy and the activities within the ministry. Clearly, there was insufficient supervision of quota allocation, despite the deputy prime minister's instructions in Document 669.

The deputy minister of the Ministry of Commerce, Mai Van Dau; his son, Le Van Thang; and 14 other officials and individuals were found guilty of bribery and abusing power, and all were sent to prison. My data is inconclusive as to whether the then prime minister, Nguyen Tan Dung, and other high-ranking officials, such as Truong Dinh Tuyen, benefited financially from the misallocation of quotas. For example, Tuyen put Dau in charge of quota allocation, and Dau later allowed transfers of quotas that effectively created the black market. Yet Dau was the highest official prosecuted. It is unlikely that Tuyen knew nothing about the misallocation of quotas, given it was his duty to supervise Dau. Furthermore, the T&G industry was one of the most important export industries at the time, and it produced significant business opportunities and profits in the early 2000s.

Analysis and outcomes from the mismanagement

At the industry level, although local firms had little power to sway distribution of quota rent, they could report corruption to law enforcement agencies and bring cases to the media. This is what A Chau did. However, A Chau used this strategy as a last resort, after it had manufactured a large garment shipment for a U.S. buyer but did not receive the quota it had paid a bribe to receive.[12] Clearly, individual firms did not desire enforcement of rules that would make the industry more productive as a whole. Competitive firms were willing to pay black-market rates for quotas because they could still earn some profit, provided they received the quotas they had paid for under the table. In this context, regulations and law enforcement was not a factor in sustaining value-enhancing rents.

A different scenario could have been possible, particularly because a large number of SOEs were engaged in both textile and garment production. If quotas had been properly managed, successful exporting firms engaged in investment and upgrading would have earned extra rents in the form of export profits, which could have been reinvested to further increase capacity. That new capacity would have then led to increased official quotas relative to their success. Further, garment exporters would have had the incentive to pay extra for locally produced textiles to boost their local content as part of the allocation criteria. This could have created market demand and incentives for production expansion in the textile sector. If SOEs had boosted their textile production, given higher market demand and financial incentives, they would have benefited from vertical integration and increased value added in their production during the early 2000s period.

In reality, however, the rents created and allocated during the quota period failed to provide incentives and pressures for investment in capability building, and resources were diverted away from capable firms. Schaumburg-Muller (2009) reports that there was little industrial upgrading after the quota period. There was an impressive increase in exports, but that was largely due to Vietnamese enterprises' flexibility in dealing with multiple international buyers for different lines of production. This flexibility occurred because Vietnamese enterprises could produce at lower costs than most of their foreign competitors in low-value garment production. Further, productive firms that could not obtain quotas had to change their business strategies. Knutsen and Nguyen (2004) point out that firms that could not gain quotas for the U.S. market reoriented toward buyers in other markets such as Japan or Europe. With higher tariffs in these markets, as compared to the United States, and with low profits, these firms struggled to stay in business, especially in the off-season, making expanding capability and upgrade impossible (Thomsen, 2007).

Overall, most quotas were given to firms and individuals willing to buy them, thus, making quota rent a redistributive rent. This rent was shared among limited firms, individuals, and the government at the expense of more productive firms. As noted earlier, these failures in the rent-management mechanism were only addressed and corrected through the justice system. A Chau's scandal of illegal trading and bribery led to court and public attention. However, the rule of law only punished the *corruption*. It was not involved in enforcing the official quotas criteria, nor did it create incentives and pressures for their effective management. From the perspective of industrial upgrading and learning, there was no developmental rent-management mechanism during this period.

5.4.5 Summary of the quota period

What is truly unfortunate about the failed allocation mechanism for quotas during the early 2000s is that the appropriate allocation of quota rents could have created valuable learning rents that supported industrialization and learning among Vietnamese enterprises, especially in the textile sector. Capacity improvement, especially increased local content and industrial upgrading, meant the T&G industry could have adopted new technology and integrated vertically to move up the value chain. Even though the redistributive rent-seeking period lasted only two years (2003 and 2004), it set the wrong foundation for the second half of the quota period. Two of the criteria in the later period were based on production performance in the previous year and connections with large U.S. buyers. Therefore, firms that benefited in the early quota period, whether through bribery or first-mover advantages, received more quotas in the following two years. With a large amount of their quota rent diverted through bribery in the first half of the quota period, and with no improved technology, productive textile and garment producers had neither enough capital nor time to improve their competitive advantage before the Vietnamese economy opened up with its 2007 entry into the WTO.

It is often expected that the rule of law creates the institutional framework to prevent rent seeking. This is rarely the case in a development context, where government officials are directly involved in the rent-seeking process. In this case study, law enforcement brought a few corrupt individuals to court, but it was insufficient to ensure developmental outcomes. The rule of law addressed some of the damaging aspects of rent distribution, but it could not recast the allocation process. Thus, there was no developmental rent management to ensure that the quota rents had growth-enhancing effects. The quota period only increased underlying political distrust among the Vietnamese populace.

This case study illustrates the complex and unregulated rent-seeking activities that occurred at both the state and firm levels in the 2001–2006 period. It highlights the (possibly deliberate) inability of the state to monitor rents and questions whether there was real intention and incentive mechanisms to boost industrial upgrading in the T&G industry, as textile producers failed to expand production capability and garment producers were unable to move up the value chain. Had the U.S. quota been allocated properly, based on criteria set out in the government documents, export quotas could have been a valuable learning opportunity to support industrial development among Vietnamese enterprises, especially in the textile sector. An analysis of this period using the DRMA framework is summarized in Table 5.4. This case study helps explain the T&G industry's continued dependence on low-cost labor and foreign inputs. In

Table 5.4 DRMA Summary of the Quota Period

Step 1: Political Context	• Document 669 formalized political will to turn quota benefits into learning rents for textile and garment firms • Informal political motives led to redistributive rents **Type of rent:** Learning rents created through quota benefits and allocation criteria
Step 2: Institution Structure	• Clear criteria of quota allocation based on performance, upgrading, use of local inputs, and reducing regional inequality • Lack of an effective mechanism to monitor and supervise quota allocation
Step 3: Market and Industry Structures	• Severe rent seeking to obtain quotas through bribery • Exchange of quotas created a black market and increased speculation on quota value • Firms that obtained quotas illegally experienced high profits when selling the quotas on the black market • A Chau sued in court as a last resort

Step 4:
Rent Outcomes
	• Missed opportunities to use quota rents to:
	  • Enhance investments and capacity
	  • Upgrade domestic firm capability
	  • Increase domestic linkages between garment and textile sectors

the next case study, I analyze Vietnam-China's border trade and the impact of China's rise on the development of the T&G industry.

5.5 Case study 2: the political economy of Vietnam-China border trade

China and Vietnam have had a long and complex trade relationship. A series of border conflicts in 1979 largely shut down border trade and social interactions in border communities through the following decade. Although such activities informally resumed in the late 1980s, the official legal framework that normalized border trade was only established in December 1999, when Vietnamese and Chinese foreign ministers signed a treaty demarcating the border between the two countries. Since then, both governments have issued a number of official documents and instructions that set the framework for trade of small volumes, tariff rates, trade by inhabitants of border areas, and preferential policies to deepen economic cooperation. Vietnam and China share a border of 2,363 kilometers; much of it passes through mountainous areas that are not accessible to large-scale trade. The long borderline crosses through China's Guangxi and Yunnan provinces and through eight provinces on the Vietnamese side. Because of the mountainous terrain crossing Yunnan Province, 80 percent of border trade occurs along the 1,020-kilometer stretch of China's Guangxi Province (Gu & Womack, 2000). In 2015, Vietnamese officials reported that there were approximately 29 official border gates, more than 15 sub-border gates, and 50 informal paths ("Red flag rising over Vietnam-China," 2015).

Vietnam's official data on trade volume at the Vietnam-China border is extremely limited and often understated due to poor government accounting and smuggling. Nonetheless, the available data suggests complex and interconnected trade integration between the two countries, resulting in chronic and large-scale trade deficits for Vietnam. In 2018, trade volume (imports and exports) between the two countries reached USD 148.3 billion, of which Vietnam's exports accounted for USD 65.15 billion; meanwhile, Vietnam imported USD 84.2 billion of Chinese goods (China General Administration of Customs, 2019). As a consequence, Vietnam incurred a USD 21 billion trade deficit with China in 2018. As an example of the rapidly deepening trade relationship, between 2008 and 2018, the total trade volume between the two countries increased almost eightfold, from USD 19.45 billion to USD 148 billion (China General Administration of Customs, 2019). These figures, though tremendous, still do not account for large quantities of smuggled goods, for which no reliable estimates exist.

In the last two decades, China has been one of Vietnam's largest trade partners and creditors. In 2017, China ranked second (only after South Korea) as Vietnam's largest creditor in trade. In the same year, more than a quarter of Vietnam's imports came from China (General Department of Vietnam Customs, 2018). Figure 5.3 demonstrates that Chinese goods made up the lion's share among

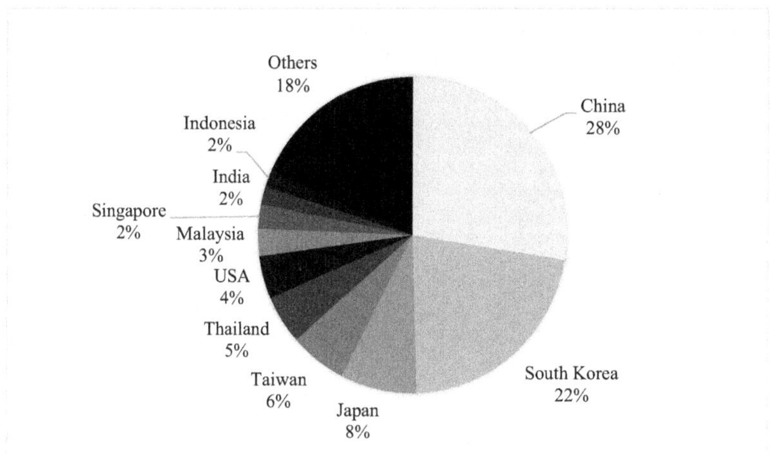

Figure 5.3 Shares of Vietnam's Top 10 Import Countries in 2017

Source: Author's compilation and calculation using data from the General Department of Vietnam Customs (2018).

Vietnam's top 10 import countries with 28 percent, followed by South Korea, Japan, and Taiwan.

The increase in trade volume between China and Vietnam has created an alarming deficit for Vietnam since 1999, especially after accession to the WTO. This is because import tariffs and administrative measures were reduced after 2007, which allowed for greater exchanges in manufactured and consumer goods. From 1999 to 2018, Vietnam's trade deficit with China increased almost 40-fold, from USD 610 million in 1999 to USD 200 billion in 2018 (China General Administration of Customs, 2019). At the height of this trade imbalance in 2014, Vietnam incurred a startling USD 43.7 billion trade deficit with China (China General Administration of Customs, 2019). Figure 5.4 illustrates Vietnam's rising trade deficit with China from 1999 to 2018.

In 2017, the General Department of Vietnam Customs (2018) estimated that imports from China were approximately USD 58.59 billion. However, the Chinese official estimate was closer to USD 72.36 billion – a gap of USD 13.77 billion between the two official numbers (China General Administration of Customs, 2019). A reporting gap between the two countries' statistical offices has occurred almost every year since the early 2010s. The most pronounced difference in reporting between the two countries occurred in 2014, when the reporting gap in Chinese imports to Vietnam was USD 19.9 billion (China General Administration of Customs, 2019; General Department of Vietnam Customs, 2018). Some Vietnamese officials and experts suggest that the import difference occurred at the Vietnam-China border and that a large portion of the difference in accounting was smuggled goods or goods sold on the border's

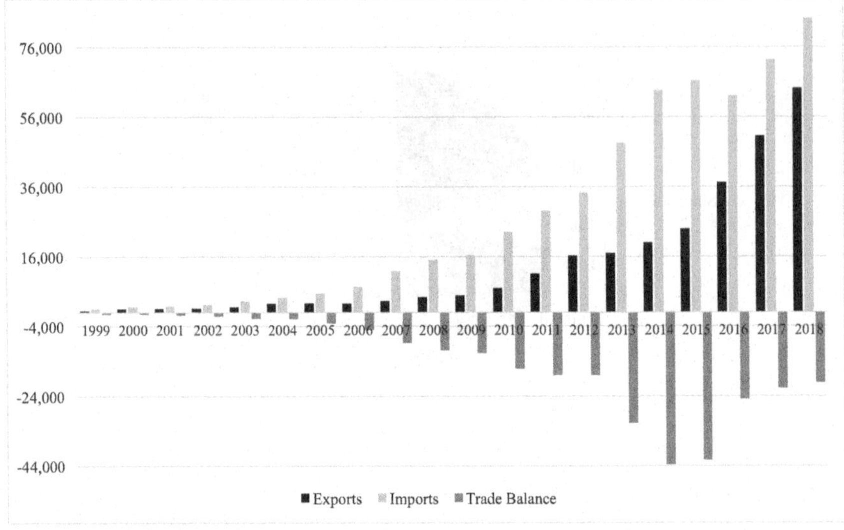

Figure 5.4 Vietnam's Trade Balance with China (in USD million)

Source: Author's compilation and calculation using data from China General Administration of Customs (2019).

black market. "There is no dispute that the difference in the trade statistics across the borderlines fundamentally results from the informal trade across the border and the inherent difficulties in measuring the volume of it," suggests one news report ("Red flag rising over Vietnam-China," 2015, p. 1).

Indeed, cross-border smuggling is a decades-old problem frequently highlighted by news media and experts. In addition, research shows that it accounts for a large share of trade volume between the two countries. Ben Bland (2012) reported from the busiest trading point between the two countries, the Mong Cai border: "As many as 1,500 vehicles traffic goods every day through the busiest unofficial crossings in Mong Cai, each paying border officials $10–$20 in bribes for right of passage" (pp. 2–3). Womack (1994) points out, "The border trade takes place in crowded, makeshift cooperative zones where officials often assess fees per porter rather than by the goods carried, and there is much smuggling (estimated at one-third of trade volume) as well as bribery and collusion of customs and border officials" (p. 496).

Vietnam has often been said to downplay its imports statistics, particularly since 2010 ("Reports about Vietnam-China trade," 2015). However, the discrepancy in the 2014 trade data was so severe that the Vietnam National Assembly held a meeting in June 2015 to discuss inconsistencies in cross-border bookkeeping and illegal trade (Chen, 2015). If the USD 19.9 billion discrepancy in imports in 2014 is accounted for as smuggled trade, as some news reporters and experts suggest, smuggling could have accounted for up to 31.1 percent of Vietnam's imported value from China that year. This indicates that smuggling and informal trade far exceed small-scale trade. Nevertheless, the Vietnamese government has had difficulty controlling illegal border activities, resulting in major negative impacts on the industrial sectors. This case study analyzes the rent-management configuration of Vietnam's border trade as well as the effects of large-scale smuggling on industrial development in Vietnam's T&G industry.

5.5.1 Political context of the border trade

The Vietnamese government's position on border trade can be understood at the international, bilateral, and national levels. First, within the international community, border trade fits into the Vietnamese government's overarching trade agenda, and the rhetoric of its market openness to global capitalists and integration within the international market. Second, border trade plays a stabilizing role in Vietnam-China diplomatic relations and is the major expression of shared interests and mutual benefits in cooperation (Womack, 1994). Consequently, relaxed border control reflects the reality that the Vietnamese government does not want to harm the general tone of its relationship with China. By default, the border becomes the prime target when tensions between Vietnam and China escalate. Along the 2,363-kilometer border, crackdowns are intermittent and often more reflective of Ha Noi's relationship with Beijing than of economic concerns of the upland region or the nation. For example, after China moored an oil exploration rig in waters off Vietnam's central coast, tensions caused border trade to stall at the semiofficial crossings for months in 2014 and early 2015 (Ives, 2015).

Third, national governments on both sides are not the major beneficiaries of border trade and thus are rarely seen as major promoters of bilateral trade via borders. Accordingly, border trade is not a leading policy concern in Ha Noi (Womack, 1994). Who, then, are the beneficiaries? The border war with China in 1979 and the closed border in the following decade severely impoverished border regions and upland ethnic minorities. From 1979 to 1989, "this period was marked by hunger and poverty in northern Vietnam. Families reverted to subsistence means, including turning to the forest for food such as roots, mushrooms, and insects, as well as for shelter from the military presence in the region" (Turner, 2015, p. 278).

Thus, for Vietnam, the reestablishment of border trade has benefited small ethnic communities and customs officials in the uplands and is a means of economic and social provisioning for a region otherwise isolated from the Kinh people and from Ha Noi's political agenda.[13] In addition, Vietnamese importers and Chinese exporters benefit from trade at extremely low tariff rates. This allows them to unfairly compete in the Vietnamese market, crowding out both local producers and exporters from other countries. The political will of Ha Noi to use border trade as a symbol of its willingness to maintain good diplomatic relations with China, coupled with trader incentives to exploit benefits of informal trade, creates a rich and complex political context. These factors weaken the government's willingness to closely enforce border activities.

5.5.2 Institutional structure of border-trade enforcement

The institutional deficiency of border control is considered the leading cause of widespread smuggling at the border. Experts frequently point out that the Vietnamese government is incapable of regulating border activities without cooperation from Chinese authorities (Chan, 2013; Hill, 1998; Turner, 2015; Womack, 1994). For example, from September 1992 to April 1993, the Vietnamese government banned 17 specific goods from China, especially through the border. However, the policy was largely ineffective, and trade in the first half of 1994 increased 14 percent over the first half of 1992 (Turner, 2015; Womack, 1994). A senior official of AGTEK pointed out: "Historically [weak enforcement at the border] has always been like this, except it has gotten worse in the recent decade." He suggests that this institutional deficiency reflects the government's weak political will to adequately address the border problem (interview, Ho Chi Minh City; May 2011).

To regulate illegal imports of Chinese goods, one must take into account: (1) the difficulty of one-sided enforcement; (2) the prohibitive resources required to control the border effectively; and (3) the social acceptance of informal trade as a way of life at the border (Bland, 2012). Cooperating with Chinese authorities to patrol the border is difficult because southern Chinese industries, workers, and traders are profiting from the trade; thus, the Chinese government, especially the provincial authorities, lacks the incentive to monitor and penalize smuggling at the border. Second, with over 1,000 kilometers of border by land and waterways, it is extremely costly for the Vietnamese government alone to crack down on smuggling, particularly when the political context does not impose pressure to act.

An informal aspect of smuggling is that it is generally accepted in certain Chinese and Vietnamese societal groups, which aggravates the difficulty of enforcing informal trade activities. Field researchers provide evidence that Vietnamese border traders dismiss the idea that smuggling and bribery are morally wrong and even regard them as socially accepted behavior (Endres, 2014; Schoenberger & Turner, 2008). Local people see smuggling as a practice that reflects the dynamic relationship between local authorities and the people: "To many local people and state agents, smuggling is just a supplement of border trade. Indeed, some borderland authorities have also deemed smuggling as an integral part of the local economic development strategy" (Chan, 2013, p. 95). There are also informal rules that determine rates of bribery in popular border areas where there is more than one point of entry. This helps keep the price of bribery to an affordable level, which sustains the informal relationship between traders and customs authorities (Eyler, 2014).

Implicitly, Vietnam's loose border control is a form of rent provision that embodies tangible and intangible benefits to the governments, customs officials, traders, Chinese exporters, and Vietnamese buyers, so long as the scale of smuggling remains insignificant. However, the USD 19.9 billion discrepancy in import values means large-scale informal trade at the border severely impacts

Vietnam's economic and industrial development. The next section discusses specific effects to the T&G industry.

5.5.3 Industry structure in the T&G industry

At the industry level, given the lack of high-quality domestic fabrics, there has been a large volume of exports from China to Vietnam, especially in textile materials. Table 5.5 shows both fabrics and textile accessories ranked in the top seven of imported commodities in 2017, indicating Vietnam's heavy trade volume and reliance on China for textile materials. According to the General Department of Vietnam Customs (2018), in 2017, imports of Chinese fabrics accounted for 10.4 percent of total imports while accessories accounted for 3.5 percent. Compared to import values from 2016, imports of fabrics increased by 11.5 percent and textile accessories by 9.6 percent in 2017 (General Department of Vietnam Customs, 2018). Vietnam continues to depend on Chinese textiles and accessories for garment exports to foreign markets.

In December 2015, Vietnam reduced tariffs with China in accordance with the Association of Southeast Asian Nations (ASEAN)-China Free Trade Area. Prior to that, there had been three trading options for Chinese textiles and accessories to enter Vietnam. The first was trading through the ASEAN block, based on its commitments with the ASEAN-China Free Trade Area. As for most other ASEAN countries, the official import tariff for Chinese textiles was 10–18 percent, depending on the category. The second option was for textiles to be imported directly from China via border trade. Large-scale imports across the border were subject to a 5 percent tariff rate. The third option was smuggling. Official statistics show that direct export via the borders (Option 2) accounted for

Table 5.5 Vietnam's Top Seven Imported Commodities from China in 2017

	Categories	*Imported value (in USD million)*	*Share of total imports (%)*	*Annual change from 2016 (%)*
1	Equipment, tools, and instruments	10,909	18.6	17.2
2	Telephones, mobile phones, and parts	8,749	14.9	42.4
3	Computers, electrical products, spare parts, and components	7,077	12.1	19.4
4	Fabrics	6,078	10.4	11.5
5	Iron and steel	4,104	7.0	–8.3
6	Textile, leather and footwear materials, and auxiliaries	2,047	3.5	9.6
7	Plastic products	1,925	3.3	29.0

Source: Author's compilation based on data from the General Department of Vietnam Customs (2018).

one-third of the trade value between Vietnam and China (Bland, 2012); however, this figure did not account for illegal trading and smuggling (Option 3).

Hill (1998) pointed out: "[S]muggling of Chinese textile products into Vietnam is reportedly widespread and has been the subject of several unsuccessful campaigns to eradicate it" (p. 33). This observation was confirmed in my 2011 fieldwork. A senior AGTEK representative and owner of a medium-sized garment factory in Ho Chi Minh City pointed out that the majority of textiles used for manufacturing were provided by foreign buyers who often sourced their materials from China, South Korea, or Taiwan. Even for the Vietnamese firms that sourced their own supplies, they often used materials and accessories from China, and a large portion was smuggled materials. The interviewee said, "We know that there is a large volume of smuggled textiles and accessories, but there is really no way to know the exact amount and cost. Chinese textiles and accessories are cheaper than Vietnam's and are of better quality and variety" (interview, Ho Chi Minh City; May 2011).

Given the lack of competitiveness, many local textile producers opted for garment production to make up for the loss in textile manufacturing. Two industry executives explained that most Vietnamese SOEs producing textiles incurred heavy losses and lacked capital and technology to upgrade production. These SOEs mostly rely on garment production to cover losses in the textile sector. Therefore, capital, labor, and resources have been reallocated to improve competitiveness in garment manufacturing at the cost of the textile sector's development (interviews, Ha Noi and Ho Chi Minh City; May and June 2011).

5.5.4 Impacts of border trade on Vietnam's T&G industry

After Vietnam entered the WTO in 2007, the garment sector grew with the influx of foreign investment and access to the global market. With the severe constraint of domestic inputs, the garment sector had to import up to 82 percent of its materials in 2007 and still up to almost 67 percent in 2017 (Table 5.3). Consequently, Vietnamese producers have reinforced their competitive advantage through low value-added production and cheap resources in labor, land, and preferential tariff rates. Thus, they have only earned profits by a small margin (Phi et al., 2014). The estimated local content ratio in the T&G industry between 2005 and 2017 is shown in Table 5.3.

The Vietnamese government's lack of control over large-scale smuggling at the border appeared to have benefited not only customs officials and small minority groups but also Vietnamese garment producers and Chinese exporters. First, cheap Chinese textiles permitted foreign and domestic garment producers in Vietnam to access inexpensive inputs and earn higher profits. Second, as a result of rising wages in the Chinese garment industry, foreign buyers diversified their supply networks and expanded into Vietnam. With informal border trade that avoided tariffs, Chinese textile exporters gained market access by supplying materials for apparel production taking place in Vietnam, despite losing foreign buyers in their own country. Thus, border trade expanded Chinese exports and increased exporters' profits through the growth of Vietnam's garment manufacturing.

The Sino-Vietnam border trade influenced the T&G industry in two ways. First, since the Vietnamese textile sector cannot satisfy the high demand for quality and quantity of the garment producers, without Chinese imports there would be bottlenecks in the supply of materials for garment production. Therefore, Chinese textiles eased the shortage of textiles in Vietnam in the short term. Second, unlike global trade, which may increase foreign investment, border trade is largely driven by market access of one country into the neighbor's economy (Womack, 1994). In the context of Vietnam-China border trade, Chinese producers competed and shrank the market demand for Vietnamese textiles. They also intensified the garment producers' reliance on and susceptibility to Chinese inputs. Here, the short-term benefit of Chinese imports required a crucial tradeoff for the longer-term development of Vietnam's T&G industry in the global value chain.

Overall, the growth of China's industrial capability, large-scale border trade, and smuggling at the Vietnam-China border have hindered Vietnam's textile sector upgrades in the global value chain in two significant aspects. First, despite its large volume of exports, the Vietnamese T&G industry is locked into labor-intensive and low value-added production as well as a limited profit margin. The country is heavily dependent on imported inputs and unable to move beyond garment manufacturing to fully integrate into the global value chain. Without vertical integration between the textile and garment sectors, Vietnam cannot generate more value-added manufacturing or participate in the more profitable segments of the value chain. This problem has been aggravated as lower-wage countries such as Bangladesh and Cambodia entered these low-cost segments of the T&G value chain and thus competed with Vietnamese garment producers for low-cost garment production. Second, Vietnam's trade with China pits the interests of garment producers against the interests of domestic textile producers as well as the long-term development of the T&G industry as a whole. Here, the negative outcomes include many local textile producers giving up on upgrading their competitiveness and either closing down their businesses or refocusing on garment production (interviews, four managers of textile companies and experts, Ha Noi and Ho Chi Minh City; April–June 2011). This reinforces the first problem by creating a cycle that deepens Vietnam's comparative advantage in low-cost manufacturing and cheap resources, besides impeding its industrial development.

The impact of China's rise on Vietnam's T&G industry has been further aggravated since December 2015, when Vietnam officially implemented its commitments to the ASEAN-China Free Trade Area. The trade agreement stipulates that Vietnam is to reduce its import tariffs for 90 percent of imported goods (7,881 product categories) from China and 10 other ASEAN countries to below 1 percent. If the Vietnam-China border trade experience is a point of reference, one could project the influence of this trade pact to industrial development in Vietnam. According to the trade treaty, Vietnam will remove trade barriers from some

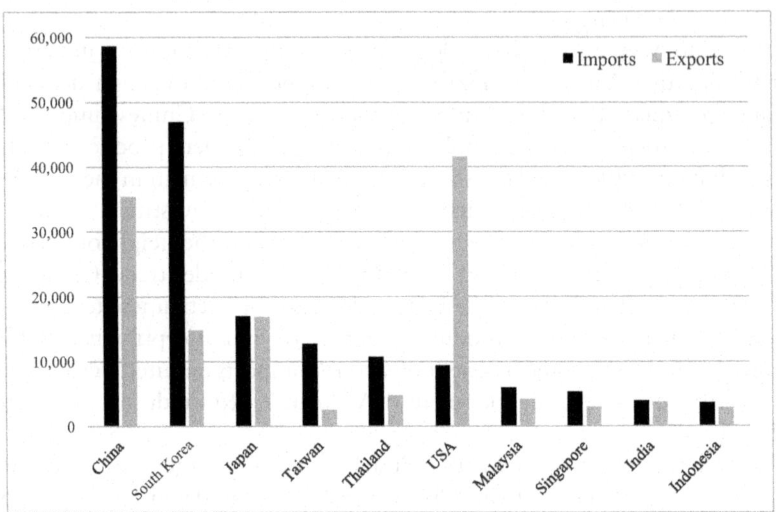

Figure 5.5 Import and Export Values of Vietnam's Top 10 Trading Partners in 2017 (in USD million)

Source: Author's compilation based on data from General Department of Vietnam Customs (2018).

of Vietnam's largest import countries: China, Singapore, Thailand, and Malaysia. These are the countries with whom Vietnam has regularly experienced trade deficit. For example, in 2017, these four countries comprised 38 percent of Vietnam's import value but only 22 percent of its export value (General Department of Vietnam Customs, 2018). The disparity between imports and exports between Vietnam and other Asian countries is shown in Figure 5.5. There has been weak local content and value addition in Vietnamese exports as well as heavy reliance on intermediary goods for manufacturing inputs (Ngo & Chi, 2017). Without trade barriers with China and industrialized countries in the region, Vietnam's domestic firms are forced to compete while their technical, organizational, and financial capabilities are still weak. This will lead to a reduction in the industrial base and competitiveness, as already seen in the T&G industry.

5.5.5 Case study summary

This case study assesses the industrialization of Vietnam's T&G industry from the perspective of the Vietnam–China border trade and the impacts of China's economic rise on the industry's development. The combination of historical, political, institutional, and industrial factors explains the industry's limited ability to raise its competitiveness, particularly in facing China's manufacturing competition and intricate border trade. A summary of this case study, using DRMA analysis is shown in Table 5.6.

The Vietnamese government's inability to protect a tariff-based policy for domestic textile producers occurred because (1) the Vietnamese government had weak political will to singularly control the border activities, (2) there were

Table 5.6 DRMA Summary of the Vietnam-China Border Trade

Step 1: Political Context	• Complex historical and political relationships with China led to Vietnam's weak political will to address smugglings at the border **Type of rent:** • Tariff-based rents created for textile producers were deconstructed • Lack of border control generated redistributive rents for customs officials, ethnic groups in the uplands, and garment producers in the T&G industry
Step 2: Institution Structure	• Vietnam could not singlehandedly enforce border trade due to its long border route with many gates, sub-border gates, and informal paths • Smuggling was accepted in some societal groups
Step 3: Market and Industry Structures	• A weak textile sector could not provide all inputs for domestic garment industry • Garment producers overcame shortages of high-quality and low-cost textiles by using illegal Chinese textile imports • Textile producers were too politically weak to lobby for better border control
Step 4: Rent Outcomes	• Missed opportunities to focus on upgrading the textile sector and to integrate garments and textile sectors

insufficient institutional structures and capacity to manage border smuggling, (3) textile producers were not able to meet market demands for inputs, and (4) garment producers continuously relied on Chinese imports for production and exports. Given this intricate political economy, Chinese exporters and Vietnamese garment producers benefited from loose border control. At the same time, Vietnamese textile producers were without incentives to upgrade when informal trade and smuggling destroyed their tariff protection.

The political economy of the Sino-Vietnam border trade and the penetration of Chinese industrial surplus in the Vietnamese market are examples of internal and external factors that destroyed the benefits of import-competing industries such as textiles and deepened dependence on foreign inputs of exporting industries, such as garments. In sum, the Vietnamese model of liberalization in recent decades has exposed its industries to excessive competition, and thus, they have become unable to reach the technological level and production scale necessary to be globally competitive.

5.6 Case study 3: the state sector and Vinatex (1990–2010s)

This case study assesses industrial development and capability building of the state sector within the T&G industry. It especially focuses on Vinatex, the largest firm in the industry, and a general corporation that manages state capital and a number of state-owned subsidiaries. Prime Minister Vo Van Kiet created

Vinatex in 1995 by grouping approximately 200 state-owned T&G firms under its umbrella (Tran, 2012). Due to a major restructuring in 2006 and again 2015, Vinatex became a privately owned corporation, though the government is still the majority owner at roughly 51 percent (Nguyen, 2015). The remaining share is owned by Vietnamese, Korean, and Taiwanese foreign investment funds. In principle, there are three types of state ownership within Vinatex: 100 percent state-owned companies (including one-member companies with limited liability), joint-stock, and joint-venture companies (Tran, 2012). In 2019, the state continues to maintain majority control over some of Vinatex's most profitable T&G companies, such as Phong Phu Joint Stock Company and Nam Dinh Textile Garment Joint Stock Corporation (Vinatex, 2019).

Vinatex's scope of operation covers all aspects in the T&G industry, including spinning, knitting, weaving, dyeing, import-export, design, education, training, media, and so on. In 2019, the Vinatex website indicated that the corporation comprised two magazines, three training colleges and universities, a research institute, one hospital, a fashion center, two yarn producing factories, eight wholly owned corporations, 12 joint-stock corporations where Vinatex has more than 50 percent ownership, and 22 joint-stock corporation with less than 50 percent ownership (Vinatex, 2019). Although Vinatex's export share in the industry varies slightly from year to year, it frequently hovers around 10 percent annually, implying that the general corporation commands approximately 10 percent share of the industry's market. For example, in 2017, Vinatex exported USD 3.2 billion, the equivalent of 10.3 percent share of the industry's total exports (USD 31 billion) ("Vinatex summarizes its business performance," 2018). Given the industry's low entry barrier, a large number of firms, and high volume of foreign investment, this is the largest share of market concentration in one business group.

In the domestic market, Vinatex has the largest market presence because many of its subsidiaries and fashion centers are renowned local names. It also frequently launches marketing campaigns to promote domestic purchases of Vietnamese brands and products. Considering Vinatex's significant role and share in the T&G industry, this case study analyzes Vinatex's structural transformation and performance as well as the government's efforts to force the general corporation to achieve both its social and economic missions. I also analyze rents and the rent-management structure within Vinatex to elucidate the process of industrial transformation in the T&G industry during the 1990–2010s period.

5.6.1 *Political context of rent management in the state sector*

The Vietnamese Communist Party's support of the T&G industry is based on the political imperative of maintaining social and political stability through employment and raising state revenues. Since Doi Moi, the T&G industry has served as an engine for job creation in Vietnam. In early 2019, the industry generated roughly 2.85 million jobs in its core sectors and related industries

("Vietnam's textile-garment industry," 2019), an increase from 2 million jobs in the early 2000s. It is in this context that Vinatex is an instrument of social policy. Vinatex employs approximately 10 percent of the total industry labor force, approximately 250,000–285,000 employees (Fujita, 2017). A senior advisor at Vinatex explained to me that Vinatex carries both social and economic responsibilities, including job creation and retention, skills training, and poverty reduction (interview, Ho Chi Minh City; October 2011). This social mission often involves bailing out its failing SOEs and using cross-subsidization across plants to maintain employment and growth. In July 2011, for example, media reported that Vinatex poured capital into its Dai Cat Tuong Garment Company, a failing company in Da Nang with 1,300 workers, to prevent it from going out of business (Tan-Toi, 2011). This was in accordance with the government's instruction to support provinces experiencing economic difficulties, thus ensuring basic incomes for people in those regions. The same advisor explained that Vinatex could not perform better financially because its social responsibilities often conflicted with its economic objectives – to maintain competitiveness and generate profits in the marketplace (interview, Ho Chi Minh City; October 2011). Indeed, the government's restructuring of Vinatex in the mid-2000s demonstrates the state's strong political will to concentrate its rent-management power in Vinatex, while forcing the general corporation into improving industrial capability in its core businesses.

The restructurings of Vinatex

Shortly after the turn of the century, Vinatex underwent a series of restructuring efforts, the first of which took place in 2006. Prior to 2006, Vinatex's authority over its subsidiaries was limited, especially when it came to distribution of profits. Le Quoc An, the chairman of Vinatex at that time, said: "Before [2006] our state companies acted independently, if they made a profit, they kept it" (Martin, 2008, p. 8). As SOEs, these enterprises were owned and managed either by the central government via its managing ministries or by provincial state bodies. However, with the help of PricewaterhouseCoopers, the Vietnamese government restructured Vinatex and transformed it into a profit-oriented holding company. Following instructions from the Ministry of Industry, Vinatex began its equitization in 2007 with the goal of completing its transformation into a joint-stock holding company by the end of 2008. The equitization would not reduce the value of the government's capital holding in Vinatex but instead issue new shares for sale to private investors to attract new capital. As a result, Vinatex now collects profits and closely manages its subsidiaries much more so than before its transformation. In the words of Le Quoc An, '[N]ow we act as a real owner' (Martin, 2008, p. 9). The restructured Vinatex is to focus its efforts in five major areas:

- Invest, produce, supply, distribute, import, and export textiles and garments
- Set up joint ventures with domestic and foreign investors

- Develop and expand both domestic and overseas markets as well as assign member companies to penetrate potential markets
- Conduct research and improve technological applications in Vietnam's garment and textile industries
- Provide technical training for workers and skill training for midlevel managers.

(Martin, 2008)

The 2006 transformation of Vinatex into a shareholding company with state ownership in a number of Vietnam's largest clothing companies suggests that the government intended the Vinatex conglomerate to lead the industry and implement its social programs.

In 2013, the ownership structure shifted once again, as Vinatex was at the center of the government's public sector reform. Prime Minister Nguyen Tan Dung signed a Vinatex restructuring plan to occur between 2013 and 2015. As part of the plan, Vinatex would retain 100 percent stake in four of its subsidiaries (instead of seven, as in 2006), reduce its stake to between 50 and 65 percent in six companies and to less than 50 percent in 20 others; and divest itself from 37 noncore subsidiaries ("Prime Minister okays restructuring plan," 2013). The plan implied that, by the early 2010s, the state was withdrawing its capital from Vinatex, thus forcing the corporation to concentrate on its core businesses. In September 2014, Vinatex launched an initial public offering, which sold 24.4 percent of the company's total shares and raised USD 58 million. In consequence, the Vietnam Investment Development Group holds 14 percent share, and property developer Vingroup holds the other 10 percent ("Vinatex raises $58 Million," 2014). The government remains Vinatex's largest shareholder with a 51 percent stake ("Vinatex raises $58 Million," 2014). Vinatex's stock sales demonstrate the government's efforts to involve more private investors with the goal of boosting efficiency and reducing public debts. This reinforces the government's desire for private investors to lead the development of the T&G industry, particularly in preparation of Vietnam's entrance into the Comprehensive and Progressive Agreement for the Trans-Pacific Partnership in 2019.

The most recent round of Vinatex's restructuring took place in November 2018, when the government transferred 53.49 percent of Vinatex's charter capital (USD 114.6 million) to the State Capital Investment Corporation (SCIC). This was a broad and bold government reform, led by Prime Minister Nguyen Xuan Phuc who shifted state ownership rights of 62 major SOEs and general corporations to SCIC based on Decision 1232/QD-TTg dated August 17, 2017. This decision empowered SCIC with the ultimate managing capacity of approximately USD 478 million in state-owned capital (State Capital Investment Corporation, 2018). SCIC was specifically tasked to execute the sale of state capital, implying the government's stern intent to equitize some of its largest general corporations. SCIC's website also mentions restructuring of SCIC-linked companies, making investment decisions, raising capital, and providing other supporting services (State Capital Investment Corporation, 2014). It is unclear how this substantial restructuring will impact Vinatex's production and performance, although it is certain that Vinatex will wield less political and economic influences now that its investment and business activities are partially managed by a separate government institution. The analyses in the remaining sections and case studies focus on the institution and industry factors influencing Vinatex's performance until late 2018, when the last round of restructuring took place.

5.6.2 Institutional and policy structure of rent creation for Vinatex and the SOEs

Before November 2018, the institutions of rent creation and allocation were structured through two state agencies and one association: Vinatex, the MoIT, and VITAS. As an institutional instrument for the government, Vinatex performed two primary functions: to create social and economic policies and manage state assets. Given these roles, Vinatex held substantial influence over the government's policy agenda. It sought rents, market share, and political power (Fujita, 2017). Indeed, it could be argued that Vinatex was one of the most influential rent seekers in the industry. For example, of Vietnam's 12 powerful state-owned conglomerates – the general corporations[14] – under the supervision of the prime minister, Vinatex was said to be one of the most powerful, followed by Petro Vietnam (interview, VITAS representative, Ha Noi; June 2011).

What was the institutional process through which rents were created and allocated to Vinatex? Until the mid-2010s, the chairman and vice chairman of Vinatex also chaired and vice-chaired VITAS, the government think tank and policy advisor for the MoIT. There has been a slight change in this arrangement. In 2019, the chairmen and vice chairmen of Vinatex and VITAS are separate personnel. However, they are all ex-government appointees deeply connected to Vinatex. For example, the current chairman of VITAS, Vu Duc Giang, was the ex-chairman of Vinatex.[15] VITAS frequently acts as the go-between that connects T&G firms with the government. Because leaders of Vinatex frequently head VITAS, by default, VITAS regularly represents the voice and interests of Vinatex in consultations with the government on development policies and strategies (Fujita, 2017). In addition, the MoIT regularly holds meetings with both VITAS and Vinatex to gather industry updates and consultations. Based on policy recommendations from Vinatex and VITAS, the MoIT adjusts policies accordingly in implementing social programs, regulating state-owned firms, and overseeing state control over the industry (interviews, three Vinatex and VITAS representatives, Ha Noi and Ho Chi Minh City; June–September 2011).

As a state-owned and profit-oriented holding company, Vinatex also actively lobbied the government for rents. For example, when the global financial crisis was at its worst in early 2009, VITAS and Vinatex industry representatives requested government financial support for Vietnamese T&G exporters, given significant decline in the international market (Business Monitor International, 2009). Their argument was that the global crisis started in the United States, Vietnam's largest export market, and thus the immediate impact on the industry was severe. The former chairman of Vinatex and VITAS, Le Quoc An, was quoted in the local media suggesting the adoption of three emergency measures. First, the government was to provide USD 295 million to support bank credit for the industry and reduce interest rates considered to be too high at the time. Second, the government would allocate 1 percent of Vinatex's export earnings to assist SOEs facing falling orders and considering layoffs. Third, the government was to budget USD 2.9 million to support international sales and marketing promotions (Business Monitor International, 2009). In response to these requests, the government introduced new tax measures in April 2009 to stimulate domestic consumption, along with measures to support textile and garment firms, especially SOEs. Under the Ministry of Finance, the value-added tax rate was reduced by half for T&G enterprises as well as on a number of selected products. The tariff payment deadlines were extended on certain types of imports, and garment companies were exempted from some categories of income tax liabilities (Business Monitor International, 2009). Finally, interest rates were lowered from 15.78 percent in 2008 to 10.07 percent in 2009 (World Development Indicators, 2018).

Through Vinatex and the MoIT, the Vietnamese government provided the public sector with rents that could potentially support new investment in technology and learning. During the 1990s and the early 2000s, the government's implicit guarantee of SOE debt, as well as access to credit via state banks, gave SOEs easier access to credit than private enterprises (Knutsen & Nguyen, 2004; Thomsen, 2007). Additionally, SOEs that already possessed critical assets, such as land and equipment, had significant advantages over private firms because these resources could be used as collateral for bank loans at low interest rates. Finally, SOEs organized under Vinatex were provided with implicit rents to develop their industrial capabilities. These subsidiaries:

- Received financial cross-subsidization if the Vinatex management decided that particular plants required short-term capital support to sustain operation and competitiveness.
- Received training, market information, and management expertise from more successful plants under the Vinatex umbrella.
- Shared experiences and trading information to identify buyers in foreign markets.

(interviews, two VITAS representative and a Vinatex senior manager, Ha Noi and Ho Chi Minh City; June and October 2011)

Vinatex also used its market position to pass business opportunities on to subsidiaries. Data collected from Thomsen (2007) found that state institutions such as VITAS, Vinatex, and the MoIT commonly mediated contacts between foreign buyers and Vietnamese suppliers, and those who obtained orders through this system were more likely to be SOEs or state-connected private companies. Foreign buyers found it easier to go through the state system because they were provided assistance with finding suppliers and administrative procedures

(Thomsen, 2007). In short, preferential treatment by the government, including the provision of credit access, land, expertise, and information sharing, helped Vinatex and its SOEs correct a number of market failures while learning the international market.

5.6.3 Effects of competition on rent management

There were two factors at the industry level that created pressure on Vinatex and its subsidiaries to invest in learning and upgrading. The first was market competition in international and domestic markets, which pressured Vinatex to maintain good relationships with its international buyers. Globally, there has been severe competition among T&G manufacturers in a number of developing countries. *Danatex* reported: "The Vietnamese apparel and textile exporters are seeing difficulties because major importers are shifting their orders from Vietnam to Cambodia, Laos and Bangladesh in order to avoid [the] 10 per cent import duty since these countries are entitled to the Most Favored Nation status with zero import duty" ("Garment-textile export," 2013, p. 2). In addition, starting in the late 1990s, foreign textile and garment producers moved into Vietnam and competed with domestic producers in both Vietnamese and international markets. The intense competition forced Vinatex to focus on improving its production capability and competitiveness.

The second factor was that Vinatex actively competed with other state-owned general corporations for rents and political supports. The Vietnamese government's backing of Vinatex came with the implicit demand that Vinatex was to maintain competitive performance through investments in new capabilities and fulfill the state's social missions in job creation and employment stability (interviews, three industry experts, Ha Noi and Ho Chi Minh City; May, June, and October 2011). The nature of these goals and the government's clear expectations on performance implied that Vinatex must put in extra effort to use the government rents effectively, such as providing training programs to garment workers and trade information to subsidiaries.

5.6.4 The state sector: rent outcomes

This section assesses whether Vinatex used rents to acquire new technology, enhance learning, or increase upstream production of textiles. A Vinatex senior officer contended that there were a number of coordination and management failures at Vinatex, largely due to inexperience and poor planning, that constrained its ability to use rents productively. This officer noted that corruption and rent seeking for personal profits were prevalent in the state sector and within the Vinatex complex structure (interview, Ha Noi; June 2011). However, an economist and industry expert on the role of the state sector in the T&G industry and a professor at the National Economics University in Vietnam both pointed out that Vinatex was relatively more productive and capable overall than many other firms in the T&G industry. These industry experts maintained that when compared to other SOEs or general corporations in other industries, Vinatex was more effective in managing rents and boosting industrial capabilities among subsidiaries. For example, Vinatex owned a growing number of garment superstores in large cities that actively promoted the brands of its subsidiaries. Some of the best firms such as Viet Tien and Phong Phu not only produced high-quality garments for international retailers but were also respected brands among Vietnamese consumers (interviews, Ha Noi; April 2011).

Another approach to assess Vinatex's ability to manage rents is to compare its SOEs' efficiency with private sector manufacturers. In earlier research, Tran (1999) finds evidence that some SOEs under Vinatex were efficient in acquiring new technologies for industrial upgrading. The author attributed this quality to the management's ability to take advantage of market opportunities and devise business strategies suitable for learning.[16] Nguyen and Le (2005) conducted a survey of 96 textile and garment enterprises, finding evidence that "there is no operating profitability difference between state and private enterprise after adjusting the land rent and export quota rent difference" (p. 309). The study also finds that total productivity of state enterprises was higher than private enterprises but lower than foreign enterprises (Nguyen & Le, 2005).

Furthermore, there were inherent benefits to state ownership that Vinatex and SOEs received, which allowed for overall high performance. Knutsen and Nguyen (2004) point out that large and small foreign buyers tended to prefer collaboration with state enterprises due to their close relationship with the government and their ability to reduce administrative hassles (Knutsen & Nguyen, 2004). A buyer reported that Vietnamese state enterprises were fairly attractive business partners because "state enterprises also have more advanced technology in place" (Knutsen & Nguyen, 2004, p. 132). These findings are confirmed by the T&G experts I interviewed. According to a senior advisor at Vinatex, in the early 2010s, Vinatex subsidiaries attracted foreign investments via joint ventures and joint-stock companies, and thus, productivity improved substantially among a number of subsidiaries (interview, Ho Chi Minh City; October 2011). Finally, in 2015, Fujita (2017) reports that 34 of the 50 largest garment exporters in Vietnam are foreign-invested enterprises, and only six Vinatex members are on the top-50 list; "[h]owever, Vinatex's three largest associated companies are ranked first, fifth, and ninth, respectively, among all garment exporters in the country" (p. 18). Thus, the data suggest some Vinatex subsidiaries are globally competitive, even with the increasing dominance of foreign investors in the industry.

Dinh Vu Polyester Fiber project

Despite the positive evaluations and evidence showing substantial development of the state sector in the T&G industry in the earlier period, in the mid-2010s, Vinatex was wrapped in Dinh Vu's scandal of mismanagement and corruption. In 2005, Prime Minister Phan Van Khai issued Decision 343/2005/QD-TTg for the Development of the Chemical Industry in Vietnam. Based on the Decision, a joint agreement was signed in 2007 to develop the Dinh Vu fiber manufacturing plant between two state-owned general corporations, PetroVietnam and Vinatex (PVTEX, 2016). The initial investment comprised 23 investors with Petro Vietnam and Vinatex holding the largest shares (PVTEX, 2016). The agreement's objective was to increase fiber and yarn production in Vietnam by 40 percent and reduce garment-producer dependence on imported materials. In 2014, Vietnamese producers consumed roughly 400,000 metric tons of polyester fiber and yarn. They imported approximately 246,000 metric tons of these materials (roughly 61.5 percent of the total consumption), mostly from China, Taiwan, Thailand, and South Korea (Mai, 2015). The cooperation agreement between PetroVietnam and Vinatex stated that production from the Dinh Vu fiber manufacturing plant would reduce Vietnam's reliance on imported fiber by 30–40 percent and increase the local content of Vietnamese-made garments ("Inaccurate study leads to trouble," 2015).

In 2008, the Dinh Vu Joint Stock Company (PVTEX) was established and jointly owned by Vinatex, PetroVietnam, and some of their subsidiaries to execute the agreement. In 2009, construction for the largest textile fiber plant in Vietnam began in Ha Phong, a major port city. PVTEX invested approximately USD 346.7 million toward the construction and importation of technology from Germany and Switzerland ("Inaccurate study leads to trouble," 2015). The manufacturing plant was designed to utilize filtered oil and other chemical materials from PetroVietnam's oil refinery plant in Dung Quat to produce polyester fiber on-site ("PVTex – Từ "Con Cưng" Của Tập Đoàn Dầu Khí," 2016).

PVTEX began trial production in 2013 and immediately suffered losses of USD 17.38 million ("PVTex – Từ "Con Cưng" Của Tập Đoàn Dầu Khí," 2016). In 2014, PVTEX started large-scale production for commercial sales and reported financial losses of USD 51.42 million. In 2015, PVTEX stopped its operation twice and produced less than 50 percent of its production capacity. Its financial losses increased, amounting to USD 62.19 million ("PVTex – Từ "Con Cưng" Của Tập Đoàn Dầu Khí," 2016). Although the manufacturing plant was designed to produce 175,000 tons of fiber and yarn per year, in 2015, PVTEX produced only 32,000 metric tons and was able to sell just 23,000 metric tons in the Vietnamese market (Mai, 2015). *Tuoi Tre News* reported that PVTEX's fiber and yarn were more expensive than those imported from abroad ("Inaccurate study leads to trouble," 2015). More importantly, buyers told the newspaper that their products had low and inconsistent quality ("Inaccurate study leads to trouble," 2015).

Considering PVTEX's substantial losses, mounting debts, and frequent stalls in operation, in 2016, the Vietnamese government investigated PVTEX's operation and financial records. State investigators concluded that there were a number of regulation violations and instances of mismanagement, causing severe financial losses to the state ("PVTex – Từ "Con Cưng" Của Tập Đoàn Dầu Khí," 2016). In November 2016, the former CEO of PVTEX, Vu Dinh Duy, who managed the company from 2009 to 2014, disappeared before the MoIT suspended his official appointment at PetroVietnam. At the end of 2016, the media reported that the manufacturing plant had ceased operations, and PVTEX was unable to repay its debts of USD 236 million in long-term loans and USD 75.4 million in short-term loans (Bui, Bach, & Dao, 2016). The MoIT said that without any new government financial support, the company could go bankrupt in the near future (Bui et al., 2016). The dream of industrializing and developing the textile industry was once again shattered through weak state capacity, mismanagement of state investment, and corruption.[17]

5.6.5 Case study summary

In conclusion, the government's preferential treatment of SOEs in the form of privileged access to land, credit, state investment fund, and quotas helped them invest and upgrade. Indeed, Vinatex is as productive and profitable as private firms, even when government rents are discounted (Nguyen & Le, 2005). Some Vinatex subsidiaries are also globally competitive, especially against foreign firms

Table 5.7 DRMA Summary for Case Study on the State Sector and Vinatex

Step 1: Political Context	• Political will to maintain social programs and political stability and to retain economic profits forced Vinatex's restructuring and performance **Type of rent:** • Learning rents created through state investment fund and policies promoting vertical integration between textile and garment sectors • Land, credit access, and equipment allocation to SOEs • Commercial opportunities channeled through state agencies and VITAS, such as connecting foreign buyers with Vinatex subsidiaries
Step 2: Institution Structure	• MoIT and Vinatex are government institutional instruments to manage the T&G sector • Vinatex sought and received government rents (land, credit access, preferential tax treatment) for its subsidiaries • Vinatex channeled rents across its subsidies (via expertise and information sharing, coordinating foreign investment, allocating business opportunities and state resources) • Weak monitoring and oversight of large state investment project such as Dinh Vu Polyester Fiber project
Step 3: Market and Industry Structures	• Competition among firms for market profits led to incentives and pressures on Vinatex for performance effort • Competition with other general corporations pressured Vinatex to maintain rents and rent seeking through capability development • Vinatex complex structure reduced its oversight on state investment among subsidiaries
Step 4: Rent Outcomes (mixed)	• Development of new capability, especially in garment production as well as domestic design, branding, and marketing • Evidence suggesting large- and small-scale rent seeking led to inefficiencies and waste of state resources

operating in Vietnam (Fujita, 2017). Despite the MoIT's weak rent management capability, as described in the quota period and in the Dinh Vu Polyester Fiber project, Vinatex has been a positive factor in moving its SOEs toward upgrading. This outcome can be explained in terms of competition within the market and among the general corporations. Effective pressure on Vinatex and its SOEs forced the efforts to increase profits, not only for moneymaking purposes, but to retain their rents and rent-seeking power within the state.

The failure of the Dinh Vu Polyester Fiber project (similar to the Quota period) highlights important aspects of industrial development in the T&G industry. First, there were complex and pervasive rent-seeking activities among government agencies, SOEs, and private producers, which weakened the state's capacity to effectively implement industrial policies. Second, the government's heavy reliance on state-owned conglomerates to execute large-scale industrial projects proved, at times, fatal. The lack of supervision and discipline mechanisms led to intentional violations of the law and mismanagement of state investment. The result was timid development in the T&G industry, largely driven by comparative advantage in low-skilled labor and heavy reliance on imported inputs such as textiles and accessories. This final case study of Vinatex and the public sector in the T&G industry, at large, demonstrates that rent creation and rent seeking may produce a mixture of developmental and redistributive outcomes. Vinatex is an illustration of such opposing forces that together limit the long-term industrialization and growth of the industry. The rent-management mechanism in the industrial development of the state sector is summarized in Table 5.7.

5.7 Observations and policy considerations

The heart of a viable industrial policy in developing countries is to develop large domestic firms that are globally competitive and technologically competent and address market failures that constrain development of these domestic firms (Khan, 2009). This chapter assessed the factors affecting learning experience in Vietnam's textile and garment industry and how that experience led to industrial development and capability building among domestic firms. The chapter also analyzed the political, institutional, and industry factors that explain the high and low levels of effort to improve competitiveness in the presence of rents and rent-seeking activities since the economic reform.

Vietnam's T&G industry is unique, as the rent-management configuration produced *mixed outcomes* in development. From the perspective of technical learning, industrial upgrade within the garment sector has been largely limited to low-skilled manufacturing and measured success in local branding and marketing. Unlike the telecom industry, T&G was quickly opened up to private investment, especially FDI. Given severe competition, domestic producers have been slow to move up the value chain, enhance value added to their production, or engage in vertical integration. The market structure included deep state involvement, forcing private and state-owned firms to compete for economic profits, leading to a great deal of competition among players in local and international markets and between the public and private sectors. The intense market competition forced effective rent management for learning and upgrading, although notable constraints and mismanagement held back greater industry development. The DRMA framework provides five observations regarding the process of technical upgrade and capability building for the textile and garment industry.

First, the industry has achieved some success in industrial development, although some of the major factors that allowed this to happen – namely, international market expansion and foreign capital – are no longer readily available due to changes in international markets. Cambodia, Laos, and Bangladesh, for example, compete aggressively with Vietnam in the global market. As well, they have the advantage of the Most Favored Nation status, which gives them zero import duty access to large markets such as the United States and the European Union. Second, there has been strong state support in the development of Vinatex and its SOEs. The government's aim of social and economic development through job creation, retention, and by addressing poverty in certain rural and mountainous areas explains state provision of rents and political support to SOEs to carry out these missions. Therefore, there has been clear political will to support Vinatex and its subsidiaries to expand and upgrade, provided they fulfill these missions and that government supports do not violate WTO rules. Political will created a stable macropolitical context for the dominance of the state sector during the 1990s–2010s period.

Third, the MoIT, which is in charge of managing the sector, primarily favored SOEs and state-connected enterprises. In addition, as evident in the quota period and the Dinh Vu Polyester Fiber project, the MoIT's lack of discipline and oversight led to damaging rent-seeking activities and redistribution of state resources. As SOEs gradually equitize, the role of the MoIT is broadening to support the private sector and oversee industry performance. However, the MoIT continues to depend on VITAS and Vinatex for policy advice and strategic vision. This relationship creates conflicts of interest and possible negative effects for private firms, because Vinatex's subsidiaries regularly compete with them in domestic and international markets. Fourth, Vinatex remains a dominant industry player and rent seeker. After being restructured in 2006 as one of the 12 general corporations, Vinatex plays a number of roles – manager of state assets, provider of economic and social benefits, industry advisor to MoIT, and market player and rent seeker in the industry. It used its close government connections to access important rents and deployed them to improve the sector's overall performance. Under Vinatex, the industry expanded and industrialized; however, corruption and rent seeking severely undermined the development of firms. Thus, an important policy question is how to better manage Vinatex to boost its productivity and value added, while allowing for the development of the private firms across different subsectors.

Finally, since Vietnam's accession to the WTO, the textile and garment industry has expanded quickly by volume but has struggled to move up the value chain. Khan (2009) argues that free trade agreements can create favorable rents, so long as other developing country exporters do not have free market access. By the time Vietnam became a WTO member in 2007, major competitors like China and India were already members, so membership did not offer substantial extra rents for Vietnam's textile and garment industry. In addition, there was less policy space to promote industrialization. As a member of the WTO, Vietnam could not use industrial policy or direct subsidies in the ways that the Asian Tigers did during their development. A VITAS senior advisor explained that Vietnam's commitment to the WTO and other mega-regionals such as the Trans-Pacific Partnership meant that the state largely left the industry to market mechanisms (interview, Ho Chi Minh City; October 2011). It will be even more challenging for Vietnam to maintain its export performance and increase employment amid fierce competition with international markets and the emergence of other developing countries. Unless Vietnamese garment producers move up the value chain, they will be under pressure to reduce prices, which will cut profits and opportunities to create new productive value in manufacturing.

5.7.1 Policy options for the industry's development

The analyses in this chapter suggest five policy directions to support the development of the industry over the next few decades. Vietnam missed opportunities to boost its competitiveness in the textile sector by allowing large quantities of cheap Chinese imports into the country during the crucial period of the industry's development: from the 1990s to 2015. However, Vietnam cannot afford to write off its textile sector. My first suggestion is to adopt *strategic policies* to raise the textile sector's competitiveness. It may be difficult to use local content requirements today, but it is possible to achieve higher domestic content in the future by developing an integrated strategy in which incentives are created for domestic textile producers to manufacture and participate in niche markets. Here, a comprehensive approach would involve upgrading equipment, relevant technologies and skilled labor, and improving output quality while maintaining competitive prices. This approach requires the Vietnamese government to play an active role in easing constraints in the credit market, increasing access to land, transferring new advanced technologies, boosting technical training for the labor force, and encouraging private investment in technical training and technology transfer. The incentives and rents offered would have to be managed carefully to ensure that performance conditions are imposed and enforced in order that local producers step up their efforts and damaging rent seeking does not derail these specific strategies. From this perspective, the government also needs to strengthen MoIT's supervision and implementation capability.

Second, the textile sector would benefit from rigorous market research to find niche markets for domestic textile production. Targeting specific niche markets may allow Vietnamese firms to develop capabilities through learning without head-to-head competition with China. Vinatex and VITAS are currently managing three research institutes charged with market research and design.

These research institutes should be given specific tasks: (1) research niche textile markets based on fashion trends in the domestic and global markets, (2) analyze and suggest the type of technology required to perform competitive production for these textile materials, and (3) develop production processes for these niche products. While Vinatex's primary objective is to support its subsidiaries, VITAS should make available research findings on market insights, technologies, and production development to all Vietnamese producers – including private ones – so these firms do not lose ground to the public sector.

Third, there must be specific mechanisms to ensure SOEs' performance, particularly in technological upgrade and enhancing value addition. They continue to have privileged access to land and capital, so the government, via the MoIT and Vinatex, must adopt strategies to reform inefficient or failing SOEs by either equitizing them or merging them with more capable firms. This will allow state resources to be channeled to more efficient enterprises. Further, Vinatex should focus on improving the capability of its subsidiaries in various stages of the value chain, not just in garment production. The general corporation should aim particularly at improving textiles production (second stage), packaging and shipping (fourth stage), and branding, marketing and sales (fifth stage). This does not imply allocating more rents for Vinatex, but it does require improving the *institutional monitoring and enforcing of conditions associated with existing rents.*

Fourth, if the government decides to use rents more aggressively for learning and industrialization, then additional institutional mechanisms are needed to link rent allocation to the achievement of particular investment, production and quality objectives, and technology acquisition. Currently, Vinatex's performance is motivated by competition in the market and with other general corporations and by the desire to reinforce its political and economic power. Both of these competitive pressures may change in ways that fail to push Vinatex toward industrial development in the next decades. Therefore, the MoIT must ensure that Vinatex uses rent effectively to carry out its responsibilities as the primary driver of the industry's industrialization and provider of jobs and opportunities for the impoverished regions of the country.

Finally, neither VITAS nor AGTEK have effectively performed as intermediaries between the state, buyers, investors, and local firms or as the industry's overall watchdogs of rent management. There is an urgent need for more neutral, even-handed, and capable associations than the current version of VITAS to act as the intermediary between government agencies and all domestic firms. The role of VITAS must go beyond supporting Vinatex and its subsidiaries. The first step toward this reorientation must be that VITAS, AGTEK, and other relevant associations are empowered to challenge (1) the MoIT's rent policies, and their implementations, as well as (2) Vinatex if it engages in unfair business practices against domestic producers. Next, VITAS and AGTEK should serve as communication channels between the government and domestic firms regarding new government policies, market constraints, new market access, and opportunities abroad. By doing this, coordination failures between firms and the state could be addressed and improved. On the issue of coordination, Vietnam could learn from the successful model used by the Taiwan Textile Federation (Weiss, 1995). In the context of diminishing policy space, it is ever more critical that the Vietnamese government employ (and actively enforce) strategic and concerted industrial policies that remove negative market externalities, provide incentives, and impose performance conditions to ensure continuous and long-term competitiveness in the T&G industry. Without building a stronger industrial capability of local firms, Vietnam could be trapped in low value-added exports and chronic trade deficits that will severely hinder its economic growth and development.

Notes

1 If the data source or newspaper provided the data in USD, I reported the same value as shown in the source. However, if VND was used in the data or in interviews, I converted the value to USD using the exchange rate of USD 1 = VND 21,000.

2 In this book, the textile sector refers to weaving, spinning, dyeing, and finishing (the upstream subsectors), and the garment sector refers to clothing and apparel manufacturing (downstream subsectors).

3 There are two types of SOEs in Vietnam: one is managed by the central government and the corresponding ministry to the industry; the other is provincial and managed by the local city or province government.

4 In Vietnam, a state-owned shareholding company represents the state and is responsible for managing the state's funds in the industry.

5 While the data include both textile and garment exports, garment production has always been the driving force of the industry exports, making up 70 percent of the industry overall capacity.

6 A seller can use a Letter of Credit as collateral for loans. It also guarantees that a shipment from the seller to the buyer will be delivered on time and for the correct amount.

7 The borrowing rates gradually declined since 2011. In 2017, the interest rate was 7.4 percent (World Development Indicators, 2018).

8 Indirect exporting occurs when foreign investors use their own textiles manufactured in Vietnam as materials for their garment production. This process reduces transaction costs.

9 The MFA quota restriction ended January 1, 2005, for all WTO members. However, Vietnam did not join the WTO until 2007, so the U.S. MFA quota applied to Vietnamese exporters until 2006.

10 The Ministry of Commerce and the Ministry of Industry were the predecessors to the present-day MoIT.

11 Author translation.

12 The owner of A Chau was also prosecuted and found guilty of bribery.

13 The lowland area of Vietnam is occupied mostly by the Kinh ethnic group, which has majority control of economic activities, political power, and policymaking in the government. This is in contrast with ethnic minorities living in the Vietnamese uplands.

14 Some of these general corporations have been transformed into state economic groups, such as Viettel.

15 As of 2017, the chairman of Vinatex is no longer appointed by the Vietnamese government; however, a closer examination of the profiles of the chairman and vice chairman reveals that they are both ex-government appointees. The same holds for the VITAS chairman and vice chairman. Because the VITAS current chairman was ex-chairman of Vinatex, these two state institutions continue to have an extremely close relationship.

16 It remains difficult to quantify Vinatex and its subsidiaries' levels of effort in raising productivity in the presence of rents, yet interviewees observed that the apparent success of some T&G producers was partly due to rents the SOEs received.

17 A major restructuring of PVTEX took place in 2017 and 2018, with a new managing board and foreign investment from Fortrec Chemical and Reliance PTE as well as some local textile and garment producers such as An Phat Holdings Joint Stock Company. PVTEX resumed production in 2018 starting with just three production lines. The new managers announced at the end of 2018 that PVTEX aims to run 15–20 of its production lines in 2019 (Tran, 2019).

References

Akter, A. (2018, February 3). Vietnamese textile and apparel industry moving towards US$50 billion by 2020. *Textile Today*. Retrieved from www.textiletoday.com.bd/vietnamese-textile-apparel-industry-moving-towards-us50-billion-2020/

Bland, B. (2012, May 29). Vietnam: China smuggling surges. *Financial Times*. Retrieved from www.ft.com/cms/s/0/e3bc38a8-9a8d-11e1-9c98-00144feabdc0.html#axzz2VCqM8Jud

Bui, H. N., Bach, D., & Dao, T. (2016, March 31). State-owned $325-million fiber plant on verge of bankruptcy. *VnExpress*. Retrieved from http://e.vnexpress.net/news/business/state-owned-325-million-fiber-plant-on-verge-of-bankruptcy-3379183.html

Buisman, L., & Wielenga, G. J. (2008). *Textile and garment industry in Vietnam: Research on garment producers in Vietnam*. Retrieved from University of Groningen, Faculty of Economics and Business.

Business Monitor International. (2009). *Vietnam textile and clothing report Q3 2009* (Industry Report). Retrieved from Business Monitor International.

Chan, Y. W. (2013). *Vietnamese-Chinese relationships at the borderlands: Trade, tourism and cultural politics*. New York, NY: Routledge.

Chen, A. (2015, July 21). What China: Vietnam trade balance figures miss, misstate and mask. *China Economic Review*. Retrieved from www.chinaeconomicreview.com/what-china-vietnam-trade-balance-figures-miss-misstate-mask

China General Administration of Customs. (2019). *China: Imports and exports by country*. Retrieved from CEIC https://www.ceicdata.com/en

Cong-Minh. (2006, December 9). De Xuat Xu Ly Bo Truong Truong Dinh Tuyen [Recommendation to discipline minister Truong Dinh Tuyen]. *Viet Bao*. Retrieved from http://vietbao.vn/Xa-hoi/De-xuat-xu-ly-Bo-truong-Truong-Dinh-Tuyen/30101043/157/

Đứng đầu Bộ Thương Mại, tôi chịu trách nhiệm về sai phạm [As the head of Ministry of Commerce, I take responsibility for the misconduct]. (2004, December 1). *Viet Bao*. Retrieved from http://vietbao.vn/Chinh-Tri/Dung-dau-Bo-Thuong-mai-toi-chiu-trach-nhiem-ve-sai-pham/20351663/73/

Endres, K. (2014). Making law: Small-scale trade and corrupt exceptions at the Vietnam-China Border. *American Anthropologist, 116*(3), 611–625.

Eyler, B. (2014, July 9). The coming downturn of China: Vietnam trade relations. *East by Southeast*. Retrieved from www.eastbysoutheast.com/fear-change-future-china-vietnam-trade-relations/

Fair Wear Foundation. (2015). *Vietnam: Country study 2015*. Retrieved from www.fairwear.org

FDI firms expand in local textile-garment sector. (2018, December 24). *Viet Nam News*. Retrieved from https://vietnamnews.vn/economy/482288/fdi-firms-expand-in-local-textile-garment-sector.html#Z4u6AJSyJttoZTU0.97

Fujita, M. (2017). *Vietnam's textile-garment industry hopes for breakthroughs in 2019* (RIETI Discussion Paper Series 17-E-121). The Research Institute of Economy, Trade and Industry. Retrieved from https://ideas.repec.org/p/eti/dpaper/17121.html

Garment and textile industry on course to conquer domestic market. (2019, March 24). *Nhan Dan Online*. Retrieved from https://en.nhandan.com.vn/business/item/7279202-garment-and-textile-industry-on-course-to-conquer-domestic-market.html

Garment-textile export: Lofty expectations for 2013. (2013, April 4). *Danatex*. Retrieved from http://danatex.com.vn/

General Department of Vietnam Customs. (2012). *2011 customs statistics*. Ha Noi: Information Technology and Statistics Deparment.

General Department of Vietnam Customs. (2013). *2012 customs statistics*. Ha Noi: Information Technology and Statistics Deparment.

General Department of Vietnam Customs. (2014). *2013 customs statistics*. Ha Noi: Information Technology and Statistics Deparment.

General Department of Vietnam Customs. (2017). *2016 customs statistics*. Ha Noi: Information Technology and Statistics Deparment.

General Department of Vietnam Customs. (2018). *2017 customs statistics*. Ha Noi: Information Technology and Statistics Deparment.

Gu, X., & Womack, B. (2000). Border cooperation between China and Vietnam in the 1990s. *Asian Survey*, *40*(6), 1042–1058.

Ha, T. (2012). *Upgrading in the global apparel value chain to improve the competitiveness of Vietnam's garment industry* (Masters Thesis). Leeds Metropolitan University, Ho Chi Minh City, Vietnam.

Hai, N. V. (2004, November 20). Ông Mai Văn Dâu đã "lợi dụng chức quyền" như thế nào? [How Mr. Mai Van Dau abused his authority?]. *Viet Bao*. Retrieved from http://vietbao.vn/Xa-hoi/Ong-Mai-Van-Dau-da-loi-dung-chuc-quyen-nhu-the-nao/40056559/157/

Hill, H. (1998). *Vietnam textile and garment industry: Notable achievement, future challenges* (Medium-term industry strategy project, research report for the Vietnam industrial competitiveness review). Ministry of Planning and Investment, Development Strategy Institute in Vietnam, and United Nations Industrial Development Organization. Retrieved from https://pdfs.semanticscholar.org/387f/9c8f4b2e5ae2e384998c76366612e355df1e.pdf

IBM Belgium, DMI, Ticon, & TAC. (2009). *Economic integration and Vietnam's development*. Retrieved from European Union-MUTRAP.

Inaccurate study leads to trouble for Vietnam's $325mn yarn plant. (2015, October 19). *Tuoi Tre News*. Retrieved from http://tuoitrenews.vn/business/31059/inaccurate-study-leads-to-trouble-for-vietnams-325mn-yarn-plant

Ives, M. (2015, June 25). When Vietnam and China bicker, traders on the border feel the bluster. *New York Times*. Retrieved from www.nytimes.com/2015/06/26/world/asia/when-vietnam-and-china-bicker-traders-on-the-border-feel-the-bluster.html

Khan, M. H. (2009, November). *Pro-growth anti-corruption and governance reforms for Vietnam: Lessons from East Asia* (Policy Discussion Paper). United Nations Development Programme Vietnam. Retrieved from https://eprints.soas.ac.uk/9922/1/Vietnam_Anti-Corruption_Governance_Mushtaq_H_Khan.pdf

Knutsen, H. M., & Nguyen, C. M. (2004). Preferential treatment in a transition economy: The case of state-owned enterprises in the textile and garment industry in Vietnam. *Norwegian Journal of Geography*, *58*, 125–135.

Le, A. Q. (2011, February). *The Viet Nam textile and garment industry develops with the market liberalization strategy of Vietnamese government*. Presentation in Ho Chi Minh City. Retrieved from Vietnam Textile and Apparel Association.

Mai, C. T. (2015, October 19). Nhà máy 7.000 tỉ đồng . . . "đắp chiếu" [7,000 trillion VND factory . . . "covered in sedge blanket"]. *Tuoi Tre News*. Retrieved from http://tuoitre.vn/tin/kinh-te/20151019/nha-may-7000-ti-dong-dap-chieu/987400.html

Martin, M. F. (2008). *U.S. clothing imports from Vietnam: Trade policies and performance* (CRS Report for Congress, Report No. RL34262). Retrieved from U.S. Foreign Affairs, Defense, and Trade Division www.policyarchive.org/handle/10207/bitstreams/19493.pdf

Ngo, C. N. (2017). Industrial development, liberalisation and impacts of Vietnam-China border trade. *European Journal of East Asian Studies, 16*, 154–184.

Ngo, C. N., & Chi, M. (2017). *Differentials in market constraints and value addition among micro, small, and medium enterprises in Viet Nam.* Retrieved from United Nations University World Institute for Development Economics Research www.wider.unu.edu/publication/differentials-market-constraints-and-value-addition-among-micro-small-and-medium

Nguyen, C. M., & Le, Q. V. (2005). Institutional constraints and private sector development: The textile and garment industry in Vietnam. *ASEAN Economic Bulletin, 22*(3), 297–313.

Nguyen, N. (2015, February 13). Vinatex plans $441m investment after IPO. *Deal Street Asia.* Retrieved from www.dealstreetasia.com/stories/vinatex-plans-441m-investment-ipo-3018/

Nieuwoudt, T. (2009, October 6). Vietnam's textile industry: Opportunities and challenges. *Ezine@Articles.* Retrieved from http://ezinearticles.com/?Vietnams-Textile-Industry-Opportunities-and-Challenges&id=3041691

Phi, T., Tran, A., & Trinh, M. (2014). *The development of the vietnamese garment industry from the viewpoint of rent management theory* (UNDP Technical Paper for Human Development Report). United Nations Development Programme, Ha Noi.

Phuoc-Vinh. (2004, December 1). Biến động giá cả, vụ tiêu cực quota: điểm nóng chất vấn [Questioning the hot spots: Price fluctuation, and unjust quota affair]. *Viet Bao.* Retrieved from http://vietbao.vn/Xa-hoi/Bien-dong-gia-ca-vu-tieu-cuc-quota-diem-nong-chat-van/40058097/157/

Prime minister okays restructuring plan for Vinatex, Vinacomin. (2013, February 23). *Hanoi Times.* Retrieved from www.hanoitimes.vn/economy/industry/2013/02/81e0694b/pm-okays-restructuring-plan-for-vinatex-vinacomin/

PVTEX. (2016). *History of foundation and development.* Retrieved from www.pvtex-dv.vn/

PVTex – từ "con cưng" của Tập Doàn Dầu Khí đến thua lỗ hơn 3.000 tỷ, Thanh tra chỉ ra hàng loạt sai phạm [PVTex: From being a favoured child of PetroVietnam to losses of over USD 144 million, investors pointed out a number of violations]. (2016, April 11). *VNMedia.* Retrieved from www.vnmedia.vn/thi-truong/201611/pvtex-tu-con-cung-cua-tap-doan-dau-khi-den-thua-lo-hon-3000-ty-546371/

Red flag rising over Vietnam: China illegal cross-border trade. (2015, June 29). *Voice of Vietnam.* Retrieved from http://english.vov.vn/Economy/Trade/Red-flag-rising-over-VietnamChina-illegal-crossborder-trade/295618.vov

Reports about Vietnam-China trade have conflicting figures. (2015, June 8). *Vietnam Net.* Retrieved from https://english.vietnamnet.vn/fms/business/132556/reports-about-vietnam-china-trade-have-conflicting-figures.html

Schaumburg-Muller, H. (2009). Garment exports from Vietnam: Changes in supplier strategies. *Journal of the Asia Pacific Economy, 14*(2), 162–171.

Schoenberger, L., & Turner, S. (2008). Negotiating remote borderland access: Small-scale trade on Vietnam-China Border. *Development and Change, 39*(4), 667–696.

State Capital Investment Corporation. (2014). *About us: Operations.* Retrieved from www.scic.vn/english/index.php/intro/11-introduction/linh-vu-hoat-dong.html

State Capital Investment Corporation. (2018, November 26). *SCIC receives the transfer of state ownership rights at Vinatex from the Ministry of Industry and Trade.* Retrieved from www.scic.vn/english/index.php/thong-tin-bao-chi/307-scic-receives-the-transfer-of-state-ownership-rights-at-vinatex-from-the-ministry-of-industry-and-trade.html

Tan-Toi. (2011, July 13). Vinatex đầu tư 50 tỷ đồng "cứu" Đại Cát Tường [Vinatex invested VND 40 trillion to "Rescue" Dai Cat Tuong]. *Bao Tin Tuc*. Retrieved from http://baotintuc.vn/doanh-nghiep/vinatex-dau-tu-50-ty-dong-cuu-dai-cat-tuong-20110712193445405.htm

Thoburn, J. (2007). Vietnam and the end of the multi-fibre arrangement: A preliminary view. *Journal of International Cooperation Studies, 15*(1), 93–107.

Thomsen, L. (2007). Accessing global value chains? The role of business-state relations in the private clothing industry in Vietnam. *Journal of Economic Geography*, 7(6), 753–776.

Tran, A. N. (2012). Vietnamese textile and garment industry in the global supply chain: State strategies and workers' responses. *Institutions and Economics*, *4*(3), 123–150.

Tran, C. N. (1999). *Technological capability and learning in firms: Vietnamese industries in transition*. Aldershot: Ashgate Publishing, Ltd.

Tran, M. (2019, January 31). Tổng kết năm 2018 PVTEX có những chuyển biến tích cực [Closing 2018: PVTEX experienced some positive changes]. *PVTEX*. Retrieved from pvtex.com.vn/

Tung-Duy. (2004, October 10). Them nhieu quan chuc Bo Thuong Mai "dinh" vu chay quota [Many more government officials in the Ministry of Commerce "involved" in quota bribery]. *Viet Bao*. Retrieved from http://pda.vietbao.vn/An-ninh-Phap-luat/Them-nhieu-quan-chuc-Bo-TM-dinh-vu-chay-quota/20333483/218/

Turner, S. (2015). Borderlands and border Narratives: A longitudinal study of challenges and opportunities for local traders shaped by the Sino-Vietnamese Border. *Journal of Global History*, *5*, 265–287.

Van-Thanh. (2004, September 19). Quota Det May Ai Ban Ai Mua? [Textile-garment's quota: Who is buying and who is selling?]. *VnExpress*. Retrieved from https://vnexpress.net/kinh-doanh/quota-det-may-ai-ban-ai-mua-2675776.html

Vietnam's textile-garment industry hopes for breakthroughs in 2019. (2019, January 14). *Vietnam Plus*. Retrieved from US-ASEAN Business Council, Inc. website www.usasean.org/council-in-the-news/2019/01/16/vietnam%E2%80%99s-textile-garment-industry-hopes-breakthroughs-2019

Vinatex. (2019). *Organization chart*. Retrieved from https://vinatex.com.vn/so-do-to-chuc/

Vinatex raises $58 million in IPO. (2014, September 28). *AmCham Vietnam*. Retrieved from www.amchamvietnam.com/vinatex-raises-58-million-in-ipo/

Vinatex summarizes its business performance in 2017 and plans for 2018 (2018, January 20). *VitaJean*. Retrieved from http://vitajeans.com/news/industry-news/vinatex-summarizes-its-business-performance-in-2017-and-plans-for-2018-106.html

Vo, K. T. (2015). *Vietnam: Cotton and products annual commodity report* (GAIN Report: VM5018). Retrieved from USDA Foreign Agriculture Service website http://gain.fas.usda.gov/Recent%20GAIN%20Publications/Cotton%20and%20Products%20Annual_Hanoi_Vietnam_3-27-2015.pdf

Vo, K. T., & Francic, M. (2018). *Vietnam: Cotton and products annual commodity report 2018* (GAIN Report Number: VM8020). Retrieved from USDA Foreign Agricultural Service website https://gain.fas.usda.gov/Recent%20GAIN%20Publications/Cotton%20and%20Products%20Annual_Hanoi_Vietnam_4-13-2018.pdf

Weiss, L. (1995). Governed interdependence: Rethinking the government-business relationship in East Asia. *The Pacific Review*, *8*(4), 589–616.

Womack, B. (1994). Sino-Vietnamese Border trade: The edge of normalization. *Asian Survey*, *34*(6), 495–512.

World Bank. (2013). *Data, lending interest rate, Vietnam* (Online Data Bank). Retrieved from http://data.worldbank.org/indicator/FR.INR.LEND

World Development Indicators. (2018). *Vietnam*. Retrieved from The World Bank https://data.worldbank.org/country/vietnam?view=chart

6 The motorcycle industry

The triangular rent-seeking relationship among Vietnam, Japan, and China

6.1 Introduction

This chapter analyzes the industrial development of the motorcycle industry in Vietnam from the mid-1990s to the early 2010s. The motorcycle industry was one of the first industries chosen as a strategic foundation for Vietnam's economic development. The Vietnamese government's strategy was to attract foreign investment while simultaneously nurturing the infant industry through import-substituting and export-promoting policies. Due to these efforts, the industry achieved a number of important milestones beginning in the mid-1990s. Prior to 2005, the motorcycle industry accounted for 3.1 percent of the total industrial production value of the country; by 2007, it grew to 23.9 percent (Ministry of Industry and Trade, 2007). After a decade of development, major foreign motorcycle makers in Vietnam established dominance, not only in the Vietnamese market but all across Asia. Beginning in 2010, they began exporting production surplus to other markets, marking a major turn of the industry – from an importing to an exporting industry. In 2018, Vietnam exported USD 408.5 million worth of motorcycles, making up to 1.5 percent of the global share (Workman, 2019).[1] The country, therefore, ranked 14th in the world for its export volume of motorcycles. Of this USD 408.5 million export value, the net export for motorcycles was USD 73.5 million, contributing to the country's export profile and growth (Workman, 2019). As foreign manufacturers established their production and supply networks, by the early 2010s, the local content ratio (percentage of domestic parts in each motorcycle) reached between 70 and 95 percent (Quoc-Hung, 2012) and remained consistently high into 2019. Although the local content percentage is high, components are largely supplied by foreign firms producing in Vietnam, not Vietnamese manufacturing firms.

The motorcycle industry provides an exemplary case study of industrial upgrading driven predominantly by foreign direct investment (FDI) starting in the early 1990s. It also offers an example of how market competition among foreign manufacturers led to significant technical learning and capacity building for local firms, despite the Vietnamese government's failure to effectively monitor rents and implement rent policies. The rent-management analyses provided in the case studies suggest that, first, market opening and free trade do not automatically provide channels for technology transfers and upgrade from advanced lead firms[2] to local firms, as prescribed by neoclassical economics (see Case Study 1). Second, in the absence of state pressure to transfer technology and know-how to domestic firms, multinational corporations (MNCs) dominate the production network and capture rents rather than provide industrial upgrade for domestic firms (Case Study 1). The case studies also illustrate the complexity and difficulty of state interventions in encouraging technological spillover from foreign lead firms to local firms (Case Study 2). This is not to dismiss the role of the state in industrial development, but rather to highlight the complexity of such a process and to inform challenges associated with economic development from the industrialization perspective.

It should be noted that firms operating in the motorcycle industry are also part of the supporting industries in Vietnam. For example, many motorcycle industry suppliers also supply components to related industries. Thus, government documents and secondary data often refer to the motorcycle industry as one of the supporting industries, which traditionally imply mechanical and electronic industries. For example, in Decision No. 12/2001/TD-TTg (Decision 12), the Vietnamese government identifies five supporting industries: (1) textile and garment, (2) leather and footwear, (3) electronics, (4) automobile and motorcycle production, and (5) mechanical manufacturing. This chapter focuses on the industrial development of the motorcycle industry, although it also references supporting industries.

The rest of the chapter is organized as follows. Section 6.2 provides background on the motorcycle industry, the stages of localization in the value chain, and the three phases of the industry's development in Vietnam. Section 6.3 reviews industry constraints on technology learning and upgrading in the capital and credit markets. Sections 6.4 and 6.5 provide two case studies using the developmental rent-management analysis (DRMA) framework. Section 6.6 discusses the current standing of the industry's development, especially after the China shock. Finally, Section 6.7 provides concluding remarks, observations, and policies implication.

6.2 Background on the motorcycle industry in Vietnam

Vietnam's motorcycle industry has achieved a number of important milestones since the mid-1990s. In 2012, motorcycle production employed approximately 20,000 workers, as well as tens of thousands of workers in supporting industries and related services. In 2018, Vietnam was the fourth-largest motorcycle market in the world, after only China, India, and Indonesia, respectively ("Vietnam August: Two-wheeler sales down," 2019). Between 2011 and 2019, the industry sold, on average, 3.1 million units each year (Nguyen, 2019). In 2018, motorcycle sales reached a record of nearly 3.4 million vehicles ("Motorcycle sales reach record," 2019). The five largest motorcycle manufacturers in Vietnam combined – Honda, Yamaha, Suzuki, SYM, and Piaggio – sold approximately 3.386 million units ("Motorcycle sales reach record," 2019). This figure implies that the five largest motorcycle manufacturers took roughly 99.5 percent of the market share, leaving a large number of foreign producers and few domestic lead firms to split the remaining 0.5 percent of the market, or 12,846 motorcycle units.

Effectively, in 2020, the industry is structured as an oligopoly market where lead manufacturers are all foreign firms. Foreign firms use Vietnam as a manufacturing base servicing the substantial demand for motorcycles in the local market. The significant sales volume of the five largest brands in Vietnam is shown in Figure 6.1. Of the five largest manufacturers, Honda lead the market with 75.9 percent of market share in 2018 (Nguyen, 2019). Given that its market share was roughly 11.9 percent in 2005, the 2018 market share shows a considerable jump in dominance, an event that Case Study 2 analyzes in depth.

Considering the motorcycle industry's rapid growth in outputs and demand, it is often forgotten that the industry did not start to develop until the mid-1990s, when the Vietnamese government launched an import-substitution policy and erected trade barriers while providing incentives to foreign investors coming to Vietnam. By the late 1990s, major motorcycle companies established trade offices and assembling plants in Vietnam, including transnational corporations: Taiwan's VMEP and Japan's Suzuki, Honda, and Yamaha. Some Taiwanese and Japanese parts manufacturers followed the lead firms and built plants in Vietnam to produce items such as tires, batteries, electric and plastic parts, and brakes. Fujita (2007) asserts that the Vietnamese motorcycle industry was dominated by foreign manufacturers in the late 1990s, creating an oligopolistic market. Foreign motorcycle firms set prices that far exceeded the costs of inputs and assembling, which enabled them to enjoy substantial rents. Table 6.1 lists major manufacturers in Vietnam, their year of business licensure, and ownership structures by country.

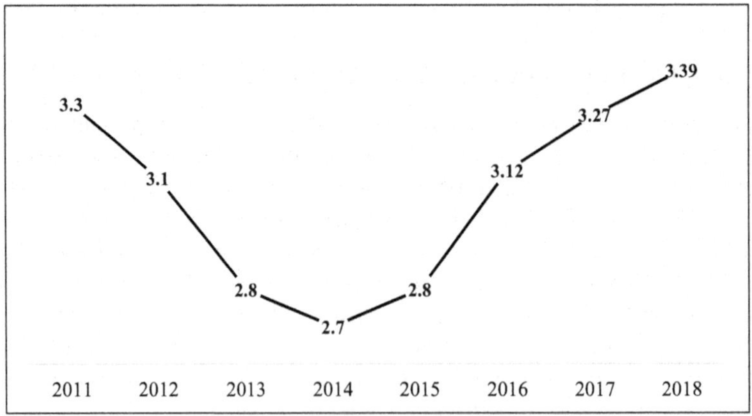

Figure 6.1 Sales of Motorcycles from Vietnam's Five Largest Brands (in millions)

Source: Author's compilation based on data from Vietnam Association for Motorcycle Manufacturers (2019).

Table 6.1 Major Foreign Motorcycle Firms in Vietnam, 1992–2017

Name of Company	*License Year*	*Ownership Structure by Country and Percent*
Vietnam Manufacture & Export Processing C. (VMEP)	1992	• Chinfon Group, producer of SYM motorcycles (Taiwan, 100%)
Vietnam Suzuki Corp.	1995	• Suzuki Corp. (Japan, 35%) • Sojitz (Japan, 35%) • Vikyno: Southern Agricultural Machinery Corp. (Vietnam, 30%)
Sufat Vietnam Corp.	1996	• Sufat Vietnam (Vietnam, 100%)
Honda Vietnam Co.	1996	• Honda Motor Co., Ltd. (Japan, 42%) • Asian Honda Motors (Thailand, 28%) • Vietnam Engine & Agricultural Machinery Corp. (Vietnam, 30%)
Yamaha Vietnam Co.	1998	• Yamaha Motors (Japan, 46%) • Hong Leong Industries (Malaysia, 24%) • Vietnam Forestry Corporation (Vietnam, 30%)
Lifan Motorcycle Manufacturing JV Co.	2002	• Chonqing Lifan (China, 70%) • Vietnam Import-Export Technology Development Co. (Vietnam, 30%)
***Kymco Vietnam**	2005	• Kymco (Taiwan, 60%) • Hoa Lam (Vietnam, 40%)
***Piaggio Vietnam**	2009	• The Piaggio Group (Italy, 100%)
***Peugeot Motorcycles**	2016	• Peugeot Scooters (France, 100%)
***VinFast**	2017	• VinGroup (Vietnam, 100%)

Source: Author's compilation based on Fujita (2008); ownership structure and firm names may have changed since 2008. (*) indicates author's data collected from secondary sources.

In an effort to speed up negotiations for the country's entry into the World Trade Organization (WTO), the Vietnamese government abolished a series of regulations restricting motorcycle imports and sales. This move boosted domestic sales of foreign-brand motorcycles and stimulated a new wave of FDI in production and component manufacturing. It also set the industry on a more market-oriented path of development. The following chronological summary of the government policies from 1995 to 2017 highlights changes in the Vietnamese policy agenda to encourage development of local firms through participation of FDI in the Vietnamese market:

- **Mid-1990s**: The Vietnamese government introduced import-subsidy policies as trade barriers but also provided incentives to attract FDI.
- **1998**: The prohibition of completely built units (CBUs)[3] and localization requirements were introduced. The local content policies meant that MNC firms had to pay high import tariffs if the proportional local content ratio was low and vice versa.

- **2000:** A new policy was enacted that required all countries exporting motorcycle parts to Vietnam to submit quality certificates from their respective countries to prevent exporting inferior quality motorcycle parts to Vietnam. The policy was implemented in response to pressure from Japanese investors to restrict smuggled motorcycles and parts from China as well as quality issues with Chinese/Vietnamese manufactured motorcycles.
- **2001**: The Vietnamese government started to implement local content policies and to audit records of Vietnamese and Chinese firms for tax evasion. Existing firms were expected to maintain at least 60 percent local parts in production. In addition, the government banned imports of 20 motorcycle parts to protect domestic industries, arguing that those parts could be made locally.
- **2002**: The Vietnamese government introduced additional controls on motorcycle parts by imposing import quotas for components. These policies were announced without notice. Because the allocated quotas were too little for Honda and Yamaha to fill their production capacity, they suspended production temporarily until additional quotas were granted. This policy came under strong criticism by FDI investors.
- **2003**: Import quotas were abolished, but the Vietnamese government enacted a policy that required FDI motorcycle manufacturers to operate according to the projections in their business plans, which they submitted to the authority when they applied for a business license. Clearly, the rapid market growth in the early 2000s could not have been envisaged in the 1990s. This policy constrained various Japanese companies from expanding production as the demand for motorcycles increased.
- **January 2003**: The Vietnamese government abandoned local content rules. This policy decision was made primarily to gain accession to the WTO.
- **2003–2005**: The Vietnamese government abandoned restrictions on motorcycle registration, including the policy limiting one resident to one registered motorcycle. A rule banning registration of new motorcycles in Ha Noi's inner districts was also revoked.
- **2007:** The Ministry of Industry issued the "Master Plan for the Development of Vietnam's Motorcycle Industry in the Period of 2006–2015, with a Vision to 2020." In the same year, the Ministry of Industry also issued the "Master Plan for Development of Supporting Industries until 2010, Vision until 2020." The master plan aimed to create new breakthroughs in the development of manufacturing industries.
- **2011**: The prime minister signed Decision 12/2011/QT-TTg (Decision 12; discussed earlier), which was designed to encourage and create conditions for domestic and foreign organizations, as well as individuals, to develop supporting industries. Decision 12 proposed several types of subsidies, including promotions for market development, infrastructure, human resource training in science and technology, and finance.
- **2016**: Decree 111/2015/ND-CP was signed and took effect in January 2016. It provided incentives in the form of preferential corporate tax,

import-export tax, value-added tax, and favorable interest rates for new investment and land rent for businesses in supporting industries. In addition, firms operating in prioritized sectors were supported by government funding and incentive policies such as investment in new research, human resources, and international cooperation.

- **2017**: Decision 68/QD-TTg came into effect in January 2017. The government budgeted VND 1 trillion or USD 47.6 million – the largest government funding package in decades – to assist supporting industries through a variety of programs such as promoting new investment, providing information and data to buyers and investors, assisting start-up businesses, encouraging technology transfer and production testing, assisting domestic enterprises in applying international standards to their production, and acquiring international certifications. For producers of metal, plastic, rubber, electrical and electronic components, the government set a target of 35 percent of domestic demand by 2020 and 55 percent by 2025.

6.2.1 Development of the local value chain

Development processes require capability development of local firms, especially from a technological standpoint. The production of a motorcycle involves numerous components as well as final-stage assembly. Therefore, capability building among local firms occurs over time, through stages within the *local value chain* (Figure 6.2). In this context, the local value chain is defined as *the chain of production that involves a network of interconnected local enterprises generating domestic value within the chain.* The aim is to develop a value chain that improves local firms' competitiveness and market integration within and across industries. As local firms move along the value chain, more value is added to their component production and final outputs. This section briefly discusses the local value chain in the motorcycle industry.

In any local value chain, technical capability moves from low to high. In Stage 1, foreign lead firms relocate their assembling facilities to developing countries and hire local workers to assemble knockdown motorcycles,[4] with all components imported from abroad. There is little technology diffusion at this stage, as assembly does not require technology transfer from advanced countries to developing ones. A number of foreign suppliers, especially those with established relationships with lead firms in their home countries, move production

Figure 6.2 Local Value Chain Development in the Motorcycle Industry

to developing countries to provide components for foreign lead firms. By doing so, they avoid import tax, reduce cost of production, and quickly respond to the demand of lead firms. These suppliers are regarded as first-tier suppliers, meaning they sell components directly to lead firms.

In Stage 2, local firms move to produce basic and low-tech components for local and foreign assemblers. In Vietnam, Vietnamese suppliers produced very simple parts for Japanese and Taiwanese assemblers first, and later for Chinese assemblers. In Stage 3, local firms become second-tier suppliers. They establish relationships to supply specific and more complex components to first-tier suppliers. Local second-tier suppliers benefit from collaboration with first-tier suppliers and lead firms. At this stage, many foreign firms transfer technology and expertise to support technical learning among local suppliers. Technology adoption and technical learning speed up, corresponding to the level of complexity of the components.

In the final two stages, local firms become first-tier suppliers, supplying complex parts directly to foreign lead firms (Stage 4) and become lead firms themselves (Stage 5). As lead firms, they produce Vietnamese-branded motorcycles. From a developing country's perspective, Stages 4 and 5 indicate high levels of technological capacity, especially when local firms become capable of designing, manufacturing, and branding motorcycles using local components and labor. This local value chain does not distinguish whether local firms supply to local industries or foreign buyers. The aim is for local firms to achieve competitiveness, first in the domestic market and then in the global market.

6.2.2 *The industry's transformation*

This chapter separates the development of Vietnam's motorcycle industry into three periods: 1990s–2000, 1998–2004, and post-2004. Figure 6.3 illustrates the periods, which correspond with two case studies in this chapter.

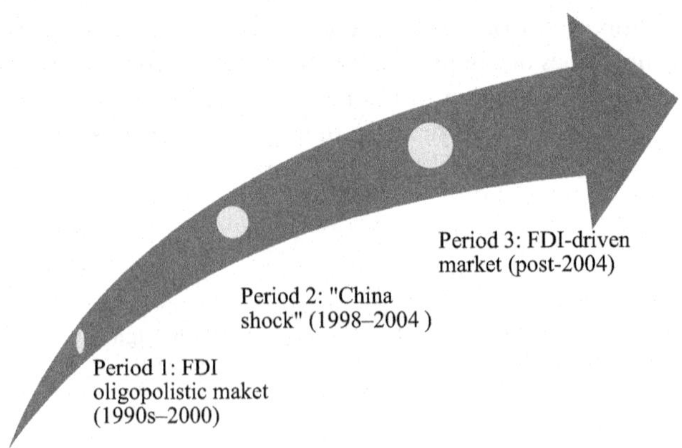

Figure 6.3 Three Periods of Industrial Development

The first period of industrial development in the motorcycle industry started in the 1990s. In the spirit of Doi Moi, the government enacted industrial programs in the motorcycle industry. One of the first measures was a series of import-substitution policies that erected trade barriers while providing incentives to attract FDI in the industry. The intention was to provide various rents to local enterprises and to foreign investors to encourage foreign transfer of technology by establishing manufacturing lines and employing local suppliers. This series of policies, however, created an unintended oligopolistic market for Japanese and some Taiwanese producers. These foreign producers imported completely built motorcycles from abroad, which kept market prices extremely high. Given the lack of competition, foreign investors were able to earn tremendous profits in Vietnam until Chinese motorcycles flooded the market during the second period, known as the "China shock" period.

The second period of the industry's development started with this large-scale penetration of Chinese motorcycles. The "China shock" experience marked an industrial transformation of domestic firms. During this period, local Vietnamese firms acted as assemblers and later as parts suppliers for Chinese-led firms as they sought profits in the low-cost market, which had remained unexploited by Japanese motorcycle manufacturers. Vietnamese firms achieved notable industrial upgrading during this period (Fujita, 2010). In the third period (post-2004), the industry took a major turn. Starting in 2005, the industry was once again largely occupied by major foreign motorcycle manufacturers, with local firms participating lower down in the production chain. The Vietnamese government removed its administrative and trade barriers to attract more FDI, especially small and medium enterprises (SMEs), but this left local firms competing directly with FDI businesses. Consequently, nearly half of local businesses went under, given their lack of competitiveness. Nevertheless, motorcycle production by foreign lead firms continued at a high growth rate, due to expansion in market demand. I analyze the industrial transformation during these periods in the subsequent case studies.

6.3 Market and industry constraints

This section reviews the market failures and constraints imposed on local firms in the motorcycle industry from the 1990s to the early 2010s. The aim is to provide context for the industry's capacity during its crucial development period as well as to inform the rent-management mechanism described in the case studies. This section focuses on the four most important constraints within the motorcycle industry: technical learning and upgrading, capital and credit markets, coordination failures, and challenges imposed by trade liberalization.

Vietnam's Institute for Industry Policy and Strategy conducted a one-time survey on the capability of local suppliers in the Vietnamese motorcycle industry in 2008. The study revealed that supporting industries were experiencing major constraints for a number of reasons. First, a large number of "low-tech" parts and components made of cast iron, steel, or plastic continued to be imported because few local companies could supply them. Second, both the engineering and technical capabilities of domestic suppliers were generally low and did not provide reliable quality, cost, and delivery (QCD). Third, domestic suppliers' ability to supply large quantities of quality parts was limited. Fourth, local producers' attention was largely focused on the cost of materials, with far less attention to costs associated with waste, defective parts, limited inventories, and inconsistent quality of inputs. Finally, local producers were unable to invest in the necessary human and physical capital to become competitive parts manufacturers (Vietnam Development Forum, 2011). My fieldwork in 2011 validates these observations: a number of my interviewees made similar remarks, which I describe below.

6.3.1 Technological learning and upgrading

Since the opening of the motorcycle industry, learning has taken two forms: (1) domestic firms collaborating with foreign enterprises and (2) domestic firms using alternative financing opportunities to upgrade technical capacity on their own. An example of the former is the Ha Noi Plastic Company. It started as Honda Vietnam's supplier, but the company increasingly developed linkages with other foreign motorcycle makers and now supplies large precision plastic parts for home appliances, such as washing machines and air conditioners. In 2010, the company purchased a 1,500-ton injection molding machine to diversify its products and to expand production capacity (Vietnam Development Forum, 2011).

Technology transfers to local firms from either FDI lead firms or first-tier suppliers can be slow and often incomplete. In 2011, I interviewed a manager of a Japanese Vietnamese joint venture and first-tier supplier to Honda Vietnam (hereafter, F1), and he explained that there was technology that his company mastered years ago, yet when this same technology was transferred to a local state-owned enterprise (SOE) and second-tier supplier (hereafter, F2), they simply could not perfect it, despite having technical assistance for a few years. In this specific case, F1 had agreed to transfer technology to F2 that used robots to run and monitor production of a few select components. After three years of technical support from F1, F2 continued to encounter multiple errors in its production using the robots. The manager expressed frustration, as F1 had produced components using this robotic technology with nearly 100 percent accuracy for years. I asked why this happened. Having had the opportunity to lead the technology transfer from F1 to F2, as well as serving on the technical support team for F2, the manager pointed out that F2 (and similar local suppliers) did not follow certain important procedures in using the technology, which caused failures in operation. He explained, for example, that F2 skipped steps in the maintenance and operation procedures and thus failed to maintain the robot (interview, Ha Noi; July 2011).

The firm managers I interviewed told me that local firms could overcome certain impediments through collaborating with foreign suppliers for transfer of technology. However, many foreign firms, especially Japanese ones, often required strict QCD and management standards *before* signing a contract with local firms for any type of technology or skills training. Achieving these strict standards might take as little as six months or as long as a few years, depending on the initial capability of the firm. In 2011, the Centre of Supporting Industries Development conducted a survey of the eight areas of support offered by foreign firms to local suppliers. Of the 18 suppliers who responded, 12 received support in areas of new product development and production and quality management. None received any support in exporting. Two local firms received support in human development, including technical training, and four received assistance for importing equipment. The statistics of the survey are in Figure 6.4. However, as mentioned above, it is often overlooked that to obtain a component supply contract with a foreign firm, a local firm must initially satisfy a strict set of criteria that requires a learning period on its own.

Examples of the second type of learning include local firms' efforts to invest in available, often secondhand equipment and technology to reduce costs and boost the technical skills of engineers and workers. These self-initiated efforts often take time and a number of failed attempts before a firm succeeds in acquiring new capabilities. However, some Vietnamese firms succeeded in developing skills that made them globally competitive using this approach,

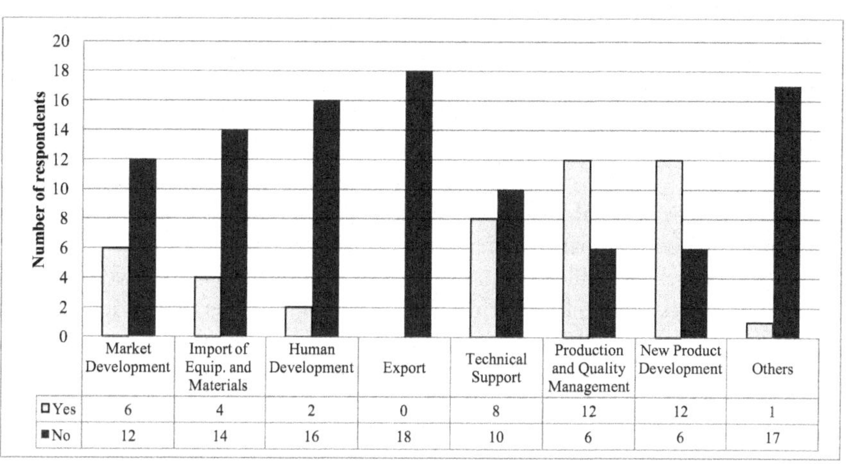

	Market Development	Import of Equip. and Materials	Human Development	Export	Technical Support	Production and Quality Management	New Product Development	Others
□Yes	6	4	2	0	8	12	12	1
■No	12	14	16	18	10	6	6	17

Figure 6.4 Areas of Support by Foreign Firms in 2011

Source: Author's compilation based on data from the Centre of Supporting Industries Development, Ministry of Industry and Trade. N = 18.

such as Hoang Phat Company and Tan Hoa Mechanical Company. Both these enterprises started out using secondhand imported equipment from Taiwan, and they slowly improved their technical capabilities to produce parts that satisfied the standards required by Japanese and Taiwanese lead firms, eventually becoming their suppliers (Vietnam Development Forum, 2011). I interviewed an expert at a Ha Noi research think tank regarding local firm upgrading efforts, and she suggested that this type of self-effort upgrading took place at a very slow pace, and enterprises were often held back by lack of capital and technical skills (interview, Ha Noi; April 2011). As a result, there were few successful firms and numerous failures.

Several interviewees pointed out that formal training or education at Vietnamese universities and technical schools did little to supply skilled labor to local firms; thus, most learning took place in the workplace (locally known as *cam tay chi viec*) (interviews, three industry experts and three firm managers, Ho Chi Minh City and Ha Noi; April–July 2011). This is another reason why investment in local suppliers' technical learning and upgrading was risky and time consuming. Two of the local firms I visited (one assembler and one supplier) confirmed that the majority of their investment in training and technical upgrading was based on (1) hiring experts, (2) learning-by-doing, or (3) asking advice from colleagues who worked in other foreign firms (interviews, Ho Chi Minh City and Ha Noi; May and July 2011). In addition to the lack of technical expertise and production know-how, there is a shortage of investment capital and problems related to obtaining bank loans for investment. The next section discusses these constraints in detail.

6.3.2 Capital and credit markets

A major constraint facing private local SMEs in Vietnam was the shortage of investment capital due to a weak credit market between the 1990s and the 2010s. Throughout the industry's development, motorcycle suppliers lacked access to long-term loans or an equity-based financing system. The issue was exacerbated by commercial banks (state-owned and private) on the one hand, who had strict collateral requirements and stringent administrative procedures to approve investment loans, particularly regarding documentation. On the other hand, SMEs were unwilling to tangle with commercial banks, given the low chance of success in meeting their requirements. This generated a vicious cycle that prevented many SMEs from entering the formal credit sector, forcing them to rely on informal credit, which then slowed learning and upgrading processes (Ministry of Industry and Trade, 2012).

A local supplier remarked in 2011 that Honda and other foreign firms were willing to provide training with the caveat of meeting their production quality standards. This owner did not have the immediate capital to upgrade his equipment, which he had purchased in the early 2000s; his technology was simply too old to meet Honda's requirements. At the time of the interview, it had taken him eight months to build a new production line to make components of the quality that Honda (and others) required. He said it would have taken less time, if he would have had extra capital to invest. He revealed that he had been in the process of negotiating with Honda Vietnam to be their supplier. However, this opportunity would have to be put on hold if Honda inspected the factory and came to the conclusion that he needed more or newer equipment. He would not be able to afford any additional investment, as his financing had been exhausted (interview, Ha Noi; July 2011). This scenario was common, according to two Vietnamese industry experts (interviews, Ha Noi; April and June 2011). It created a two-way problem: local suppliers lost this chance to sign a contract with a lead supplier, and Honda could not get all the components needed for production expansion in Vietnam.

To address such bottlenecks, the Vietnamese government instituted banking reforms with the aim of easing lending practices. Agreed upon between Japan and Vietnam in 1999, the Private Sector Promotion Action Plan, or so-called Miyazawa Plan, included an official decree on lending guarantees, a decree liberalizing transactions involving land-use rights, and the establishment of the stock exchange center (Ministry of Industry and Trade, 2012). Other key milestones for improving the financial environment for SMEs included the creation of a two-step loan fund[5] and a credit guarantee fund[6] (Richards, Harvie, Nguyen, & Nguyen, 2002). In the early 2010s, the government also proposed to improve the regulatory framework on lending, mortgaging, and leasing as well as pending banking sector reform that would provide SMEs with greater access to credit (interview, Ministry of Industry and Trade official, Ha Noi; July 2011).

Overall, the Vietnamese government's use of private financial institutions rather than state-owned commercial banks to provide investment capital for domestic firms had several shortcomings (see Richards et al., 2002). First, coverage of the two-step loan fund and credit guarantee fund were not sufficiently targeted to have meaningful effects on parts suppliers. Second, the broad coverage encouraged rent-seeking activities by enterprises looking to access these funds even though their business operations had little relation to the development of the motorcycle and supporting industries. Third, SMEs faced a number of difficulties the banking reforms largely ignored: insufficient corporate financial information, inadequate evaluation capacities of banks, and strict collateral requirements. Finally, the impact of these reforms on the domestic private sector remained limited because private firms often could not secure access to land-use rights, which would be their most valuable source of collateral. By contrast, most SOEs could lease public lands from the government. This gave them a significant advantage over the private domestic sector in securing loans for investment (Richards et al., 2002). In summary, the capital and credit markets were major constraints for the motorcycle industry because private SMEs faced enormous difficulties in gaining access to the capital and land needed to upgrade their capability.

6.3.3 Coordination failures

The Vietnamese government and the motorcycle industry also suffered a number of coordination failures in the policies that protected industry start-ups. Consequently, supports for industrial learning and capacity building turned out to be inadequate. Two instances between 2001 and 2004 illustrate this failure. In 2001, the government started to implement new local content policies: firms were expected to use at least 60 percent local parts in their production. The policies also introduced new standards for manufacturing plants (Nguyen, 2005). The government also banned imports of 20 motorcycle parts to protect domestic industries, arguing that these parts could be produced locally (Jalaluddin, 2002). In reality, locally made parts did not meet foreign firms' quality standards. Thus, the local content policies created a problem by obliging foreign firms to buy local products that did not meet their need, forcing them to stop production. This policy created bottlenecks for both foreign firms and local suppliers. Chinese and Vietnamese lead firms went so far as to import complete knockdown motorcycles, assemble them in Vietnam, and then falsely claim that the local content requirement was met.

In the second example, in 2003, the Vietnamese government enacted a policy requiring foreign motorcycle manufacturers to operate within the projections of the original business plans they presented to the ministry in the 1990s. However, rapid and unexpected market growth in the early 2000s caused foreign assemblers to exhaust their planned production before the end of the year (Agence France Presse, 2002). Under the new policy, companies were constrained from producing more despite increased market demand. The policy came under severe criticism by the foreign business community and was abolished in April 2005, as a result of intergovernmental negotiations (Agence France Presse, 2002). For an outline of the policies from 1990 to 2005, see Table 6.2.

Table 6.2 History of Rent Policies, Pre-1990 to 2005

Year	*Content*
Before 1990	Import restrictions on CBUs
1997	Further restriction of imports of CBUs; local content requirements introduced
January 2011	Imposed proportional import tariff on motorcycle parts based on local content ratio
2002	Raised import tariff
September 2002	Set quotas on imports of component sets; relaxed quota requirement in November 2002
2003	(1) Abolished quotas on CBUs
	(2) Imposed administrative restrictions on imports in accordance with previously approved business plans
2004	Normalized import tariff on components
2005	Removed administrative restrictions on imports based on business plans

Source: Adapted from Nguyen (2006).

The events that took place between the late 1990s and the early 2000s illustrate the government's severe coordination failures that created bottlenecks and setbacks for both foreign and domestic enterprises. The policy failures suggest that the Ministry of Industry and Trade (MoIT) was disconnected from the reality of the industry, so its policies did not reflect the actual capabilities or needs of foreign and local firms. Vietnamese local suppliers could not possibly produce enough parts, let alone quality parts, for foreign manufacturers without an appropriate period of learning and upgrading. As a result, there were drastic price fluctuations of motorcycles during this period.

6.3.4 Challenges imposed by trade liberalization

The opening of the Vietnamese market to foreign investment and international trade, starting in 2007, imposed critical challenges for domestic firms. Due to various trade commitments, especially in the WTO, the ASEAN+3 and the ASEAN-China Free Trade Area,[7] the Vietnamese government could no longer use the import-substitution strategy and other industrial policies employed between 1998 and 2006. From the industrial development perspective, trade liberalization not only intensified competition in the domestic market but also worsened the policy space needed to support domestic firms' competitiveness. In particular, protections against the ASEAN-China trade block were completely removed in 2015 through the creation of the ASEAN-China Free Trade Area. This trade pact involves zero tariff rates for 7,881 product categories, or 90 percent of imported goods for ASEAN members and China, Vietnam's largest trade partner. Commenting on the rapid rate of trade liberalization and growing number of trade agreements between Vietnam and other ASEAN nations, Ohno (2008) points out the "great concern for Vietnam since ASEAN is the strong production base of Japanese products such as automobiles and electronics" (p. 1), and Vietnam would be forced to switch from producing and assembling their own products to importing similar products from neighboring countries. Such a phenomenon would create considerable negative pressure on the country's trade balance (Ohno, 2008).

Ohno's warning and prediction were partially fulfilled. In the motorcycle industry, unable to compete with foreign competitors, domestic firms saw their market share shrink dramatically. In 2007, while many foreign manufacturers achieved phenomenal growth rates, given a rapid demand expansion for motorcycles in the Vietnamese market, the market share of Vietnamese lead firms shrunk from about 13 percent in the 1990s to roughly 2 percent (Fujita, 2007). During my fieldwork in 2011, one local assembler remarked that the local business in motorcycle assembly was like a car about to run out of fuel. He was pessimistic about both his business and the overall business environment for local firms. The market for low-cost Vietnamese motorcycles was nearly nonexistent, with foreign manufacturers continuously introducing low-cost models to compete in the low-end market segment (interview, Ha Noi; July 2011).

In her fieldwork, Fujita (2010) reported that the number of local assemblers decreased from 51 in 2002 to 28 in 2006. Additionally, between 2002 and 2006, 28 manufactures left the motorcycle industry, although 12 new ones entered the market in that period (Fujita, 2010). By 2012, many Vietnamese motorcycle assemblers either went out of business or were bought out by foreign firms (Quoc-Hung, 2012). Quoc-Hung (2012) reports further that the number of local firms and suppliers shrunk from 56 firms in the early 2000s to less than 30 in 2012, of which there was only *one* 100 percent Vietnamese-owned lead firm operating. One of the lead firms that closed down, the Hoa Lam Company, had once been well respected with a well-known brand: Halim. Hoa Lam largely left the market after selling most of its stake to Kymko Vietnam, a Taiwanese-based motorcycle maker (Quoc-Hung, 2012). In 2018, local motorcycle producers' market share shrank further to less than 0.5 percent, from 2 percent in 2007, as they struggled to find their own niche in a market dominated by foreign producers in all consumer segments and income groups ("Motorcycle sales reach record," 2019). Finally, although Vietnam's export volume increased dramatically after Vietnam joined the WTO in 2007, imports of machine and industrial inputs also grew in the same period, and thus there has been insignificant trade surplus (Figure 1.5).

Thus far, this chapter has provided an overview of the motorcycle industry and the constraints holding back processes of industrial upgrading and capacity building from the late 1990s to the early 2010s. The following sections offer two case studies that analyze the Vietnamese government's efforts to generate technological catch-up and to allocate learning rents that decisively changed the dynamic of the motorcycle industry from 1995 to 2004. The first case study assesses the emergence and failure of learning rents in the first period of the industry's development from 1995 to 2000. The second case study reviews the industry's transformation that occurred when Chinese motorcycles penetrated the Vietnamese market in the early 2000s. It also examines the learning effects and how Vietnamese firms reorganized from local assemblers to parts suppliers for foreign firms. The objective of the case studies is to assess how the three factors of rent management – political, institutional, and industry organization – impacted the structure of incentives and pressures to ensure effort for learning and industrialization in the motorcycle industry. The development of the industry during the 2010s was very much impacted by the mechanisms of rent management and their outcomes in the earlier period. The case studies provide the historical and political economy contexts that determine the paths of industrialization of the motorcycle industry in contemporary Vietnam.

6.4 Case study 1: the failure of learning rents (1990s–2000)

In the 1990s, in an effort to enhance industrialization, the Vietnamese government chose to champion the motorcycle industry for industrial development. It launched an import-substitution policy that erected trade barriers and provided incentives to attract FDI, in particular Japanese and Taiwanese MNCs. The primary purpose of this policy was to enhance learning-by-doing as well as to transfer technology in components manufacturing to Vietnam's motorcycle industry. According to interviews with government officials and industry experts, the Vietnamese government used tax breaks for foreign companies, provided subsidized land, protected intellectual property rights, and imposed tariffs on imports of fully assembled motorcycles (four interviews, Ha Noi and Ho Chi Minh City; April–July 2011).[8] These policies implicitly created rents for foreign investors investing in Vietnam. Because these policies were designed to improve skills, training, and technology in the domestic motorcycle industry, these rents were, in effect, *learning rents*.

Attracted by the large and growing market, several foreign motorcycle manufacturers in Taiwan and Japan began importing completely built motorcycles, incomplete knockdown motorcycles,[9] and complete knockdown motorcycles – new and used – from their home countries. Foreign lead firms had incentives to extract learning rents: they could enter the Vietnamese market and secure profits in the absence of domestic competition. The percentage of import values from CBUs made outside of Vietnam between 2000 and 2005 is detailed in Table 6.3. The table illustrates the substantial percentage of CBUs imported into Vietnam prior to 2001, when components manufacturing was limited. In 2000, 95.45 percent of the total imported value was from CBUs made in lead firms' home countries. Separate parts that did not come with the completely built kit accounted for only 4.45 percent of imported value.

With a number of reputable foreign lead firms in Vietnam, several foreign parts suppliers followed them to Vietnam to provide high-quality components. Thus, foreign lead firms did not have to collaborate with local suppliers for parts. In addition, despite high tariffs imposed on foreign motorcycles (new and secondhand), many were imported into Vietnam throughout this five-year period (Intarakumnerd & Fujita, 2008). In an oligopolistic market occupied mostly by foreign suppliers and lead firms, foreign motorcycle producers were able to set high prices to offset high import tariffs and enjoyed substantial profits (Mishima, 2005).

Table 6.3 Import Shares of Completely Built Units and Separate Parts, 2000–2005 (by percentage)

Year	*2000*	*2001*	*2002*	*2003*	*2004*	*2005*
Completely built units	95.45	88.16	64.17	27.98	0	0.23
Separate parts	4.45	6.76	31.63	55.54	87.9	86.5

Source: Author's calculation and compilation based on data from Ministry of Industry and Trade (2007).

6.4.1 The political context of learning rents

The political context in this period had two relevant characteristics. First, the Vietnamese government was interested in attracting FDI to take advantage of foreign capital, expertise, and technology, as explained above. Second, Japanese manufacturers (particularly Honda, Suzuki, and Yamaha) were successful in lobbying the Vietnamese government – in this case, the prime minister and the MoIT – to implement policies that served their economic interests, including tax reductions and the enforcement of intellectual property rights. An interviewee who worked at the MoIT explained that between the 1990s and 2005, Japanese investors had significant leverage to negotiate the terms of their investments in Vietnam[10] and were supported by the Japanese government through organizations such as their embassy, the Japan International Cooperation Agency, and Japanese manufacturing associations. To prevent local firms from imitating, adopting, and adapting Japanese motorcycle models and technologies, Japanese investors insisted that the Vietnamese government implement tighter controls over intellectual property rights. These investors argued that the Vietnamese government's commitment to intellectual property rights protections would encourage more Japanese investors into Vietnam. The Vietnamese government obliged (interview, MoIT official, Ha Noi; July 2011). In essence, the political context that set the policy agenda was driven by two parallel though somewhat contradictory forces: to upgrade the domestic industry using FDI and to meet Japanese investor demands as conditions for investment in the Vietnamese market.

6.4.2 Implementation mechanisms

At the institutional level, one major problem lay in the approach used to negotiate licenses with Japanese investors. Technology transfers were not part of license negotiation, despite the Vietnamese government's intention to use FDI for development of the industry. I asked two MoIT officials about this failure. They pointed out that in the late 1990s, the Vietnamese government was inexperienced in negotiating with foreign investors, including not understanding how to negotiate specific conditions for capital and technology transfers. Instead, as they looked to the Asian Tigers for lessons, they thought local content policies and import restrictions on motorcycle parts would be sufficient to force technical spillovers from FDI. However, the Vietnamese context was different from the Asian Tigers. After the 1980s, Japanese investors were much more cautious in sharing their expertise in production operation and management (interviews, Ha Noi; July 2011 and September 2012).[11] In sum, at the institutional level, the MoIT failed to create pressure for technology diffusion as intended by the learning rents.

The second institutional failure was the Vietnamese government's inability to coordinate rent policies in line with its development agenda. In many instances, the government devised a number of rent policies and regulations to implement them but failed to make sure the rents produced value-enhancing outcomes. I explain the coordination failure in Section 6.3.3 and will provide another example here to highlight this point. In 2002, in an effort to force Japanese firms to produce motorcycles in Vietnam rather than import them, the MoIT introduced import quotas that reduced imported motorcycles without advance notice. Announced on September 4, 2002, and taking effect immediately, the MoIT slashed the number of sets (one set makes one motorcycle) that firms could import annually from 2.5 million to 1.5 million. Furthermore, of the reduced quota, 600,000 sets were allocated among the seven foreign manufacturers, with the remaining 900,000 sets divided among 55 Vietnamese assemblers (Fujita, 2007). The quota allocation clearly favored local assemblers over foreign ones. This move prompted a storm of protest from three of the foreign manufacturers – Honda, Suzuki, and Yamaha – which had each based their annual assembling targets for joint-venture operations in Vietnam on the larger quotas. Assembly lines at Honda's plant in the Vinh Phuc province, northwest of Ha Noi, halted on September 18 because it ran out of parts; a month later, Yamaha stopped production at its plant on the outskirts of the capital for the same reason (Agence France Presse, 2002).

Even so, many local assemblers did not benefit from the quota policy. Also during this time, domestic firms were audited for possible tax fraud in their claims of localization ratios in the earlier period. Those under investigation by the tax authority were not permitted to obtain import quotas to continue production, leading to discontinued production for a majority of local assemblers in 2002 (interviews, two local assemblers, Ha Noi; July 2011). In this case, both foreign and local firms suffered from lower production output because of the MoIT's abrupt quota policy. As a result of this supply shortage, motorcycle prices surged, harming both producers and consumers. The government then backtracked by lifting import quotas at the beginning of 2003. The ministry's coordination failure was partly due to introducing policies on very short notice. Hence, neither domestic suppliers nor foreign lead firms had enough time to adjust their operations accordingly. Furthermore, the quota policy did not provide adequate resources and incentives to domestic firms to engage in the necessary investment and learning. As a result, not only did domestic suppliers fail to learn or upgrade their capability but the government also frustrated foreign investors.

6.4.3 Industry structure in the post-reform period

At the industry level, two particular aspects of the industry structure had damaging consequences for learning efforts. The first was that market competition was such that foreign firms had an incentive to exploit market profits without motivation or pressure to collaborate with local suppliers. For example, in the late 1990s, there were no Vietnamese-brand motorcycles, and Japanese motorcycles were in great demand among the Vietnamese upper class due to their reputation for quality and durability. As the Vietnamese population and economy grew, demand for motorcycles increased. Therefore, foreign manufacturers, particularly Japan's, benefited from a substantial market demand and, thus, high profits. There was no need for Honda, Suzuki, or Yamaha to engage in price competition in the Vietnamese market (interview, industry expert from Japan, Ha Noi; June 2011). In addition, the market was large enough so that competition with Taiwan-based SYM had negligible effects on price. Thus, foreign investors lacked incentives and pressures to reduce costs by sourcing components from local suppliers, and they did not perceive the need for any systematic technology transfer to the few local partners in the joint ventures. For example, Honda did not develop a specific business model in the Vietnamese market during this period (Nguyen, 2006); instead, it simply opened an assembling plant that built imported knockdown motorcycles.

The second failure in rent management within the industry structure was due to strict Japanese (and other foreign) quality criteria, which discouraged technology transfers from foreign investors to local firms. Given the gap in technological capability, it was near impossible for Vietnamese firms to learn Japanese technologies and production techniques on their own. A senior Japanese researcher who specializes in Vietnam's motorcycle industry was quite vocal in reporting that Vietnamese firms were not competent to learn sophisticated Japanese technology or to meet the strict operation and quality standards of foreign lead firms and suppliers. He said that Vietnamese workers were not skilled, disciplined, or organized enough to absorb the high-level technical training from Japanese firms, and until Vietnamese suppliers could meet the standards of production, it would be difficult to collaborate with Japanese firms based in Vietnam (interview, Ha Noi; June 2011).[12]

However, this argument is flawed because Japanese investors failed to acknowledge that the rents provided to them through various protections and tax incentives were, in fact, instruments to compensate for collaborating with local firms and transfers of technology and expertise. In reality, these rents were not intended to guarantee high profits for Japanese and Taiwanese investors; rather, they were offered as necessary subsidies for providing in-house training to local suppliers.[13] Without the motivation of technology transfers on the part of the Vietnamese government, Japanese investors never would have obtained business licenses and government incentives and, thus, would not have made substantial earnings in the Vietnamese market.

6.4.4 Outcomes: a lost opportunity

From 1995 to 2000, Vietnam failed to achieve significant technology transfers and industrial upgrade. Although there were numerous local firms engaged in the production of replacement parts, these firms were largely outside the procurement networks of foreign lead firms. In 1998, Japanese manufacturers held nearly 75 percent of the market in Vietnam (Intarakumnerd & Fujita, 2008), but they offered little, if any, technology transfers or training. As a result, only a few local suppliers, mostly SOEs that had joint ventures with foreign lead firms, became parts suppliers for simple, low-tech components. In 2006,

Table 6.4 Part Procurement Structure of Japanese Motorcycle Firms by Percentage in 2006

Parts	*In-house*	*Domestic purchase*				*Imports*					
		JP	*TW*	*VN*	*Other*	*JP*	*TH*	*Indo*	*Mal*	*TW*	*Other*
Engine	6.3	14.3	16.1	**5.4**	0.0	2.7	47.3	4.5	1.8	0.9	0.9
Exhaust	0.0	50.0	50.0	**0.0**	0.0	0.0	0.0	0.0	0.0	0.0	0.0
Body	0.8	32.0	44.3	**9.0**	9.0	0.0	3.3	0.0	0.0	0.8	0.8
Electric	0.0	75.0	7.1	**10.7**	3.6	0.0	0.0	3.6	0.0	0.0	0.0
Others	0.0	15.2	24.2	**36.4**	0.0	12.1	6.1	3.0	0.0	0.0	3.0

Source: Author's compilation using data retrieved from the Ministry of Industry and Trade (2007).

JP = Japan, TW = Taiwan, VN = Vietnam, TH = Thailand, Indo = Indonesia, Mal = Malaysia. The MoIT did not specify what "Other" means.

local suppliers played only a minimal role in complex component manufacturing for foreign lead firms, even though the required localization ratio was extremely high (60 percent as of 2001). For example, in 2006, Vietnamese firms provided only 5.4 percent of engine parts, 9 percent of electrical parts, 10.7 percent of body parts, and 0 percent of exhaust systems. For a breakout of the percentage of local suppliers that participated in the procurement chain for Japanese manufacturers, see Table 6.4. The table illustrates the limited diffusion of technology.

From the local value chain perspective, Vietnam only completed the first stage: local assembling during the 1995–2000 period. It was only at the start of the second stage that local firms became basic and low-tech components suppliers for local and foreign assemblers.

6.4.5 Case study summary

On the whole, the failure of learning rents during the first period was primarily due to three reasons. At the political level, while there was clear political will to attract foreign investment and production expertise for local firms through several policy measures, influential Japanese investors lobbied to define the conditions for entry into the Vietnamese market, thus undermining rent policies. At the institutional level, the government failed to negotiate specific conditions of technology transfers and to coordinate implementation of rent policies. Last, insufficient market competition and strict Japanese quality criteria created weak incentives and pressures for foreign-local partnerships. The outcome was a period of rent extraction, in which foreign motorcycle makers successfully reaped large profits and gained nearly the whole Vietnamese market while little technology diffusion and training took place. The Vietnamese government's rent strategy, therefore, was largely unsuccessful. For a summary of the rent-management mechanism of the first case study, see Table 6.5.

Table 6.5 Summary of the Motorcycle Industry's First Period

Step 1: Political Context	• Political will to use FDI for industrial upgrading • Lobbying and pressures from foreign investors to meet investor demand for intellectual property rights protection **Type of rent:** Learning rents created by giving tax breaks, subsidized land, and protection of intellectual property rights to foreign firms as compensation for transfers of technology and expertise to local firms
Step 2: Institution Structure	• Failure to negotiate with foreign investors to ensure technology transfers • Uncoordinated rent policies and implementation
Step 3: Market and Industry Structures	• Large market with high-profit margins and no local competition • Insufficient initial capability of local firms to meet Japanese standards for collaboration
Step 4: Rent Outcomes	• Rapid growth, mostly in domestic assembling of foreign motorcycles • Slow local upgrading and learning • Completion of Stage 1 and start of Stage 2 of the local value chain

6.5 Case study 2: the China shock (1998–2004)

After 1998, the Vietnamese government maintained three types of policy interventions that provided *learning rents* for local firms: (1) local content requirements, (2) tariffs on imported components, and (3) prohibitions on the import of CBUs. These policies were distinguishable from previous ones, which largely aimed to draw foreign investment. One effect of prohibiting CBUs was an increase in imports of complete knockdown units to be assembled by local firms. These policies were meant both to pressure foreign lead firms and suppliers to collaborate with local suppliers and to purchase local materials and parts. Indeed, these policies put pressure on Japanese firms to increase their local content ratio. Given this context, in the late 1990s, Chinese and Vietnamese lead firms aggressively sought to capture the low-cost market segment, which had been largely neglected by Japanese and Taiwanese firms.

6.5.1 Political context and the institutional structure of the China shock

At the first level of DRMA, the rent policies reflect the Vietnamese government's political will to create learning rents for local firms in order to boost technical learning and industrialization. Vietnamese leaders at the time were in agreement that the economy had to be reformed in order to acquire the new industrial capability that would then develop the country (interviews, an ex-chairman of Vietnam Chamber of Commerce, an industry expert, and an MoIT official, Ha Noi; April–July 2011). However, at the institutional level of rent management, rent policies failed because these policies were neither carefully designed nor implemented.

Starting in 1998, Chinese-made knockdown motorcycles were both legally and illegally imported into Vietnam. Illegal importing occurred across the borders between the two countries. Chinese and Vietnamese assemblers falsely claimed to meet the required percentage of local content (up to 60 percent) so as to avoid the taxes imposed by the local content requirement (Intarakumnerd & Fujita, 2008). Because Chinese motorcycles were sold at much lower prices than Japanese motorcycles, Chinese and Vietnamese assemblers quickly captured a large market share. At the same time, there was a surge in the number of local firms – up to 51 – to assemble knockdown motorcycles imported from China and to provide parts for Chinese lead firms (Mishima, 2005).

The impact of these Chinese motorcycles was enormous. They lowered the average price of low-cost motorcycle models from USD 1,321 (before 2000) to around USD 472 (in 2000) and then to USD 297 (in 2001) (Fujita, 2007). As a result, by 2001, Chinese-Vietnamese motorcycle firms had captured 80.5 percent of the market. Fujita (2007) referred to this phenomenon as the "China shock" period.[14] The market share of Chinese-Vietnamese enterprises are grouped together in Table 6.6, in the "Chinese & Local firms" category.[15] According to the data, the market share for this group jumped from 13.5 percent in 1998 to 75.2 percent in 2000 and to 80.5 percent in 2001. This vertical rise clearly shows the effect of market penetration by Chinese imported motorcycles, or the China shock.

Had the local content policy been strictly enforced, Chinese manufacturers would not have succeeded in penetrating the Vietnamese market. Fujita (2007) noted that during the China shock period, there was virtually no local content in imported Chinese motorcycles, and thus, they should have been subject to high import tariffs. In other words, Chinese firms were involved in rent-sharing arrangements with local companies. Owners of two Vietnamese assembling companies reported that to justify their claims on local content, they imported secondhand production lines from China but never actually produced the

Table 6.6 Market Share by Assembler (in percentage)

Year	*1998*	*1999*	*2000*	*2001*	*2002*	*2003*	*2004*	*2005*
Honda[a]	67.2	63.1	19.4	11.9	19.4	33.3	35.7	36.9
Chinese & Local firms	13.5	23.8	75.2	80.5	65.1	37.8	29.6	35.7
Suzuki	7.2	3.6	1.0	1.4	2.2	4.0	4.9	4.1
VMEP (SYM)[b]	11.7	4.2	2.3	3.3	7.4	13.6	15.6	7.5
Scooter Completely Built Units	0.4	2.5	1.1	1.7	3.4	3.7	1.0	2.7

Source: Author's compilation using data retrieved from the Ministry of Industry and Trade (2007).

a Market share includes sales of motorcycles from both Honda Vietnam and imported Honda brand from abroad.

b VMEP is Vietnam Manufacture & Export Processing Co., Ltd.

components on their own. The production lines existed largely to falsify tax audits about the local components in Chinese motorcycles assembled in Vietnam (interviews, Ha Noi; July 2011). As a result of the government's failure to enforce the local content policies, some Vietnamese and Chinese assemblers captured the benefits of rents meant for domestic suppliers and assemblers that met the local content requirement.

The penetration of Chinese manufacturers into Vietnam's motorcycle industry established Chinese supply networks and disturbed the established rent-seeking relationship between Japanese MNCs and the Vietnamese government. It also accidentally enhanced the opportunity for local firms' participation in foreign supply networks. The structure of the motorcycle industry helps explain this industrial transformation.

6.5.2 Industry structure during the China shock

At the industry level of the DRMA, there were two important rent-management factors at work: the introduction of simpler Chinese technology, which more closely matched local firm capabilities when compared to Japanese technology, and greater market competition, which forced transformation of the foreign supply network.

Type of technology and local firms' ability

Prior to the China shock period, there was no clear distinction among the local firms since they all had insufficient financial resources and capabilities necessary to participate in the Japanese and Taiwanese value chains (Mishima, 2005). The China shock period inadvertently created a substantial demand for standardized parts for Chinese motorcycles, raising the demand for low-cost suppliers. Consequently, local firms that had previously produced replacement parts or engaged in related industries entered into production of motorcycle parts by collaborating with Chinese firms (Fujita, 2007). In addition, Chinese technologies were better suited to the basic technical, organizational, and learning abilities of local assemblers and suppliers. The Chinese components were mostly *standardized*, in the sense that they were not customized to specific models. Hence, one component could be used for a number of different Chinese knockdown models. Furthermore, neither the Vietnamese nor the Chinese assembly firms demanded strict quality or delivery requirements from their suppliers (interviews, two local firm managers, Ha Noi; July 2011). This type of production process in the Vietnamese market is referred to as the *local Chinese chain*.

The relaxed quality standards of the Chinese lead firms allowed imitation and copying across local firms, as entry barriers and financing requirements were low. As a consequence, the number of local suppliers in the industry began to grow steadily. Given the drastic increase in market share, some local assemblers started to produce parts in-house and to source other parts from Taiwanese, Chinese, and Vietnamese suppliers (Fujita, 2007). In 2003, local firms achieved an average local content ratio of 63 percent (Van-Nam, 2012). In-house production of parts was often achieved in collaboration with foreign firms, mainly Chinese ones. Among the five local firms surveyed by Fujita in 2005, three revealed that China was the source of their technology for the production of motorcycles and core components. Two firms listed South Korea and Taiwan as additional sources. At this time, the local factory that held the largest market share among local assemblers had a joint venture with a Chinese firm for mass production of motorcycle parts (Fujita, 2007).

Data from my fieldwork in 2011 confirmed that extensive collaboration between Vietnamese and Chinese firms was largely due to how easy it was to imitate Chinese technology. In addition, low quality standards demanded by Chinese and local lead firms allowed local suppliers to participate in the local Chinese chain. Two owners of Vietnamese lead firms told me in interviews that they sourced certain components to local suppliers due to low cost, despite already owning factories that could produce these parts. The interviewees also indicated that it was much easier to collaborate with Chinese firms than Japanese counterparts because Honda and other foreign firms deemed their production operation lacking in quality and capacity (interviews, Ha Noi; July 2011).

Market competition: transformation of the Japanese production chain

Seeing their market share significantly diminished, Japanese manufacturers made serious attempts to recapture the market in 2002. Consequently, the Japanese supply chain underwent a significant transformation, as the local Chinese chain started to take on a clearer shape. There were three important factors underlying the transformation within the Japanese chain. First, the Vietnamese government's local content policy, introduced at the end of 1998, came into effect at the beginning of 2001. Second, Japanese manufacturers needed to reduce production costs in order to compete with Chinese motorcycles. And third, Japanese investors realized the profit potential in the low-cost motorcycle market, which motivated the production of budget motorcycles. All these factors pressured foreign lead firms to utilize local suppliers in order to meet the local content policy and lower the cost of components.

In 2002, Honda launched the Wave Alpha, its first budget motorcycle model. Priced at USD 510, the Wave Alpha cost nearly one-third of the previous models and was only slightly more expensive than Chinese motorcycles. It immediately attracted a large number of Vietnamese consumers and was favored by local buyers for its affordability and higher quality over Chinese motorcycles. Honda's reputation for reliability and durability also boosted consumer confidence in choosing the Wave Alpha over similar Chinese models. The Wave Alpha expanded Honda's market share from 11.9 percent in 2001 to 36.9 percent in 2005. This success continued into the early 2010s. Both Honda and Chinese firms experienced drastic shifts in their market position between 1998 and 2004 (Figure 6.5).

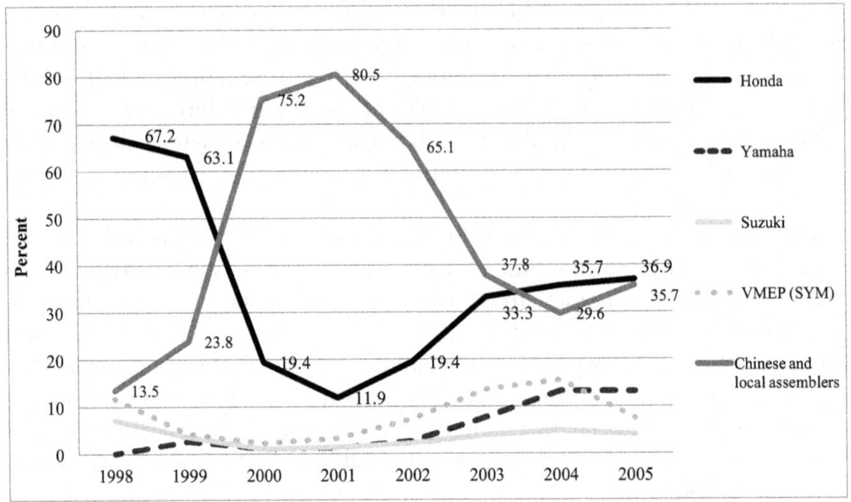

Figure 6.5 Market Share of Major Firms During the China Shock Period, 1998–2005

Source: Author's compilation based on data from the Ministry of Industry and Trade (2007).

When compared with its two most popular predecessors – the Super Dream and the Future – Honda's success with the Wave Alpha was considerable. With the introduction of the Wave Alpha into the Vietnamese market, Honda saw a high volume of production in its Vietnamese manufacturing plants (Figure 6.6).

In developing the low-priced Wave Alpha, Honda imposed substantial cost-reduction targets and announced it was ready to switch suppliers, regardless of nationality, provided that alternative suppliers met Honda's required standards and their costs were lower (Nguyen, 2006). First-tier suppliers initially responded to Honda's pressure for cost reduction by replacing imported parts with parts produced by Japanese second-tier suppliers in Vietnam and eventually with parts sourced from Taiwanese and Vietnamese second-tier suppliers (Ohara & Sato, 2008). In her survey in 2004 and 2005, Fujita (2008) interviewed six first-tier suppliers from Japan, Taiwan, and Korea. These suppliers used a total of 162 second-tier suppliers, at least 106 of which were Vietnamese firms. This was a major shift in the supplier network as compared to the earlier period, when there were only a handful of local firms supplying to foreign assemblers. This transformation marked the industry's significant advancement from the second stage of the local value chain to the third and fourth stages, when local firms became suppliers for first-tier suppliers and, in some cases, for the foreign lead firms. In sum, the competition for market power among Japanese and Chinese firms was the second important rent-management factor that affected allocation of rents. It provided important opportunities for local suppliers to enter the Japanese production chain.

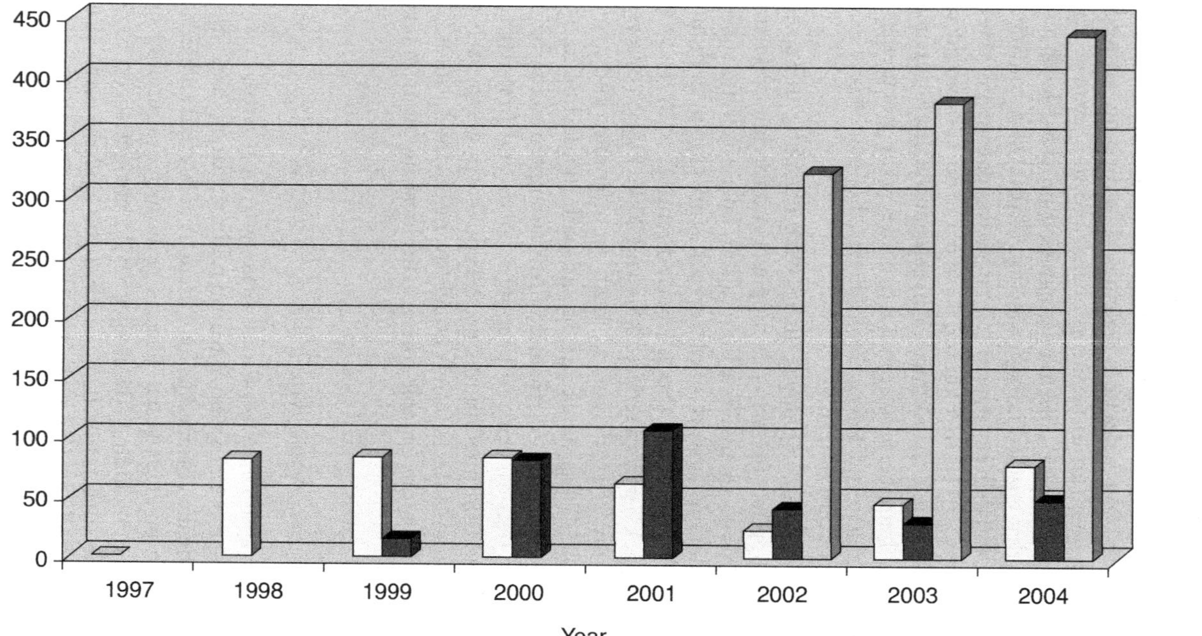

Figure 6.6 Wave Alpha versus Super Dream and Future (in thousand units)

Source: Nguyen (2006, p. 5).

6.5.3 Outcome: from local assemblers to parts suppliers for foreign firms

Before the China shock period, Japanese lead firms largely purchased components from Japanese and Taiwanese suppliers, along with a limited number of local suppliers (Figure 6.7). During the China shock, Vietnamese firms created their own production and supply chains by collaborating with Chinese firms. Starting from 2005 and after the China shock, local second-tier suppliers were able to supply components for foreign first-tier suppliers, which allowed for deeper integration into foreign supply networks and technical learning by local firms. This was mostly due to the introduction of Honda's Wave Alpha and Japanese manufacturers' cost-reduction strategies. These events allowed local suppliers in the Chinese chain to be incorporated into the Japanese chain as first- and second-tier suppliers. The new integration provided local suppliers additional upgrading that enabled mass production of parts in accordance with Japanese quality, cost, and delivery standards (interviews, managers of three local suppliers, Ha Noi; July 2011). In addition, Japanese firms also provided their local suppliers with training in product management, quality assurance, and technical skills. As local suppliers took more active roles in the procurement networks of Japanese, Chinese, and Taiwanese producers, they gained new technical skills, expertise, and capacity over time.

In the local value chain, Vietnamese firms were engaging in Stages 3, 4, and 5 as lower-tier suppliers for first-tier suppliers and foreign lead firms and becoming local lead firms themselves. Fujita (2007) demonstrates significant changes in the production network of motorcycles in Vietnam in Figure 6.7. In the figure, the "Before 'China shock'" period represents 2001–2002, and the "After 'China shock'" period reflects 2004 and 2005. Fujita's observations were confirmed by my 2011 fieldwork. Both an assembler and a supplier observed that after the China shock period and with the decline in demand for Chinese motorcycles, some Vietnamese firms attempted to upgrade their technical and production capacity to become second- and first-tier suppliers, while other firms continued to pursue the cost-cutting approach or did nothing. Many of these latter firms eventually went out of business, as they failed to compete with more capable foreign and local suppliers (interviews, Ha Noi; July 2011).

The negative impact of inadequate time horizon

The developmental transformation of local firms was short lived, however. A local assembler during the China shock period told me that, in 2002, the Vietnamese government finally enforced its local content policy and audited alleged fraudulent cases from previous years. The tax audit halted a number of local assemblers' production, including his, as they could not get access to import quotas for motorcycle parts while being audited. He said the audit lasted for more than a year, during which time his production nearly came to a full stop

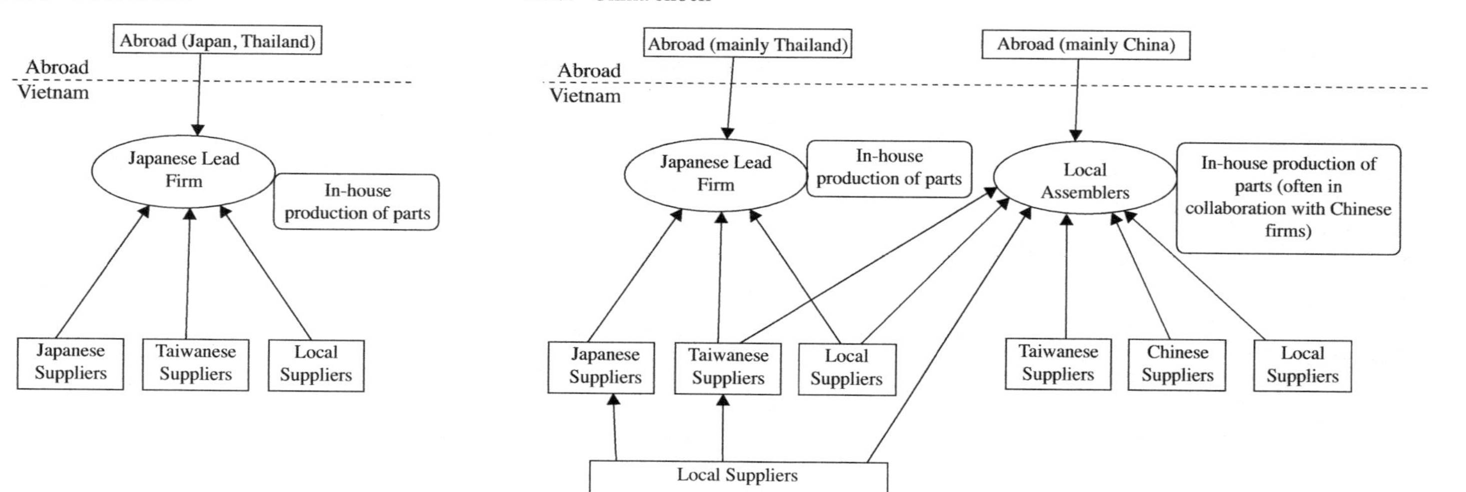

Figure 6.7 Value Chains within Vietnam's Motorcycle Industry

Source: Fujita (2007, p. 15).

(interview, Ha Noi; July 2011). By this time, foreign manufacturers were aggressively trying to recapture the market with new low-cost models, such as the Wave Alpha. Many Vietnamese assemblers struggled in the low-cost market segment. The few local assemblers who performed well pursued a low-pricing strategy by relying on Chinese counterparts for components instead of producing them in-house. They were either incapable or not interested in building their own brand or distribution networks (interviews, two local firm managers, Ha Noi; July 2011).

The Vietnamese assemblers who focused on building their own brands via upgrading and technological adoption, such as Hoa Lam Company and Sufat Vietnam, faced tremendous difficulty in competing with foreign competitors, as conditions enabling them to engage in learning began to change. To avoid bankruptcy in 2004, Hoa Lam Company joined a venture with the Taiwanese lead firm Kymko (Quoc-Hung, 2012; "Taiwanese giant stirs scooter market," 2005). To do so, Hoa Lam stopped production of its Vietnamese-brand motorcycle, the Halim, as Kymko began producing its branded motorcycle using Hoa Lam's production facilities (Quoc-Hung, 2012). In my interviews, local business owners cited Sufat Vietnam as the only local firm that continued to pursue Vietnamese-branded motorcycles, but it struggled to compete with foreign firms. At the time of the interview, Sufat was facing operating losses (two interviews, Ha Noi; July 2011). In sum, the time horizon for local firms' learning was cut short when the Vietnamese government began enforcing local content policy. The policy enforcement did not protect local suppliers or allow them time to learn and develop capability. The rapid decrease in the number of local assemblers and suppliers, coupled with the reemergence of Japanese and Taiwanese motorcycles, highlights the insufficient time horizon for local firms to reach the highest level of the local value chain.

6.5.4 Summary: the China shock period

In summary, at the macropolitical level, there was clear support for the industrialization of the industry via a number of rent policies, including localization requirements, import tariffs, and prohibition of CBUs. At the institutional level, however, the Vietnamese government failed to implement these policies, which led to the emergence of the China shock period. In reality, the rent-management factors that motivated technical collaboration and technology transfer came from within the industry itself and from the government's failure to stop illegal Chinese imports. This resulted in an influx of Chinese producers and the establishment of a new local Chinese chain, whose technologies were more appropriate to the capabilities of local firms. Consequently, a number of dynamic local firms emerged. In addition, the market competition between Japanese and Chinese lead firms forced a meaningful integration of local firms into foreign supply networks. A DRMA summary of the China shock period is shown in Table 6.7.

Table 6.7 DRMA Summary of the China Shock Period

Step 1: Political Context	• Clear political will to protect and boost upgrading in the industry, reflected in protection policies that generated learning rents **Type of rent:** Learning rents based on local content requirements, import tariffs, and import prohibition of CBUs
Step 2: Institution Structure	• Failure to implement rent policies and to enforce border controls against illegal Chinese motorcycles
Step 3: Market and Industry Structures	• Availability of simple modular technologies • Cost-cutting strategies by Chinese and Japanese producers in competitive motorcycle market
Step 4: Rent Outcomes	• Important but short-lived industrial upgrading for local firms • Transformation of Japanese production chain and emergence of the local Chinese chain • Local suppliers moved into third- or second-tier supplier networks of foreign lead firms • Insufficient time horizon for Vietnamese suppliers to become assemblers of Vietnamese-brand products • Some completion of Stage 3 and start of Stages 4 and 5 of the local value chain

6.6 Demand-driven and FDI-led market (post-2004 period)

After the China shock period, the motorcycle industry experienced three major events: (1) an FDI-led growth period due to foreign firms recapturing the Vietnamese market, (2) the removal of trade restrictions and administrative regulations to embrace FDI and principles of market liberalization, and (3) the emergence of new policies aimed at promoting supporting industries. These major events rearranged the structure of the motorcycle industry and market position of domestic manufacturing firms.

6.6.1 FDI-led development

After Honda and the other foreign manufacturers regained their market share, the industry experienced a sustained FDI-led development period. The number of local lead firms and suppliers shrank substantially, as foreign manufacturers took over and expanded production. As mentioned earlier, of the 51 Vietnamese firms surveyed by Fujita between 2001 and 2006, 35 left the industry, 16 continued motorcycle assembly, and 12 new firms entered the market (Fujita, 2010). As Vietnam experienced high economic growth, motorcycle production and sales continued to grow at a high rate. In 2000, these 51 local firms assembled and produced 1.37 million units, taking more than 80 percent of the market share (Fujita, 2010). However, changes in consumer preference for quality motorbikes, the launch of Honda's Wave Alpha, enforcement of the local content rules, and new regulations requiring all motorcycle lead firms to produce certain key components in-house meant that between 2005 and 2008, the number of local firms declined between 30 and 40 percent, with production dropping to roughly 800,000 units per year (Fujita, 2010). By 2011, this number diminished further to 380,000 motorcycles sold by Vietnamese firms (Quoc-Hung, 2012). In 2011, two Vietnamese assemblers told me they expected (correctly) the market share in the low-cost market segment to continue to diminish, unless the government intervened with supporting measures. One assembler said that his company was trying to find ways to adapt to the inevitable change – to become a second-tier supplier for Japanese lead firms (interviews, Ha Noi; July 2011). As mentioned earlier, sales of domestic vehicles were less than 13,000 in 2018 (Nguyen, 2019).

The structure of domestic firms also changed during this FDI-led growth period. In contrast to 2001, when a majority of local firms were small, there was a rise of relatively large-scale firms in 2006. For instance, in 2001, "more than half of the motorcycles sold were produced by assemblers producing fewer than 20,000 units of motorcycles per year" (Fujita, 2010, p. 9). However, toward the middle of the 2000s, production was concentrated in larger firms. For example, four firms produced more than 100,000 units in 2005 (Fujita, 2010). Overall, as the market became more concentrated, local firms were forced to engage in economies of scale in production, and many smaller, less resourceful firms were forced to exit the industry. This restructuring not only resulted in fewer domestic firms operating as lead firms or suppliers in the production chain, it also led to the disappearance of Vietnamese-branded motorcycles in the market.

6.6.2 *Changes in policy direction focusing on the supporting industries*

Starting in 2005, the Vietnamese government began to gradually liberalize the economy in anticipation of Vietnam's accession to the WTO. To do this, the government removed prohibitions on motorcycle imports, repealed local content requirements, and reduced tariffs on imported components. Furthermore, Vietnam engaged in a number of trade agreements, notably the ASEAN+3, the ASEAN-China trade bloc, and the Comprehensive and Progressive Agreement for Trans-Pacific Partnership, which required the government to further dismantle industrial policy framework and allow more foreign access to the Vietnamese market and key industries. In addition, the government relaxed regulations on motorcycle registrations so that resident drivers could register more than one motorcycle under one name. In essence, the government's efforts to loosen the market using both trade and administrative policies, together with the introduction of low-cost motorcycles by foreign manufacturers, substantially expanded motorcycle production and sales. The expansion has been long lasting, from the mid-2000s through 2019 (see Figure 6.1).

During the post-China shock period, the Vietnamese government also moved toward developing a set of policies to support the industrial sectors at large, instead of aiming at the motorcycle industry alone. The 2007 Decision 34/2007-QD-BCN (Decision 34) was the master plan for development of supporting industries until 2010 though it also provides the government's vision of the industry until 2020. Based on Decision 34, responsible ministries were to devise policies and instruments to carry out the general government master plan. As the decision came to an end in 2010, the government reviewed its policy effectiveness. A report from the Vietnam Development Forum (2011) pointed out that a major shortcoming of Decision 34 was the government's overly broad definition of "supporting industries." It encompassed nearly every part of the value chain, from materials to marketing. For instance, it lumped the textile and garment industry with mechanical industries (such as electrical and electronics) and the automobile industry. This broad definition made it difficult to create targeted policies, such as focusing on technological adoption and industrial upgrading (Van-Nam, 2012). Given Vietnam's limited capabilities and resources, such a large scope did not help the government lift constraints in important sectors or provide meaningful support for upgrading of Vietnamese manufacturing firms.

Decision 12/2011-QD-TTg (mentioned above), signed by the prime minister in February 2011, provided a policy framework for developing supporting industries. At its inception, local investors were particularly hopeful that it would offer meaningful assistance for certain important sectors. However, an industry expert at a Ha Noi research think tank and official with the MoIT indicated that the decision largely failed to assist financially weak local suppliers who still lacked the technical capability in industrial manufacturing (interviews, Ha Noi; April and July 2011). The same MoIT official participated in drafting Decision 12. She remarked that its content was too general to be effective, especially since the decision was embedded in other bodies of law with higher authority, such as the Enterprise Law (Decree 56/2009/ND-Cp and Decision 105/2009/QD-TTg). This means that if there is a conflict, Decree 56 and Decision 105 take precedence over Decision 12. Further, the official pointed out that Decision 12 contained very few provisions to assist local businesses that go beyond the policies previously established to support SMEs (interview, Ha Noi; July 2011).

The government intention to develop supporting industries was renewed in the mid-2010s and once again manifested in Decree 111 (effective in 2016) and Decision 68 (effective in 2017) – both mentioned in Section 6.2. Decree 111 was important in that it created a clear legal framework for the development of the supporting industry. Subsequent government decrees, in fact, referred to and relied on it to create a road map for policy supports for manufacturing firms ("Legal update: Decree 82," 2018). For example, Circular 1/2016/TT-NHNN stipulates that small- and medium-sized enterprises may borrow up to 70 percent of the capital they need if investing in supporting industries ("Government gives incentives," 2016). In actuality, the decree's assistance to Vietnamese firms has been limited – only one firm is reported to receive government assistance in 2018 (Wirjo & Cheok, 2017).

Unlike previous government policies, Decision 68 came with a set budget of approximately USD 47.6 million to subsidize local firms (Quynh-Nga & Hoa-Quynh, 2018). The decree was given priority to create conditions for domestic firms to become suppliers for major foreign manufactures such as Honda, Samsung, and LG. It reinforced the government's conviction that Vietnam is to become a component supplier instead of an assembling destination for MNCs ("Supporting industry to receive assistance," 2017). As mentioned, the decree specifies a number of practical measures designed to assist supporting industries. For example, on the basis of the decree, the MoIT and Samsung signed a memorandum of understanding on training Vietnamese firms to help improve production and quality. A program involving Samsung training Vietnamese information technology firms commenced in 2018. The program comprised eight cohorts of 25 Vietnamese professionals, trained by Samsung across 12 consecutive weeks ("Businesses should play major role," 2018). This is possibly the largest training program between Vietnamese firms and a lead foreign manufacturer to date. It is still too early to conclude the decree's effectiveness, however. During my 2016 interviews, two government officials expressed cautious optimism that perhaps progress will be made to enable capability building for local firms in industrial manufacturing (interviews, Ho Chi Minh City and Ha Noi; June and July 2016).

In summary, there have been major changes in the motorcycle industry since 2004, especially from policy and industry organization standpoints. Institutionally, the government relaxed trade and administrative restrictions, which enhanced market demand for motorcycles. The result was a period of FDI-led growth in which foreign firms captured almost all of the market. In addition, local firms had to restructure their production organizations – a small number of local assemblers scaled up production, while others became suppliers or left the industry entirely. Finally, the Vietnamese government devised and implemented measures to assist supporting industries, but many of them were overly broad and ineffective. The result of these policies demonstrated the Vietnamese government's willingness to support industrial sectors, though they struggled to make far-reaching impacts. This highlights the immense challenges of creating rent policies that support home-grown domestic capacity in the context of weak state institutions and intense foreign competition. Nonetheless, the government and the MoIT, in particular, seemed aware of their mistakes and shortcomings. With Decision 68, they appeared to make progress in policy design and implementation (interviews, two MoIT officials, Ha Noi and Ho Chi Minh City; June–July 2016).

6.7 Observations and policy options

Since the beginning of its industrialization in the mid-1990s, the Vietnamese motorcycle industry successfully attracted foreign investors from abroad and achieved important technological upgrading. The industrial experience can be understood through the DRMA framework. It suggests that at the highest level, there was clear political will to use FDI as an instrument to develop technical learning and adopt foreign expertise and technology. This political will, however, was diluted at the implementation stage, partly because the government was uncoordinated and ill-informed about market dynamics. Government agencies such as the MoIT did not understand the progress that local suppliers were achieving. They implemented policies resulting in the loss of a number of development opportunities. One was the failure to push Japanese and other lead firms to collaborate with local suppliers; another was a failure to support local firms, so they could compete with foreign motorcycle manufacturers after the China shock. As a result, foreign brands continued to control the majority of the motorcycle market while Vietnamese manufacturers attracted only a small portion of the low-income market segment.

The government's failure to keep Chinese firms out resulted in market competition between Chinese and Japanese firms, although it also (1) induced cost competition that allowed local suppliers to join the production value chain; (2) allowed local firms to upgrade their technical capacity through the availability of more appropriate technology from China; and (3) gave local firms the opportunity to quickly learn through collaboration, first with Chinese lead firms and later with Japanese assemblers and suppliers. These three factors, combined with the political will of the Vietnamese government, define the rent-management mechanisms that enhanced learning effort and transformation of local enterprises.

The DRMA suggests three important observations. First, the process of technology transfer from foreign investors does not take place voluntarily or automatically. In order for rent policies to become growth enhancing, government subsidies in the form of learning rents offered to foreign investors must be accompanied by credible pressure to transfer technology and production know-how to local firms. If necessary, the state can create conditions wherein foreign investors understand that rents are provided *in exchange* for investment in local learning and diffusion of technology. In the Vietnamese experience, these pressures came not from the government but from market competition, particularly between Japanese and Chinese firms, in a context where the latter effectively "stole" rents created for the former. This experience suggests that, despite the state's inability to implement rent policies, market competition among foreign investors – in a context where rents existed in the domestic market – produced positive effects for local learning. This was based on a fortuitous and short-lived set of conditions in which local firms were dynamic and flexible in adapting to and learning the new technology and know-how from foreign partners.

Second, there were no powerful local rent seekers lobbying the government for more favorable rent allocation. In this sense, the motorcycle industry is different from the textile and garment industry or the telecommunications industry. In these industries, state corporations – VNPT, Viettel, and Vinatex – were effective in utilizing their political connections to seek rents from the government, improve their competitiveness through industrialization, and assert their market power in the economy. In the motorcycle industry, however, MNCs, notably Honda, Yamaha, and Suzuki, managed to capture substantial rents early in the industry's development due to (1) limited domestic competition in the late 1990s, (2) flexible and adaptive business strategies to recapture the market from 2000 to 2005, and (3) effective rent seeking through the Japan International Cooperation Agency and business associations in Vietnam. As a result, the motorcycle industry remained an FDI-dominated industry, while local firms struggled to overcome market failures, accumulate technical capacity, and compete with foreign firms operating in Vietnam.

Third, the second case study indicates that there was some technological upgrading in the industry because the rent-management mechanism operating in the China shock period created accidental and positive learning effects. However, this type of rent-management mechanism was problematic, as it occurred randomly and benefits were limited and fleeting. Since 2007, Vietnam's economic growth occurred largely due to input expansion and less so from local capacity development. This growth dynamic is vulnerable because it is not based on industrial strength and capacity of the domestic industries. In fact, Vietnam's productivity, measured by total factor productivity, was consistently negative from 1997 to 2009, with the exception of 2001. It plummeted to 0.5 and 0.4 from 1997–2000 and 2006–2009, respectively (Figure 1.7). Meanwhile, the implementation of WTO obligations in 2007 and the ASEAN-China Free Trade Area in 2015 exerted significant competition pressure on local enterprises. Kenichi Ohno (2008) predicted that "if local capability in technology and management remains as weak as today, a large segment of indigenous industries is likely to shrink or even disappear under severe competitive pressure, and Vietnam will be locked into the position of producing low-value goods with the dominance of foreign firms" (p. 1). The motorcycle industry provides a clear example of this undesirable scenario and the difficulty of changing it in subsequent decades.

6.7.1 Policy recommendations

As international integration deepens, Vietnamese enterprises must greatly improve their capability if they are to survive and compete with global competitors. To realize Vietnam's vision for an industrialized motorcycle industry and supporting industries, local firms must achieve not only simple expansion of low-value component production but also higher productivity and technical capability. This requires Vietnam to modify its manufacturing model to one that focuses on value-added production and skilled manufacturing. In this context, my analysis provides seven suggestions for a developmental strategy as the industry moves forward.

First, there must be genuine *political will* to boost the development of supporting industries by recognizing their importance in Vietnam's industrial development.[16] This requires the Vietnamese government to acknowledge the urgency by creating effective and meaningful rents and a rent-management framework that can address issues facing local producers and suppliers: capital shortage, an ineffective credit market, difficulties in learning and transfer of technology, and uncoordinated policies among state agencies. Second, but no less important, the MoIT, the Ministry of Planning and Investment, the Ministry of Science and Technology, and other governmental agencies must take a practical approach in strengthening rent-management capabilities and in being up-to-date with local firm needs and development. The Vietnamese government must make informed rent policies, so subsidies target enhanced learning and technology acquisition specifically. Once rents are created and include both incentives and pressures for learning, the key to rent management from the state's perspective is to: (1) monitor rent performance under the MoIT, (2) negotiate with foreign investors to transfer expertise and technical learning, and (3) renegotiate rent policies if current ones are deemed ineffective. Monitoring could be based on specifying, in advance, clear performance criteria, timing, and expected results. Large and important investment projects should be closely supervised, but with flexibility to allow some conditions to be modified to ensure high performance.

Third, the Vietnamese government's rent-management capability requires a radical reorganization of institutions to deepen support for industries. For example, in Malaysia, industrial projects are designed, implemented, and supported by the Ministry of International Trade and Industry, and in Thailand, they are within the Ministry of Industry. The ministries in both countries have several under-agencies that carry out a number of tasks like conducting market research, promoting technological adoption for local firms, and coordinating with other ministries for policy planning and implementation. To prioritize and coordinate supporting policies and activities, these ministries also have national committees headed by top political and business leaders in their respective industries. In Vietnam, the initial process of conferring the primary responsibility and authority to the MoIT and building its necessary policy-making ability is incomplete. Budgeting and staffing of the MoIT's Centre of Supporting Industries Development remains very modest. This center should be the leading agency charged with real power and resources to promote supporting industries. Unfortunately, in my interview with the manager of the center, she admitted that its power is currently limited to policy advice and drafting official documents. It does not yet have the power to meaningfully influence policies and assist firms in supporting industries (interviews, Ha Noi; July 2011 and July 2016)

Fourth, as argued in the preceding two chapters, new industrial upgrade at the firm level is a prerequisite for sustaining growth. Despite the high local content ratio in motorcycles sold in Vietnam, there has always been a major gap in technological capacity between local suppliers and foreign manufacturers. Therefore, it is critical that the government step in and speed up the process of technological adoption and adaptation for local firms, as this process does not happen automatically. In this context, the development of larger and more sophisticated local suppliers in the industry must proceed in tandem with the development of supporting industries. If Vietnam is to thrive in Stage 5 of the local value chain and engage with research and development, the government must devise Schumpeterian rents to support investments in R&D. It is also critical to create mechanisms that support industry consolidation through mergers and acquisitions, in order to develop larger and more capable local suppliers with the necessary scale and sophistication to compete with MNCs and liaise with the MoIT.

Fifth, trade and FDI continue to play important roles in Vietnam's industrial development by transferring technology and collaborating with local firms so technical learning and adaptation can occur. This process is by no means automatic; thus, it requires a system of incentives and pressures at the government or the market level to induce technology transfers and learning. The government should opt for a mix of industrial-linkages between local enterprises and foreign firms and a leapfrogging strategy to create independent, high-tech SMEs.[17] In addition, the Vietnamese government will need to negotiate more skillfully with foreign investors to ensure that they commit to transfer expertise and technology on a larger and more systemic scale, while they benefit from policy-created rents, Vietnam's low-cost labor force, and its large consumer market.

Sixth, the China factor plays an important role in the development of Vietnamese industrial sector. While the China shock forced important industrial transformations in the motorcycle industry in the second period, illegal and inexpensive Chinese components remain a threat for local suppliers, as they compete unfairly in the Vietnamese market. In 2017, Vietnam imported a total of USD 58.59 billion worth of goods and merchandise from China, of which almost 70 percent serve production in manufacturing industries, and 18.6 percent are equipment and machinery (General Department of Vietnam Customs, 2018). According to Tran Anh, owner of equipment manufacturing firm Vikyno & Vinappro Company, there are supporting industries that have a high potential for entry by foreign manufacturers, especially Chinese ones, but these are also areas where Vietnamese suppliers could participate competitively (Bich-Diep, 2011). If the Vietnamese government loses sight of illegal mechanical imports from China, these products will unfairly compete with local suppliers, making it difficult to boost the development of Vietnam's mechanical industry. The China factor must be taken seriously because penetration of Chinese goods has reduced demand for domestic industrial inputs in the Vietnamese market.

Finally, starting in 2012, the market demand for motorcycles in major Vietnamese cities was close to saturation, so excess production in Vietnam has prompted foreign manufacturers to find ways to export to other developing countries. For example, in 2017, Honda produced 3.14 million motorcycles in Vietnam, of which 2.17 million units were sold in the domestic market. The company exported 131,000 CBUs and other accessories, together earning USD 331 million in export revenue. Compared to the previous year, the 2017 export revenue was up 11 percent (Le, 2018). In 2018, Vietnam exported USD 408.4 million worth of motorcycle units, thus taking a 1.5 percent share of the global motorcycle market (Workman, 2019). This export activity is beneficial for Vietnam because it increases export revenue, creates new jobs, and deepens collaboration between local and foreign firms. Therefore, a policy structure that provides incentives for motorcycle lead firms to increase exports should be considered, along with a clear set of expectations. Policies in this area are important, as they could open up the possibility for Vietnam to become a large exporter of motorcycles in the international market.

To conclude, the success or failure of an industry often depends on interaction and compatibility among a number of rent-management mechanisms that rely on the state, firms, and market dynamics. Sharing risks in technology acquisition and targeting industrial upgrading require institutions to provide appropriate profit incentives as well as political ability to overcome resistance from interest groups within the economy. Given Vietnam's commitment to global and regional integration, the motorcycle industry's next phase of development requires more informed and coordinated rent policies that could bring local firms to the next level of technological and organizational capabilities. This will place them well within global and regional supply networks.

Notes

1 If the data source or newspaper provided the data in USD, I reported the same value as shown in the source. However, if VND was used in the data or in interviews, I converted the value to USD using the exchange rate of USD 1 = VND 21,000.
2 Lead firm is defined as the motorcycle manufacturer whose brand comes with the motorcycle. For example, Honda, Suzuki, Yamaha are all known lead firms. Their motorcycles bear their name.
3 Completely built units (CBUs) are motorcycles fully assembled abroad and exported to Vietnam as a complete unit.
4 Complete knockdown motorcycles are motorcycles produced in the country of origin that are knocked down completely into parts and imported by another country, in this case Vietnam. The assembling process in Vietnam requires more skills from local workers than for incomplete knockdown motorcycles (discussed later in this chapter).
5 An agreement for a two-step loan fund was signed between the Japan Bank for International Cooperation and the Vietnamese government in 1999. It provided long-term credit to Vietnamese SMEs through participating financial institutions, such as joint-stock commercial banks. It was expected that 70 percent of the beneficiaries from this fund would be private SMEs.
6 The credit guarantee fund for SMEs aimed to encourage financial institutions to lend to SMEs by absorbing a part of the credit risk, thereby alleviating borrowing constraints as a result of insufficient collateral.
7 ASEAN countries include Brunei, Cambodia, Indonesia, Laos, Malaysia, Myanmar, the Philippines, Singapore, Thailand, and Vietnam. ASEAN +3 includes all members of ASEAN plus China, Japan, and South Korea.
8 Official data for these subsidies are not available.
9 Incomplete knockdown motorcycles are motorcycles that are partially disassembled in the country of origin.
10 One interviewee explained that Taiwanese investors did not have as much negotiating power, given the smaller size of their investments. In addition, Japanese brands were much more popular in Vietnam, and thus the market demand for Japanese-made motorcycles was considerable (interview, MoIT official, Ha Noi; July 2011).
11 As an alternative to using local suppliers, they used Japanese suppliers and partners, or set up in-house production in Vietnam.
12 This observation only applies to the period between the 1990s and the 2000s. In the third phase, Honda was more collaborative with Vietnamese suppliers, partly due to improvements in local firms' industrial capability.
13 In the late 1990s, there were a number of small-scale local firms, and even households, that were engaged in production of replacement parts, such as pistons, piston rings, cylinders, gaskets, crankshafts, valves, and sprockets. Some of these producers had been making

machinery parts since the government's central planning period (before 1986), while others entered the market in the late 1980s, as the demand for motorcycle parts increased (Fujita, 2007).

14 I interviewed Fujita Mai in July 2011. She explained that the term "China shock" was a literal translation from Japanese, and it was widely used at the time to illustrate the phenomenon of Chinese goods' penetration in low-cost market segments in other developing countries.

15 This category is needed because Chinese companies refused to take part in a Vietnamese government survey or in author interviews.

16 Given the need to upgrade the entire industrial sector, policies that promote the motorcycle industry must converge with ones devised for supporting industries. At present, the government should focus on the supporting industries, more so than the motorcycle industry itself.

17 An example of a leapfrogging strategy would be a firm skipping steps in the stages of its development.

References

Agence France Presse. (2002, October 30). Vietnam lifts motorbike import tax. *CNBC Africa*.

Bich-Diep. (2011, August 12). Phát triển công nghiệp phụ trợ: "Nói khá nhiều, làm rất ít" [Developing supporting industry: "Plenty of talkings, lack of doings"]. *BaoViet Securities*. Retrieved from www.bvsc.com.vn/News/2011812/160982/phat-trien-cong-nghiep-phu-tro-noi-kha-nhieu-lam-rat-it.aspx

Businesses should play major role in supporting industries. (2018, April 18). *Saigon Times*. Retrieved from https://english.thesaigontimes.vn/59371/businesses-should-play-major-role-in-supporting-industries.html

Fujita, M. (2007). *Local firms in latecomer developing country amidst China's rise: The case of Vietnam's motorcycle industry* (Discussion Paper No. 97). Institute of Developing Economies. Retrieved from https://ideas.repec.org/p/jet/dpaper/dpaper97.html

Fujita, M. (2008). *Value chain dynamics and growth of local firms: The case of the motorcycle industry in Vietnam* (Discussion Paper No. 161). Institute of Developing Economies. Retrieved from www.ide.go.jp/English/Publish/Download/Dp/161.html

Fujita, M. (2010). *The diversity and dynamics of industrial organization: Transformation of local assemblers in the Vietnamese motorcycle industry* (Working Paper No. 230). Institute of Developing Economies. Retrieved from www.ide.go.jp/English/Publish/Download/Dp/230.html

General Department of Vietnam Customs. (2018). *2017 customs statistics*. Ha Noi: Information Technology and Statistics Deparment.

Government gives incentives to small firms to invest. (2016, February 15). *VietnamPlus*. Retrieved from https://en.vietnamplus.vn/government-gives-incentives-to-small-firms-to-invest/88934.vnp

Intarakumnerd, P., & Fujita, M. (2008). Coping with a giant: Challenges and opportunities for Thai and Vietnamese motorcycle industry from China. *Science, Technology & Society*, *13*(1), 35–60.

Jalaluddin, A. (2002, March 13). Vietnam motorcycle market: Imports spurt growth. *Frost & Sullivan Market Insight*. Retrieved from ww2.frost.com/

Le, H. (2018, May 28). Honda dominates 72% of Vietnam's motorcycle market. *Saigon Times*. Retrieved from https://english.thesaigontimes.vn/59971/honda-dominates-72-of-vietnam's-motorcycle-market.html

Legal update: Decree 82 on new concepts of industrial parks and their incentives. (2018). *ACSV Legal*. Retrieved from https://cdn-se.mynilead.com/2c8bf258f12ee1b2538bb25067eaf6e3/assets/media/legal-update-decree-82-on-new-concepts-of-industrial-parks-and-their-incentives_1547448284.pdf

Ministry of Industry and Trade. (2007). The master plan for the development of the motorcycle industry. *Ministry of Industry, Institute for Industrial Policy and Strategy*. Retrieved from www.grips.ac.jp/vietnam/VDFTokyo/Temp/Doc/2007/JWG_Keydoc_FinalEMay31.pdf

Ministry of Industry and Trade. (2012). *Research and evaluation of the development potentials of the supporting industries in Vietnam*. Ha Noi: Ministry of Industry and Trade, Center of Supporting Industry Development.

Mishima, K. (2005). The supplier system of the motorcycle industry in Vietnam, Thailand and Indonesia: Localization, procurement and cost reduction processes. *National Graduate Institute for Policy Studies*. Retrieved from www.grips.ac.jp/vietnam/KOarchives/doc/EB02_IIPF/9EB02_Chapter8.pdf

Motorcycle sales reach record in 2018. (2019, January 13). *Vietnam Plus*. Retrieved from https://en.vietnamplus.vn/motorcycle-sales-reach-record-in-2018/145082.vnp

Nguyen, T. D. (2005). *Honda knowledge transfer and the role of the local supplier responsiveness* (Ph.D. Thesis). Graduate School of Economics, Kyoto University, Kyoto, Japan.

Nguyen, T. D. (2006). Chinese motorcycle penetration into Vietnam and the existing motorcycle makers: A study of Honda Company. *Economics Bulletin*, *13*(4), 1–9.

Nguyen, T. D. (2019, January 22). Motorbikes still the vehicle of choice in Vietnam. *VN Express*. Retrieved from https://e.vnexpress.net/news/business/data-speaks/motorbikes-still-the-vehicle-of-choice-in-vietnam-3872250.html

Ohara, M., & Sato, Y. (2008). *Asian industrial development from the perspective of the motorcycle industry* (Discussion Paper No. 182). Institute of Developing Economies. Retrieved from www.ide.go.jp/English/Publish/Download/Dp/182.html

Ohno, K. (2008). *Vietnam-Japan Monozukuri partnership for supporting industries: For leveling up Vietnam's competitiveness in the age of deepening integration*. Paper presented at the Seminar on Action Plan for Development of Supporting Industry in Vietnam, Ha Noi. Retrieved from www.grips.ac.jp/vietnam/KOarchives/doc/EP23_monozukuri.pdf

Quoc-Hung. (2012, March 11). Các nhà sản xuất xe máy tính chuyện tiến vào thị trường khu vực [Motorcycle producers plan to penetrate regional markets]. *Saigon Times*. Retrieved from www.thesaigontimes.vn/72840/Cac-nha-san-xuat-xe-may-ti%CC%81nh-chuye%CC%A3n-tien-vao-thi-truong-khu-vuc.html

Quynh-Nga, & Hoa-Quynh. (2018, January 28). Govn't incentives, business initiatives boost support industries. *Vietnam Economic News*. Retrieved from http://ven.vn/govnt-incentives-business-initiatives-boost-support-industries-30823.html

Richards, D., Harvie, C., Nguyen, H., & Nguyen, V. L. (2002). The limping tiger: Problems in transition for SMEs in Vietnam. In C. Harvie & B. C. Lee (Eds.), *The role of SMEs in national economies in East Asia* (Vol. 2). Cheltenham, England: Edward Elgar Publishing Limited.

Supporting industry to receive assistance from the state. (2017, March 4). *Vietnam Law & Legal Forum*. Retrieved from http://vietnamlawmagazine.vn/supporting-industry-to-receive-assistance-from-the-state-5740.html

Taiwanese giant stirs scooter market. (2005, January 18). *Vietnam Breaking News*. Retrieved from www.vietnambreakingnews.com/2005/01/taiwanese-giant-stirs-scooter-market/

Van-Nam. (2012, May 24). Mỏi mòn trông chờ công nghiệp phụ trợ [Endless wait for supporting industries]. *Saigon Times*. Retrieved from www.thesaigontimes.vn/77083/Moi-mon-trong-cho-cong-nghiep-phu-tro.html

Vietnam Association for Motorcycle Manufacturers. (2019). *Sales data.* Retrieved from http://vamm.org.vn/sales-data/

Vietnam August: Two-wheeler sales down 5% while Yamaha is down 24%. (2019, September 18). *MotorCycles Data.* Retrieved from https://motorcyclesdata.com/2019/07/08/vietnam-motorcycles/

Vietnam Development Forum. (2011). *Survey on comparison of backgrounds, policy, measures and outcomes for developement of supporting industires in ASEAN (Malaysia and Thailand in Comparison with Vietnam)* (1st ed.). Ha Noi, Vietnam: Publishing House of Communication and Transport.

Wirjo, A., & Cheok, D. (2017). Supporting industry promotion policies in APEC: Case study on Viet Nam. *Asia-Pacific Economic Cooperation.* Retrieved from http://publications.apec.org/-/media/APEC/Publications/2017/6/Supporting-Industry-Promotion-Policies-in-APEC-Case-Study-on-Viet-Nam/217_PSU_Final-Report_Case-Study-on-Supporting-Industry_Viet-Nam.pdf

Workman, D. (2019, September 10). Motorcycle exports by country. *World's Top Exports.* Retrieved from www.worldstopexports.com/motorcycles-exports-country/

7 Industrial transformation and rent seeking

Lessons for development

7.1 Introduction

Successful industrial development among third-world countries is rare. Over the twentieth century, only a handful of countries made the leap to industrialization comparable with the United States and Europe. This is because industrialization requires resources, state planning, coordination, resilience to external shocks, and sustained performance of firms. It also involves articulated industrial strategies that demand government-created incentives and conditions for high performance, while also addressing existing industrial and political constraints. Such requirements are extremely difficult to achieve in the context of intense global competition, weak state capacity, low levels of skilled labor, underdeveloped credit markets, and timid domestic demand for goods and services.

In this context, Vietnam's industrial development features a number of important characteristics. First, under conditions of controlled economic reform, the Vietnamese government managed rent seeking by coupling state intervention with gradual market openness in the industrial sectors. A lack of developed rules of law, weak contract enforcement, and inconsistent property protection enabled rent seeking to occur side by side with monopolistic behaviors, cronyism, and corruption. However, the growth and development in the telecommunications industry, and to some extent in the textile and garment (T&G) and motorcycle industries, suggests that rent seeking also reduced the impacts of institutional and market failures. This is especially true where the interplay of politics, institutions, and markets incentivized strong efforts and performance by firms.

Second, technological learning and upgrading occurred, but the intensity varied widely across sectors and firms because they required time, capital, and effort from workers and business owners. For economic transformation in industrial manufacturing, success or failure frequently depends on whether markets, institutions, and political conditions encourage long-term investments. In this context, Vietnam's growth and industrialization appears uneven across industries, particularly given the government's ad hoc policies, changing global market conditions, and frequent fluctuations in opportunities and challenges in the local market.

Third, Vietnamese state-owned enterprises (SOEs), especially the state general corporations and economic groups, played a dominant role in rent seeking. They unfairly competed with small and medium enterprises (SMEs) in the private sector. In many instances, rent-seeking activities resulted in the capture of state resources without productivity gains. These rents can be described as *redistributive rents*. Many experts interviewed during my fieldwork (2011, 2012, and 2016) called for reforms of these SOEs, given their persistent inefficiencies and the distortions they inflicted in the domestic market. However, in some instances in the T&G and telecom industries, SOE rent-capture strategies offered growth enhancement. In these instances, rent seeking delivered developmental outcomes when captured rents were used to invest in industrial capacity, new technology adoption and know-how, solutions to market and institutional failure, and exploration of new business opportunities abroad. Much could be learned from the ways Vietnamese SOEs competed against each other, and how some SOEs were encouraged to use rents for productive activities that led to industrial development.

Finally, in opening its own market to the forces of global and regional integration, Vietnam encountered a great number of opportunities and challenges. Globalization is not automatically a winning strategy for developing countries, especially if exports reinforce poor countries' comparative advantages and fail to include higher value-added production over time. By and large, and with a great deal of nuance, market openness and integration were favorable for Vietnam's economic growth, which allowed the country to achieve middle-income status in 2008. Whether this economic transformation will continue its developmental path, and whether Vietnam can avoid a middle-income trap, will depend considerably on political, institutional, and economic factors. In the context of dynamic and evolving global markets, changing geopolitics, and shifting domestic political settlement, Vietnam needs to continually assess its rent-management configuration so that its industrial policy can truly boost the competitiveness of its firms in the international market. The DRMA framework and case studies offered herein provide the theoretical foundation, analytical tools, and critical assessments necessary for policy considerations both now and in the future.

7.2 Summary of results

A significant observation emerging from this research is the analytical view that rents can be developmental and growth enhancing, if the configuration of rent management incentivizes industrial upgrade and conditions firm performance. In the telecommunications industry, for example, factors included a strong political commitment to develop the industry, the presence of effective institutions that monitored competition, strong incentives offered to firms with industrial ability, pressure from market competition, and relatively high levels of initial capacity and resources for production expansion. In the T&G industry, relevant factors determining rent-management mechanisms included rent competition among general corporations within the state sector, which forced the state-owned general corporation Vietnam National Textile and Garment Group (Vinatex) and its subsidiaries to strive for greater competitiveness. In addition, there was competition among SOEs, domestic private enterprises, and foreign investors to export to the international market. This competition created credible pressures to boost capacity in the low-skilled garment sector.

In the motorcycle industry, rent management was driven by a political commitment to develop the industry in the late 1990s and early 2000s, followed by effective market competition between Chinese and Japanese manufacturers in the Vietnamese market. Vietnamese firms were also flexible and adaptive to the changing market dynamics forced by global and regional integration. In some cases, rent seeking allowed local firms to capture additional profits from market opportunities that later became investment capital for technical capacity. The following sections summarize the different rent-management mechanisms identified in the case studies and offer observations about the configuration of factors that were either growth enhancing or growth reducing in the Vietnamese context.

7.2.1 Factors affecting rent management in Vietnam

The three factors identified in the DRMA – politics, institutions, and industry organization – that affected the structure of incentives and pressures are highlighted in Table 7.1. The plus (+) sign indicates positive effects and conditions in terms of growth-enhancing outcomes; the minus (–) sign indicates negative or negligible effects. The plus and minus (+/–) signs together imply that the factors created a combination of positive and negative effects. The signs are simplified indicators of the many nuanced effects of particular factors and conditions. As discussed in Chapters 4, 5, and 6, the positive and negative effects can vary a great deal in each case study, and the signs do not indicate equal effects in different cases. For instance, while the political commitment and support for upgrading had positive effects in both the telecommunications and T&G industries, the scale of support and outcomes achieved were more significant for Viettel in

Table 7.1 Summary of the Case Studies

Case No.	*Industry*	*Case Study*	*Politics*	*Institution*	*Industry Organization*
1	Telecom	VNPT Monopoly	–	–	–
2	Telecom	Viettel	+	+	+
3	Telecom	3G Adoption	+	+	+
4	T&G	Quota Period	–	–	+/–
5	T&G	China Factor	–	–	–
6	T&G	Vinatex/State Sector	+	–	+/–
7	Motorcycle	Oligopoly by Foreign Firms	+	–	–
8	Motorcycle	China Shock	+	–	+/–

telecom than for Vinatex in T&G. Finally, what constitutes a positive or negative factor itself depends on overall conditions of the sector, policies that created rents, capabilities of the firms, and types of technology at issue.

The shaded rows are the more successful cases of technological upgrading, although the degree of success, again, varies widely. The unshaded rows are relatively unsuccessful cases: rent seekers captured rents without any effect on upgrading and productivity improvement. Thus, the relevant industry lost opportunities during the period studied. For instance, in the T&G industry, there were more successful technology adoptions and industrial development in the case of Vinatex (shaded row) than in the quota period (unshaded row). Generally speaking, the successful cases show two or more factors or conditions with plus signs, and the unsuccessful cases show at least two factors or conditions with minus signs. Based on the insights provided by the case studies, I offer the following observations.

7.2.2 Growth-enhancing rent-management mechanisms

When all three factors affecting rent management provide positive support for effort in technology acquisition, an effective rent-management mechanism can emerge, even if individual factors do not work perfectly alone. This observation is exemplified by successful cases in the telecom industry (Case 2: Viettel and Case 3: 3G Adoption). There were formal and informal learning rents provided to the firms; and the state was relatively capable of managing rents and regulating competition within the industry. In addition, there were strong internal incentives to enhance profits, pressures from competition, the possibility of foreign entry, and sufficient initial capabilities of the firms to upgrade. This combination of factors created an effective rent-management mechanism for the industry to industrialize and develop. Therefore, these two case studies are closest to the optimal scenario of rent management for development.

In other words, meaningful industrial development requires stable political commitment to develop the industries. The commitments are then manifested in state-directed rent creation (such as industrial policies) and effective implementation that combines both incentives and compulsion for firm performance. The rents should be created in a competitive market environment to avoid redistribution. They should also account for a firm's capacity to adopt, adapt, and learn new technology. Finally, market opportunities, such as a strong market demand for goods and services, allow firms to take risks, invest, learn, make mistakes, and eventually become competitive.

In any configuration of rent management, rent seeking by firms and connected interests is inevitable. It is often followed by rent creation and distribution. Some rents eventually manifest in the form of learning and Schumpeterian rents, while others could be redistributive or monopolistic rents. Oftentimes, a combination of rents emerges. The aim of development policy and governance is to ensure that when rent seeking and rent creation occur, they are directed toward productive activities, ensuring developmental outcomes. The two case studies in the telecom industry (Viettel and 3G Adoption) demonstrate this exact combination of rent seeking in the public sector.

7.2.3 Developmental rent-management mechanisms with institutional failures

If a state cannot fully manage its policy-created rents to ensure growth-enhancing outcomes – because of failures at the implementation level – growth-enhancing outcomes may still be possible if other factors support firm development. The case studies in Chapters 5 and 6 suggest that developmental outcomes are still possible (1) if the political conditions are resistant to unproductive rent capture, (2) if the firms have initial capability for learning, (3) if there is an adequate time horizon to support technology adoption, and (4) if there is sufficient pressure on firms (either from market competition or other disciplining mechanisms) to put in high levels of effort and performance.

For instance, Vinatex (Case 6) had weak state commitment and poor rent-management capability from state agencies that monitor and enforce rents (i.e., the Ministry of Industry and Trade and the Vietnam Textile and Apparel Association). However, there was a political commitment to keep Vinatex competitive in order to further the government's social objectives. In addition, Vinatex was motivated to sustain its political support from the state, relative to other general corporations and state economic groups (SEGs). There were also incentives for profits from international markets and pressures from competition in the private sector. Together, these factors ensured that government rents facilitated capacity building among SOEs.

In the case of the China shock period that affected the motorcycle industry (Case 8), the Vietnamese government was again incapable of managing rents in line with its formal policy objectives because of institutional weaknesses. Thus, rent seeking was rampant. Here, developmental outcomes were achieved because the political will to support the motorcycle industry created an overarching policy environment of supportive rents, even if they were not effectively managed as learning rents. More importantly, there were also market incentives to make a profit, and effective market competition from Chinese and Japanese manufacturers. Finally, the institutional weaknesses of enforcing border controls had an accidental positive effect: it allowed less-sophisticated motorcycles and Chinese technology to penetrate Vietnam, which created the opportunity for Vietnamese firms to become component producers and suppliers. However, this positive outcome was short lived. The time horizon for local firms to develop industrial capacity was inadequate, given the vulnerable combination of factors that produced the learning outcomes.

7.2.4 Growth-reducing rent-management mechanisms

If there are too few factors supporting learning efforts at the three levels in the DRMA, the result could be rent capture in the form of redistributive rents or monopoly rents, and the consequent loss of development opportunities. For instance, in the case of VNPT (Case 1), the policy rents created had the character of monopoly rents and thus failed to induce industrialization because they offered VNPT insufficient incentives to upgrade. Rents were also granted without sufficient pressure from state leaders and without a state-disciplining mechanism linked to productive outcomes. There was also no competition in the market at the time to pressure VNPT to upgrade.

Similarly, the quota period (Case 4) analyzed in the T&G industry provides an example of a missed opportunity. In this case, the state was not only incapable of managing rents but was so corrupt that it extracted rents from the industry. Although there were formal rents created by policy, producers could not access these rents to improve their industrial capability or expand investment in the textile sector despite dynamic market conditions supportive of learning and upgrading. In this configuration of conditions, government officials and local and foreign firms engaged in rent-seeking schemes to obtain quotas for exports in ways that were beneficial for some but damaging to the industry overall.

In the case of the Vietnam–China border trade discussed in Chapter 5 (Case 5), there was a failure to generate incentives and pressures for upgrading at all three levels of rent management, leading to lost opportunities and heavy dependence on imported materials. The state was incapable of protecting rents because it could not control illegal materials imported from China. This led to unfair price competition in the domestic market and redistribution of rents to smugglers and other unproductive rent seekers. At the same time, Vietnamese textile manufacturers lacked the capability to immediately compete with Chinese suppliers because they were unable to upgrade their technical skills, adopt and learn from advanced technologies, or enter joint ventures with foreign investors to learn from them.

Finally, in the motorcycle industry case study analyzing the initial entry of multinational corporations (Case 7), foreign lead firms were provided rents without conditions from the state or pressures from the market to transfer technology and know-how to domestic firms and workers. Consequently, despite the political commitment of the state to develop the motorcycle industry, there were insufficient conditions to ensure a transfer of learning and technology from foreign multinational corporations to Vietnamese suppliers.

7.3 The role of the state and policy implications for Vietnam

Despite the high and sustained growth rate, Vietnam's growth process was not linear; much of it took place during a period of pervasive rent seeking and ad hoc rent policies. Nonetheless, some learning and technological upgrading took place, but it was with a great deal of inconsistency across sectors and firms due to internal rent seeking among vested interests and the varied ability of Vietnamese firms to absorb new technology. In addition, the state sector, including some powerful state-owned conglomerates, engaged in large-scale rent seeking and rent distribution. The private sector, which initially did not get significant rents or state supports, achieved some industrial development, though it was limited in relation to the government's SOE-centric agenda. The strength of the private sector suggests that Vietnam would benefit from encouraging industrial competitiveness of private firms, especially among SMEs.

The rent-management analyses in Chapters 4, 5, and 6 suggest that there was not one unique and successful configuration of rent management that worked in all industrial sectors. Instead, a successful synthesis included one or more of these factors: (1) political will and competition among political and economic interests supporting industry development, (2) effective formal and informal institutional structures of rent allocation and implementation, (3) incentives for profits and pressures from market competition, (4) effective use of a time horizon to develop firm competitiveness, and (5) the initial capability of firms and workers to learn new skills and technologies. Now that Vietnam has reached middle-income status, it should avoid ad hoc industrial development, aiming instead to formulate practical and developmental rent-management strategies to move the country toward the next stage of development and avoid the middle-income trap.

In this context, government policies should focus on five important areas. First, the ability of the private sector to take risks in technology acquisition is absolutely vital for Vietnam's development. However, as previous chapters suggest, the Vietnamese private sector has weakened from intense pressure from foreign firms and large SOEs. If this decline continues, it is likely to damage Vietnam's economy and its ability to continue learning and developing new industrial capability. From this perspective, the state's rent strategies need to focus on promoting *domestic enterprise development and the local value chain*. Here, the most important task is to address the critical constraints and bottlenecks identified throughout this book: access to credit and capital markets, low technical and managerial skills, weak linkages and communications between the state and firms and between international buyers and domestic sellers, heavy reliance on imported materials, outdated machines and techniques, and inadequate production expertise.

It is critical that Vietnamese firms increase value added in production to move into the more profitable segment of the value chain (Khan, 2009; Masina, 2010; Ohno, 2008). There must be a policy focus on upgrading technical and organizational capabilities at the firm level. To accomplish this, the playing field between the state and private sectors has to be leveled to a greater extent. SOEs cannot indefinitely drive technology acquisition and capability development, given their monopolistic characteristics and access to political rents. Next, any policy has to ensure an overall mix of conditions such that rents go to those who can put in the most effort in learning technical skills and improving capabilities. This may involve instituting performance benchmarks, making rent beneficiaries accountable for performance, and specifying time limits for protections to avoid unlimited redistribution of rents and to ensure that rents are not captured in unstable conditions with limited time horizons. The success of these measures is highly dependent on the rent-management capabilities of the state, especially government institutions such as the Ministry of Industry and Trade and Ministry of Planning and Investment, as well as central and local business development agencies. In addition, in the context of weak institutional capabilities, the government should focus on policy interventions that not only create rents but competition among firms and industries to force industrial development efforts.

Investors in developed countries frequently oppose rent policies, arguing that they discriminate against foreign firms. Vietnam has done well in resisting this pressure. In the early stages of industrialization, competition with foreign firms should be introduced gradually so as to promote collaboration, allow local firms to gain technical capabilities, and increase exports. However, excessive avoidance of competition can be counterproductive – a point strongly made by Case Study 1 of the telecom chapter. Additionally, international trade agreements have made rent creation through trade restrictions more difficult since Vietnam committed to open its domestic market to a number of trade partners. The focus should be on providing rents to domestic firms through other mechanisms, such as reducing the cost of skills training and higher education, enhancing information sharing within the local value chain, adopting and diffusing new technologies from abroad through active technical research and development institutes, and introducing and coordinating local firms with investment opportunities in the international market. These policies are generally welcomed, as they reduce training and operation costs for foreign investors while supporting local firms in their efforts to upgrade and penetrate international markets.

Second, while exports remain a significant source of income, it is difficult for any developing country to sell labor-intensive products in foreign markets without the danger of being trapped in established supply chains and trade networks. To become an exporter of high-skill and high-value goods, Vietnam must reexamine and address the factors that constrained it. This is a difficult problem. Any national development strategy must consider that the Vietnamese market has been flooded with materials and imports from industrially advanced countries, increasingly from China and South Korea. In effect, this reality limits the opportunity of local firms to build their capacity gradually and add value in their manufacturing activities. Once again, rent policies have to create opportunities while resisting pressures from foreign imports. It may be difficult to raise tariffs today, but government procurement plays a key role in the national economy and could be directed toward supporting domestic firms. Further, a national campaign to raise consumer awareness about purchasing Vietnamese-made products is inexpensive and might create genuine demand for Vietnamese goods. Meanwhile, a set of development policies could focus on developing Vietnamese-owned trading houses providing not only trade deals but also business and technical advice. They would be the brokers and advisors for domestic small and medium manufacturers, connecting them with buyers abroad.[1] These trading houses could also help domestic firms overcome knowledge barriers, improve expertise in trade and logistics, and bridge the information gap between Vietnamese exporters and international buyers.

Third, Vietnam needs stronger business associations; it also needs state agencies to create greater linkages and embeddedness among firms, government agencies, training institutes, and universities. Rodrik (2004) underscores the "need to embed private initiative in a framework of public action that encourages restructuring, diversification and technological dynamism beyond what market forces on their own would generate" (p. 1). So far, as with the Vietnam Textile and Apparel Association, most Vietnamese associations are strongly connected to the government or to SOEs and thus fail to represent the private sector. Creation of – and support for – more effective private and independent associations operated and represented by businesses in the private sector will be vital for constructive dialogue and information-sharing among government agencies and industries. It would also help the state to devise practical policies that address realistic issues in the private sector and support business activities and growth. In addition, there should be a feedback loop among firms, training institutes, and universities. The private sector could communicate its needs for specific skill sets desired from the labor force. Additionally, technical knowledge and applied university research with commercial value could be shared with and adopted by firms.

Fourth, the China factor is important enough to be separately considered, given the challenge it poses to the industrialization of Vietnam from the influx of cheap, often illegal, and frequently below-market-price imports. So far, the Vietnamese government has neither addressed the issue nor remedied its negative effects. This is due largely to the state's lack of political will to confront China, and its own weak monitoring and enforcement capacity in targeting illegal cross-border trade. The Vietnamese government must devise new strategies to address the negative effects caused by Sino-Vietnam trade. Otherwise, the Vietnamese economy will be forever overshadowed by China and miss many more opportunities to develop its own industrial base.

Policy solutions must especially focus on capacity development of domestic firms in *niche markets*, where Chinese goods are not as competitive. Some Chinese producers are reluctant to accept small orders, given the benefits of scaled production – a beneficial market opening for small and medium manufacturers in Vietnam. In the next few years, Vietnam should also find ways to take advantage of the Comprehensive and Progressive Agreement for Trans-Pacific Partnership, which does not include China but involves major trade partners such as Japan, Australia, and Canada. Finally, Vietnam could tap into and leverage foreign investors' desires to reduce production from China while maintaining a manufacturing base in the Asian region. A policy strategy that combines foreign investors' eagerness for an alternative Asian industrial base with the production of niche products that avoids head-to-head competition with Chinese producers could substantially reduce China's impact on Vietnam and open new opportunities in areas not yet exploited by large-scale Chinese manufacturing.

Finally, the question of how to effectively reform the state sector in Vietnam needs to be addressed, although such a complex issue is beyond the scope of this book. Nevertheless, the rent-management analyses in the empirical chapters suggest that to improve the state sector, Vietnam needs rigorous and effective policies that *promote competition* and *information disclosure* to improve accountability and public scrutiny. In addition, rents, if given, must come with clear conditions for performance, discipline mechanisms for nonperformance, and specific time horizons for when benefits will end. It is also key to monitor and discipline SOEs that thwart competition and monopolize industries with unproductive and speculative activities. The government also needs to manage conflicts among the general corporations and SEGs. If it does not, the current round of public sector reform is likely to fail just like the previous ones: equitization has largely created incentives for SOE managers to capture rents based on their monopoly or oligopoly position in the domestic market and their advantageous access to state capital and land (Pincus, 2009). The suggestions here require a two-pronged approach: (1) a high level of political will on the part of Vietnamese leadership to override powerful interests that would block or modify meaningful reforms and (2) a fostering of industrial development across industries.

7.4 Lessons for development

For developing countries, the heart of viable industrial and technology policies is to address the many market failures that constrain domestic firms from technical learning and upgrading. This will promote the development of globally competitive and technologically competent domestic firms. However, globalization has brought fundamental shifts in what poor countries can and cannot do to foster industrialization. In the past, trade policies were the principal instruments for industrial promotion. Unfortunately, the lowering of trade barriers, the proliferation of bilateral and regional trade agreements, and more stringent World Trade Organization rules on issues such as domestic-content policies and the protection of intellectual property rights have constrained the types of trade (or rent) policies that are beneficial to promote development (Haque, 2007). For example, along with lower trade barriers, the bilateral trade agreements between Vietnam and other developed countries usually contain provisions related to foreign direct investment (FDI), capital account liberalization, intellectual property protection, and labor and environment standards. In addition to new rules governing international trade, the context and design of industrial policies were profoundly impacted as a result of changes in global value chains and the rise of international trading networks. All this has increased barriers for new firms entering the world market and global production chain. These changes have arguably constrained the policy space that developing countries had available in devising rent strategies, but they have not removed the space entirely.

The difficulty in studying economic development is not about coming up with the most thorough and extensive laundry list of policies but to identify areas of constraints and externalities that can be corrected, given a country's political economy. Furthermore, policymaking is contextual; there is no blueprint of "good policies" that all countries should adopt. The choice of industrial specialization and relevant rent policies have to be determined according to an individual country's circumstances and existing capacity. The challenge is to measure policy-amenable variables with those that are exogenous, so that the overall configuration of factors affecting rent management can ensure conditions for effective learning and the development of capabilities. It is a challenge, but an entirely possible one. The Vietnamese experience provides useful examples for such an endeavor. For all its success and failures over the last three decades, Vietnam offers five constructive lessons for development. Principally, the research findings and observations below present a forceful theoretical challenge to neoclassical economics and the limitations of its policy suggestions.

7.4.1 *Privatization versus competition in the state sector*

The neoclassical literature on public sector reforms frequently attributes state failures or weak governance to the performance of the state sector, particularly SOEs. A common solution suggested by neoclassical economists is to privatize SOEs and industries. The underlying assumptions are that free-market competition would ensure efficient allocation of resources, production of desirable goods and services, and technological investments for the long term. This policy suggestion assumes away issues of imperfect competition that are frequently seen in developing economies. For example, not all firms have equal market power and access to inputs. In some countries, previously protected industries like telecommunications saw a few large private firms exploit their political and economic power to form an oligopoly market, with price determined by market power and marketing campaigns, not by competitive market mechanisms. In this context, privatization of the public sector may deepen market concentration and enhance the power of existing large firms rather than promote better or fair market competition. In addition, this does not guarantee better efficiency, higher productivity, or greater effort in industrial upgrading. The outcome indeed may involve more rent seeking and redistribution among vested interests with or without the state's involvement.

The Vietnamese experience in the telecommunications industry provides a different and more constructive perspective to the debate on public sector reform. Two case studies (Cases 2 and 3) demonstrate that credible competition for political favors, rents, and market dominance within the public sector were sufficient to ensure efforts, technology upgrades, and performance from state-owned conglomerates. Given the need for large economies of scale in the investment of telecom infrastructure, the Vietnamese government intentionally restricted licenses to a few state-owned general corporations. Additionally, foreign telecom providers were allowed to partner with local firms to provide technology, expertise, and capital. Further, government rents helped solve market failures in the labor market, financed new investments, and encouraged technology adoption from abroad. Thus, the successful development of the telecom industry in Vietnam was partly due to the government enforcing credible competition among large SOEs, which pressured them to adopt new technology in order to gain (or sustain) market power. The Vietnamese experience offers an important lesson: *successful development of firms and industries in developing countries can occur in the private and public sectors, even with the prevalence of rent seeking.* This happens when firms are (1) pressured to put in the greatest effort, (2) incentivized with market opportunities and profits, and (3) provided the resources for solving market constraints and learning.

7.4.2 *Global value chain participation versus local value chain development*

Using a state capitalist model, the Vietnamese government employed a combination of state control and market openness to promote the country's development. After the 1986 economic reform, some sectors – such as the T&G and motorcycle industries – were initially protected. However, liberalization quickly forced the government to open up these industries to foreign access, including the domestic market and export activities. These early industry experiences in liberalization were negative. In the T&G sector, although export volume was high, Vietnam found itself trapped in the low-value segment of the global value chain: garment production. Vietnamese producers still rely heavily on China and other advanced countries for inputs such as textile and accessories as well as for design and marketing.

In the motorcycle industry, liberalization policies allowed foreign producers access to a large Vietnamese consumer market. Competition among foreign firms increased the pressure to produce low-cost motorcycles, which led Vietnamese firms to join the low-value segment of the production chain. However, similar to the T&G sector, high-tech inputs continue to be imported from abroad or sourced from foreign suppliers operating in Vietnam. The result is that foreign motorcycle makers from Japanese and Taiwanese firms control over 99 percent of the Vietnamese market. After 30 years of development, Vietnam has failed to produce a competitive brand of domestic motorcycle to benefit from the vast demand in transportation.

In stark contrast with neoliberal theory on trade, these examples demonstrate how liberalization policies fail to provide sufficient incentives and opportunities for domestic firms to develop capabilities sufficient to compete with foreign producers in their own markets. As just noted, both the T&G and motorcycle industries continue to rely on inputs and expertise from abroad; thus, a large segment of profits and value added are earned by foreign multinationals. The benefit of trade openness is limited – it mostly encourages low-skilled and low-tech production. This is very much in contrast to the telecommunications industry. Foreign investors were forced to sign business cooperation contracts and partner with Vietnamese firms allowing for credible upgrading and technology adoption in crucial stages of the industry's development.

Here, the Vietnamese experience suggests a second important lesson. Local firms partaking in the global production network via trade and FDI does not guarantee industrial development. Furthermore, technical learning does not occur automatically; rather, it requires tremendous financial investment, time, and effort. In actuality, any opportunity for high profits and value added requires that domestic firms be capable and competitive in the first place – an unrealistic expectation in developing countries. The challenge for industrial development is in the gradual transformation in technical and productive capacities that lead to the absorption of foreign technology, expertise, and business opportunities. Vietnam's case studies suggest a solution to this challenge. They indicate that local firms frequently acquire technical learning by providing intermediary goods for the domestic market via local supply networks. This is an important insight: it suggests that developing countries' rent policies must utilize their domestic market when promoting local firms' industrial capacity. In other words, *domestic firms' participation in the competitive local value chain is a gateway for the learning and industrial upgrading necessary for success in the profitable segment of the global value chain.*

7.4.3 Technological change as the driver of growth and development

In the context of globalization and regional integration, developing competitive capability requires both technology transfers from advanced countries and domestic ability to adopt and adapt the new technologies. This process infers a number of conditions: (1) the resources needed to purchase or attract foreign technology,[2] (2) the ability of the local firm to adopt the technology, and (3) the speed of adapting the technology in the local firm's production process such that new productivity and capacity emerge. The third step is the most unknown because it requires significant effort from domestic firms to invest long term in the technology and to successfully integrate the technology into their production processes.

In Vietnam, technology transfers from foreign firms to domestic firms have been largely positive since Doi Moi, although not without complications. In the motorcycle industry, starting in mid-2010s, Japanese firms were more willing to provide training for domestic component producers when the local firms joined their supply chain (interviews, MoIT official and two local firms, Ha Noi; June–July 2016). However, few Vietnamese firms were able to satisfy the initial requirements to become suppliers. This is because Japanese buyers usually required local firms to set up an entirely new production line to match their quality and safety standards. In the electronics manufacturing industry, American, Korean, and Chinese investors have little interest in training or transferring technology and production knowledge. Most electronics lead firms recruit suppliers based on existing capacity and price. The expectation is that Vietnamese suppliers should be competitive on their own when bidding for contracts with foreign lead firms (interviews, four local firm managers in the electronics industry, Ha Noi and Ho Chi Minh City; June–July 2016). This expectation implies that foreign knowledge and technological capability should already be in place. Hence, in a globalized component supply market, market exchange takes place on the basis of existing comparative advantage and price, not on the basis of transfers of technology and know-how, as suggested in neoclassical economics.

The case studies in the T&G and telecom industries provide two contrasting experiences related to technology adoption: T&G relied on foreign direct investment, and telecom relied on direct technology transfer via purchasing. In the T&G industry, foreign investors producing textiles in Vietnam frequently held exclusive expertise and techniques. Because of liberalization, international investors were allowed to operate 100 percent foreign-owned textile facilities in Vietnam. In these production plants, knowledge of advanced dyeing and production techniques for high-end textiles were held exclusively by foreign managers and investors. Local workers were hired for manual and basic production with little training; without training, there was no spillover of foreign experience to the domestic market (interviews, four local firms and two T&G experts, Ha Noi and Ho Chi Minh City; April–September 2011).

Meanwhile, the telecom industry provides evidence of the successful transfer of foreign technology via direct purchase of technology, coupled with domestic effort to adapt the technology into production. Viettel, a military-owned telecom producer, acquired new technology and knowledge for design and production through the purchase of technology licenses from abroad. They succeeded in producing telecom devices at comparable market prices to their Chinese counterparts. This required Viettel to come up with the initial capital to procure the new technology, plans to organize its production, and a time horizon that would allow it to learn from mistakes and failed experiments. Viettel's experience suggests that local firms must be ready to invest substantial capital and human resources to cushion failure as part of the learning process. For Vietnamese SMEs, acquisitions of foreign technology and expertise are risky and require up-front and long-term capital, which is often unrealistic for domestic firms. The government's rent policies could be crucially helpful in narrowing the gap in investment and human capital for these firms.

Vietnamese industries offer the third lesson for development: *where local firms rely on foreign direct investment for technology transfers, the scale of technology adoption is negligible, and the time required is too long.* Developing countries need to develop national systems of innovation that focus on purchasing technology from abroad, boosting human capital via education and skills training, and providing local firms with financing options for new investment such that they could make the risky investment in advanced technology on their own over the long term.[3]

7.4.4 *China's effects and integration within the global value chain*

Globalization and regional integration have brought opportunities and challenges to the development of poor countries. On the one hand, market openness and trade liberalization allow developing countries to boost exports, revenue, and economic growth based on existing comparative advantages. On the other hand, competition with foreign firms undermines opportunities for domestic firms to develop capabilities that may lead to additional comparative advantages. The challenge is further aggravated by the rise of China and its robust industrial capacity. Its businesses produce everything from low-skilled products to advanced manufactured goods at varieties of scale. As a result, China has become the greatest barrier to industrial development for poor countries.

Vietnam lags behind China's development by more than 10 years. Therefore, the country's industrial development is heavily dictated by its relationship with China.[4] Until 2017, China was consistently Vietnam's largest trade partner and creditor.[5] In 2017, Vietnam incurred a trade deficit of USD 23.19 billion with China, an amount equivalent to 10.35 percent of Vietnam's gross domestic product (GDP) (General Department of Vietnam Customs, 2018). In industrial manufacturing, Vietnamese producers faced severe challenges. China's industrial capacity was superior to Vietnam's in terms of scale, product quality, and price. Thus, much of China's industrial surplus found its way to Vietnam through the Sino-Vietnam border. In the T&G sector, Chinese manufacturers had a clear advantage in textile manufacturing: their products were cheaper and of higher quality. Therefore, Vietnamese producers depended largely on Chinese fabrics and accessories for their textile production. Despite a large volume of garment exports, Vietnam's T&G producers had only profited from the low-skilled and low-profit segment of the production chain. Meanwhile, China's textile producers continued to access foreign markets indirectly through Vietnamese garment production and thus profited from Vietnam's exports.

The influence of China's rise is also visible through intense competition in the motorcycle market. In the early 2000s, illegally imported Chinese motorcycles cut short market demand for Japanese motorcycles. They forced Japanese lead firms, most notably Honda, to develop cheaper models to compete with Chinese motorbikes. Honda and other foreign lead firms eventually took the high-end segment of the motorcycle market, yet still offered lower-cost models for the growing middle-income Vietnamese consumer. In the low-cost market segment, the persistent presence of low-cost Chinese motorcycles, unreasonably cheap due to illegal border trade, deprived Vietnamese motorcycle producers from attracting low-income Vietnamese households with their home-built, Vietnamese-branded motorcycles. After numerous trials, Vietnam's local producers failed to develop competitive domestic products to reap the significant opportunities and benefits of Vietnam's substantial demand for motorbikes.

The Vietnamese experience illustrates how difficult it is for a government in a developing country to avoid relying on Chinese imports, especially when China severely cuts short market demand for production of intermediary and final goods by local firms. This problem not only deepens developing countries' substantial trade deficit with China, as seen with Vietnam (Figure 5.4), but also reduces market opportunities for poor countries to industrialize and develop any comparative advantage. More importantly, the Chinese government wields considerable economic influence to maintain its status as the largest trade partner and creditor for poor countries. The China factor was not an issue for Japan and the East Asian newly industrialized economies during the early decades of their development. However, it is the most prevalent challenge for developing countries today. The fourth lesson is implied here: *developing countries are facing a new but extremely complex development problem, given substantial competition with*

China for foreign capital and market demand at home and abroad. Scholarship on economic development must incorporate and assess the China factor seriously so as to confront its potent advantages both in regional and global markets. Unfortunately, there is no one-size-fits-all solution when it comes to the China challenge. Policy solutions for developing countries must be nuanced and context specific, as politics, geography, resources, and capability heavily influence the practical strategies available to each developing nation. The DRMA provides an analytical instrument to assess the appropriate policy options, given a country's political economy.

7.4.5 A model for development

Vietnam's hybrid use of market competition, liberalization, and state control of strategic sectors has resulted in mixed success for industrial development, despite positive economic growth overall. The country's economic transformation is taking place in tandem with pervasive rent seeking and rent allocations among and across state agencies, SOEs, and connected businesses. From this perspective, Vietnam illustrates how growth can happen in a rent-seeking society, thanks to specific interplays of politics, institutions, and market conditions, even with the lack of rules of law, enforceable contracts, and property protections. This subject is of substantive interest among political economists and one still far from being well understood (Gray, 2013; Khan & Jomo, 2000; Ngo, 2016; North, Wallis, & Weingast, 2009).

The case of Vietnam also provides evidence that rent-seeking dynamics vary between industries due to political, institutional, and industry structures as well as the technology characteristics required to develop the industry. In other words, the context of the industry's political economy matters in explaining the rent-seeking processes and development outcomes. The rent-management analyses offered in this book render a serious warning against making assumptions about the nature of a country's "development model" based solely on analysis of one or a few sectors. Different rent-seeking systems involve different development mechanisms. If we jump to quick and generalized conclusions, we risk grossly misidentifying causes of economic difficulties, possible remedies, and paths to development.

From this perspective, a final lesson is suggested: *when state capacity is weak, a policy agenda that seeks to eliminate rent creation and rent seeking entirely could backfire by undermining the capacity of firms and industry to overcome weak institutions.* In the context of economic transformation, a growth-enhancing development strategy is not a result of simply eliminating rent seeking and rent policies. Economic development is the result of the difficult and time-consuming process of strengthening state capacity, technology upgrading, and human development. Given the incentive structure of political elites, the question for the future remains: can Vietnam and other developing countries move toward a full and "open access" (or democratic) society and away from the "personal rules" that characterize the different avatars of a rent-seeking society? Although this book does not answer the question directly, it provides robust evidence of the underlying conditions that have amplified or hindered such a move.

Notes

1 Domestic large firms often employ consultants and trade experts in-house.
2 Neoclassical economics suggests that foreign investors would automatically transfer technology and know-how to local firms.
3 This strategy was implemented successfully in Taiwan during the early stages of the country's industrialization (see, for example, Wade, 1990).
4 Vietnam is not alone in its perilous dependence on China.
5 In 2017, South Korea surpassed China as Vietnam's largest trade creditor, with Vietnam experiencing a USD 32.14 billion trade deficit with South Korea.

References

General Department of Vietnam Customs. (2018). *2017 customs statistics.* Ha Noi: Information Technology and Statistics Deparment.

Gray, H. (2013). Industrial policy and the political settlement in Tanzania: Aspects of continuity and change since independence. *Review of African Political Economy, 40*(136), 185–201.

Haque, I. U. (2007). *Rethinking industrial policy* (Dicussion Papers No. 183). UNCTAD, Investment, Technology and Enterprise Development Division. Retrieved from http://unctad.org/en/Docs/osgdp20072_en.pdf

Khan, M. H. (2009). *Pro-growth anti-corruption and governance reforms for Vietnam: Lessons from East Asia* (Policy Discussion Paper). Retrieved from United Nations Development Programme Vietnam website https://eprints.soas.ac.uk/9922/1/Vietnam_Anti-Corruption_Governance_Mushtaq_H_Khan.pdf

Khan, M. H., & Jomo, K. S. (2000). *Rents, rent-seeking and economic development: Theory and the Asian evidence.* Cambridge, England: Cambridge University Press.

Masina, P. P. (2010). Vietnam between developmental state and neoliberalism: The case of the industrial sector. In K. S. Chang, B. Fine, & L. Weiss (Eds.), *Developmental politics in transition: The neoliberal era and beyond* (pp. 188–210). New York, NY: Palgrave Macmillan.

Ngo, C. N. (2016). Local value chain development in Vietnam: Motorcycles, technical learning and rents management. *Journal of Contemporary Asia, 47*(1), 1–26.

North, D. C., Wallis, J. J., & Weingast, B. R. (2009). *Violence and social orders: A conceptual framework for interpreting recorded human history.* New York, NY: Cambridge University Press.

Ohno, K. (2008). *Vietnam-Japan Monozukuri partnership for supporting industries: For leveling up Vietnam's competitiveness in the age of deepening integration.* Paper presented at the Seminar on Action Plan for Development of Supporting Industry in Vietnam, Ha Noi, Vietnam. Retrieved from www.grips.ac.jp/vietnam/KOarchives/doc/EP23_monozukuri.pdf

Pincus, J. (2009). Vietnam: Sustaining growth in difficult times. *ASEAN Economic Bulletin, 26*(1), 11–24.

Rodrik, D. (2004). *Industrial policy for the twenty-first century.* Retrieved from Centre for Economic Policy Research website http://econpapers.repec.org/paper/cprceprdp/4767.htm

Wade, R. (1990). *Governing the market: Economic theory and the role of government in East Asian industrialization.* Princeton, NJ: Princeton University Press.

Index

Note: Page numbers in *italic* indicate a figure, page numbers in **bold** indicate a table, and page numbers followed by an 'n' indicate a note on the corresponding page.

Printed in the United States
by Baker & Taylor Publisher Services